JUDICIAL
INDEPENDENCE
AT THE
CROSSROADS

JUDICIAL INDEPENDENCE
AT THE
CROSSROADS
An Interdisciplinary Approach

STEPHEN B. BURBANK
BARRY FRIEDMAN
EDITORS

With special thanks to:
American Judicature Society
Brennan Center for Justice

SAGE Publications
International Educational and Professional Publisher
Thousand Oaks ▪ London ▪ New Delhi

For information:

Sage Publications, Inc.
2455 Teller Road
Thousand Oaks, California 91320
E-mail: order@sagepub.com

Sage Publications Ltd.
6 Bonhill Street
London EC2A 4PU
United Kingdom

Sage Publications India Pvt. Ltd.
M-32 Market
Greater Kailash I
New Delhi 110 048 India

Printed in the United States of America

Library of Congress Cataloging-in-Publication Data

Judicial independence at the crossroads: An interdisciplinary approach
/ editors, Stephen B. Burbank, Barry Friedman.
    p. cm.
Includes bibliographical references and index.
    ISBN 0-7619-2656-9 (cloth) — ISBN 0-7619-2657-7 (pbk.)
    1. Judicial process—United States. 2. Judicial power—United States.
3. Judges—United States. 4. Courts—United States.   I. Burbank,
Stephen B.   II. Friedman, Barry.
    KF8775 .J825 2002
    347.73'12—dc21   2002001365

This book is printed on acid-free paper.

02 03 04 05 10 9 8 7 6 5 4 3 2 1

Acquisitions Editor:	Alison Mudditt
Editorial Assistant:	Mishelle Gold
Copy Editor:	Amy Kazilsky
Production Editor:	Diane S. Foster
Typesetter:	Rebecca Evans
Proofreader:	Toni Williams
Indexer:	Molly Hall
Cover Designer:	Ravi Balasuriya

Contents

Part IV: Comparative Dimensions

Part I

RECONSIDERING JUDICIAL INDEPENDENCE

∾ Chapter 1

Introduction

Stephen B. Burbank
Barry Friedman
Deborah Goldberg

What do we mean when we speak of "judicial independence"? One might think the answer was obvious. After all, the phrase is invoked regularly by proponents and opponents alike. When emerging democracies seek to emulate the success of the United States in preserving the rule of law, an independent judiciary is often at the top of their wish list. Yet, in the United States itself, presidential candidates joust over the extent to which judges should be accountable to popular will. Meanwhile, the rights of countless litigants—not just criminal defendants and civil liberties plaintiffs, but ordinary citizens and corporate entities in mill-run legal disputes—are thought to depend on some notion of an independent judiciary available to rule on difficult and often controversial issues.

Although great interest exists in the subject of judicial independence, most scholars work only sporadically in this area and without well-defined research agendas. Legal scholars have a great deal to say about policy debates concerning the judiciary but few of them consider whether their ideas and solutions play out in empirical reality. Political scientists have data on courts, but few of them attempt to relate those data directly to the specific problem of judicial independence. Historians accumulate valuable information about the judiciary, but most of it remains cabined-off from policy debates. There is no literature on judicial independence; rather, there are "literatures."

Believing that the debate about judicial independence has produced more heat than light and that scholars in different disciplines have been talking past one another, we convened a conference of some 30 prominent academics with backgrounds spanning four disciplines to discuss what we know, and ought to know, about judicial independence. The American Judicature Society and the Brennan Center for Justice at New York University cosponsored the conference, which was held at the University of Pennsylvania Law School March 31 through April 1, 2001. Additional funding was provided by Bristol-Myers Squibb Company, Deer Creek Foundation, the Open Society Institute, and the Institute for Law and Economic Policy.

A fundamental premise of the conference was that, despite the assumption that the ground of judicial independence has been plowed and replowed, we know far less about the subject than we should. Participants (see Appendix), each of whom wrote a short paper in advance, were asked to consider what questions needed to be asked and answered, what gaps existed in our knowledge, and what research strategies were promising. The working sessions confirmed our intuition, producing a host of good ideas and more rigorous thinking on the subject than one usually encounters in existing literatures on the subject. It remains to disseminate some of the fruits of the enterprise.

We have chosen eight of the papers produced for the conference and asked the authors to expand them for this volume, fleshing out ideas already expressed and reflecting new insights and perspectives gained at the conference. We also added a chapter, authored by the academic organizers of the conference, setting out the major challenges to progress and sketching fruitful avenues of research.

At the core of the conference sat the puzzle of exactly what we mean—or could possibly mean—by the phrase "judicial independence." "Independent from what?" was a typical reaction, and every bit of common wisdom on the subject was challenged. For example, the desire for judicial independence may reflect an aspiration that judges decide cases free from outside influence and consistent with the governing law and facts of a case. Yet, the common intuition of the participants was that wholly unaccountable judges are as likely to deviate from what the law might demand as follow it. Thus, *some* amount of accountability seems essential to ensure judicial adherence to popularly specified legal norms and therein lies a dilemma.

Professor Edward Rubin's chapter challenges the traditional view that such a thing as judicial independence exists, separate and apart from independence that modern governments use for a variety of different purposes, and in varying degrees, in structuring the institutions of government. This way of looking at judicial independence may help to understand the variety of arrangements we make for judges in the country as a whole.

Both Rubin's chapter and that of Professor Terri Peretti suggest that this perspective may be thought a better approach than attempting to read into the Constitution words that are not there ("judicial independence"), let alone a normative proposition that is so flatly contradicted by the existence of numerous powers that are there.

Even if Rubin is correct, it is likely that there will be a need in the future, as there has been in the past, for a specification of the particular roles and functions of judicial independence. Professor Lewis Kornhauser's chapter suggests potentially helpful lines of inquiry, particularly when considered together with Rubin's chapter and other contributions that point away from a monolithic view of judicial independence as applied to courts or judges and from exclusive focus on the judiciary.

Of course, understanding how to make judges independent requires having some sense of what it is that motivates judges, a problem that has proved quite intractable for scholars. The most basic work in economic modeling and cognitive psychology requires knowledge of the "utility function" of relevant actors. For example, when political scientists study the legislative process, they are able to operate with some simple notion of what motivates legislators. They want to be reelected and to enact laws that comport with their understanding of what is best for society. But students of judicial behavior concede that judges are more complex actors and that we do not have a very good handle on what motivates them in performing the judicial function.

This can be self-defeating for the entire project of understanding judicial independence. Thus, the framers of the United States Constitution decided that life tenure (with removal only by impeachment) and compensation that could not be diminished would shelter judges from the influences that affect most politicians. Yet, evidence suggests that judges—human beings after all—are responsive to community pressure and have a normal desire to be liked and admired and sometimes they act from partisanship, ideology, or the desire for advancement. If this is the case, life tenure may not begin to yield the sort of independent institution to which we aspire. Professor Peretti's chapter is less a call for new research, although it is that, than for those participating in scholarship and policy debates about judicial independence to take on board the wealth of existing research, much of which contradicts or casts in doubt factual claims made by scholars and policymakers.

Even if we understand what motivates judges, common wisdom may be backward on how to ensure we get out of those judges what we desire. Political societies tend to rely on formal rules to structure governmental institutions. What the conferees revealed, however, is that formal rules often have perverse consequences and informal norms often are the most durable and significant determinants of judicial behavior. To take one example of the former, the (apparently) progressive move in judicial politics is toward "merit selection" of judges who then run unopposed in up-or-down retention elections. Although the idea is to insulate judges from partisan politics and thus make them more independent, research suggests that it is very easy for interest groups to target judges they dislike in these elections in which judges run on their record.

Thus, the reasons for Professor Charles Franklin's conclusion about the fragility of nonpartisan institutions seem to apply with equal or greater force to retention elections. A group unhappy with a judge's views on tort reform can attack the judge on the basis of a decision in a death penalty case and knock the judge off the bench. This sends a message to all the other judges up for retention or reelection, potentially chilling their judicial behavior. Conversely, as Professor Charles Geyh demonstrates, informal norms may be the best protection of judicial decisional autonomy.

Judges are not passive actors who go about their business with neither the intent nor ability to influence their own political fate. Although the traditional wisdom in the legal academy sees judges as largely reactive and limited to the cases before them, research suggests that judges might act far more strategically in deciding cases. Thus, when judges interpret statutes, they are bound to do so in a way that furthers the intent of the body that enacted them. Yet, evidence suggests that judges have opinions about outcomes and decide cases, including those involving statutory interpretation, in a way consistent with their own ideology. However, judges are also savvy: If they depart too far from the wishes of other political actors, they will be overruled. Professor Charles Cameron's chapter calls for systematic quantitative analyses testing the hypothesis that an ideologically unified legislature and executive will be willing and able to rein in a judiciary that does not share their ideology. It may be that judges cleverly split the difference, deciding cases close to the result they would prefer but far enough away from their first preference to avoid being overruled. Or consider that the public does not keep track of everything judges do; it follows only the "salient" cases. The hypothesis is that judges might thus play to public opinion in the visible cases while pursuing their agendas in less visible ones.

Perhaps the most important and least understood aspect of judicial independence is the relationship between public opinion and judicial decision making. Professor Franklin suggests that knowledge about judicial independence would be enhanced if we knew the sources of information available to the public in voting for judges. The lack of understanding runs in both directions: Do judges cater to, or are they even aware of, public opinion? And does the public watch and react to what judges do? In the common wisdom of judicial independence, the answer to the first question ought to be no but the second regrettably is yes. As it turns out, this may be exactly backward. What evidence there is suggests that a remarkable number of high-profile decisions comport with public opinion. At the same time, it seems the public has very little clue what the judiciary is up to. This juxta-position of results presents serious normative questions about whether judges are paying too much attention to public opinion and whether the public is paying too little attention to what judges are doing. It also presents a real set of questions about how the public forms its opinion of judges. After all, in most states in the United States, judges stand for some form of election.

An important insight emerged from the conference repeatedly: Policy debates and academic research about the judiciary should separate high—or constitu-tional—courts from other courts. Most academic research either conflates the two or deals exclusively with one or the other (usually high courts). Moreover, the problem plagues the current debate about federal judicial selection, in which many are laboring under what the American Judicature Society has termed the mistake of "treat[ing] all federal judicial appointments as if they were appoint-ments to the Supreme Court" (American Judicature Society, 2001). Yet, the intu-ition is that high courts by their very nature inevitably are, and perhaps are meant to be, policymakers of a very different sort from lower courts. According to the tra-ditional view, trial and intermediate appellate courts deal with the gritty facts of ordinary cases. It is here, specifically, that we seek decisions rendered on those facts free of any outside influence. High courts and constitutional courts, by con-trast, are more likely to deal with broad questions of public policy. Although we may want those judgments rendered in a forum different from that of ordinary politics, we may not want them entirely immune from democratic accountability.

Finally, the conferees spent substantial time talking about how to study judi-ciaries and the benefits of comparative approaches. We considered three specifi-cally. The first went to the question of natural experiments: Judiciaries operate in different locations under different sets of rules. For example, within the United States, different selection and retention systems exist in otherwise similar states and even within the same state. What, if anything, can we learn from comparative studies? Second, there is history. Over time, our approaches to judicial selection and retention—and our expectations of what we want from judges—have varied widely. What can we learn from cross-historical study? Professor Lee Epstein's and her colleagues' chapter offers a powerful critique of existing scholarship and advances a set of testable hypotheses based on more reliable data, more compre-hensive variables, and more realistic assumptions about political behavior.

Third, judiciaries around the globe are developing along different models, in very different cultures. A consensus emerged that norms of judicial independence may not be universal and that we could profit from comparative international studies. Professor Epstein's hypotheses about domestic retention and selection systems drew inspiration from the study of constitutional courts in other coun-tries. Professor Kim Lane Scheppele's discussion of soviet-style positivism, to-gether with her suggestion that judicial review may be all that matters for judicial independence, put in somewhat different perspective calls in this country for "strict construction" of statutes and of the Constitution itself.

The scholars who attended the conference arrived skeptical that much traction could be gained on this subject. They left with a very different view. As the following chapters suggest, as the transcript of the conference reveals, and as the numerous suggestions that were made for research projects indicate, much of what we think we know may not be correct, and we may learn a great deal from research on questions that have yet to be addressed. Judicial independence, as a rhetorical concept, will continue to play a prominent role in democratic politics. Our hope is to look beyond the rhetoric of political debate and expand the horizons of both scholars and policymakers so that judicial institutions can be designed in a way that permits them to meet reasonable social aspirations.

∞ Reference

American Judicature Society. (2001). Clinton's legacy or Bork's? *Judicature, 84,* 224.

Chapter 2

Reconsidering Judicial Independence

Stephen B. Burbank
Barry Friedman

๛ Introduction

Judicial independence exists primarily as a rhetorical notion rather than as a subject of sustained, organized study. Many scholars assume that a judiciary with at least some independence is important to the protection of property rights and individual liberty, not to speak of the maintenance of the structure of democratic governance itself. But legal writing on the subject all too often seems part of a polemical debate between contending camps. Very little of this work even acknowledges the existence of state courts, let alone considers how the variety of arrangements governing state judiciaries might affect general theories of judicial independence. Meanwhile, the political science literature has not been immune to its own brand of extremism, much work failing to acknowledge that different courts may play different roles and, more generally, viewing the question of judicial independence in all or nothing terms.

Good, serious work about judicial independence is available in both the legal and political science literatures, but there is too little of it, and too often the products have been like ships passing in the night. Our goal in this chapter is to reinvigorate research about judicial independence by taking account of the contributions of multiple disciplines without being captive to the traditions of any of them. We are indebted not only to those whose work is presented in this volume or cited here, but to all of the participants in the conference out of which this volume has emerged (see Appendix). Interdisciplinary scholarship is fashionable. Too often it has the appearance of window dressing. Hopeful that we may avoid such criticism ourselves, we take an interdisciplinary approach because we are persuaded that it offers the best hope for genuine understanding of, and wise public policy concerning, the role of the judiciary in American society.

∾ What Do We Mean By Judicial Independence?

This section attempts to achieve a degree of rigor, on the one hand, and of flexibility, on the other hand, that is missing from most public policy debates about, and much of the legal and political science literatures on, judicial independence. Many people simply assume that there is agreement about what judicial independence is, thereby relieving them of the duty to state precisely what they mean when invoking the term. Many others are quite clear what they mean by judicial independence, but their definitions are so obviously the product of the academy that they are ill suited for the practical business of government. Still others capitalize on the multiplicity of possible meanings of judicial independence, with the same result.

These barriers to understanding and hence to progress tend to reflect, and to some extent may be due to, three anterior and fundamental shortcomings. The first is a common failure to recognize or faithfully to incorporate in analysis the fact that, when the mists of rhetoric have parted, in no modern political society of which we are aware is judicial independence itself a goal of government. That is, those responsible for the formal structures of government, and for the informal norms that fill up their interstices, do not seek whatever degree of independence they favor for the judiciary because they believe that judicial independence is itself normatively desirable. Rather, *judicial independence is a means to an end (or, more probably, to more than one end)* (Burbank, 1999; Kornhauser, this volume).

The second and third shortcomings are related to, at least in the sense that they may be encouraged by, the first. Thus, and second, discussions of judicial independence often proceed on the erroneous premise, stated or unstated, that judicial independence and judicial accountability are discrete concepts at war with each other, when in fact they are complementary concepts that can and should be regarded as allies. This supposed dichotomy between independence and accountability is a favorite target of legal scholars in search of a paradox; when it is found to be present, many political scientists regard it as proof that judicial independence is a myth (or a hypothesis not confirmed). The instrumental view of judicial independence urged here, on the other hand, requires no dichotomy and sees no paradox, because it proceeds from the premise that judicial independence and judicial accountability are different sides of the same coin (Burbank, 1996, 1999).

The third shortcoming in many discussions of judicial independence is the erroneous assumption that judicial independence is a monolith. Most legal scholars who write about judicial independence know nothing and care less about state courts. Their incentive structures or utility functions reflect the prominence and prestige of the federal courts in general, and of the Supreme Court of the United States in particular (Posner, 1995). To their great credit, political scientists have not similarly dispensed with those courts that conduct the great majority of judicial business in this country. At the same time, however, much of the high profile political science work on judicial independence has similarly concentrated on the Supreme Court, attention that may be due to some of the same incentives operating in the legal academy but that surely also reflects the current perceived need for practitioners of the science to quantify and measure, and their need for data with which to do so.

Whatever the reasons for the failure of most scholars of the subject to consider, let alone study, state courts and federal trial and intermediate appellate courts, the insight that judicial independence is a means to an end (or ends) and not an end in itself suggests that the quantum and quality of independence (and accountability) enjoyed by different courts in different systems, and indeed by different courts within the same system, may not be the same. To that extent, *judicial independence is not a monolith.* Indeed, it could be otherwise only if the architects of, and the major players in, the governments of all American polities had the same attitudes toward and aspirations for their judiciaries and for every court within their judicial system. Both history and a comparison of the arrangements that different states have made and now make for their courts tell us that this cannot be so. The point is also clear when one tries to imagine a general theory of judicial independence and takes account of experience in different (foreign) legal systems, as it does when one tries to conceive a general theory of independence as a tool of modern government.

We shall briefly develop each of these points in an attempt to clear away the vast underbrush that obscures a clear view of the subject.

Judicial Independence Is a Means to an End (or Ends)

No rational politician, and probably no sensible person, would want courts to enjoy complete decisional independence, by which we mean freedom to decide a case as the court sees fit without any constraint, exogenous or endogenous, actual or prospective (Seidman, 2001). Courts are institutions run by human beings. Human beings are subject to selfish or venal motives, and even moral paragons differ in the quality of their mental faculties and in their capacity for judgment and wisdom. In a society that did not invest judges with divine guidance (or its equivalent), the decision would not be made to submit disputes for resolution to courts that were wholly unaccountable for their decisions. One implication of this proposition is that we need law to constrain judges rather than judges to serve the rule of law (Chase, 2001).

As the reference to the rule of law may suggest, completely independent courts in this sense would also be intolerable because they would render impossible the orderly conduct of the social and economic affairs of a society. Citizens would not and could not long turn to courts for the resolution of their disputes if the result of each case were an immaculate conception, worthless for the governance of future conduct. In such a world, an opportunity to appeal to a higher court would represent insult added to injury, which helps to explain why, even in systems in which first instance courts are in theory not constrained by precedent, such as Italy, they do not lightly depart from the law as previously articulated by a higher court (Cappelletti, Merryman, & Perillo, 1967; Guarnieri, 2001).[1]

Thus, once a political society accepts the importance of law for the prospective governance of human affairs, courts cannot be accorded complete decisional independence. In societies that divide responsibility for making such law among different institutions, similar considerations require the creation of a hierarchy of authority providing decision rules for the resolution of conflict between or among those institutions. Unless such rules always privilege the views of the society's courts, complete decisional independence is for that reason also impossible.

In fact, most developed political societies privilege law made by legislatures. In such societies, courts have the obligation to interpret and apply (subject to constraints found in a written or unwritten constitution) legislative law, with which obligation complete decisional independence is obviously and fatally inconsistent (Hazard, 2001).

No American federal or state court of which we are aware has ever enjoyed complete decisional independence and if that is what judicial independence is taken to mean, as a historical matter it is, indeed, a myth. Moreover, and more important for present purposes, consideration of just the formal arrangements governing American courts reveals that the aspirations of those responsible for their creation and continued operation could not have included complete decisional independence.

Consider the federal courts, not because of their prominence or prestige, but because they appear to enjoy the greatest measure of judicial independence of any American courts.[2] The Constitution confers on Congress the power to impeach and remove Article III judges from office. It is true that a very strong norm has developed against using this power in reaction to the content of judicial decisions (and hence to coerce different decisions in the future). We should remember, however, that the result in the early 1800's impeachment trial of Justice Samuel Chase, which is regarded as generative of the norm, was very close (Friedman, 1985; Hurst, 1950; Rehnquist, 1992).

The Constitution also confers on Congress the power to determine which, if any, lower federal courts will exist and, as interpreted, which if any of the cases and controversies enumerated in Article III they will be enabled to hear,[3] and even the appellate jurisdiction of the Supreme Court is subject to exceptions and regulations Congress may prescribe. Although the triumph of judicial review and judicial supremacy in the 19th century may have helped to persuade Congress that it would be unconstitutional to strip the judges of the Commerce Court of their offices when it abolished that court early in the 20th century, it did abolish the court and could take similar action in the future (Burbank, 1999; Carpenter, 1918; Friedman, 1998).[4]

Congress' formal powers to control or influence the decisions of the federal courts are not confined to the impeachment process, court stripping, and the regulation of original and appellate jurisdiction. For Congress also decides how many judges will comprise a given federal court. Some scholars conclude that Congress has added justices to the Supreme Court directly to affect decisions on matters of great importance to it (Friedman, 2001; Friedman, 1985; White, 1996; but see Geyh, this volume). Again, the fact that the failure of Roosevelt's 1937 court-packing plan has generated (or confirmed) a strong norm against the use of the formal power does not negate its existence or (entirely) eliminate the shadow it may cast (Burbank, 1999; Friedman, 2000).[5]

All of this would probably suffice to persuade one new to the study of our institutional arrangements that the federal judiciary is the weakest and hence "least dangerous" branch. Yet, we have not even considered that which prompted Hamilton so to describe it in *The Federalist No. 78*, namely that Congress wields the power of the purse (controlling the budget of the federal courts), and the executive wields the power of the sword (being responsible for the enforcement of judicial decisions). Nor, of course, have we considered state court systems, in most of which the judges of at least some courts must stand for some form of election and serve terms far shorter than life.

These formal exogenous constraints are potent evidence against any assertion, explicit or implicit, that the "judicial independence" we use as a label to describe the result of the arrangements made for the federal judiciary means, or could possibly have been intended to mean, complete decisional independence. It is also likely that the architects of those arrangements envisioned and thus took into account endogenous constraints on decisional independence. Law itself may have been thought to function as such a constraint, at least to the extent that it was (sincerely) believed to be determinate and discoverable (as opposed to indeterminate and judicially created) (Burbank, 1999). The existence in the Constitution of both the Supreme Court and the Supremacy Clause suggests others, to wit, a hierarchy of authority and at least the beginnings of institutional hierarchy.[6]

For these purposes it is not necessary to agree about—and we do not here seek to identify—the goals that the architects of the federal (or any other) court system actually did seek to achieve in providing the measure of judicial independence they did, or that the architects of the future should seek to achieve. Professor Rubin's general approach, reflecting the modern administrative state, causes him to dismiss the contemporary relevance of separation of powers and to highlight the due process values served by decisional independence (Rubin, this volume). Professor Scheppele's awareness that due process, however important, may yield nothing more than arid formalism and her concern with constitutional courts in developing democracies cause her to highlight judicial review (Scheppele, this volume). The framers of the United States Constitution appear to have sought to achieve both goals in making the arrangements they did for the federal judiciary (Burbank, 1999).

The United States is not the same country it was in 1787 and although our Constitution has changed very little in the intervening years, the same cannot be said about our notions of law and lawmaking. Moreover, as we have seen, the Constitution would provide very little protection against an executive and legislature intent on controlling the decisional independence of the federal courts. Finally, change rather than permanence has been the norm in the architecture of the arrangements that formally determine state court independence (Epstein, Knight, & Shvetsova, this volume). This suggests to us that, as the ends to be achieved change, so (subject to federal or state constitutions) may the means.

Judicial Independence and Judicial Accountability Are Different Sides of the Same Coin

In previous work positing as the central goal of the architects of federal judicial independence the enablement of judicial review, one of us explored the implications of the fact that the legal arrangements whose consequences are described by the terms "judicial independence" and "judicial accountability" are separately situated in the Constitution. That might lead one to maintain that "judicial independence and judicial accountability are analytically discrete concepts, at least as they concern the federal judiciary" (Burbank, 1999).

Even on those terms, however, the argument would be difficult to maintain. That is because, as a concept that describes the consequences of legal arrangements, judicial independence invites attention to that which it denies, a process that quickly directs attention to the importance of context and purpose.

Once one has formulated the concept of judicial independence in light of its purposes, it becomes clear that, at the federal level, "the article respecting impeachments" is *not* the "only provision" that confers power, the exercise of which would deny the power of federal courts to make decisions free of executive or legislative control. Indeed, the impeachment article has become a virtual dead letter for that purpose but, as we have seen, the political branches are hardly without alternative weapons.

To some extent, confusion on this matter may arise from the restricted meaning of "judicial accountability" that follows from consideration of the limits history has imposed on the federal impeachment power. But again, as a purposive legal concept, judicial independence is not so restricted, and in thinking about the level of executive or legislative control or influence that is compatible with a desired level of independence, we are thinking about accountability. The same is true in states with elective systems, where the inquiry also includes the level of popular control or influence. (Burbank, 1999)

The temptation to place judicial independence and judicial accountability in opposition may be difficult to resist if one views the problem of independence for judges as a unique phenomenon. The truth is that, to the contrary, independence is a tool used by those responsible for the structure and operation of many government institutions (Rubin, this volume).[7] This perspective instantiates, and thus highlights the importance of, an instrumental approach to the concept of independence. Moreover, to the extent that we are not hostage to history and that constitutions permit, viewing the judiciary as one part of a complex governmental apparatus seems to us to hold more promise of yielding a specification of what it is we seek from courts today, and the balance between independence and accountability that we must afford them in order to get it, than an account that is stuck in 1787 or that disembodies courts (usually through apotheosis) and their independence.

Both the realization that judicial independence and judicial accountability are different sides of the same coin and the knowledge that achieving the proper balance between them is not a challenge unique to the judiciary should assist in identifying and understanding the complex set of informal norms and understandings that may have more practical importance to judicial independence (and accountability) than any formal rules. Insisting on the traditional dichotomy or on the uniqueness of the judiciary, to the contrary, obscures the processes of inter-action and dialogue that we know characterize institutional relationships in other systems, both ancient (Stevens, 2001) and very new (Scheppele, this volume), and that we believe also characterize such relationships in this country (Friedman, 1993).

Finally, viewing judicial independence and accountability as the joint product of purposive legal and political arrangements helps one to understand the weak-nesses of another traditional dichotomy encountered in the literature: that between the independence of an individual judge and the independence of the court or judicial system of which that judge is a member.

> The capacity of the judiciary, federal and state, to function independently of control by the executive and legislative branches . . . requires the capacity of individual judges to enjoy [a measure of] extrainstitutional independence. It also requires that the judiciary, as a system of courts, function and be per-ceived to function according to law. This in turn requires that individual judges yield some intrainstitutional independence. (Burbank, 1999)

Judicial Independence Is Not a Monolith (Unless the Ends Are Always and Everywhere the Same)

We have suggested that the utility function of academics helps to explain the preoccupation of scholars, particularly legal scholars, with federal courts in gen-eral and the Supreme Court in particular. Normative scholarship gravitates toward institutions perceived to be prestigious and influential because good scholarship may have an impact on the work of such institutions and because that is where, even for scholarship that does not seek to have such an impact, the pres-tige and influence of legal scholars are thought to lie. In part for the same reasons, such institutions attract empirical study and thus generate the data that contem-porary political scientists require for their work.

If this is correct, it helps to explain why those who write or participate in policy debates about judicial independence tend to refer to it as if it were a monolith, a concept having the same meaning everywhere and at all times. That tendency is, in any event, unsurprising to the extent that the individual in question treats judi-cial independence as an end in itself. Moreover, such a unitary goal would natu-rally take its shape from that which those harboring it know best, to wit, federal judicial independence (and the independence enjoyed by the Supreme Court in particular).

Of course, few scholars labor under this fallacy in fact, well recognizing the possibility that, even if they do not pause to inquire why, the quantum and quality of judicial independence (and accountability) may vary dramatically between courts in the United States. One reason they may not pause to inquire, however, has to do with a normative commitment to judicial independence on the federal model. Such a normative commitment constitutes both a further disincentive to study state court systems (were it needed!) and an impediment to an instrumental understanding of judicial independence.

Even if one is predisposed for normative reasons to the federal model, an instrumental view of judicial independence (and accountability) requires attention to what it is that we seek from courts and to possible differences in that regard between the various court systems in the United States and between courts within the same system. Although the inquiry must attend to both formal (including constitutional) and informal constraints on changing the arrangements we make for courts and judges that bear on their independence and accountability, it simply will not do to read into constitutions protections that are not there or to pretend that informal norms will last forever. Here, as elsewhere in the American legal landscape, comparative scholarship is most valuable for the light it sheds on domestic institutions and here, as elsewhere in scholarship that attends to functional relationships, it is useless to proceed as if nothing had changed since 1787.

On this view, rather than, for example, simply dismissing as defective state court systems in which judges are not appointed and do not enjoy life tenure, and before seeking to bring about change in such systems, we need to try to make precise what it is we seek from courts, the degree of decisional independence (and accountability) that is necessary or desirable in order to achieve that end, and the arrangements, formal and informal, that are best calculated to yield that quantum of independence (and accountability). Although unable to elaborate this research agenda in great detail here, we set forth below some possible distinctions that may be helpful, if only in burying more deeply all three of the fallacies with which we are concerned in this section: that judicial independence is an end in itself, that it is in opposition to judicial accountability, and that it is a monolith.

Federal Versus State Courts

From an instrumental perspective, the assertion or assumption that the only suitable arrangements affecting judicial independence (and accountability) for courts in the United States are those that have been and are made for federal courts implies not only that the latter are appropriate given the roles and functions of federal courts but that for these purposes, no relevant differences between federal and state courts (or federal and state judges) exist. Putting to one side evaluation of the federal arrangements, the hypothesis, in other words, is that nothing is different about the roles and functions of state and federal courts, or the influences affecting their judges, that should cause those responsible for the rules that determine decisional independence (and accountability) to make different choices. A thorough evaluation of this hypothesis would be an enormous undertaking, requiring a detailed investigation of the various state court systems, the business they conduct, and their place in the larger political landscapes in which they are situated. The present occasion permits only the suggestion of some general considerations that may be useful in testing it.

Having said that we were putting the appropriateness of federal arrangements to the side, our first consideration nevertheless brings that question back on the scene. We raise it, however, because the federal model is likely to provide the baseline for comparative analysis of judicial roles and functions. The question is the significance, if any, that should be accorded the fact that the makers of the Constitution provided only for a Supreme Court, leaving to Congress the decision whether to create lower federal courts and if so, to define the scope of their subject matter jurisdiction. Whatever the makers thought Congress was likely to do (Geyh, this volume), the arrangements they made that formally determined the decisional independence (and accountability) of the federal judiciary would clearly and surely apply only to a high court, one moreover operating under a constitutional provision (the Supremacy Clause) that can (but need not be) read to contemplate judicial review.[8]

Whatever the implications of the Supremacy Clause for judicial review, its chief bite lies in the hierarchy of authority it establishes between federal and state law and the obligation it imposes on all courts, federal and state, to respect that hierarchy. With the acceptance of judicial review, that obligation extends to striking down state and federal laws found to be inconsistent with the federal constitution. Thus, unlike the situation in a number of modern democratic societies, in which a separate constitutional court exists with a monopoly on constitutional decisions and whose members are subject to selection and retention arrangements quite different from the members of other courts (Guarnieri, 2001; Scheppele, this volume), every court in the United States is a constitutional court.

To permit the consideration of the federal business of state courts to drive the inquiry into their roles and functions would be, however, again to exalt (in this case, without having separately evaluated) the federal model of arrangements bearing on decisional independence (and accountability). Moreover, and apart from the availability of Supreme Court review of the decisions of state courts on federal questions, the federal legislature and executive lack obvious means to control the decisions of state courts (other than by prescribing the governing law), to that extent negating the primary historic functional justification for the federal arrangements. Of course, it may be that within a given state effective performance of the role of state constitutional judicial review might be thought to require functionally equivalent decisional independence. The question would then be whether the federal arrangements are the only or the best means to bring it about (Burbank, 1999; Hurst, 1950).

Finally in this aspect, particularly if testing the hypothesis proceeds, explicitly or implicitly, by comparison of state with federal judicial roles and functions, we think it may be important to pay close attention to differences in lawmaking powers and to structural differences. The common lawmaking power of the courts of most states has long been recognized as extensive (whether as a power to make law or simply to find it). At least since early in the Republic, the federal courts have not been thought endowed with comparable power as to questions of federal law, and their ability to bring about functionally similar results in state law diversity cases has been seriously constrained since 1938 (Burbank, 1987; Jay, 1985). Moreover, recent scholarship suggests that structural differences between state and federal courts call for very different limitations on their authority. (Hershkoff, 1999, 2001).

Trial Versus Intermediate Appellate Versus Supreme (High) Courts

We can never know whether, although it seems unlikely that, the makers of the Constitution would have fashioned different arrangements bearing on decisional independence (and accountability) for the lower federal courts than for the Supreme Court if they had established the former in that document rather than leaving decisions concerning them to Congress. If we knew the answer to that question was negative, however, we still would not know much of significance for testing the hypothesis set forth above. For, as we have seen, the formal protections of decisional independence in the Constitution are dwarfed by those formal powers that could be used to control or influence decisions, and informal arrangements and understandings reached in their shadow may be far more significant to the quantum and quality of federal judicial independence (and accountability).

Rather, we have raised the question as one means of encouraging attention to the notion that, because different courts within a given judicial system may play different roles, the arrangements we make for them that bear on their decisional independence (and accountability) may appropriately vary. Thus, for example, one might explore whether the same degree of insulation from political and private influence appropriate for a trial court, deciding questions of fact and applying law in a hierarchical system of precedent, is appropriate for an appellate court whose primary role is the creation of precedent binding both in the case before it and in other similar cases.

The importance of judicial role is also a message carried by comparative scholarship exploring the etiology and functions of constitutional courts in emerging democracies (Scheppele, this volume). Indeed, it is a message that seems to us likely to emerge from empirical and historical study of the means by which the members of different American courts within the same system have been and are selected, retained, or both (including their terms of office).

As an example, data gathered throughout the country by the American Judicature Society indicate that, in at least ten states, different selection systems are used for members of trial and appellate courts. Careful study of those state systems, which we strongly encourage, may reveal that one reason for the differences was their architects' belief that different judicial functions warrant different degrees of judicial independence (and accountability) (American Judicature Society, 2000).[9]

To take another example, when the question is federal judicial selection, there is a tendency to conceive of the role of the president, the Senate, or both in monolithic terms. Yet, as a number of studies clearly reveal, both have played very different roles in connection with nominations and confirmations to seats on the district courts, the courts of appeals, and the Supreme Court (Goldman, 1997). In a system in which, from a political science perspective, accountability is front-end loaded in the appointment process, the role differences of those responsible for selection thus have potentially significant implications for the quantum and quality of decisional independence (and accountability), and they may be due at least in part to views about differences in the roles and functions of the courts to which appointments are to be made.[10]

In studying the possible implications of role difference within a court system for the arrangements that bear on decisional independence (and accountability), it will be important to attend to both formal institutional structure and actual practice, to the allocation of power that is supposed to exist and to that which does exist. These inquiries will require attention to the theory and practice of precedent and of appellate review within the system. Moreover, in connection with the role of trials courts, it will be important to consider the role of the jury.

As suggested, one hypothesis such work might explore is that both a strong tradition of binding authority and a hierarchical structure providing more than one opportunity for review can act as powerful checks on decisional independence and, to that extent, reduce the need for other forms of decisional accountability.[11] That hypothesis would not pass unchallenged by political scientists, many of whom reject, if only because they cannot measure, the constraining force of law. Perhaps, however, the reminder that political science has told us very little about the independence and accountability of courts other than the Supreme Court, coupled with attention to the point that even on that court "judges often agree with one another, no doubt because the law is clear and they follow it" (Peretti, this volume), will help to soften positions. Progress of that sort would be facilitated if legal scholars reciprocated by reading the political science literature and paid attention to the part that politics plays in judicial decision making.

This discussion has suggested a number of considerations that seem to us important in pursing the possible relevance of different judicial roles for the arrangements that determine the quantum and quality of judicial independence (and accountability). The first is the importance of attending to changes in the roles and functions of a court over time. The second consideration, related to the first, is the importance of not permitting theory or formal structure to obscure actual practice. The third consideration, related to the second, is the importance of not permitting the extraordinary to obscure the ordinary.

We have speculated that the makers of the Constitution may have regarded law as a consequential constraint on decisional independence and that such an attitude may have affected the choices they made concerning the formal arrangements bearing on such independence (and accountability) in the Constitution. We have also noted, however, that attitudes toward law and lawmaking, particularly by judges, have changed since 1787, developments that could affect one's views about the appropriateness of those arrangements today. Moreover, wherever one looks in the federal judicial hierarchy, there have been substantial changes in the work and role, including the power, of the courts over time (Burbank, 1997; Hartnett, 1997; Songer, Sheehan, & Haire, 2000).[12]

Of course, just as it is important not to permit, for instance, the theory or tradition of appellate review (i.e., published opinion after full briefing and oral argument) to obscure the reality (i.e., judgment order after page-limited briefing and no oral argument), so is it important not to forget that, at least in terms of numbers, ordinary cases surely dwarf extraordinary cases, with judges usually agreeing about that which they are pleased to call "the law." Perhaps most important, as we have seen, the formal arrangements in the Constitution that could be used to constrain decisional independence dwarf the formal protections and both may pale in significance to informal norms and understandings reached in their shadow.

It may be that, at the end of the day, there is a core to the notion of judicial independence, an irreducible normative essence that must be present in any political system for a court to operate as such. The very statement of the proposition gives us pause, however, and a review of the fallacies described in this chapter well suggests the problems with, and the limitations of, any effort to identify such a core.

Foremost is the fact that judicial independence is not an end in itself but a means to an end, which requires that the inquiry focus on the goal(s) to be achieved in determining the quantum and quality of independence (and accountability). Is there a goal that any enlightened architect of any judicial system would want courts in that system to be able to achieve and for which a measure of decisional independence would be necessary? In addition, the realization that judicial independence is not a monolith requires that the search for a core, and the consideration of social and political goals, comprehend (and consider differences between) at least all courts within a given system. Finally, acceptance of the need to achieve a balance between independence and accountability, a pervasive challenge of institutional architecture, requires that attention to history and formal arrangements be tempered by a realistic appraisal of the practical needs of modern government.

All of this suggests what comparative scholarship on judicial independence confirms, namely, the daunting obstacles that any attempt to develop a useful general theory of judicial independence. The obstacles may appear less formidable, and the enterprise more tractable, to the extent that one assimilates other lessons of such scholarship. One such lesson, confirming an insight from comparative institutional scholarship, is that it is a mistake to measure a court's judicial independence (or accountability) exclusively by formal arrangements (Georgakopoulos, 2000; Ramseyer, 1994). Another, confirming the clear implication of an instrumental perspective, is that there are likely to be more ways than one to bring about the same measure of independence (and accountability).

∽ What Motivates Judges?

Even if we can clarify the end(s) to be achieved and hence what we want courts to be independent of, matters are more complicated yet. This is because of a fact well understood in the political science literature, yet usually not discussed in the legal literature on the subject. When people talk about judicial independence, and when they design judicial systems attempting to ensure a measure of independence, the focus typically is on external forces. Judges are given certain guarantees—such as salary or tenure—so that others cannot control the courts on which they sit. Rules, formal and informal, exist about actions others may legitimately take affecting the judiciary.

The overlooked fact in many discussions of judicial independence is that judges are human. Being human, they are motivated by incentives (Baum, 1994; Posner, 1995). In planning judicial systems, we usually address only the most base of these incentives. For example, both criminal law and ethical codes bar taking money to render a particular decision, and in the United States these seem to work. Similarly, designers of selection and retention systems, aware that judges want to win elections, may seek to prevent abuses to which that incentive can lead, although no satisfactory solution has yet been found. But these concerns—monetary gain and keeping one's job—barely scratch the surface of what might motivate judges and what therefore should be considered in a serious discussion of judicial independence.

In the language of economics, that which motivates judges is included in the judicial utility function, by which is meant the things that judges find personally rewarding, some of which they may seek to maximize. We know very little about the judicial utility function as opposed to that of other public officials. Perhaps this is because the potential motivations of other public officials are so much more transparent. Perhaps, however, lulled by the mythology of an independent judiciary, we are loath to concede that judges are human in ways that matter to court decisions. Yet, if we are to be successful in designing judicial systems to achieve our instrumental goals, it is necessary to take account of what motivates judges and allow for—or attempt to control—those motivations.

Just as we may want different things from different courts, even courts within the same judicial system, so may judges in different systems, and at different levels, have different utility functions. Assuming, then, that we want judges independent and accountable in different ways in different contexts, we must work with or against the grain of the judicial utility function in those contexts.

This section does three things. First, it explains why the nature of law makes the judicial utility function come into play so dramatically. Second, it discusses an idea that has preoccupied political scientists, namely that judges decide (or vote in) cases consistently with their personal preferences. Third, and most important, it brings to the surface other factors that would seem to be important but that have received insufficient attention in the literature. It is in this third area that the most work remains to be done.

Law's Indeterminacy

Ever since the turn of the 20th century, there has been considerable turmoil within the legal profession—and sometimes in the broader public—about the determinacy of law. The fight is over the question whether cases are decided by law or whether there is enough room for discretion that judicial preferences ultimately decide cases. It is easy to see why this question is so important and controversial. Our entire idea of a "government of laws and not of men" seems in a superficial way to turn on law's determinacy. Yet, first the Legal Realists, and then the Critical Legal Studies movement, made hash of strong claims for the determinacy of law.

Happily, the controversial nature of this question far outstrips its difficulty, at least in the realm in which the question presents itself for serious thinking about judicial independence and accountability. Any good lawyer can answer this question. We suspect the answer would go something like this: "Some cases are so easy that it is not worth going to court. In many others the correct decision under the governing law is or should be clear. But even easy cases can have angles that afford space for judicial discretion. And, of course, cases that make their way up to the highest state and federal courts often involve undecided issues, inviting arguments that move in opposite directions."

In addition to understanding that the decision of many cases requires an exercise of discretion, a good lawyer knows that the higher the stakes, the more indeterminate the law may appear. Why is it that the same legal question may seem more or less determinate depending on whether $100 or $100 million dollars is at stake? There are two answers, one that may be troubling and one that ought not to be. On the troubling side, when enough is at stake, good lawyers will think of arguments as to why the seemingly obvious is not so. But this appears less troubling if cast in a different light: Our willingness to accept legal answers, even answers that might not seem right on serious reflection, is a function of how much is at stake. Sometimes, when enough is at stake, we rethink how the law should operate.

This suffices for us to conclude that, as most practicing lawyers no doubt understand, there is leeway in the law and because judges are human, some decisions will depend in part on who sits on the bench. If this were not true, it would be difficult to explain the current level of concern about who is selected for judicial positions. We do not think our judges are venal, implacably biased, or corrupt. We just realize that the identity of the judge matters and that this understanding is essential in a consideration of judicial independence. Law's indeterminacy requires that we think seriously about the mix of accountability and independence and that we take the judicial utility function into account.

Political Science and Judicial Ideology

Political scientists have seized on the insight that there is room for discretion in the decision of cases, to make the claim—usually quite forcefully—that judges decide cases based on their attitudes or beliefs. The "attitudinal model" has been developed most fully and famously by Professors Jeffrey Segal and Harold Spaeth, but a vast literature exists on the subject (Segal & Spaeth, 1993; Spaeth & Segal, 1999). The conclusion of this literature is that it is possible to show, with a high degree of confidence, that judicial decisions are the product of attitudes or ideology (and that it is not at all clear what role law plays in them).

This research is problematic for reasons we discuss, but it is important first to determine whether its main conclusions matter. How could they not matter? Although attitudinal studies are a cottage industry in political science, once all this was explained to a good lawyer, the likely response would be, as a federal judge stated, utter lack of surprise (Wald, 1999). Everyone knows that who sits on the bench matters to some extent.

The important question is, rather, to what extent judicial identity matters, and attitudinal studies to date do not provide the answer. The problem these studies encounter is controlling for law in the models. Until law is successfully taken into account—a task that is exceedingly difficult but worth pursuing—it is impossible to understand the relative role played by ideology.

In order to perform attitudinal studies, one must be able to "operationalize" law, by which we mean reduce it to a variable (or variables) that can fit into a regression. Good attempts have been made (George & Epstein, 1992; Spaeth & Segal, 1999), but thus far, success has been elusive. The models tend to make errors such as confusing what constitutes "law" with what constitutes "facts." The mistake is understandable, both because this is sometimes a confusing question and because the task of capturing law—which by its nature is always evolving—is a difficult one. But given the failure to operationalize—and thus control for—law, it is an error to conclude from these political science studies that judging is all politics (or attitudes) and no law.

Most attitudinal studies focus on the Supreme Court, but given the necessity of controlling for law, the lower courts are a far more fruitful place to work. Everyone understands that the Supreme Court is, and should be, far less constrained by law than other courts. Lower courts, on the other hand, likely exhibit far more obedience to legal commands. It would be extremely useful to know just how much decisional force, for example, precedent provides in the appellate and trial courts. Some good work is being done in this area (Cross & Tiller, 1998; George, 1998; Revesz, 1997), but too little.

A reason that attitudinal studies focus on the Supreme Court highlights the difficulty with research in this area. If one wants to test the hypothesis that ideology or attitudes, not law, decide cases, one must have a measure of a judge's ideology or attitudes. In order to develop a robust measure, one must have a great deal of information about a judge. Not only is collecting such information expensive, but researchers are uncertain precisely how to specify ideology. Accordingly, researchers tend to rely on proxies. A common proxy of attitudes or ideology is derived from editorial coverage about a judge when nominated to the bench (Segal & Cover, 1989). Although this measure can be applied to Supreme Court justices, who garner substantial attention when nominated, it simply will not work for most judges. Thus, resort is had to another proxy, commonly the party of the president who appointed the judge (Revesz, 1997). This measure also is problematic, because there are reasons other than ideology that might lead a judge to remain loyal to the appointing president (or that president's party). As a result, we lack a reliable measure for most cases in which law might matter.

Assuming something other than law does affect judicial decision making, it would be valuable to know what aspects of judicial experience have an impact and in which way. If the goal is policy reform, it is not helpful simply to say that judges are affected by ideology or attitudes. It would be interesting to know if factors such as the gender or race of the judge tended to affect outcomes and in what kinds of cases. Similarly, does prior work experience, such as prosecution or criminal defense, color the way judges see cases before them (Sisk, Heise, & Moriss, 1998)? The suggestion is not that we disable judges from hearing certain cases, but the information might suggest reasons for and ways to diversify the bench.

The Judicial Utility Function

Perhaps most important, most of the studies to date typically make insufficient (if any) effort to control for the many factors that might be in a judge's utility function (Baum, 1994; Posner, 1995). One might happily concede that there is room for judicial discretion and that in that space cases are decided. But if the task is designing judicial systems, instead of just studying them, that does not tell us very much. We need to know what motivates judges so that we can allow for it. Attitudinalists would have us believe that judges are all about imposing their policy preferences on the law. But to those who work with and appear before judges, that just seems too simple. The question is: What factors motivating judges might stymie (or enhance) the best efforts to construct a judiciary that is optimally independent (and accountable)?

Getting and Keeping the Job

At the top of the list in most scholars' minds are factors related to the selection and retention of judges: Judges want to secure the job and keep it. When scholars think about judicial independence, they probably should think more about retention than selection, however. Once on the bench, judges are more likely to respond to the influences that determine if they keep their jobs tomorrow than to those responsible for giving them the job yesterday. Some studies suggest that judges are faithful to those who appoint them (Peretti, 1999). But for obvious reasons, it is difficult to tease out whether any such apparent fidelity is a function of presidents selecting those of like minds or federal judges feeling constrained by the appointments process. Our intuition is that it is the former, not the latter.

Perhaps this could be studied, for example, by determining whether judges who have strong subsequent motivations—such as seeking a promotion—tend to remain as faithful as those without such apparent motivations. But this would be difficult to do. Moreover, any such research must account for the different roles of those responsible for appointment. In the federal system, it is necessary to account for the role that both the president and Senate may play in the nomination and confirmation of judges to different courts. States have far more variation.

Clearly, we do not know nearly enough about how judges respond to retention measures. This is important, as most judges in this country periodically face some sort of reelection or retention process. Equally important, informal norms and recent history seem as likely to play a role as formal retention structures. Judges may stand for reelection or retention, but if it is virtually a sure thing—either because there is no opponent or retention rarely is denied—it likely will not affect judicial behavior. On the other hand, a close retention election of a colleague might well induce greater sensitivity among all judges in a jurisdiction or at a particular level.

This complexity may make it easier rather than more difficult to study the issue because thorny reelection or retention races can mark a point around which changes in judicial behavior might be observed. In any event, we need a great deal more information about whether judicial behavior shifts in response to upcoming reelection or retention events. Our intuition is that, if such a shift occurs, it is likely to be in high salience cases. Certainly, the limited studies to date and anecdotal information about judicial behavior in criminal and death penalty cases are disturbing, going to the heart of our notion of judicial independence (and accountability) (Georgakapoulos, 1999).

The Judges' Communities

Judges likely are influenced by a host of factors that rarely show up in discussions of judicial independence and even more rarely are a subject of sustained study. We tend to assume that federal judges, with life tenure and a guarantee against salary reduction, are the most independent. Yet, if judges care about things other than salary and keeping their jobs, this should be only the beginning of the analysis. Indeed, once salary and tenure are guaranteed, ironically the door is open for many other factors to influence judicial behavior.

Judges live in a variety of "communities" that might influence their behavior. It is possible to imagine these as ever-expanding concentric circles in which the judge is embedded. Start with family, move to personal community, be it friends, the neighborhood, the club, or the religious community, move out once again to the professional community, then to the political community, and so on. For some judges, the relevant community may not necessarily be in existence; it may be posterity (Posner, 1995). The point is that judges, being human, likely respond to the forces that shape their self-image.

Some scholars acknowledge the importance of understanding the judicial utility function (Baum, 1994; Georgakopoulos, 2000; Posner, 1995; Schauer, 2000), but few of whom we are aware have done anything to study it systematically. The reason for this may be its complexity coupled with disciplinary unfamiliarity. To understand these mechanisms, scholars must explore the psychology of judicial behavior—itself an underdeveloped area. Consider the behavior of southern judges during the civil rights movement. There have been suggestions that appellate judges managed to act in ways that furthered civil rights more than trial judges and that federal judges outstripped their state counterparts (Bass, 1981). The differential behavior of state and federal judges may be attributable to selection or retention systems, but it also could be a function of institutional culture and the perceived community or audience to which the judge was playing. The differential behavior of trial and appellate judges may reflect on community as well. This might suggest that trial judges, whose decisions are more clearly linked to the judge that rendered them, felt the influence of social pressures more acutely. We do not pretend to have an explanation. The example only makes the point that this is a fruitful area for study.

The Judges' Environments

Although a judge's self-defined community may be difficult for society to control, judges work in environments that include factors susceptible of influence. Although such factors receive some attention in the relevant literatures, we are unaware of systematic studies that examine the potential of policy change.

One relevant factor is caseload. Caseload might affect judicial decision making in at least two ways. One obvious way is in the sheer number of cases a court must consider and decide. Some have suggested that the judicial utility function includes leisure (Posner, 1995), which suggests that judges will react in various ways to the change in the number of cases they are hearing. The reaction is not altogether predictable, however. One judge may have a fixed amount of time he or she is willing to work; if so, an increasing caseload will decrease deliberation. Alternatively, the judge might expand output with input, although perhaps not in the same amount (Parker, 1999).

But there is another way in which caseload could influence judicial behavior, one possibility being the mix of cases that a court hears. Consider criminal cases, in which the court balances claims of individual right against societal needs. A judge who hears drug cases all day long may become quite jaded about claims of unlawful police conduct. A judge who hears those claims remote from the crime—such as a federal judge sitting in habeas corpus—may be more sensitive to a claim of right. But now take that same federal judge and give him or her a seemingly ever-expanding docket of federal criminal cases and that judge's view of the habeas cases may shift. This is but one illustration of a common problem one faces when thinking about proposals to give some of the work of courts of general jurisdiction to specialty courts.

Possibly other unstudied aspects of a judge's environment could have an impact on a judge's independence (and accountability). Little research exists, for example, on the question of how much lawyers or parties affect judicial independence. It is a familiar phenomenon in the administrative law literature that agencies may become "captured" by the parties that appear before them. Some sorts of litigation draw lawyers as repeat players, and courts of limited jurisdiction are particularly likely to see the same lawyers over and over. There has been valuable research regarding the impact of repeat lawyers and clients on judicial decision making (Songer et al., 1999). The most prominent example, which we discuss below, is research documenting the success rate of the solicitor general (SG) before the Supreme Court (Epstein & Knight, 1998).

This discussion of the many factors that might affect judicial behavior and hence the mix of independence and accountability brings us back to the distinctions with which we began this chapter.

Take, for example, the point that most discussions of judicial independence fail to distinguish between higher and lower courts, that is, fail to recognize that judicial independence is not a monolith. There are reasons to think that appellate courts, whose primary concern is legal questions (and as one moves to high courts, legal questions in which policy looms large), should—as a normative matter—be more tied to public opinion than trial courts. Public opinion presumably should not influence findings of fact, and, with rare exception, trial courts do not knowingly fail to follow the law as it is generally understood. But the broad contours of the law ought not to stray too far from the bounds of public acceptance, or perhaps it is more accurate to say that respect for law may depend on popular acceptance.

Now, combine this line of analysis with the understanding that a judge's community may well influence judicial independence. It becomes apparent that having trial judges stand for election could be a very bad idea, whereas this might be less problematic for appellate judges. We do not mean to suggest that trial judges should be appointed. Nor do we necessarily endorse elections for appellate judges. We only mean to question traditional wisdom in this regard. Similarly, there is room to question the move to retention elections for judges. Emerging research suggests that it is easier for interest groups to pick off appellate judges who stand for retention by focusing on specific decisions. This could bring to appellate judging an evil we presumably seek to avoid: bias toward individual litigants such as death penalty petitioners. But judges have suggested that partisan races are not as bad because there is a candidate to run against. Moreover, from the perspective of voters, party identification at least is a clue to, or proxy for, judicial ideology. Our point is that research in this area is important and that the research results ought to be brought to bear on the design of judicial selection and retention systems. Too often institutional design in this area proceeds in an information vacuum.

Similarly, more attention should be directed to the nature of the cases a court hears and the impact that selection and retention methods may have on the decision of those cases. For example, our argument suggests reasons why courts of general jurisdiction might be preferable to specialized courts, so that judges have a diverse portfolio on which to fall back. In particular, we would question the not uncommon practice of separating civil and criminal jurisdiction. On the one hand, there is something to be said for specialization. On the other, criminal cases regularly are high profile and there is reason to think the court that hears a mix of cases is less likely to let popular opinion influence decisions in individual cases.

∽ What Constrains Judges?

It is apparent that courts and judges, even those that seem most "independent," are subject to various influences. This section looks at some of those influences in a more systematic way. Our goal is to show that all courts and all judges are embedded in an ever-expanding field of influence and to ask whether, normatively, those influences are desirable. What emerges from this section are the understanding that judicial independence necessarily is tempered and the question whether any given tempering influence ought to be encouraged or, if possible, neutralized.

Judges' Superiors

Courts are hierarchical. We expect some decisions of most courts to be taken to a higher court for review, and we expect courts to follow the decisions of the courts above them. Thus, we limit independence in the name of fidelity to the orderly progress of the law. Even this familiar hierarchy, however, presents difficult questions that researchers are only now beginning to face. For example, should lower courts follow the precedent of the higher court or attempt to predict what the higher court would do in this case (Caminker, 1995; Dorf, 1995)? This question has greatest bite in connection with the role of trial courts and is all the more complex if one takes into account changing membership on appellate courts. Suppose the trial court believes that precedent has become tenuous because of the addition of new judges with different views on the appellate court. What does fidelity to law require?

Similarly, because appellate courts cannot give the same amount of attention to all the cases that come before them, how do they decide which cases receive closer scrutiny? Are those decisions based on the nature of the question presented, which is how we commonly envision review under law (Kornhauser, 1995)? Or do courts (or members thereof) look for signals, such as whether the court below was more liberal (and voting in a liberal way) or more conservative (and voting in a conservative way) than the appellate court (Cameron, Segal, & Songer, 2000; McNollgast, 1995)?

Depending on which of these occurs, we are operating under very different models of judging and judicial independence. To the extent law is the primary deciding factor in these cases, we have a familiar hierarchical legal system. But to the extent lower courts are trying to guess the preferences of higher courts, and higher courts are reviewing based on ideology and outcome, then law is not the chief determinant of outcomes; rather, it is ideology and reversal rates.

Judges' Colleagues

Judges on collegial courts could not be entirely independent; they must operate in conjunction with their colleagues. The question then concerns the extent to which they act relatively autonomously or whether they act strategically in order to influence outcomes. It is theoretically possible that on collegial courts judges simply vote their individual understandings of the law, letting the chips fall where they may. But there is reason to believe that this model bears little relationship to reality.

Judges regularly alter their views in response to those of their colleagues. Some of this no doubt is intentional strategic behavior. Take opinion writing as an example. It is common knowledge, and makes common sense, that in drafting Supreme Court decisions, the justices deviate from their ideal point in order to attract enough votes to hold a majority (Epstein & Knight, 1998; Maltzman, Spriggs, & Wahlbeck, 2000). In other instances, the motive for modifying one's views may be more subtle and difficult to understand. In this regard, evidence indicates that judges sitting on appellate panels in the District of Columbia Circuit vote differently depending on the political composition of the court (Cross & Tiller, 1998; Revesz, 1997). For example, a judge appointed by a Democratic president is more likely to vote for an environmental group and against industry if there is at least one other panel member appointed by a Democratic president. Alternatively, with two other panel members appointed by Republican presidents, the sole Democratically appointed judge tends to go along with a decision against the environmental group (Revesz, 1997). Whether this reflects a norm of consensus under certain circumstances, or is simply a psychological reaction against dissenting, is difficult to know.

One may question whether this practice of altering votes moves beyond the bounds of individual cases (Maltzman, Spriggs, & Wahlbeck, 2000) and whether it is appropriate in either instance. In order to reach normative judgments, it would help to know more. No doubt the idea of trading votes across cases would be anathema to most legal scholars. Nonetheless, empirical evidence suggests bloc voting by justices of the Supreme Court (Maltzman et al., 2000) and there is anecdotal evidence that informal vote trading has occurred. Perhaps if the circumstances were better understood, the normative picture might be more appealing. For example, suppose a justice goes along in a case that he or she does not believe is very important, as part of a process of persuading a colleague to join a decision he or she views as critical. Note how the way we feel about this is inextricably intertwined with the way we view the job of these judges and their court. Should the primary concern be the direction of the law or individual justice in a given case?

Other Actors

The judiciary is part of a system of government that includes other actors whose actions likely will constrain judicial decision making. Academic discussion of this takes two forms. First, some scholars consider the weapons available to the more political actors to discipline judges should they be discontent about the direction of judicial decision making (Segal, 1997). This line of inquiry is brought into play primarily with regard to constitutional cases, in which legal decisions of the judiciary are understood to be final absent constitutional amendment. Second, other scholars deploy a game theoretic analysis of judicial decision making that suggests that when other actors can respond to judicial decisions, courts will act strategically to achieve as much as they can without being overturned. This analytic perspective is most common in statutory interpretation or similar cases in which we grant legislative bodies the authority to disagree with judicial decisions and change them prospectively (Eskridge, 1993; Eskridge & Ferejohn, 1992; Ferejohn & Weingast, 1992).

Note that the constraints arguably placed on courts in these situations are not purely a function of avoiding discipline or the overturning of judicial decisions. Courts also have an interest in seeing that their decrees are enforced, that the rules they set down win adherence (Canon & Johnson, 1999). Thus, even courts and judges who are unlikely to face discipline may well adjust their determinations, privileging the feasible over the ideal.

We do not know how common these practices are. Theory in the area is abundant; empirical information is elusive. Part of the problem is the phenomenon of "anticipated response." It may not actually require an expression of congressional discontent for the Supreme Court to alter its practices, just as the Court need not necessarily strike down disfavored enactments. Actors in both institutions are capable of engaging in rational calculations about what the response might be to a given action (Peretti, 1999; Stimson, MacKuen, & Erikson, 1995). Thus, the dynamic that constrains courts may be difficult to locate.

Quite dramatic evidence indicates Supreme Court responsiveness to one government actor, although it is difficult to know what exactly to make of it. Many studies have documented the influence of the solicitor general of the United States at the Supreme Court. The Court is far more likely to take cases when requested to do so by the SG. In addition, the SG typically has a high win rate in the Court, both in cases in which the United States is a party and in cases in which the Court seeks the SG's views as friend of the court (amicus curiae) (Epstein & Knight, 1998). Two very different interpretations result from this evidence, however. Some scholars suggest that the SG's legal acumen and familiarity with the Court explains the influence of the office. But it is equally plausible that the Court understands the critical role the executive plays, both in enforcing judicial decisions and in mustering public opinion concerning Court decisions, and so pays heed to the executive's representative before the Court (Iaryczower, Spiller, & Tommasi, in press; Martin, 2001).

The Public

Finally, the public's influence on courts and other government actors complicates, but is an essential ingredient of, an assessment of how independent (and accountable) courts and judges are in fact. Much research investigates public reaction to judicial decisions, seeking to answer the following sorts of questions: How aware is the public of judicial decisions (Franklin & Kosaki, 1995; Hoekstra, 2000)? Is public support for courts a function of specific decisions or more diffuse factors that protect the courts even when they encounter public resistance (Caldeira, 1986; Caldeira & Gibson, 1992)? Do courts pay attention to public opinion in rendering decisions? Does public opinion constrain the actions that other branches may take against courts and—again—is this a function of agreement with individual decisions or a broader view about judicial independence?

The evidence to date is that the public pays little attention to judicial decisions, but this may be a good thing. Studies suggest that popular approval of courts may rest on the public's impressions remote from judicial decisions (Caldeira, 1986; Caldeira & Gibson, 1992). The more the public knows about individual decisions, the more public opinion comes to depend on specific outcomes (Franklin & Kosaki, 1995). On the other hand, as matters now stand, a small number of salient cases tend to have a large impact on public opinion. Perhaps mechanisms for enhancing public understanding of the judicial process would influence attitudes unrelated to specific outcomes.

Answering these questions is critically important. Even in robust separation of powers models, public opinion is likely to be the ultimate constraint on what action can be taken against judges. In state systems in which judges are account able to voters, the influence is more immediate. Finding the right balance between independence and accountability in any system, however, requires that we understand how the public understands courts.

Thus, courts may be constrained by other actors in many possible ways. Our picture of exactly how these forces operate to influence judicial decision making is poorly developed. But even if we had perfect information, we still might be at a loss to know precisely how to fit it into a model of judicial independence (and accountability).

The problem, at the level of theory, rests in the definitional questions we addressed at the outset. Particularly, it reflects the tension between accountability and independence. Many of the influences on courts and judges described here come from forces quite central to American democracy. We might decry legislative reaction to judicial decisions, but the fact is that we call ourselves a democracy and it is in legislatures that the democratic impulse is most keenly felt. (Interest group influence is felt in legislatures as well, but that too—for better or worse—is an established feature of our system.) Without a clear normative understanding of the appropriate balance between independence and accountability, it is impossible to label a set of influences in or out of bounds.

Consider, in this regard, the question of executive influence on the judiciary. Suppose the solicitor general's success rate is a reflection of judicial attentiveness to the wishes of the president. Think about this in the context of civil rights litiga tion conducted in the 1950s and 1960s. A "rights essentialist" strategy common in constitutional scholarship would take a dim view of courts adjusting rights in light of the preferences of the current administration (Levinson, 1999). Yet, judges know full well that implementation of judicial remedies may require executive enforcement. Ultimately, both rights enforcement and judicial legitimacy may de pend on executive concurrence or acquiescence. Moreover, the executive more likely reflects pragmatic political concerns, if not popular will itself. And yet again, ought rights to depend on any of this?

The point is not that judicial decision making necessarily should yield to exter nal constraint, any more than that executive failure to enforce the law necessarily is illegitimate. Rather, it is to make clear that the tensions that play themselves out daily in real cases are merely exemplary of unresolved problems at the level of democratic theory. Moreover, broad generalizations about rights and democratic accountability are unlikely to be helpful in resolving the very practical political issues involved in questions of judicial independence (and accountability). Democratic theory as it is implemented daily in the United States is textured and nuanced, and sweeping propositions are not likely to be helpful.

๑๙ Conclusion

Notwithstanding the wealth of different approaches to judicial selection and retention in the United States and around the world, many cannot resist the temptation to bless one as correct, thereby condemning the others. Yet, this reconsideration of what we mean by judicial independence, of what motivates judges, and of what constrains them strongly suggests that there is no single correct answer to the problem of selection and retention or, more generally, to the problem of judicial independence (and accountability). Taking as working hypotheses that systems have their strengths and weaknesses and that formal arrangements are but one part of the puzzle, both research and public policy should focus on situation-specific analysis without losing sight of the larger contexts in which the courts and judges whose independence (and accountability) are in question do their jobs.

Our goal has been to develop a set of tools by which to assess different practices and an agenda for research. If we have asked more questions than we have answered, all the better. Discussions of judicial independence (and accountability) have partaken more of slogans than they have of analysis. The analysis offered here should suffice to put to rest some shibboleths and to put in context some existing research findings. We hope that, in addition, our approach illuminates fruitful avenues for research in the future.

At the least, it should now be clear that judicial independence is a means to an end and not an end in itself. It remains for different polities to define what it is that they want from their courts and the measure (or quality) of judicial independence they believe is necessary or appropriate in order to secure it.

It should also be clear that, in thinking about the measure (or quality) of judicial independence that is necessary or appropriate to the attainment of particular goals, a polity should not treat judicial independence and judicial accountability as dichotomous but rather as different sides of the same coin. That is not just because a denial of independence necessarily entails accountability but also because a modern polity's goals for its judiciary will almost surely include functions that require a measure of accountability, just as they do a measure of independence.

The third shibboleth that we hope to have put to rest is the notion that all polities should seek the same measure (or quality) of judicial independence (and accountability) and that they should do so for all courts within their judicial systems. Both history and existing practice tell us that, even if this were normatively desirable, it has not been accomplished. The instrumental view of judicial independence (and accountability) taken here casts the normative proposition in serious doubt.

The knowledge that even within the American system—generally thought to accord the greatest measure of judicial independence—other actors possess numerous formal powers that could reduce decisional independence to insignificance (and increase accountability accordingly) reveals that selection and retention arrangements are but one part, and perhaps not the most important part, of the landscape of judicial independence (and accountability). We are just beginning to grasp the importance for both research and policy making of understanding the roles and limits of informal arrangements, including customs (Geyh, this volume). The enterprise must attend to the possibility that a distinction between formal and informal arrangements is artificial because of the shadow cast by power even when it is not exercised.

We deem it likely that understanding of this sort will help to explain why it is that theoretical approaches to, and purely normative treatments of, judicial independence (and accountability) that are restricted to formal selection and retention arrangements usually do not faithfully represent the landscape, and why it is more generally that little in this area is what it seems to be. Such understanding will not suffice, however, either fully to appreciate the current state of judicial independence (and accountability) in a given system or to know what changes in formal or informal arrangements would be necessary to alter the mix. For that purpose, we have argued, it is necessary to confront what it is that motivates judges and what constrains them.

We happily acknowledge the possibility "that a society cannot function without myths that capture its aspirations" (Burbank, 1999). It is, however, the business of scholars to expose rather than to trade in myths, and policymakers should trade in them only when the benefits outweigh the costs. Perhaps the biggest myth underlying traditional treatments of judicial independence in the legal literature has been the myth that those appointed to the federal bench are transformed by life tenure and nondiminishable compensation into superhuman beings not subject to the temptations and motivations that entice or drive the rest of us. In recent years, this myth has been in competition with another story, which we believe also to be a myth, emerging from the political science literature. According to that story too, federal judges are different from the rest of us, not because they are immune to self-interest, but rather because they are slaves to one such interest, the desire to maximize partisan or ideological preferences.

Once it is recognized that selection and retention arrangements may be a small point at which to stick in taking the measure of judicial independence (and accountability), the importance of refining and expanding the terms of this debate between lawyers and political scientists, as well as the implications of the enterprise for policy making, should be clear.

As to refinement, a critical distinction that has been missing from most of the studies to date concerns the different motivations and different constraints that may operate in different courts: federal and state, trial, intermediate appellate, and high. Like independence and accountability, motivation and constraint are different sides of the same coin. Thus, the additional studies we encourage may reveal that law as it is generally understood and the possibility of appellate review constrain decision making in many lower courts to a degree that renders if not insignificant, then unproblematic, whatever motivation the judges of those courts have to maximize their partisan or ideological preferences. They may also reveal that traditional role expectations, generated by the circumstances of selection and the culture of judging, have an influence on such motivation.[13]

Our discussion has only begun to suggest the many motivations other than the desire to maximize personal preferences that may contribute to judicial behavior. Yet, no less than partisanship or ideology, such motivations should be considered by policymakers when seeking to determine the mix of formal and informal arrangements best calculated to lead to the mix of judicial independence and accountability deemed necessary to secure what they want from a court and its judges. For that purpose, policymakers need the help of scholars. The biggest payoffs, we believe, are likely to come from attention to the effects that money and public opinion have on judicial behavior. The two are not unrelated and, although the former looms larger in selection and retention systems that require periodic voter approval than where they do not, if only because they are related no system is immune to the influence of both. No such research can hope to contribute to progress, however, unless those conducting it are willing to temper the purity of majoritarian or countermajoritarian theory with an appreciation, fueled by a knowledge of history and of the role of law in politics, of that to which reasonable polities can aspire.

As federal judicial selection becomes one of the most contentious political issues in Washington, as the states of the United States confront judicial election and retention election campaigns drowning in dollars and misleading advertisements, and as many nations and supranational organizations struggle with their own questions of judicial review, the need for fresh thinking and research has never been greater.

∾ Notes

1. There are likely other reasons having to do with the incentive structure in a career judiciary (Georgakopoulos, 2000; Ramseyer & Rasmusen, 2000).

2. Some regard the fact that decisions interpreting federal statutes can be effectively overruled by the enactment of subsequent legislation as relevant to the subject of judicial independence. Although one can certainly imagine a court avoiding a particular decision because of concern that, in light of a high likelihood of override, the decision would be an embarrassment or a futility, the phenomenon seems to us best considered as part of the allocation of lawmaking power.

3. The text is literally accurate, see U.S. CONST. art. III, § 1; Palmore v. United States, 411 U.S. 389, 400-01 (1973), but here as elsewhere where congressional action requires legislation, the executive is involved.

4. Congress has also, albeit infrequently and not in modern times, sought to exercise decisional control over the Supreme Court by regulating its calendar and appellate jurisdiction (Carpenter, 1918; Rehnquist, 1992).

5. More subtly, Congress can use the power *not* to add judges to overburdened lower courts as a means to discipline those courts for unpopular decisions or simply to keep them busy and out of trouble. Similar motivation probably helps to explain the refusal of early Congresses to heed the pleas of the Justices of the Supreme Court that they be relieved of the onerous business of riding circuit (Jacob, 1962).

6. See U.S. CONST. art. III, § 1; art. VI. Recent scholarship on the history of the struggles for judicial review and judicial supremacy, however, cautions us about inferences in that regard from the time of the founding (Friedman, 1998). A recent decision exploring the history of precedent in this country is another reminder not to retroject modern views to that period. See Hart v. Massanari, 266 F.3d, 1155 (9th Cir. 2001).

7. Once one recognizes that, from an instrumental perspective, judicial independence is not unique, the possibility emerges both that theoretical work on independence confined to the judiciary is incompletely specified and that, as William Ross has observed, historical inquiry so cabined may miss trends that tend to affect the independence of other institutions of government as well (Ross, 2001).

8. "This Constitution, and the Laws of the United States which shall be made in Pursuance thereof; and all Treaties made, or which shall be made, under the Authority of the United States, shall be the supreme Law of the Land; and the Judges in every State shall be bound thereby, any Thing in the Constitution or Laws of any State to the Contrary notwithstanding." U.S. Const., art. VI.

9. It is a separate question whether careful normative analysis would support current differences, particularly to the extent that they reflect the proposition that greater decisional independence (less accountability) is more appropriate for high courts than for trial courts.

10. A similar perspective may help to understand the recent phenomenon, referred to in Chapter 1 in this volume, of "treat[ing] all federal judicial appointments as if they were appointments to the Supreme Court" (American Judicature Society, 2001, p. 224).

11. In comments at the conference, Professor Scheppele likened a typical court structure to an inverse pyramid, pointing out how increasing the size of the court as one goes up the system could moderate the effect of individual partisanship, ideology, or both.

12. Thus, the federal judicial hierarchy may resemble an inverted pyramid, but as proportionally fewer and fewer cases proceed up the pyramid and are fully considered by a

superior court, the potential for the system effectively to constrain the decisional independence of inferior courts declines (Burbank, 1997).

13. Of course, studies that seek to determine the extent to which, if at all, law and appellate review constrain the implementation of personal preferences must be alert to other myths, or at least to stories that are out of date. To the extent, for instance, that the law is either generally or in specific areas indeterminate and there is little prospect of effective appellate review, the suggested distinction among trial, intermediate appellate, and high courts may lose some of its force, particularly in an age of massive aggregated cases. Moreover, even though formal arrangements may remain the same, both the circumstances of selection and the culture of judging may change, and rather than constraining motivation to implement personal preferences, they may enhance it (i.e., by putting a premium on ideological purity). This, it seems to us, is a valuable perspective from which to view changes in federal judicial selection, including shifts in the balance of power among those involved in that process, over the past decades. It may help to explain why it has become more difficult to distinguish the process used to nominate and confirm justices of the Supreme Court from that used for positions on the lower federal courts.

୧୨ References

American Judicature Society. (2000). *Judicial selection in the States: Appellate and general jurisdiction courts.* Available: http://www.ajs.org/Judicial%20Selection%20Charts3.pdf

American Judicature Society. (2001). Clinton's legacy or Bork's? *Judicature, 84,* 224.

Bass, J. (1981). *Unlikely heroes.* New York: Simon & Schuster.

Baum, L. (1994). What judges want: Judges' goals and judicial behavior. *Political Research Quarterly, 47,* 749-768.

Burbank, S. B. (1987). The costs of complexity. *Michigan Law Review, 85,* 1463-1487.

Burbank, S. B. (1996). The past and present of judicial independence. *Judicature, 80,* 117-122.

Burbank, S. B. (1997). The courtroom as classroom: Independence, imagination and ideology in the work of Jack Weinstein. *Columbia Law Review, 97,* 1971-2009.

Burbank, S. B. (1999). The architecture of judicial independence. *Southern California Law Review, 72,* 315-351.

Caldeira G. A. (1986). Neither the purse nor the sword: Confidence in the Supreme Court. *American Political Science Review, 80,* 1210-1226.

Caldeira, G. A., & Gibson, J. L. (1992). The etiology of public support for the Supreme Court. *American Journal of Political Science, 36,* 635-664.

Cameron, D. M., Segal, J. A., & Songer, D. (2000). Strategic auditing in a political hierarchy: An informational model of the Supreme Court's certiorari decisions. *American Political Science Review, 94,* 101-116.

Caminker, E. H. (1995). Precedent and prediction: The forward-looking aspects of lower court decisionmaking. *University of Texas Law Review, 73,* 1-82.

Canon, B. C., & Johnson, C. A. (1999). *Judicial policies: Implementation and impact.* Washingon, DC: Congressional Quarterly Press.

Cappelletti, M., Merryman, J. H., & Perillo, J. M. (1967). *The Italian legal system: An introduction.* Stanford, CA: Stanford University Press.

Carpenter, W. S. (1918). *Judicial tenure in the United States with especial reference to the tenure of federal judges.* New Haven, CT: Yale University Press.

Chase, O.G. (2001, March/April). *A speculation on judicial independence, triadic disputing, and cultural legitimacy.* Paper presented at a conference sponsored by the American Judicature Society and the Brennan Center for Justice, University of Pennsylvania, Philadelphia, PA. (see Appendix)

Cross, F.B., & Tiller, E.H. (1998). Judicial partisanship and obedience to legal doctrine: Whistleblowing on the Federal Courts of Appeals. *Yale Law Journal, 107,* 2155-2176.

Dorf, M. C. (1995). Prediction and the rule of law. *University of California Los Angeles Law Review, 42,* 651-715.

Epstein, L., & Knight, J. (1998). *The choices justices make.* Washington, DC: Congressional Quarterly Press.

Eskridge, W. N. (1993). The judicial review game. *Northwestern University Law Review, 88,* 382-395.

Eskridge, W. N., & Ferejohn, J. A. . (1992). The Article I, Section 7 Game. *Georgetown Law Journal, 80,* 523-564.

Ferejohn, J. A., & Weingast, B. R. (1992). A positive theory of statutory interpretation. *International Review of Law and Economics, 12,* 263-279.

Franklin, C. H., & Kosaki, L. C. (1995). Media, knowledge, and public evaluations of the Supreme Court. In L. Epstein (Ed.), *Contemplating courts* (pp. 352-375). Washington, DC: Congressional Quarterly Press.

Friedman, B. (1993). Dialogue and judicial review. *Michigan Law Review, 91,* 577-682.

Friedman, B. (1998). The history of the countermajoritarian difficulty, part one: The road to judicial supremacy. *New York University Law Review, 73,* 333-433.

Friedman, B. (2000). The history of the countermajoritarian difficulty, part four: Law's politics. *University of Pennsylvania Law Review, 148,* 971-1064.

Friedman, B. (2001). *The history of the countermajoritarian difficulty, part two.* Unpublished manuscript.

Friedman, L. (1985). *A history of American law* (2nd ed.). New York: Simon & Schuster.

Georgakopoulos, N. L. (1999). *A case study in judicial consistency.* Unpublished manuscript.

Georgakopoulos, N. L. (2000). Discretion in the career and recognition judiciary. *University of Chicago Roundtable, 7,* 205-225.

George, T. E. (1998). Developing a positive theory of decisionmaking on U.S. Courts of Appeals. *Ohio State Law Journal, 58,* 1635-1696.

George, T. E., & Epstein, L. (1992). On the nature of supreme court decision making. *American Political Science Review, 86,* 323-337.

Goldman, S. (1997). *Picking federal judges.* New Haven, CT: Yale University Press.

Guarnieri, C. (2001). Judicial independence in Latin countries of Western Europe. In P. H. Russell & D. M. O'Brien (Eds.), *Judicial independence in the age of democracy: Critical perspectives from around the world* (pp. 111-130). Charlottesville: University of Virginia Press.

Hartnett, E. (1997). Why is the Supreme Court of the United States protecting state judges from popular democracy? *Texas Law Review, 75,* 907-987.

Hazard, G. C., Jr. (2001, March/April). *Judicial independence: A structure for analysis.* Paper presented at a conference sponsored by American Judicature Society and the Brennan Center for Justice, University of Pennsylvania, Philadelphia, PA. (see Appendix)

Hershkoff, H. (1999). Positive rights and state constitutions: The limits of federal rationality review. *Harvard Law Review, 112,* 1131-1194.

Hershkoff, H. (2001). State courts and the "passive virtues": Rethinking the judicial function. *Harvard Law Review, 114,* 1833-1940.

Hoekstra, V. J. (2000). The Supreme Court and public opinion. *American Political Science Review, 94,* 89-100.

Hurst, W. (1950). *The growth of American law: The law makers.* Boston: Little, Brown.

Iaryczower, M., Spiller, P. T., & Tommasi, M. (in press). Judicial decision making in unstable environments: Argentina 1935-1998. *American Journal of Political Science.*

Jacob, H. (1962). The courts as political agencies: An historical analysis. In K. N. Vines & H. Jacob (Eds.), *Studies in judicial politics* (pp. 9-50). New Orleans, LA: Tulane University Press.

Jay, S. (1985). Origins of federal common law: Part one. *University of Pennsylvania Law Review, 133,* 1003-1116.

Kornhauser, L. A. (1995). Adjudication by a resource-constrained team: Hierarchy and precedent in a judicial system. *Southern California Law Review, 68,* 1605-1629.

Levinson, D. J. (1999). Rights essentialism and remedial equilibration. *Columbia Law Review, 99,* 857-940.

Maltzman, F., Spriggs, J. F., & Wahlbeck, P. J. (2000). *Crafting law on the Supreme Court: The collegial game.* New York: Cambridge University Press.

Martin, A. D. (2001). *Statutory battles, constitutional wars: Congress and the Supreme Court.* Unpublished manuscript.

McNollgast. (1995). Politics and the courts: A positive theory of judicial doctrine and the rule of law. *Southern California Law Review, 68,* 1631-1683.

Parker, P. E. (1999). Is a lower caseload the same as a lower workload? Opinion characteristics of the Burger and Rehnquist courts. *The Justice System Journal, 20,* 299-316.

Peretti, T. J. (1999). *In defense of a political court.* Princeton, NJ: Princeton University Press.

Posner, R. A. (1995). *Overcoming law.* Cambridge, MA: Harvard University Press.

Ramseyer, J. M. (1994). The puzzling (in)dependence of courts: A comparative approach. *Journal of Legal Studies, 23,* 721-747.

Ramseyer, J. M., & Rasmusen, E. B. (2000). Skewed incentives: Paying for politics as a Japanese judge. *Judicature, 83,* 190-195.

Rehnquist., W. H. (1992). *Grand inquests.* New York: Morrow.

Revesz, R. L. (1997). Environmental regulation, ideology, and the D.C. circuit. *Virginia Law Review, 83,* 1717-1772.

Ross, W. G. (2001, March/April). *Suggestions for future research on judicial independence.* Paper presented at a conference sponsored by the American Judicature Society and the Brennan Center for Justice, University of Pennsylvania, Philadelphia, PA. (see Appendix)

Schauer, F. (2000). Incentives, reputation, and the inglorious determinants of judicial behavior. *University of Cincinnati Law Review, 68,* 615-636.

Segal, J. A. (1997). Separation-of-powers games in the positive theory of Congress and courts. *American Political Science Review, 91,* 28-44.

Segal, J. A., & Cover, A. D. (1989). Ideological values and the votes of U.S. Supreme Court Justices. *American Political Science Review, 83,* 557-565.

Segal, J. A., & Spaeth, H. J. (1993). *The Supreme Court and the attitudinal model.* New York: Cambridge University Press.

Seidman, L. M. (2001, March/April). *The impossibility of judicial independence.* Paper presented at a conference sponsored by the American Judicature Society and the Brennan Center for Justice, University of Pennsylvania, Philadelphia, PA. (see Appendix)

Sisk, G. C., Heise, M., & Moriss, A. P. (1998). Charting the influences on the judicial mind: An empirical study of judicial reasoning. *New York University Law Review, 73,* 1377-1500.

Songer, D. R., Sheehan, R. S., & Haire, S. B. (1999). Do the "haves" come out ahead over time? Applying Galanter's framework to decisions of the U.S. Courts of Appeals, 1925- 1988. *Law & Society Review, 33,* 811-832.

Songer, D. R., Sheehan, R. S., & Haire, S. B. (2000). *Continuity and change on the United States Courts of Appeals.* Ann Arbor: University of Michigan Press.

Spaeth, H. J., & Segal, S. A. (1999). *Majority rule or minority will: Adherence to precedent on the U.S. Supreme Court.* New York: Cambridge University Press.

Stevens, R. (2001). Judicial independence in England: A loss of innocence. In P. H. Russell & D. M. O'Brien (Eds.), *Judicial independence in the age of democracy: Critical perspectives from around the world* (pp. 155-172). Charlottesville: University of Virginia Press.

Stimson, J. A., Mackuen, M. B., & Erikson, R. S. (1995). Dynamic representation. *American Political Science Review, 89,* 543-565.

Wald, P. M. (1999). A response to Tiller and Cross. *Columbia Law Review, 99,* 235-261.

White, G. E. (1996). Salmon Portland Chase and the judicial culture of the Supreme Court in the Civil War era. In J. M. Lowe (Ed.), *The Supreme Court and the Civil War* (pp. 37- 45). Washington, DC: Supreme Court Historical Society.

Part II

THE MEANING OF JUDICIAL INDEPENDENCE

Theoretical Dimensions

Chapter 3

Is Judicial Independence a Useful Concept?

Lewis A. Kornhauser

ை Introduction

This chapter has two theses. First, I argue that the confusion over the meaning of judicial independence cannot be eliminated. Second, I argue that judicial independence is not a useful, analytic concept. It does not promote either our understanding of how courts function or the design of desirable judicial institutions. Debate over these issues of understanding and design would advance more quickly if we abandoned the use of the concept: Jurisprudential debates over judicial independence would explicitly address the controversial theories of adjudication that underlie current debates, while inquiries into the effects of various institutional features on judicial performance would proceed without a fruitless diversion into the role of judicial independence.

These two theses are related. The ineliminability of definitional issues provides one reason that the concept of judicial independence is not useful. Consequently, the discussion begins with the question of definition. I then proceed to discuss the utility of the concept in social science and constitutional design.

This chapter grows out of a very brief essay and remarks made at the Brennan Center and American Judicature Society conference on Judicial Independence held at the University of Pennsylvania at the end of March, 2001. It owes much to the discussion at the conference. Steve Burbank and Barry Friedman commented on an earlier draft. Copyright 2001 Lewis A. Kornhauser.

怀 Definitional Issues

Discussions of judicial independence occur in a wide variety of contexts that range from public debates over decisions in individual cases and political debates over the appropriate structure of court systems to technical discussions in the social science literature—especially political science—and in law reviews.

The differing domains of these discussions suggest the source of some of the confusion in the definition of "judicial independence." Specifically, the differing domains suggest two dimensions along which one might classify definitions. First, judicial independence might be a property attributable to the decision of individual cases, to a particular judge, or to a system of adjudication as a whole. One might think that, in principle, the definition of judicial independence of a decision in a single case should be the primary definition with the definition of the independence of a single judge derivative of this basic definition and the definition of structural independence derivative of the idea of the independence of a single judge. The following discussion will suggest that this hierarchical arrangement of definitions is not necessarily followed.

Second, the definition of judicial independence might differ with the nature of the theory in which it is embedded. So, we might expect the definition of judicial independence to differ in social science studies of adjudication from those in legal studies. Not only are social scientists apt to have different explanatory aims than legal scholars but also legal scholars are more likely to advance normative theories than social scientists. This division between legal and social scientific definitions explains much, but not all, of the definitional confusion. The disciplinary division does not provide a complete explanation because definitional confusion persists within each discipline.

Legal Definitions

Lawyers, judges, and legal academics deploy the term "judicial independence" in a wide variety of contexts. Its use generally complements and contrasts with a set of related terms—"power" generally, "separation of powers," and the "rule of law." An adequate definition of judicial independence should thus satisfy at least two conditions. First, it should identify an analytically useful concept that isolates an important feature of adjudicatory practice or adjudicatory institutions. Second, the definition should clarify the relation of judicial independence to at least these three other concepts. The distinctions between these concepts may, in the end, prove subtle but a definition that treated judicial independence as synonymous with one of these terms, say "separation of powers," would be less appealing than one that distinguished between them but suggested their conceptual connections. I shall thus proceed initially by investigating the relation between these four concepts.

I begin with the relation of judicial independence to power. Note first that power is an attribute of a court rather than of a judge. We speak of the independence of courts but, in many theories, this concept is derivative of the concept of an independent judge. From this theoretical perspective, then, the two concepts differ. The idea of independence does, however, suggest that an independent judge is not subject to the "power" of another individual or institution. How one understands this lack of subjection will depend, of course, on one's concept of power, itself a notoriously controversial concept.

One may, nonetheless, see that independence is neither necessary nor sufficient for power. An independent court may have little power. Consider, for example, British courts. The independence of the British judiciary is generally uncontested but its courts are much less powerful than, for example, U.S. courts. Conversely, a dependent court may be quite powerful. The European Court of Justice exercises extraordinary power. If its judges were subject to the control of the governments of their native states, the judges would not be independent even though the Court would remain a powerful institution.

Consider now the relation of the concept of judicial independence to that of the separation of powers. These two concepts are often conflated. As before, the separation of powers is a structural concept whereas judicial independence apparently has a sense at the level of the individual judges. Even at the structural level, however, the two concepts are distinct as one may perceive by two different routes.

First, one may consider the British experience. Both the theory and practice of British government deny the significance of the separation of powers. In theory, at least prior to Britain's entry into the European Union, parliament's sovereignty was unquestioned. Moreover, the highest court in Britain is an agency of the parliament. An intermixture of executive and legislative powers also exists. Yet, British judges are generally regarded as independent; that independence is sustained both by statute and by the political and legal cultures in Great Britain.[1]

Second, separation of powers and judicial independence have different functional roles. Separation of powers provides a check on government power; it regulates the relation among government institutions and between the government and the citizenry. The concern for judicial independence, by contrast, arises regardless of the identity of the litigants before the courts. Independence is generally regarded as a virtue in the adjudication of disputes between private individuals as well as of disputes between the government and private citizens.

The differences between these concepts emerge from an analogy to an ordinary language use of "independence" that underlies both the legal and social science definitions of "judicial independence." Specifically, judicial independence relies on the idea that judges are not subject to the influence of some other actor(s); they are the authors of their own decisions. This sense of independence points to the distinction between separation of powers and judicial independence. Judicial power concerns the set of decisions that the judge has the authority to resolve; but a judge may have authority to resolve a question yet not be free of the influence of other agents. Similarly, the rule of law requires that judges exercise their authority in a particular way. A judge might exercise authority impartially in the relevant sense for the rule of law even if or perhaps *because* of influence by some other actor.

Legal definitions of judicial independence qualify this ordinary language sense of independence as freedom from influence. We may approach the qualification in either of two ways. First, the judge should only be free of "inappropriate" influence. Second, and related, the judge need not be free of the influence of *all* individuals. The parties may influence a judge through legal arguments that persuade judges and that are offered orally in court or in papers submitted to the court; such persuasion does not constitute "inappropriate" influence. Arguments offered *ex parte* might be inappropriate though we may not characterize the exercise of this sort of influence as compromising judicial independence. Similarly, judges who take bribes are subject to inappropriate influence. Neither lower court judges who follow the decisions of superior courts nor state supreme court justices who are persuaded by the rulings of courts outside their jurisdiction are subject to inappropriate influence. Most important, judges who render judgment on the basis of commitment to some set of moral and political principles are not subject to inappropriate influence.

The nature of inappropriate influence and the identity of actors who may influence the judge differ with the normative theory of adjudication from which the definition of judicial independence emerges. A theory of adjudication specifies the content of the obligation to decide a case. The obligations in turn determine what constitutes inappropriate influence from various individuals. As theories of adjudication differ widely in the content of these obligations, they also differ dramatically in their characterizations of judicial independence. Moreover, the disagreement over normative theories of adjudication accounts for the ineliminability of confusion over the definition of judicial independence.

Consider, for example, sketches of three theories of adjudication: "mechanical" jurisprudence, H. L. A. Hart's positivist theory, and Ronald Dworkin's theory of adjudication as interpretation. Hart's theory postulates two modes of judicial decision. One mode corresponds to the main idea in the theory of "mechanical" adjudication—the judge identifies the legal rule that governs the case by tracing its pedigree and then applies that legal rule straightforwardly to the case at hand.[2] In this mode, the parties may point the judge to relevant statutes, regulations, and case law, but no other influence by anyone is legitimate. If no legal rule governs the instant case, the judge, on Hart's theory, must exercise discretion. Again, in the exercise of this discretion, the judge may respond to the arguments of the parties but not to arguments or other forms of influence that others might exercise. Moreover, the judge, though exercising discretion, may not act arbitrarily. He or she must render a judgment that promotes the end of the statute or makes "good" law; he or she may not simply act capriciously. Thus, when the law is clear, the resolution of the case should not depend on the identity of the judge who decides the case. Conversely, when the law is unclear and a judge may exercise discretion, the Hartian concept of judicial independence does not imply that the decision will be independent of the identity of the judge who decides the case.

In Dworkin's theory, by contrast, the judge, after rendering a decision, must interpret the political history of the jurisdiction in which he or she sits to make the law of that jurisdiction the "best it can be." The theory imposes an obligation on the judge to make the law "the best it can be."[3] The decision must result from a legal theory that both fits the past political history of the jurisdiction and casts that political history in a favorable light. Of course, the judge's interpretation must reflect his or her own moral and political views, but this interpretation of philosophical commitment and judicial decision does not reduce the independence of the judge.

Social Science Definitions

Social science definitions of judicial independence rely on the same underlying, ordinary language sense of "independence" as legal definitions: Judicial decision should be free of "inappropriate" influence. In the social science context, however, theories are usually concerned with judicial independence from the influence of partisan politics on judicial decision. Again, the nature of the excluded influence is not clearly specified.

Political scientists and legal academics, for example, generally consider the federal judiciary in the United States as the paradigmatic case of judicial independence. The life tenure of these judges and the insulation of judges from retribution through compensation are generally identified as the indicia of this strong independence. These structural features of the federal judiciary are designed to insulate federal judges from the day-to-day pressures of partisan politics.

Yet the federal judiciary is not free of influence from partisan politics. That influence is exercised in several ways. First, partisan politics seems to influence the selection of judges. The appointees of George Bush and Ronald Reagan differ systematically from appointees of Lyndon Johnson, Jimmy Carter, and Bill Clinton. Second, Congress has the power to define the jurisdiction of the courts as well as to determine its caseload through the budgetary process. An explicit withdrawal of jurisdiction does not subject any particular judge to the influence of partisan politics, but it does ensure that those cases that Congress withdraws from the jurisdiction of the courts are resolved in response to partisan politics. Third, if positive political theory is correct, courts in general and the Supreme Court in particular will consider the views of the political branches in rendering decisions. On these strategic accounts, the views of the political branches may severely constrain the courts from rendering the judgments that they desire.

The example of the federal judiciary suggests that political scientists generally have a structural conception of judicial independence rather than a concept of the independence of an individual judge. Yet the empirical literature that finds that the political views of judges systematically influence the decisions that they render relies for its rhetorical force on a conception of the independence of an individual judge. A judge who espouses a particular set of political views may have been appointed—indeed probably was appointed—because he or she held those views and because those supporting the appointment believed that, after appointment, he or she would act independently.

३ Understanding Courts and Society

I argue in this section that the concept of judicial independence is not a useful analytic concept for the understanding of courts or society. As in the discussion of definitions, one must distinguish the legal project from the social science project. Crudely, the legal project seeks to justify political institutions generally and legal institutions in particular; it is thus a normative rather than a positive project. Social science, by contrast, has primarily an explanatory aim; it seeks to understand the origin, operation, and effects of social institutions, including legal ones.

In both the legal and social science projects, judicial independence plays an intermediate role. No one values judicial independence intrinsically. Legal theory advocates the promotion of judicial independence only because it furthers some other, more fundamental goal. Similarly, judicial independence is neither a primitive term in social theories nor the primary phenomenon to be explained.[4] It is intermediate to some other phenomenon or goal. Definitional confusion undermines this intermediation function of the concept of judicial independence.

Judicial Independence in Legal Theory

In legal theory, the concept of judicial independence is instrumental or, as noted in the definitional discussion, an artifact of an underlying theory of adjudication. Phrased differently, we believe that an independent judiciary will apply legal rules to resolve disputes better than a "dependent"judiciary would.

This characterization of the claim for an independent judiciary poses an obvious question: Against what criteria ought we to measure the performance of a judiciary? I want to identify several different criteria that embody criteria implicit in standard discussions of judicial performance and the rule of law. The first two criteria concern the treatment of a given case. *Litigant anonymity* requires that the decision of a case be independent of the *names* or *identities* of the litigants.[5] The result of a contract dispute should not depend on the identities of the litigant. It should not matter, for example, whether defendant is a prominent politician or businessman rather than the owner of a marginal business. One can, of course, imagine a "dependent"judiciary so constructed to satisfy this requirement.

Adjudicator anonymity requires that the decision of a case be independent of the identity of the *adjudicator.* A plaintiff's right to recover on a claim should not depend on which judge hears the case.[6] Notice that, again, a dependent judiciary might meet this criterion. After all, adjudicator anonymity requires only homogeneity in the decision criteria of judges. A perfectly dependent judiciary, one that decides cases exactly as the political branch would desire, would do so uniformly; that is, *every* judge would be subject to the same pressures.

Conversely, judicial independence may not guarantee either adjudicator or litigant anonymity. Freedom from inappropriate influence by others does not guarantee that a particular judge, or an entire bench, will be impartial so that litigant anonymity is not guaranteed. Moreover, even if all judges are impartial (and independent), this independence does not guarantee that they will be impartial in the same way.

In many instances, the concern for judicial independence reflects a concern about consistency across cases and, hence, across time. The two case-specific criteria, however, have consequences for consistency across time. A system that satisfies both litigant and adjudicator neutrality, for example, will treat like cases alike. Similarly, such a system would be, to some extent, predictable. Once one case had been decided, future litigants, or potential litigants, could predict the decision in relevantly similar cases. Of course, a system in which judges decided as the political branch desired would be predictable as well. Moreover, as Ramseyer's and Rasmusen's (1997) study of Japan suggests, if the political branch is ideologically (and otherwise) stable, it would be predictable in a way that permitted litigants and potential litigants to plan. The evil one must guard against here is *arbitrary*, not ideological, decision.

Judicial dependence threatens anonymity and predictability, then, only in certain circumstances. Different judges, for example, might be beholden to different politicians. Alternatively, the *set* of politicians—say the governing coalition—to whom judges respond changes sufficiently frequently to make planning difficult.

Adjudicator and litigant anonymity have rhetorical appeal in normative discussions of judicial obligation even though neither goal clearly follows from prevailing normative theories of adjudication such as Hart's or Dworkin's. Even if one accepts the legitimacy of these forms of anonymity, however, the argument above shows that judicial independence is neither necessary nor sufficient for their achievement. It is thus unclear in what way reference to judicial independence advances a debate.

More generally, different theories of adjudication will identify different normative goals that one ought to promote through the design of a judicial system. It seems unhelpful to argue indirectly over these through discussions of judicial independence rather than to argue directly about the desirability of the underlying theories of judicial independence. More strongly, because a conception of judicial independence is derivative of the normative theory of adjudication, the concept cannot guide a choice between competing theories.

Judicial Independence in Social Theory

In the social science literature, judicial independence generally serves as an "independent variable" with which the analyst hopes to explain some significant measure of social performance such as economic performance or the well-being of the population.[7] Judicial independence, however, is not directly observable. In empirical studies, then, the analyst has to use some proxy for independence. These proxies generally consider various structural features of the judiciary. The most common indicia are the appointments process and the length of term that the judge may serve. Judicial systems, of course, vary greatly in these structural features. Many of the societies in which these systems are embedded apparently perform equally well in terms of the social performance measures.

The concept of judicial independence does not help in the design of political structures that foster social stability or economic development. Two reasons suggest why: (a) Judicial independence is not a necessary condition for either stability or development; and (b) a wide variety of structures of adjudication that might qualify as independence are sufficient to foster either stability or development.

Consider the nonnecessity claim first. The work of Ramseyer and Rasmusen (1997) argues that Japan does not have an independent judiciary. Though modeled on the judiciary in civil law countries that preserve judicial independence through the creation of a bureaucracy, the Japanese judiciary appears to be subject to partisan influence in ways that go beyond the structural features of appointment and term. Ramseyer and Rasmusen argue specifically that judicial decisions adverse to the governing party have a detrimental effect on the career of the judge who renders the decision.

Japan nevertheless has a stable government as well as a spectacular record of economic development over the last 50 years. Ramseyer and Rasmusen argue that the dominance of the Liberal Democratic Party in Japanese politics and governance has substituted for the independence of a judiciary.

Consider now the problem of multiple realizability. Court systems with very different structural features provide sufficient independence to promote both political stability and economic development. It is probably sufficient to note that the judicial systems of the OECD countries differ in many structural features, yet these countries have high levels of both political stability and economic development.

The nonnecessity and insufficiency of judicial independence for the achievement of these broad social goals suggest that the emphasis on independence in the design of judicial institutions is misplaced. It may be that specific structural features in the design of judicial institutions promote economic well-being (or some other social goal), but neither the identification of that structural feature nor the clarification of its role in promoting the social goal runs through a concept of judicial independence.

Similarly, concepts of judicial independence play little, if any, role in the explanation of how judicial institutions function either in isolation or in relation to other political and social institutions. The abstract concept, because it is unclear and contested, does not help isolate specific features or clusters of features of adjudication that explain performance. A more sensible approach would focus directly on the structural features of these institutions as explanatory instruments without reference to the concept of judicial independence.

෨ Conclusion

The concept of judicial independence does not further the development of normative theories of adjudication, does not advance understanding of the functioning of extant judicial systems, and does not aid in the design (or improvement) of judicial institutions. The concept fails in these regards for somewhat different reasons.

It fails to decide between normative theories of adjudication because the concept of judicial independence derives from these theories rather than stands outside of them. Each normative theory of adjudication ascribes a different meaning and importance to judicial independence. Consequently, judicial independence has no clear meaning distinct from the theory of adjudication in which it is embedded.

A similar confusion besets the concept of judicial independence when deployed within the explanatory and design projects. In the design context, judicial independence is neither necessary nor sufficient for the achievement of a variety of social goals that it is thought to promote. Consequently, the concept of judicial independence cannot guide our design of institutions. In the explanatory project, the abstract concept does not single out specific features or clusters of features of judicial institutions as essential explanatory elements. The concept of judicial independence thus does not further our explanatory aims.

I conclude with a simple answer to the question of the chapter's title: The concept of judicial independence is not useful. Legal debates over adjudication, debates over the design of judicial institutions, and the explanation of the emergence and performance of various judicial institutions would be clearer and progress more rapidly if we abandoned the concept.

∞ Notes

1. On judicial independence and the separation of powers in Great Britain, see Robert Stevens (2001). Stevens argues that the British judiciary is independent individually but dependent structurally. That argument illustrates the confusion that plagues the literature. If structural independence and individual independence both fall under the concept of judicial independence, then we need to know the conceptual connection between them. If the two concepts of structural and individual independence are unrelated, grouping both under the rubric of judicial independence only breeds confusion.

2. In Hart's theory, the judge traces the pedigree of a given rule to determine that it is valid law and then applies the rule. The mythological theory of mechanical jurisprudence does not specify the procedure for determining the prevailing rule.

3. See Dworkin (1986).

4. A social scientist might seek to explain the pattern of jurisdictions that have independent judiciaries. This explanatory aim, however, will arise only if the theorist believes that judicial independence is significant. The text asserts that the significance of independence is never intrinsic.

5. In some instances, of course, the outcome of a legal dispute might depend critically on the identity of a party. In a dispute over an estate, a party might claim to be the son of the

testator, and proof of that claim obviously depends on his identity. This conditioning of the case outcome on identity seems unproblematic even when one espouses the value of litigant anonymity.

6. Adjudicator anonymity might apply only to legal questions in an adjudication, only to factual questions, or to both. Most discussions assume that the identify of the adjudicator should not affect legal decisions. Many legal rules, for example, address the discretion of the fact finder. Thus, a ruling in a negligence case might say that "on these facts, no reasonable person could conclude that defendant was negligent." The contrary ruling, of course, that a reasonable person could conclude that defendant was negligent, suggests that finders of fact might reach different conclusions on this issue and that this difference would be legally acceptable.

7. Some of the empirical literature on courts in political science challenges legal claims of judicial independence in which judicial independence is understood as adjudicator anonymity. These studies show that judicial ideology is a statistically significant predictor of the outcome of cases (Revesz, 1997; Cross & Tiller, 1998). These studies generally use the party affiliation of the President who appointed the judge as a measure of the judge's ideology. These studies do not undermine claims of judicial independence that rely on normative theories of adjudication that do not endorse adjudicator anonymity.

⌒ References

Cross, F. B., & Tiller, E. H. (1998). Judicial partisanship and obedience to legal doctrine: Whistleblowing on the Federal Courts of Appeals. *Yale Law Journal, 107,* 2155-2176.

Dworkin, R. M. (1986). *Law's empire.* Cambridge, MA: Harvard University Press.

Ramseyer, J. M., & Rasmusen, E. B. (1997). Judicial independence in a civil law regime: The evidence from Japan. *Journal of Law, Economics & Organization, 13,* 259-286.

Revesz, R. L. (1997). Environmental regulation, ideology, and the D.C. circuit. *Virginia Law Review, 83,* 1717-1772.

Stevens, R. (2001). Judicial independence in England: A loss of innocence. In P. H. Russell & D. M. O'Brien (Eds.), *Judicial independence in an age of democracy: Critical perspectives from around the world* (pp. 153-172). Charlottesville: University of Virginia Press.

Independence as a Governance Mechanism

Edward L. Rubin

Judicial independence is often regarded as one of the glories of the Anglo-American tradition. Older than democracy, it served as the bulwark within which were nurtured such rights as due process, habeas corpus, and freedom from self-incrimination. It remains today essential to our federal judiciary, as a source of the high regard in which our courts are held, and as a justification for the extensive role that they have been able to assume. For all these reasons, and others, we tend to treat judicial independence as a unitary concept, a linguistically embedded word pair with a single meaning.

On consideration, this would appear to be an unwise analytic strategy. It assumes an organic connection between the relationship of independence and the institution of the judiciary that may not be either exclusive or inevitable. Independence, after all, refers to a technique of governance that is regularly deployed in many parts of the modern administrative state. To treat independence as intrinsically judicial reflects the jurocentric character of American legal scholarship, which is certainly something that requires justification. To treat the judiciary as intrinsically independent is an artifact of the idea that government consists of three separate branches, an idea that is common but by no means obvious. Both

I want to thank Stephen Burbank and Catherine Struve for their help with this chapter, and the Smith Richardson Foundation for its assistance with the research that serves as the background for the first section of this chapter. A more detailed discussion of the subject matter, particularly in that section, will appear in my forthcoming book, *Onward Past Arthur: Rethinking Politics and Law for the Administrative State*.

aspects of the connection, moreover, focus attention on questions about whether the judiciary is in fact independent or what degree of independence it should be granted. But this ignores the more basic question about what the concept of independence really means, as an operational matter. The judiciary, after all, is part of the government, acts in close conjunction with other governmental units, and generally contributes to the maintenance of a single governmental system. Before discussing the matter of judicial independence, therefore, we need a general theory of independence as a tool of governance. We need to know what independence really means, to explore the different contexts in which it can be deployed, and to assess its advantages and disadvantages in each of those contexts. This chapter briefly outlines such a theory, discusses judicial independence from the perspective of that theory, and specifies some lines of future research that the theory suggests.

⟫ Branches, Networks, and the Images of the State

We commonly think of our government as being divided into three branches—the executive, the legislative, and the judicial. This arborescent image of government evolved during the English Civil War and gradually replaced the older image of the state as human body over the course of the 18th century (Vile, 1967). The idea that independence, as a tool of governance, relates uniquely to the judiciary is a product of this image (Gwyn, 1965; Spurlin, 1969); we think of the judiciary as a separate branch and assert that it must be kept independent of the other two branches, which are political in nature, if it is to act in the fair and neutral manner we expect (Bickel, 1962; Dworkin, 1986).

In a work that is currently in progress, I argue that this three-branch imagery is an infelicitous way to envision the modern administrative state. The argument, stated briefly, is that the three-branch image describes the government of the premodern era, when this image was developed, but no longer corresponds to our current situation. About 700 years ago, the government of European states, or protostates, consisted of three groups of relatively equal size—the legislature, the judges, and the king's household. A centralized administration, staffed by university-trained lawyers and clerics, was already beginning to develop, but it was still small enough to be combined with the king's household, yielding three components of roughly commensurate size (Bloch, 1961; Richardson & Sayles, 1963; Strayer, 1970; Warren, 1973, pp. 241-395). Today, of course, this is no longer the case. Although the size of the legislature, the judiciary, and the chief executive's personal staff have increased only incrementally and in rough proportion to the state's increasing population, the central administration has grown to gigantic proportions. In the United States, it numbers several million people—two orders of magnitude larger than the remainder of the government.

The three-branch metaphor simply cannot capture this reality. Where are all these millions of administrators to be placed? The traditional answer is that they are part of the executive branch. But the reference to branches suggests that we are envisioning a tree, and what tree has one branch that is a hundred times larger than the others? Moreover, it is well known that administrative agencies regularly perform legislative and judicial functions in addition to executive ones, which means pieces of this one edematous branch must now reach over and intertwine with the two diminutive ones (Strauss, 1984). Worse still, many American administrative agencies are not under the president's control at all; they are independent agencies, which means that the president appoints their leading officers but cannot remove these officers without a showing of good cause (Bernstein, 1955; Pierce, Shapiro, & Verkuil, 1999, pp. 91-108; Welborn, 1977). The Brownlow Commission that Franklin Roosevelt established to assess these developments was highly disconcerted by this "haphazard deposit of irresponsible agencies and uncoordinated powers," which it described as "a headless fourth branch" (The Brownlow Commission, 1937, pp. 39-43; Rohr, 1986, p. 153). This additional image halves the size of the overgrown executive branch and produces another of roughly equal proportions, but it suggests the grotesque idea, perhaps resulting from an unconscious reversion to the human body metaphor, that the other three branches have heads appended at their ends.

The resulting image is too odd to be useful and too ugly to enjoy. Perhaps more important, it denies or underemphasizes the reality of the administrative state. We all know that the officials with whom we deal on a daily basis, who make decisions that govern our lives, are not elected but appointed; they are not chosen from among the general population but on the basis of specialized training and internal promotion through the hierarchy; they are not supervised or controlled by elected officials, or by the traditional constraints of common law, but only by other appointed officials like themselves. But we are psychologically committed to believing that we still live in the nation that the framers envisioned, that elections give us complete control over our government, that appointed officials are constrained by law, that each branch can check the others and thereby protect us from government oppression or excess. We want to issue blistering, unmodulated condemnations at the all-too-obvious divergences from this image, treating them as products of narrowly focused interest groups, Washington politicians, and, of course, the bureaucrats themselves (Howard, 1996; Jacoby, 1973; Johnson & Libecap, 1994). These are the diseased elements that have changed the shape of our government; if we could only extirpate them, we could return to our principles and our traditions.

It is nothing more than a political fantasy, of course. The administrative state is the product of a 1000-year-long evolution and a 200-year-long period of dominance. It responds to powerful social needs, performs essential functions, and partially constitutes our sense of who we are. We can no more eliminate it, or significantly reduce its size, than we could cut large segments from the trunk of a living tree. What we need to do, and what we desperately want to do, is make this government more effective, more efficient, and more fair. The three-branch metaphor provides a means of expressing our vague dissatisfactions but does nothing to implement these more genuine commitments.

The three-branch metaphor is not only descriptively inaccurate as an image of government, but it is also inappropriately static. Although it certainly proclaims the contested notion that the executive, legislature, and judiciary are supposed to be separate, it obscures the principal purpose of this notion, which is the control of abuse. The branches of a tree do not control each other; they just sit there separately. Control is important in the modern state, but it involves a complex, dynamic interaction between different parts of government that the three-branch image does nothing to illuminate. In addition, the image coagulates each part that it identifies into an opaque, woody mass, rather than revealing their articulated structure in a way that would enable specific decisions and communication pathways to be traced, evaluated, and, if necessary, reconfigured.

Perhaps the image would serve as a more useful heuristic if more attention were paid to plant biology, the subject that it metaphorically invokes. After all, what tree consists exclusively of branches? Virtually all trees have a trunk, and the trunk is generally far larger than any branch. The trunk, then, is the missing element that serves as the analogue of our massive administrative agencies. Introducing it into the metaphor resolves virtually all the aesthetic difficulties that the advent of the administrative state creates. The independent agencies are not a branch at all but part of the trunk; they are headless only in the sense of having no definitive endpoint because the trunk terminates, quite naturally, by dividing into branches. These agencies, together with the presidentially supervised agencies, naturally combine executive, legislative, and judicial functions because all three of the branches that represent these functions feed into, and grow out of, the trunk. Most important, the addition of the trunk eliminates the disproportion among branches by enabling us to remove the presidentially supervised agencies, as well as the independent agencies, from the executive branch. What remains in this branch is the chief executive and his immediate staff—in the United States, the president, his personal staff, his immediate advisors, White House Counsel, and perhaps the Office of Management and Budget (Patterson, 2001). Thus reduced, the executive branch is now approximately the same size as the other two and produces a much more harmoniously proportioned tree.

Nifty as this solution may appear, it represents only a marginal improvement. Although it acknowledges the central role of the administrative apparatus, its continuing Arcadianism remains an ongoing denial of the complex, instrumental character of the modern state. In addition, the image fails to conform to our commitments because a tree trunk's primary purpose is to supply and elevate the patulous branches, whereas the administrative apparatus is the essence of our governmental system. It is also as unclear how branches would control the trunk as how they would control each other; on the basis of the image, the trunk itself appears to the mind's eye as a uniform, impenetrable mass. Perhaps the metaphor could be developed further through a more technical use of plant biology. We might inquire about the correlative of the roots that are appended to the lower end of the administrative trunk, or trace the operations of the agencies in terms of xylem, bark, and annual growth rings. But the image, even as elaborated, seems too organic, and insufficiently articulated, to facilitate a detailed, effective analysis of the administrative state.

In *A Thousand Plateaus,* Deleuze and Guattari (1987, pp. 3-25) level a general attack against the arborescent imagery that, in their view, dominates all Western thought. The tree, they suggest, is unitary, logical, and hierarchical—three qualities that rank very low in the value system of any French postmodernist. In its place, they propose the rhizome, a widely dispersed root structure characteristic of fungi, or, to pick a more appetizing example, strawberries (Deleuze & Guattari, pp. 5-7). Rhizomes, according to Deleuze and Guattari, are interconnected and heterogeneous; they exhibit multiplicity, not uniformity, because they consist of an undefined number of linkages; they are resilient and undifferentiated, reforming after being broken; the pathways through them lead back into themselves rather than outward toward their boundaries; they have no deep structure that can be traced but only a multidimensional complexity. The human mind, Deleuze and Guattari suggest, is more accurately pictured as a rhizome than a tree. The marionette and the puppeteer form a rhizome, and if one believes that the interconnected strings of the marionette end in the organic unity of the puppeteer, one must remember that the puppeteer exercises control through a set of nerve fibers whose structure resembles those strings (Deleuze & Guattari, p. 8).

This seems like a more promising metaphor than the tree trunk for the administrative apparatus, which indeed displays the characteristics of interconnection and multidimensional complexity. It suggests the possibility, moreover, of eliminating the tree metaphor entirely, by incorporating its three traditional branches of executive, legislature, and judiciary into an all-inclusive rhizome. Our sense that these entities are the structural superiors of administrative agencies can be at least partially counteracted by dissolving the unitary image of each branch into its component parts. Thus, Congress is composed of committees, each of which is linked to the administrative agencies through a set of complex interconnections; viewed in this manner, the hierarchical structure, like the distinction between the puppeteer and the marionette, begins to dissolve.

Several difficulties beset Deleuze and Guattari's rhizome metaphor, however. To begin with, they themselves assert that the bureaucracy is tree-like and regard any rhizome features it possesses as an unplanned, quasi-revolutionary perturbation of its predominant structure (Deleuze & Guattari, 1987, pp. 18-20). This position, however, seems driven by hostility toward Western, capitalistic culture; in one of their odder passages, they claim that Asian bureaucracy resembles a rhizome and that only Western bureaucracies display hierarchical, arborescent characteristics. This claim need not be taken as definitive, however, because the book virtually invites the use of its metaphors for purposes that its authors did not intend. Unfortunately, rhizomes are just as bucolic as trees. Although they may represent a lesser inducement to nostalgia—relatively few romantic poems depict the poet wandering amidst the rhizomes—they do not genuinely confront the instrumental modernity of our administrative state. A second difficulty is that the imagery is so remote from the ordinary usage of the state's participants that it represents a heavy interpretive overlay, and certainly lacks the intuitive appeal that metaphors are supposed to possess. Finally, although the rhizome image succeeds in opening up the internal operations of administrative agencies, it provides few further insights; Deleuze and Guattari are too vague in their description, and the rhizome itself seems too organic in its actuality, to promise a framework for the microanalysis of modern governmental institutions.

My suggestion is that we replace the idea that government consists of three branches with the image of a network of interconnected institutions. The network, of course, is a conceptual emblem of our times, just as trees and human bodies were emblematic in the premodern era. We model the delivery of electric power as a network; we describe the firms that distribute radio and television programs as networks; we call our computer communication system the Internet, a term invented by Bob Kahn and Vint Cerf for the internetworking of networks (Segaller, 1998, pp. 109-113); we refer to the process of making contacts with other people as networking. The image thus possesses a familiar modernity that at least partially counteracts our tendency to import premodern notions into a modern world where they no longer apply. More important, it avoids the implication that administrative agencies represent an unnatural tumescence of the executive branch and provides us with a means of understanding the internal structure and external connections of the institutions that constitute the bulk of modern government.

A network consists of a series of units, or lumps in engineering's elegant terminology, that are connected to one another through a series of linkages.[1] The units receive information, or inputs, and transmit information, or outputs, only through these linkages. Put another way, whenever a unit receives or transmits information, that event is represented by a linkage to another unit. Each unit's role, or task, is to transform inputs into outputs by means of some process or program that has been developed by that unit or installed in the unit when it was created or reformed. A unit can be made less responsive to inputs by applying a bias to it, that is, a steady-state signal that inputs can only overcome when they achieve a certain magnitude.

Units can exist at any level of magnitude; more precisely, the network model can be applied at successively larger or smaller scales, depending on the process that is being studied. Thus, if one is studying international relations, nation-states can be treated as the interacting units. If one is interested in the operation of a particular nation-state, it will be necessary to penetrate below this level and regard each major governmental institution within the nation as a unit of its own. Going further, each of these institutions can be regarded as a network, with its separate divisions or offices acting as the interacting units. One can go as far down as the individual, or as far up as the planet Earth; beyond those limits, one leaves the realm of social science and enters individual psychology at one end and science fiction at the other. There is, of course, no restriction on the ability of a unit at one level of analysis to interact with a unit at a different level; all that is required is a linkage through which signals can be transmitted. The U.S. Drug Enforcement Agency, for example, interacts directly with the government of Colombia. Because interaction in fact occurs at different levels, there is also no absolutely definitive way to distinguish one unit from another; often, however, the members of the government themselves define the boundaries of institutions and these defined boundaries can be used by the observer.

Modeling the U.S. government according to the modern image of a network, as opposed to the premodern image of a tree, provides a means of understanding the structure of our modern state.[2] At the highest level, the units are Congress, the federal judiciary, and each of the major agencies, such as the Department of Labor, the Department of Defense, and the Federal Reserve Board. The presidency would appear as a separate institution, consisting of the president and his immediate staff such as the Office of Management and Budget or the National Security Council.[3] Each of these, of course, could be further analyzed as a network of subordinate units. The fact that the president supervises the executive agencies is no reason to model these agencies as part of the presidential unit. They operate as separate organizations and are generally recognized as such. Whatever control the president exercises over them can be represented by the nature of the communication linkages that run between the president and these agencies.

Another issue in describing modern government involves the boundary between government and nongovernmental individuals or institutions, the notorious public-private distinction. The arborescent imagery that serves us so poorly as a description of the administrative state serves us poorly in this area as well. Despite an occasional intertwining of roots, a fairly clear boundary exists between a tree and the rest of the world. In contrast, the boundary between the government and society is certainly complex and almost certainly unclear; in a democratic regime, government interacts with society in myriad ways and generally with a wide range of intermediate institutions—government grantees, government delegates, advisory committees, political parties, private suppliers of governmental services, and so forth—whose position as governmental or nongovernmental is a matter of considerable ambiguity.

The network image provides a much more accurate way to model these relationships. It portrays the government as a group of interrelated units, whose structural relationships at any given level are represented by the nature of the signals that flow among them. This image can be extended, without any alteration, to incorporate society in its entirety; all that is needed is to model the remainder of society as a larger group of similar units that are similarly interrelated. The boundary between government and nongovernment, or public and private, can then be represented as a conventionally drawn line that demarcates one particular group of units. There is no implication that the group of units demarcated in this manner have any particular shape or any particular pattern of interaction. The line can be as convoluted as one likes, and the density of signals that flow across it, from a government unit to a nongovernmental one, can be as great as between any two units of the government.

᠗ The Structure of Independence

The signals that flow through the linkages between the units of the U.S. government, or between the government and nongovernmental units, can be analyzed as verbal statements. Although these signals sometimes represent actual transfers of resources, even such transfers are usually implemented by written or oral statements. Following Austin's (1962) taxonomy, as modified by Searle and Habermas (Habermas, 1984, pp. 273-338; Searle, 1969), we can distinguish between informative, performative, and regulative or expressive statements. Informative statements (Austin's locutions) describe a state of the world; performative statements (Austin's illocutions and, to some extent, perlocutions) act in the world by making promises, making requests, or issuing commands. Regulative or expressive statements (the remainder of Austin's perlocutions) express one's moral or emotional views. Such signals, of course, can apply to any particular performance of the receiving unit, to its general pattern of performance, or to some aspect of that general pattern.

Modern government, as Weber (1978, pp. 217-226) observed, is organized hierarchically; according to the network model, this hierarchical structure is implemented by the performative signal of a command flowing from one unit of the network to another. A command is a definitive instruction issuing from one unit that is authorized to control or supervise the second unit, and control is exercised by means of such commands. Congress, the president, and the judiciary all issue commands of various kinds to administrative agencies. Congress commands the Labor Department, by means of legislation (the Occupational Safety and Health Act), to inspect factories without a warrant and eliminate dangerous conditions; the president commands the Department, by means of a direct order, to implement this statute assiduously; the Supreme Court commands it, by means of a decision in a litigated case (*Marshall v. Barlow's*, 1978), to stop conducting warrantless searches because they violate the constitution. If any of these commands is disobeyed, the recipients of the command can be disciplined in various ways. We usually think of commands as being enforced by dismissal of the disobedient subordinate, but only the president has this authority. Congress and the courts have different sanctions at their disposal, and these generally prove equally effective. Moreover, as Hart (1961, pp. 18-25) points out, commands generally carry a normative expectation of obedience quite apart from any sanction that is attached to them.

In addition to commands, other types of signals flow through the network of modern government and between that network and nongovernmental units. Some of these are also performatives but consist of promises or requests rather than commands. Institutions that stand in a collegial, rather than a hierarchical, relationship to one another, such as two executive agencies or an executive agency and an independent agency, may need to work together and may, therefore, request action on the other's part or promise action on their own. For example, the comptroller of the currency, a subordinate of the secretary of the treasury, and the Federal Reserve Board, an independent agency, work together to examine national banks (Federal Reserve Bank of New York, 1987; Malloy, 1988, pp. 1-79). This need to work together often means that informative, rather than performative, statements flow between the two institutions. Such statements might relate to the subject matter that each agency is regulating or it might relate to the agency's own planned activities. Both Congress and the president receive massive amounts of information from administrative agencies, sometimes because it is required by law, sometimes in response to requests, and sometimes because the agency chooses to transmit the information on its own. Finally, regulative or expressive statements regularly flow through the governmental network; they can be transmitted either to the unit whose action constitutes their subject matter or to some other unit. The Comptroller might say to the Federal Reserve or to the president, for example, that he appreciates the Federal Reserve Board's cooperative attitude in coordinating bank examinations. In the network model, governmental units affect one another by means of signals. Dependence, whatever it is taken to mean, is one such effect; in order for one governmental unit to depend on another, in any sense that we might reasonably employ that term, it must receive signals from that other unit. Independence, as a structural feature of government, is therefore produced when the signals from one unit to another are interfered with in some manner. This clarifies the distinction between independence and neutrality, a separate matter that is frequently conflated with it. Decision makers are neutral if they are indifferent about the consequences of their decisions; decision makers are independent if they are not affected by any signal from another actor. An umpire for a baseball game is neutral if he or she does not care which team wins the game; he or she is independent if no one on the field or in the stands can influence his or her calls. The two considerations can operate separately, although they often occur in conjunction. For example, the umpire has lost both neutrality and independence if one team offers a bribe to decide in its favor, but only neutrality is lost, and not independence, if he or she has bet on one team. Racist judges are perfectly independent; no signal from any other actor induces them to decide against minority group litigants. They are entirely self-motivated.

Neutrality is not even desirable in most governmental situations because we generally want public officials to care about the results of their actions. What is undesirable, and what we attempt to prevent, are decisions based on personal gain or on factors that we deem to be irrelevant. Public officials are supposed to act on behalf of their constituencies and thus act improperly if they decide on the basis of a bribe (Noonan, 1988; Rose-Ackerman, 1999). For exactly the same reason, it is regarded as improper for them to act on the basis that their decisions will improve their own financial positions (*Gibson v. Berryhill*, 1973; *Tumey v. Ohio*, 1927; *Ward v. Village of Monroeville*, 1972). In contrast, we are not concerned if a judge's decision will improve his or her position, financial or otherwise, as a member of the general public. As critical legal studies, feminist, and critical race theory scholars have pointed out, public decision makers often act, or can be seen as acting, to improve the status of their own social class, gender, or race (Austin, 1989; Horwitz, 1977; West, 1988), but our concept of required neutrality does not reach these effects. Similarly, prejudice against an individual or group may be considered a forbidden breach of neutrality by the decision maker if that attitude is deemed irrelevant by law or public morals. It is currently considered improper for a public official to explicitly disfavor blacks or Jews, but this was not true with respect to blacks in early 19th century America, nor with respect to Jews in medieval Europe, and it is currently not improper for officials to express distaste for criminals. But our concept of neutrality only reaches outright and explicit prejudice; the collection of attitudes that every individual possesses is regarded as too complex and obscure to serve as the basis of a legal rule (with respect to adjudication, see *FTC v. Cement Institute*, 1948; *Friedman v. Rogers*, 1979; *Laird v. Tatum*, 1972; *Marshall v. Jerrico, Inc.*, 1980).[4] In general, neutrality, although an important concept, is a limited one, and reaches only extreme situations such as a direct financial interest in the outcome, or an explicitly and strongly stated prejudice that is deemed legally improper.

Independence is a much broader concept and applies to any situation in which the signals that a governmental unit receives are interfered with in some fashion. There are a wide range of mechanisms by which such interference can be produced. First, signals can be prohibited or attenuated. Second, these effects can be either specific or global. Third, the mechanisms by which the effects are produced can be either direct or prophylactic. All these possibilities, and others perhaps, need to be considered in order to develop a comprehensive theory of independence as a governance technique.

The most basic method of achieving the independence of one unit from another is to forbid the transmission of certain signals between the two units. Rather than being a uniform phenomenon, as the term judicial independence might suggest, this method varies greatly, in both theory and practice, based on the types of signals that are prohibited. The lowest level of independence is achieved by forbidding one unit to transmit the performative of a command to another unit. This precludes direct or hierarchical control of one unit by the other. A second and higher level of independence is achieved when the first unit is also not permitted to transmit an informative signal, or a noncommand performative signal, to the second. Although an informative signal is not a means of direct control or supervision the way a command is, it is often a means of influence. A noncommand performative, such as a request for information, might also be prohibited because it too can function as a means of influence; it places the recipient in a position of either acting as if it has something to hide or of revealing something that it really does want to hide. Finally, the highest level of independence between two units is achieved when one unit is not only forbidden to issue commands—other performative signals and informative signals to the other—but also forbidden to issue regulative or expressive signals about the second unit, either to that unit, some other unit, or both. The basis for this prohibition, clearly, is that a unit can be influenced by approval or disapproval, particularly if those sentiments are emitted by another unit with which it must cooperate, or are transmitted to a unit which exercises, or could exercise, supervisory control over it.

In addition to prohibiting signals directly, it is also possible to attenuate them, thus reducing their effect without sacrificing so much of the control or coordination that the signals provide. Although this may seem to be a desirable compromise, it is not easy to achieve. An outright prohibition can be stated and monitored much more easily than some incremental reduction. One means of achieving an incremental reduction is a norm, that is, a widely shared understanding that a given unit is not supposed to transmit signals to another unit or is only supposed to do so under certain circumstances. The implementation difficulties with this approach are obvious. Another means is to ensure that the unit receiving the signal that one wants to attenuate is also receiving signals from other units as well. For example, we may be concerned about the signals that an administrative agency is receiving from the industry it regulates, but we may be unwilling to prohibit such signals entirely due to their information value. We could try to attenuate the signals from the industry by declaring a norm that industry representatives are only supposed to communicate with the agency in situations that are crucial to the industry's well-being, or that agency officials are only supposed to listen to industry representatives under such circumstances. A preferable alternative might be to create settings in which the agency officials also receive signals from opposing sources, such as environmental groups.[5] Precisely how this can be accomplished is, of course, an interesting question.

A third way to attenuate signals is to apply a bias to the unit receiving the signals, the term bias being used in the engineering sense of a steady state input (Dorny, 1993, pp. 534-539). The most common form of bias is expertise of one kind or another, a sense of the correct way to reach a decision based on some sort of specialized training. This produces a steady state signal from within a given unit that tends to drown out inputs from other units. The strongest biases are produced by training in the natural sciences, such as physics or chemistry, because these are the areas in which we are most convinced that we can achieve objective truth. Next in order are the applied sciences such as medicine or engineering. Such scientific expertise, however, is relevant to a fairly limited range of government decisions. When we are concerned with the correctness of procedures rather than results, legal training provides a fairly strong bias. In other areas, we can rely on training in law, public policy, business, or social science, but given our disagreement about the validity of these fields, the resulting bias is frequently a rather weak one. Moreover, as debates about the relevance of scientific knowledge, or the difference between substance and procedure remind us, expertise-based biases may be difficult to justify or sustain in complex situations.

The prohibition or attenuation of signals can occur either specifically or globally. The most global prohibition, so extreme that it is essentially unknown to modern government, would be to prohibit a governmental agency from receiving any signals at all, from any source. At the other end of this spectrum, a particular type of signal from a particular source can be prohibited. Intermediate positions, obviously, are to prohibit various categories of signals from various categories of institutions. For example, so-called independent agencies, such as the Federal Trade Commission or the Securities Exchange Commission, may not be given commands by the president but can receive other performative signals as well as informative and expressive signals. In addition, they can receive commands, and many other types of signals, from Congress.

Attenuation of signals is clearly a less extreme approach than outright prohibition, but it may involve more severe restrictions because it is more difficult to tailor with precision. Precatory norms against receiving signals tend to be stated in fairly general terms, and this generality may be required for their effectiveness. Countervailing influences may be similarly general in their scope. Biases are probably the hardest form of attenuation to apply with specificity because the internally generated signal based on expertise tends to apply to the entire range of signals that the unit receives from other sources.

Aside from the direct prohibition or attenuation of signals, independence can also be achieved through indirect, or prophylactic, means. In order to ensure that one unit does not issue commands to another, the first unit might also be forbidden from taking actions that are not in themselves commands but that resemble the sanctions that can be imposed for disobedience to a command. Thus, the first unit might be forbidden to dismiss members of the second unit for any reason at all, and not just for disobedience. Similarly, it might be forbidden from cutting the budget of the second unit, or reducing the salaries of individuals within that second unit, or restricting the second unit's authority, or denying it permission to obtain better facilities. Obviously, these prohibitions can be highly inconvenient if the first unit is the one that normally makes such decisions; thus increased independence can only be obtained at a price that the society may or may not be willing to pay.

This network model of government is a heuristic, of course. It is not intended to be a demonstrable truth, but rather to free us from the three-branch model, which no longer fits the modern world very well because of its premodern origin but seems like an objective description of reality because of its familiarity. By doing so, it can facilitate an approach that I have described elsewhere as microanalysis (Rubin, 1996). For present purposes, the important feature of this approach is that it dissolves generalized terms such as judicial independence into their component parts, or alternatively, replaces statements of status with descriptions of relationships. Thus, one can no longer say that a particular governmental institution is "independent"; the question is necessarily from whom is it independent and by what specific means is such independence achieved. Which signals are precluded and what signals are allowed? Precisely what is the path of particular types of decisions and how is that path affected by these prohibitions?

From the microanalytic perspective that the network model facilitates, it becomes clear that the mechanism of independence, or rather the prohibition or attenuation of certain signals that a governmental unit would otherwise receive, is used frequently in American government, at levels ranging from the lowest to the highest and in a wide variety of situations. Given the obvious disadvantages of forbidding, or drowning out, otherwise desirable signals in an interconnected network, why is this the case? The answer, again suggested by microanalysis, is that the mechanism serves a number of valuable governmental purposes. It is an essential part of the repertoire of an administrative state, an important technique in carrying out the complex tasks of modern governance.

Clearly, the dominant use of independence is to insulate particular decisions and particular decision makers from signals that other persons or institutions, within government or outside it, would otherwise issue to them. Beyond this quasi-tautological generalization, nothing more can be safely said without further microanalysis. It is a common view that the purpose of independence is to achieve neutrality in decision making or to insulate the decision maker from the political process (Senate Commission on Governmental Affairs, 1977). But this is much too general to be useful. As discussed above, neutrality is a practical standard only in the most extreme situations because attitudes and judgments are ubiquitous. Politics is similarly ubiquitous and no general prohibition of it, however defined, can constitute a coherent standard. In order to understand the purpose of insulation, or independence, in modern government, a much more detailed examination of the subject is required.

ᴏᴏ Judicial Independence

The subject matter of this chapter and this volume is the independence of the judiciary. At the outset, the point made in the previous sections should be reiterated. The microanalysis facilitated by the network model suggests that independence is not an inherent feature of the judiciary, either as a descriptive or a normative matter. Rather, it is a technique of governance that is widely deployed in a modern state and that serves a variety of functions. The question, therefore, is entirely open. Should the judiciary be independent and if so, to what extent?

We might begin this inquiry by considering the functions of the judiciary. The most classic function is to adjudicate claims between private parties or between a private party and the government. In such adjudications, the overriding concern is that the matter be decided fairly, which means that the court must apply established legal rules to the dispute. This does not mean that courts always reach their conclusions by interpreting the legal rule in question, and it certainly does not mean, as Dworkin (1977, p. 81) asserts, a definitively correct interpretation is invariably available. Quite often, courts reach their conclusions on the basis of public policy considerations, that is, by deciding what they think is best for the nation (Baum, 1990; Carp & Rowland, 1983; Schubert, 1974).[6] When they do rely on the interpretation of an established rule, that interpretation will often be contested or contestable. What fairness means, in this context, is simply that courts must act on the basis of some authoritative text, that they must make a conscientious effort to apply that text, to whatever extent they deem it applicable, and that they should not rely on extraneous considerations to reach their result. If a court is deciding a contractual dispute between two parties, it must identify the applicable statute or common law principle, it must not reach a decision that violates this principle, and it must not decide on the basis of some other consideration, such as the wealth or religion of the litigants.

These requirements of fairness are embodied in our concept of due process. Because the Supreme Court has managed to becloud this issue over the course of the past 30 years, it requires some further explanation. According to the Court, the due process clause applies whenever a liberty or property interest is at stake, with liberty interests being established by the due process clause itself, property interests being established by state law, and the applicable procedures being again established by the due process clause.[7] But the Court has never offered any rationale besides a fairly simple-minded textualism for articulating such a convoluted doctrine.[8] In fact, due process is a basic component of our political system, and its content can be derived by considering that system's underlying premises. One such premise is that groups of people can protect themselves through the political process by securing the passage of general rules, and those groups that lose out in this process must accede. But because individuals cannot influence the political process, fairness demands that they be treated in accordance with the general rules that this process has produced. Thus, the due process guaranty applies whenever the government imposes disadvantages on individuals.[9]

A second premise of our system is that procedural protections are the means by which we ensure that individuals are treated in accordance with generally enacted rules. These protections include notice and a hearing, to give each party a chance to present its position, an impartial decision maker, and a decision on the record, that is, on the basis of relevant considerations (*Goldberg v. Kelly*, 1970; *Mathews v. Eldridge*, 1976).[10] Again, due process does not demand that decisions exclude public policy considerations or require that they flow logically and definitively from the applicable rules. But it does demand a certain type of decision making, specifically decision making that is constrained by the established procedural protections. For the legislature to impose disadvantages on specific individuals, as the U.S. Congress did during the McCarthy period, is a violation of due process because a legislative body is not set up to conduct this type of decision making; although it might provide satisfactory notice and operate satisfactory hearings, its decision makers do not restrict the kinds of information they consider or reach their decision on the basis of a previously established general rule.

Independence is a mechanism that is designed to ensure that a decision maker provides the due process protection of a decision on the record (Friendly, 1975; Redish & Marshall, 1986). It does so, as stated above, by restricting various kinds of signals from various governmental units or private parties. Courts regularly adjudicate disputes involving specified individuals, and often resolve such disputes by disadvantaging these individuals in some fashion. When they do so, they are subject to due process and required to provide its protections to those who are disadvantaged, or potentially disadvantaged. There is thus good reason to employ the mechanism of independence with respect to court adjudications; in fact, it would probably be impossible to satisfy the demands of due process without it. Neutrality, discussed above, is a separate due process requirement but, as stated, it is much more limited, and the only decided cases that apply this principle are those in which the adjudicator has a financial stake in the outcome (*Gibson v. Berryhill*, 1973; *Tumey v. Ohio*, 1927; *Ward v. Village of Monroeville*, 1972).

Judicial independence in adjudicatory decisions is established by two sets of mechanisms, the first general and the second specific. The most common general mechanism is to attenuate signals from nonjudicial units by applying a bias to the judicial system in its entirety. This is accomplished by the formal mechanism of appointing only legally trained people to the judiciary and by the informal norm recognizing that the judiciary's tasks are technical ones that require such legal training. The major exception, in the judicial system, is the jury, a nonexpert body that is assigned to determine disputed factual questions and set the level of the disadvantage that will be imposed on a losing defendant. In addition to these direct mechanisms are several indirect, or prophylactic, mechanisms. With respect to the federal judiciary, the best known are life tenure and salary protection for judges (Redish & Marshall, 1986).[11] These are, of course, formally established by our highest law, the Constitution. Additional prophylactic mechanisms are protection against reduction of staff and physical facilities and protection against changes in job conditions, such as the judge's location or subject matter jurisdiction. In some cases, these nonconstitutional protections are statutory whereas others are entirely informal. Since 1980, for example, the federal government has provided fairly elaborate protections in this area (*Judicial Council's Reform & Judicial Conduct and Disability Act of 1980*).[12] Each circuit has a circuit council consisting of the chief judge and an equal number of circuit and district judges elected by all the judges in the circuit; the council then selects a circuit executive who serves at its pleasure and who administers the personnel system, the budget, the physical facilities, and other aspects of judicial operations.[13] The establishment of systems such as this may be nearly as important as the constitutionally specified protections in ensuring judicial independence.

As stated above, general mechanisms may be effective, but their disadvantage is that they typically apply to an entire government unit and cannot distinguish between different roles or different types of tasks within those roles. This limits their value for the judiciary because adjudication is only one of the judiciary's roles and because the importance of independence varies with different types of adjudications. In general, the more serious the potential disadvantage that can be imposed on the individual, the more stringent the due process protections that we deem required and the greater the level of independence that we need to implement them. This means that the highest level of independence will be required in criminal cases in which the individual's liberty is at stake. To begin with, performative signals from any other unit in the government are forbidden, and such signals from any nongovernmental source are unauthorized; no nonjudicial unit is authorized to order a court to reach a particular decision or follow a particular decision-making strategy. This prohibition applies to noncommand performatives as well as to the more obvious case of commands. Thus, the chief executive is not only forbidden to instruct a court to decide a case in a particular manner but is also forbidden from requesting information about the case or offering advice about its outcome. Even within the judicial system, the trial court's superior can only issue performative signals that improve the individual's position; signals to the trial court that would disadvantage the individual, by reversing an acquittal for example, are forbidden by our concept of double jeopardy. Performative signals from nongovernmental units are equally forbidden, of course, as they are for almost any other governmental function.

Informative and expressive signals from governmental units are also forbidden. First, no unit may transmit information to the court regarding the subject matter of a pending trial. Criminal courts have stringent rules for the acquisition of information related to a trial and will not pay attention to information supplied outside those rules, or use such information as a basis of decision. Of course, the court may, in accordance with its procedures, request or demand information from a governmental agency, but that is an entirely different kind of signal, essentially a performative signal from the court to the agency to supply information that the court deems relevant. Second, governmental units are generally forbidden from issuing expressive signals regarding pending criminal trials. This particular prohibition is implemented by a norm rather than a formal rule. There is no stated rule forbidding a public official from commenting on the conduct of a criminal trial, but the official who does so will generally earn the disapprobation of his or her colleagues and may be punished for the indiscretion by his or her structural superior, or in the next election. Informative and expressive signals from private parties are also forbidden; in fact, they often constitute a crime.[14] In addition, judges are expected to ignore them and juries are instructed to do so. The receipt of such signals by jurors can lead to the declaration of a mistrial and is often the reason for venue changes (*Federal Rules of Criminal Procedure for the United States District Courts*, 1988, Rule 37).

Civil trials are granted a somewhat lower level of independence, even if there is more at stake for society as a whole, because the potential disadvantages imposed on individuals are less severe. Thus, the Microsoft antitrust litigation, which was likely to produce a palpable effect on the American economy, was held to lower standards than the trial of some minor crook who is accused of stealing a few hundred dollars because only money—however much of it—was at stake. The institutional or prophylactic protections are of course the same; these apply to all adjudications by a court. Moreover, because due process is still at stake, performative signals from nonjudicial units of government are prohibited. There is no absolute restriction on performatives, including commands, from superior judicial units, however; any decision, including one that benefits the defendant, may be appealed but such commands can only be issued as part of the regular appeal process.

Another difference between civil and criminal trials is that informative signals may be transmitted to the court during a civil trial by nonjudicial governmental units or by private parties. Because the due process requirement of decision on the record still applies, these views must be presented by means of a formal procedure, namely amicus briefs, and the court is free to preclude such briefs or ignore their content.[15] Intervention is a related procedure; it involves the participation of another party, rather than the mere transmission of a signal, but it necessarily involves various signals from the intervening party, and is therefore governed by similarly formal procedures.[16] But other governmental units, such as administrative agencies, also establish rules for the transmission of informative signals[17] and most units are free to ignore such signals. Expressive signals from other nonjudicial units may be considered acceptable, particularly if the defendant is a large corporation such as Microsoft; certainly, the informal norm against such signals is weaker. It may be the case that the less important the case, the stronger the informal norm. This relationship, which would appear perverse if the operative issue were judicial power, becomes sensible when one recognizes that the real issue is due process. In an obscure case, there is no justification for another governmental unit to transmit expressive signals because only the status of the individuals involved is at stake. But in important cases, in which major issues of public policy are at stake, expressive signals are deemed acceptable because these signals are understood to relate to the case's implications, not to the fate of the particular individuals who are before the court. The extreme version of this is public interest litigation. In *Brown v. Board of Education* (1954), few people really cared where Linda Brown went to school; the issue was American apartheid and thus people felt as free to express their views about the case as they did when the same issue came before Congress in the debate over the Civil Rights Act.[18]

Beyond these signal-specific prohibitions that are granted to judges, a further level of prohibition is provided to jurors in both civil and criminal cases. This includes the prohibition against receiving any informative or expressive signal from any member of the public or from other members of the jury prior to the completion of the case. Such prohibitions are difficult to enforce because they involve indirect as well as direct communication and because they apply to all members of the public, and not only to interested parties. In some cases, such as newspaper stories about the case, any effort to restrict the signal by imposing sanctions on the person generating it would not only be impractical but would collide with constitutional provisions, such as the right of free speech, and common law privileges, such as the privacy of spousal communication. Instead, therefore, the undesired signals are excluded by procedures such as prohibiting jurors from discussing the case, voir dire to determine whether any juror has received such signals, or, in extreme cases, sequestration of the jury. The purpose of these rather elaborate procedures is to compensate for the jurors' lack of an expertise bias. It is assumed that a legally trained judge can edit out irrelevant material, such as a newspaper article stating facts that have not been established in court, or a spouse's view about the merits of the case. But it is also assumed that jurors who lack legal training cannot do this and that these more elaborate mechanisms are needed to ensure their independent judgment.

Having noted the way that judicial decisions are insulated from signals issued by nonjudicial governmental units and private citizens, microanalysis requires further consideration of the way that these decisions are insulated from signals issued by units within the judiciary itself. To reiterate, the primary concern is adjudication, with its capacity to impose disadvantages on specified individuals. This means that the locus of concern, and the locus of the protection that independence is intended to secure, is the individual adjudicator, the person or panel that is actually deciding whether a particular person fits within a common law or legislatively established category such as thief, tortfeasor, or contract breacher. Signals from other officials within the judiciary might thus create fairness problems that are similar to those created by signals from nonjudicial officials; we would not want the chief judge of a supreme court commanding trial judges to find a certain defendant, or a certain type of defendant, guilty. Of the institutional protections, the expertise bias is only of value in protecting judges from signals issued by their bailiffs; with respect to signals issued by other judges, it is of course useless. Job tenure and salary protection, on the other hand, are of even greater value because dismissals, suspensions, penalties, and related forms of discipline typically issue from an official's hierarchical superior, which in this case would be other judges. It is generally unseemly for the legislature to discipline an ineffective or recalcitrant official, even in an agency with no independence, but it is standard for the official's superior to impose such discipline. The job and salary protection provided to judges, whether through civil service or more particularized provisions, is crucial to the fairness of the adjudicatory process.

Signal-specific prohibitions within the judiciary are also extensive. Of course, a superior court may command a trial court to reverse its decision, but only by means of an elaborate, highly formalized procedure that must be initiated by the disadvantaged person,[19] and that is specifically designed to increase, not decrease, our certainty that the person fits the established category. With respect to substance, moreover, certain types of trial court determinations, such as factual findings in bench trials, receive highly deferential treatment.[20] Other commands from members of the judiciary are as fully prohibited as are commands from members of nonjudicial governmental units. What is notable is that noncommand performative, informative, and expressive signals are prohibited to a greater extent. Much of the Model Code of Judicial Conduct, for example, is devoted to implementing this prohibition and its restrictions exceed those imposed on ordinary government officials.[21] Expressive statements about pending cases that are only prohibited to other officials by informal norms are prohibited to judges, and violation of this norm could lead to dismissal of a judge for cause.

The prohibition of performative, informative, and expressive signals to the judiciary applies only to decisions in specific cases, however, and not to signals about the judiciary's general performance. It is considered acceptable for public officials to transmit informative signals and expressive signals to the judiciary; for example, a legislator can provide information to the judiciary about the extent of medical malpractice and condemn the judiciary for being too lenient with defendant physicians, or he or she can note the number of offenders on probation who commit additional offenses, or issue a public condemnation of the frequency with which the judiciary grants probation. Similarly, it would be considered quite proper to condemn the general performance of a particular state's judiciary as reflecting racial prejudice and to document that condemnation with statistics about the differential treatment of the races in question. Such statements are part of our accepted political discourse; the judiciary's performance is a matter of public concern, and nonjudicial officials are entitled to speak to such matters, whether or not they have a direct role in the selection of judges. Even judges are allowed to make such statements (Model Code of Judicial Conduct, 1990), although the norm is that they must be more circumspect than other government officials.

Performative signals to the judiciary about its general performance are also considered acceptable. Any legislation that alters the substantive rules for the adjudication of some category of cases may be regarded as such a signal, as Kim Scheppele (this volume) suggests. For example, the enactment of a bill increasing liability for medical malpractice, or increasing criminal sentences for particular offenses, commands the judiciary to be tougher on physicians and criminals. Such commands can only be issued by the formal process of legislation, but the reason for this restriction lies in our concept of representative government, not in the concept of judicial independence. Perhaps it can be argued that command via legislation is entirely irrelevant to the issue of judicial independence because the concept of independence refers to judges' willingness to follow the law; if the law changes, the argument would go, then a fully independent judge should of course change his or her position. Microanalysis, however, would begin by noting that legislation is homologous with other types of signals and would be slower to dismiss its relevance on the basis of such a categorical distinction. This leads to the recognition that the introduction of a bill with broad support may function as a performative statement, even though it is never enacted (see Scheppele, this volume). It would thus produce an impact on the judicial decision-making process, without ever constituting the law that judges are supposed to follow in our system of government. It might, for example, function as a threat, which is another type of performative; the sponsors are telling the judiciary to change their pattern of decisions or they will change the law. The extreme version of this threat is a jurisdiction-stripping bill, which is directed to the judiciary per se and represents a direct expression of legislative displeasure.

Such threats to the judiciary, like commands in the form of legislation, are considered part of the ordinary political process. That is only true, however, if they are directed to the general pattern of decision. Legislation designed to command that a particular individual be subject to some disadvantage, whether criminal or civil, is a bill of attainder, and both Congress and the state legislatures are prohibited from enacting such provisions by the Constitution itself, even apart from the additional prohibition that is embodied in the due process clauses of the Fifth and Fourteenth Amendments.[22] A threat to enact such legislation would be considered improper because legislators are not supposed to introduce obviously unconstitutional bills, and would be an empty one in any event. In addition to these commands and threats, other performative signals are also deemed permissible, but only when directed to the general pattern of decisions. For example, a legislator or administrative official can request that the judiciary supply statistics about its medical malpractice decisions or sentencing practices, or can promise the judiciary that he or she will introduce legislation to increase the budgetary allocation to the prison system if the judges hand out stiffer sentences.[23]

The reason for this differential treatment of signals regarding specific cases and signals regarding the judiciary's general performance is our concept of fair adjudication. As stated, adjudication involves the potential imposition of disadvantages on individuals who cannot protect themselves politically and must therefore meet the requirements of due process, including a decision on the basis of the evidence introduced in a contested hearing. But the general pattern of judicial decisions involves a group, not individuals, and the protections of due process do not apply in this context. Thus, if physicians, as a group, are subject to disadvantageous legislation, or condemnations by individual legislators, that simply indicates that they have lost out in the political process that we rely on to distribute general benefits and burdens. The inclusion of criminals and racial minorities in the foregoing examples may undermine our equanimity about the fairness of this political process, but that is a matter to be considered in the context of general governmental structure or equal protection of the laws.

As noted above, it is common to state that judicial independence is designed to insulate judges from politics. Microanalysis of the mechanism reveals why this is not quite accurate. The statement, after all, depends on the meaning of the word politics. If this word is defined to include decisions based on ideology, or on general policy considerations such as national wealth maximization or social equality, the statement is simply false. As just discussed, the judiciary's general performance is an appropriate subject for political debate and decision. The prohibition or attenuation of signals from nonjudicial sources does not apply to this debate, nor does it preclude judges from deciding cases on the basis of their own ideology or policy considerations. If politics is taken to mean the mechanisms that render government accountable to the populace, the statement is only partially correct. Certainly, precluding signals from elected officials regarding the outcome of specific cases insulates the judiciary from instructions based on these officials' desires to satisfy the populace and secure their reelection. But it fails to insulate the judiciary from signals regarding its general performance, and it does insulate the judiciary from instructions based on motivations that have nothing to do with accountability, such as the personal ideology or prejudices of the official. What insulation is designed to achieve, as stated above, is compliance with our concept of due process.

ᙣ Judicial Nonindependence and Nonjudicial Independence

Thus far, only the adjudicatory function of the judiciary has been considered. Although this certainly constitutes the bulk of the judiciary's role, it does not constitute the entirety. Courts are assigned a variety of other tasks that vary in content from one American jurisdiction to another. In the federal system, for example, judges participate in drafting the Rules of Civil Procedure, the Rules of Evidence, and the criminal law sentencing guidelines. Microanalysis indicates that the mechanism of independence is not deployed with respect to these nonadjudicatory functions. Of course, the bias applied to the judiciary and the prophylactic means of ensuring independence remain in place. As stated, these must be applied to the institution as a whole, and the predominance of adjudication in the judiciary's range of tasks requires that these features be included in the general institutional design. But the particularized means of ensuring independence—those that affect specific signals—are typically not employed, and this tends to destroy any independence that the institutional mechanisms would otherwise secure.

Consider, for example, the federal judiciary's role in drafting the Rules of Civil Procedure. By statutory authorization, the chief justice of the United States appoints an advisory committee to develop the initial draft. This draft, if approved by the advisory committee and two intermediate bodies, is submitted to the Court, which has authority to revise it. Once the Court approves the draft, it is submitted to Congress, which is given a seven-month period in which to reject the proposed rule by legislation (Burbank, 1982; Friedenthal, 1975; Lesnick, 1975; Struve, in press).[24] If such legislation is enacted, it supercedes the proposed rule and can thus be regarded as a direct command to the Supreme Court to alter its draft in a prescribed manner; the authority that Congress possesses renders the Court its direct subordinate with respect to the Rules.[25] Moreover, the fact that the performative of a direct command is authorized implies, as a matter of both necessity and normative judgment, that most other kinds of signals are allowed as well. The draft that goes to the Supreme Court is published and, thus, is available to interested parties. This allows members of Congress to issue noncommand performative, informative, and expressive signals to the Court when it is deciding whether to accept, modify, or reject the draft. Because Congress can ultimately disapprove the draft, a statement by a member of Congress that expresses disapproval of some provision, or offers information to improve it, will often be deemed relevant by the various participants in the rule-making process, including the Court. There is, moreover, no particular norm against issuing such statements. The cumulative effect of these commands and other signals is, of course, to eliminate independence. When it promulgates the Rules of Civil Procedure, the Court is in a position analogous to an ordinary administrative agency. It may have somewhat more independence because of its prestige or as a residual holdover from other areas but, like the agency, it is directly subordinate to Congress.

The explanation of this difference between adjudication and rule drafting relates, once again, to our concepts of fairness and due process. Adjudication is subject to the requirement of due process because it brings state power to bear against specified individuals who have no access to the political process and, therefore, must be protected by being treated in accordance with general rules. The rules for civil procedure, evidence, or criminal sentencing are themselves general rules; they do not affect specified individuals but large numbers of persons, typically every person subject to the jurisdiction of the federal courts. Thus, the considerations that apply to ordinary legislation, or to signals to the judiciary regarding its general performance, apply to these rules as well.

Not only is it the case that the judiciary is not always granted independence, but the converse situation is true as well—nonjudicial institutions are often granted independence in our governmental system. This is most obvious when a nonjudicial body carries out genuine adjudications, that is, makes decisions about specified individuals that can potentially impose burdens on those individuals. In our current governmental system, at both the federal and state levels, the vast majority of adjudications are not carried out by the courts but by administrative agencies. These adjudications include the refusal to grant benefits, the termination of existing benefits, the refusal to grant licenses, the termination of existing licenses, and the imposition of injunctions or fines. Typically, these adjudications are carried out according to distinctive procedures that distinguish them from civil trial. For example, there is no right to a jury, oral hearings may not be provided, and many rules of evidence are eliminated in cases in which oral hearings are employed.[26]

In the federal system, many of these adjudications are carried out by administrative law judges (ALJs) (Mashaw, 1981). Originally called hearing officers, ALJs have acquired more and more of the functional and symbolic features of Article III judges during the past several decades. At present, the mechanism of independence is provided for adjudications conducted by ALJs to a considerable extent, although not as fully as it is provided for adjudications conducted by the federal judiciary. Like Article III judges, they cannot be dismissed for failing to follow orders, but only after a formal showing of malfeasance. However, the standard that governs their dismissal, which is "for cause,"[27] is weaker than the impeachment standard of "high crimes and misdemeanors." ALJ salaries are set independently of agency recommendations,[28] again a lesser but analogous protection to that provided for Article III judges. They do not have full protection from changes in working conditions or jurisdiction; such changes can be effected by agency officials based on the same considerations of economy or efficiency that they apply to other agency staff, but ALJs' particular case assignments cannot be prescribed in this manner, nor can they be given assignments that are "inconsistent with the duties and responsibilities as administrative law judges."[29] ALJs are partially protected by the bias of professional training, but this bias is probably weaker than it is for federal judges. Because administrative procedure is more informal and the subject matter of an ALJ's decisions more focused and almost exclusively statutory, the law-trained person's area of expertise—procedure, and common law—will be relatively less important than substance, in which case nonjudicial agency officials will have greater expertise.

With respect to mechanisms that are signal specific, there is a general prohibition against direct commands by other members of the agency, or any other government officials, regarding the decisions of ALJs.[30] With respect to the general pattern of decisions, the situation is a bit more complex. As noted above, commands to judges about their general pattern of decisions can only be issued in the form of statutes. It is clear that ALJs can be similarly commanded by regulations adopted by the agency in accordance with a formalized procedure.[31] The question of whether ALJs can be commanded by other means arose in 1981 when the Social Security Administration announced a program to provide additional review for the decisions of those ALJs who were granting disability benefits at excessively high rates. The program was challenged by the ALJs themselves, on the ground that it violated their decisional independence under the Administrative Procedure Act (*Association of Administrative Law Judges v. Heckler,* 1984). Faced with a conceptually complex issue, the trial court fudged; having stated that the ALJs "persuasively demonstrated that [the agency] retained an unjustifiable preoccupation with allowance rates," it held that the agency, in response to the initiation of the litigation, had "shifted [its] focus, obviating the need for any injunctive relief." It is a rare thing in American jurisprudence for a court to find for the plaintiff on the facts and then hold that the plaintiff's remedy is the filing of its own complaint. Given that the program was clearly directed to the general pattern of decisions, and not to specific cases, a better rationale for the decision would have been that a general command of this sort, by virtue of its generality, represents substantive change in the governing regulation, and should have been adopted through the formalized procedure that applies to such regulations.

Other types of signals from governmental units to the ALJs regarding the outcome of specific cases also tend to be prohibited. Thus, it would be considered improper for any government official, including one in the ALJ's own agency, to request information about a case under consideration, to offer information outside the hearing procedures that constitute the record for decision, or even to express an opinion about the way a particular case should be decided. Prohibition of such signals, generally designated as ex parte contacts, is specified at length in the Administrative Procedure Act.[32] The Act provides that an ALJ may decide the case against a person who initiates an ex parte contact,[33] which clearly indicates that the prohibition is directed at the mere communication of information or expression of opinion outside the formal record.

The technique of granting independence is not limited to adjudication or to concerns about fairness. Independent agencies, at both the federal and state levels, are granted their eponymous independence by prohibiting one particular official, the chief executive, from issuing commands to them in situations in which he would otherwise be able to do so. This is generally achieved by precluding the chief executive from removing the political appointees who head the agency, except for specified causes such as incompetence or malfeasance (Bruff, 1987; Miller, 1986; Welborn, 1977).[34] It is obviously a much more limited form of independence than the independence granted to an adjudicatory decision maker; it does not prohibit the chief executive from transmitting noncommand performative, informative, or expressive signals; it does not prohibit direct commands from the legislature; and it does not, of its own force, place any limitations on the agency's ability to consider signals from private parties. Thus, the purpose is not to protect the agency from all political direction, but only from the more intensive direction that the chief executive, as a unitary and hierarchical superior, would otherwise be able to impose.

Another example of partial independence in the administrative state is the civil service system.[35] Civil service employees may be given commands by their superior, but they must be appointed from a pool of persons whose eligibility is not determined by the superior,[36] and they may not be removed by their superior except in limited circumstances, and with elaborate procedures.[37] This allows legislators to restrict the kinds of commands that the superior can give to the subordinate within the administrative hierarchy. For example, the political appointee who heads a federal agency can tell his or her civil service subordinates to adopt a particular strategy but cannot order them, under threat of dismissal, to alter a legislatively established policy. If so ordered, they are entitled to refuse, and any sanction that is imposed for their intransigence will ultimately be reversed by the president or the courts. Of course, this process of vindication comes at a high cost to the subordinate, who may therefore be inclined to obey the agency head's unjustified orders, but the process of becoming involved in such a confrontation, and ultimately losing it, imposes significant costs on the agency head as well and may deter the issuance of a forbidden order.

The civil service criteria for eligibility may or may not confer the additional independence of a bias on the employees, depending on the nature of the credential. An engineering degree provides a highly robust steady state signal that will often be strong enough to drown out most signals coming from outside the agency, even from a political appointee who heads the agency. Very few political heads of a transportation agency would have the temerity to tell their subordinates, who must be engineers according to the civil service rules, how to build a bridge. On the other hand, an undergraduate degree, although it may be a valuable credential in professionalizing the agency, may have no ability to create an effective bias.

The policy that underlies these various mechanisms for granting limited independence to administrative agencies is not fairness at all but efficiency or effectiveness. We want these agencies to be politically accountable, but we feel that explicit presidential or gubernatorial intervention would interfere with their ability to develop and deploy their expertise, and thus impair their effectiveness as expert decision makers. Because the concern is efficiency, not fairness, the distinction between signals regarding a particular decision and signals regarding the general pattern of decisions is not operative; both types of signals are prohibited.

Of course, some of the agency's decisions that are insulated from the chief executive's direction involve fairness considerations. But if fairness were the only concern, or even the primary one, a specific prohibition would suffice, and the agency would not need to be separated from hierarchical control in such a global fashion.

This point is underscored by the much more extensive independence that is granted to the Federal Reserve Board in carrying out its monetary control function. At present, the Fed controls the money supply—the amount of cash, checkable accounts, and certain other assets available in the nation—by buying and selling government securities on the open market.[38] When it buys securities, it simply makes an entry in the account of the financial institution from which it is buying; because money is nothing more than the Fed's promise to pay, this increases the money supply. When the Fed sells securities, it cancels part of the financial institution's account, thereby destroying money and decreasing the money supply. The buy or sell decisions are made by the Fed's Open Market Committee, a group of high-ranking Fed officials who meet in Washington on a regular basis.

It would be difficult to think of many government decisions that are more remote from the issue of fairness to individuals than the decisions of the Open Market Committee. Increasing or decreasing the money supply produces highly diffuse effects on the general economy, such as a decrease in the inflation rate, an increase in the supply of credit, or an increase in investment. No blunter, less effective instrument could be imagined to punish a specific individual, or even a specific group of individuals. The real concern with respect to the money supply is obviously not fairness but efficiency; decisions regarding the money supply have important effects on the nation's general economic growth rate. Yet the decisions of the Fed's Open Market Committee are granted a higher level of independence than any decisions other than adjudications, in which fairness considerations predominate (Cargill, 1990; Corder, 1998; Miller, 1998). To begin with, the governors of the Federal Reserve System, who constitute a significant portion of the Open Market Committee, are appointed to 14-year terms and can be removed only for cause; other members of the committee are civil service employees with similar levels of protection. Moreover, these officials receive salary protection and working conditions protections that may exceed that of the federal judiciary because the Fed, unique among federal agencies, funds itself.[39] Consequently, it does not require, and does not receive, any legislative appropriation, which means that the Fed itself is in control of its personnel and resource budget. No public official outside the Fed has the authority to reduce the salary of any Fed official, to decrease his or her staff, downgrade his or her amenities, or transfer him or her to another position (Greider, 1987; Saint Phalle, 1985). These protections are amplified by the strong bias applied to the decisions of the Open Market Committee. Control of the money supply is widely regarded as a matter of economic expertise, and almost all the members of the committee are trained economists, a form of specialized training that is regarded as being technical and task relevant, like the legal training of federal judges.

In addition to these institutional protections, the Fed's Open Market operations receive highly robust signal-specific protections. Because the Fed is an independent agency, the president may not issue a direct command to any Fed official. Because it does not receive a budget appropriation from Congress, Congress cannot issue a command to increase or decrease the money supply backed by a threat of a funding cut; it could act by legislation, but it has never done so, and the likelihood of any such legislation being passed in the foreseeable future is very low. Because the concern is efficiency, not fairness, no distinction is made between signals regarding a specific decision and signals regarding the general pattern of decisions. For the same reason, however, there is no real prohibition against informative or expressive signals from public officials to the Federal Reserve. Any legislator is welcome to lecture the Fed about the state of the economy or heap abuse on it for its monetary control decisions. The Fed is structured, however, so that it is able to ignore such signals with impunity.

Nor are all these protections unique to the United Sates, with its independent agency structure. In recent decades, virtually all industrialized democracies have provided a similar level of protection to the agency, usually a central bank like the Fed, that is responsible for monetary control (Miller, 1998, pp. 433-434). The reason, as Geoffrey Miller has discussed, is that these nations regard monetary control as too tempting a target for short-term political manipulation. A chief executive or majority party that wanted to burnish its image for an upcoming election could inflate the currency, creating a temporary economic boom, the ill effects of which would only be felt after the election (Havrilesky, 1993; Morris, 2000; Wooley, 1984). To prevent this sort of behavior, and increase the likelihood that the crucial economic decisions regarding monetary control will be made in an efficient manner, the United States and other nations have used the mechanism of independence to insulate the relevant decision maker from the control of elected officials.

Still another example of the way that the mechanism of independence can be used for nonadjudicatory decisions that implicate efficiency, not fairness, is the Defense Base Closure and Realignment Act of 1990.[40] The end of the Cold War, the change in defense strategy by military analysts, and the effort to balance the federal budget brought an awareness that the United States had an excessive number of military bases and that a significant number should be closed. But most bases are economic mainstays of the community where they are located, a phenomenon that has very little to do with the base's military necessity. Legislators often win or lose elections based on their ability to secure or retain such valuable economic assets for their constituents; thus, any effort to close military bases runs into determined opposition from the affected state's delegation, the classic pork barrel scenario that ends up sacrificing public interest to particularized benefits

(Ferejohn, 1974). Congress enacted the Base Closure Act to prevent itself from succumbing to these political pressures, the image of Ulysses lashing himself to the mast as he passes the Sirens being an inevitable metaphor (Elster, 1984). The statute established an "independent commission" of eight members, appointed by the president, that would make base closure decisions according to stated criteria. Members of Congress could not provide information to the Commission or participate in any other way as individuals; after the Commission reached its decisions, it was required to submit the results to Congress, which could disapprove them as a body, by joint resolution.

As these various examples indicate, the separation of powers is simply the wrong way to think about judicial independence in a modern state. The concept of independence and the institution of the judiciary have no necessary connection; rather, as the network metaphor suggests, independence is a mechanism that can be deployed for virtually any kind of governmental institution. What determines its use is not the identity of the institution, but the purposes that it is capable of serving. One such purpose is fairness, an issue that arises with respect to both individuals and groups. Fairness to individuals centers largely on the issue of adjudication, which is the mechanism we employ when the state is deciding whether to impose disadvantages on specified individuals. In this context, the decision maker, whether court or agency, is generally granted extensive independence; for judges, this independence is granted against members of their own so-called branch as well. When the court is not engaged in adjudication, and fairness is not a consideration, this independence can be eliminated without offending our political or legal values.

But independence is not always linked to fairness, any more than it is linked to the judiciary. It is not a necessary aspect of our efforts to provide fairness to groups, for example.[41] On the other hand, independence is often a mechanism that is deployed to achieve other goals, such as efficiency. Control of the money supply is a function in which efficiency considerations have suggested that the decision maker should be granted a very high level of independence, one that is virtually as extensive as that granted to adjudicators, and perhaps greater in certain ways. The same considerations have led to the creation of other agencies with lesser, but still significant levels, of independence such as the FTC and the FCC. These uses of independence have nothing particular to do with fairness or with the judiciary.

It is true that when the Supreme Court held, in the case of *Humphrey's Executor v. U.S.* (1935), that granting partial independence to a federal agency did not offend the Constitution, one of the rationales of the decision was that the agency in question (the FTC) exercised "quasi-judicial functions." But as the fudge factor prefix of "quasi" suggests, the Court was simply at sea; it had no framework for analyzing the structure of the administrative state and thus fell back on the outdated three-branch metaphor. The Court must have been thinking of the judiciary's role as an adjudicator because that is the context in which courts are granted independence. Although it is certainly true that the FTC does engage in some adjudication, independence was granted with respect to the entire agency, which exercises significant policy making, investigative, prosecutorial, and other nonadjudicative functions. It is easy enough to grant independence to the particular section of an agency that carries out adjudications without granting any independence to the agency in general. The Court's use of the term quasi-judicial for the entire agency is therefore meaningless and the decision, with its implicit reliance on the three-branch metaphor, explains nothing. If the conclusion that it reached is still good law, it is for other reasons.

ᥣᥣ Prescriptions for Judicial Independence

Thus far, it has been argued that the network metaphor provides a better description of modern government, a better way to understand how the mechanism of independence is deployed in various governmental contexts. The primary argument is that the metaphor facilitates microanalysis of these various uses and thus allows for a functional, detailed description that the unitary concept of judicial independence, and its underlying three-branch metaphor for government, only obscures. The next question is whether this network-based microanalysis can be used to frame recommendations for the issue that this book addresses. The prescriptive task of framing recommendations is a defining role of legal scholarship, and thus questions of this nature arise whenever legal scholars address a particular aspect of governance.

As indicated above, the independence granted to the judiciary is generally a product of our concern for fairness in adjudication, with our concept of fairness in this context being embodied, for the most part, in our understanding of the due process clause. The most extensive level of independence that our system grants to any court is that granted to the federal judiciary, that is, to Article III courts. This serves as a baseline for assessing the fairness of other judicial institutions in the United States (Redish & Marshall, 1986). Of course, it may be the case that the federal judiciary itself does not satisfy the requirements of the due process clause, that even our most extensive level of independence is inadequate. This would be an unusual result in American jurisprudence because constitutional standards rarely require more than the best prevailing practice.[42] The possibility should not be dismissed, but because it would represent a conceptual departure, it is a more difficult inquiry that will be deferred until after we consider the more accessible question that takes our best available practice as a baseline. The question may be stated as follows: Does it violate our conception of fairness, as embodied in the due process clause, to grant a court a level of independence that is lower than that granted to the federal judiciary?

The most notable differences between state and federal judges occur at the institutional, or general, level. To begin with, many state judges are elected, rather than being appointed (Berkson, Beller, & Grimaldi, 1981; Carrington, 1998; Dubois, 1980). Second, those that are elected, plus many of those who are appointed, do not have life tenure but hold their position for a term of years.[43] Although they generally cannot be dismissed except for cause during this term, they are subject to nonrenewal of their position without a showing of cause, either because the authority who appointed them (the governor, the legislature, or a special commission) has the option to appoint someone else to the position or because they must stand for reelection (Elliott, 1957; Webster, 1995). These variations from the baseline established by the federal judiciary raise important issues about the degree of independence that state judges receive and the resulting fairness of their adjudications.

Election, as opposed to appointment, would not appear to compromise our requirement of fairness. It is certainly true that politics may enter into the election process, but there can be little doubt that it enters into the appointment process as well. Ever since the end of John Adams's administration, the sort of judges that a person will nominate for appointment has been an issue in presidential campaigns; in recent years, it has also been a major issue. Similarly, votes on presidential nominations are an important issue in many senatorial campaigns. Thus, the kind of person who is selected to be a judge, whether by appointment or election, is often determined by political considerations. As noted above, however, political effects of this sort are not what we generally mean by judicial independence; all judges are affected by their own ideology, and any claim that they decide cases on the basis of the law alone, without any ideological or political consideration, would be rapidly dismissed by almost all observers. What independence means, in this context, is whether the person or group of persons who select the judge have any ongoing ability to transmit signals to that judge as a result of that selection process. There is no reason to assume that either method, of its own force, would produce this effect; so long as judges have life tenure, they may freely ignore the views of those who were responsible for selecting them for their position. In fact, the level of independence may be marginally greater in the electoral situation because it is possible that the same entity that appoints a judge may have the authority to remove him or her for cause but impossible for any electorate to exercise this second function.

Once life tenure is eliminated, however, the situation changes dramatically, as Lee Epstein notes (see Epstein, this volume). It is widely assumed, and not only by public choice scholars, that government officials are strongly motivated to retain their positions. Judges, being no different from other government officials in this regard, are likely to be quite responsive to signals from the entity with the authority to deny them this position once their designated term has ended. Commands, and even noncommand performatives, can be prohibited in this situation by an outright ban; it is easy enough to provide that the government official who appoints a judge—the governor, for example—does not have the authority to order the judge to decide a case in a particular manner. Appointment authority is only tantamount to command authority if the appointment is at will, which is very different from a term of years. Informative and expressive signals are much more difficult to prohibit, particularly because the traditional way of prohibiting expressive signals is by informal norms, but mechanisms for doing so clearly exist. In the case of appointment, the government officials who appoint the judge may be explicitly prohibited from issuing an informative signal, and the informal norms that operate to provide life-tenured judges with independence may also operate in the case of judges appointed for a term of years.

Elections are a different matter. Although it is not possible for the electorate, as a body, to transmit an informative signal to a judge—how would a general mass of citizens give the judge any persuasive information about a particular case—it can certainly transmit an expressive signal. Such signals can be extremely influential, whether the judge must stand for reelection after a term of years or is subject to periodic or ad hoc recall (Adamany & Dubois, 1976; Croly, 1995; Pinello, 1995; Stumpf, 1998). Consider, in our current tough-on-crime environment, a judge who feels that the case against a person who is probably guilty of a heinous crime should be dismissed because the crucial evidence was illegally obtained, or a judge who wants to sentence a whole category of youthful offenders to alternative sentences, knowing that at least one of these offenders will probably commit a serious crime at some time in the future. Or consider a judge in the pre-World War II South who feels that a black man accused of raping a white woman should receive an acquittal notwithstanding the verdict because the evidence was insufficient. To these dramatic examples may be added the more frequent case of the judge whose ordinary decisions incrementally produce a general impression that he or she is soft on Communism, soft on crime, or soft on any other issue on which the public wants him or her to be hard. Not only are these expressive signals likely to be influential, but there is probably no informal norm against transmitting them and they are impossible to prohibit. Public officials may be forbidden or discouraged from expressing opinions about judicial performance as part of the understood obligations of their government position. But there is no practical way to prohibit the general public from expressing such opinions, and it would probably violate the First Amendment even to try.

Thus, the problem with elected judges is not the oft-stated one that it politicizes the judicial role. Any method of selection will do that and, besides, the role is inherently political by virtue of the judge's attitudes. The real problem is that an electoral regime inevitably exposes judges to expressive signals from the general public. The strong influences that result could deny fair adjudications to individuals who are potentially subject to disadvantages. Perhaps it would go too far to assert that judicial elections violate the due process clause, given the long history of this mechanism and the traditional nature of due process, at least with respect to civil trials. But these influences do indicate that judicial elections violate our general sense of fairness and should be abolished as a matter of policy.

A second institutional question involves salary and resources protection. Here again, many states depart from the federal baseline. To begin with, salary protection is found in only a minority of states, a situation that some would rank with elected judges as a major risk to judicial independence. But microanalysis suggests that salary protection may not be as critical as is sometimes assumed. Of course, lowering a specific judge's salary would constitute a powerful signal to that person, but the process is too cumbersome to be used with respect to an individual decision, and civil service rules would generally preclude its use with respect to the general pattern of decisions by an individual judge. By and large, salary reductions can only be imposed on the judiciary as a whole. As such, it is an extremely crude means of sending signals and it is not necessarily an effective one. It is certainly possible to construct a scenario in which the legislature or chief executive punishes a judiciary whose decisions antagonize the public, but the actualization of this scenario is a bit more difficult to envision. An elected official who interfered with the decisions of the judiciary in such an obvious fashion might be taking a greater political risk than one who tolerated the judiciary's unpopular stance. Moreover, the judiciary's response, when confronted in such an obvious manner, might well be recalcitrance, particularly if the salary reduction were only a modest one, which would probably be the case.

On the other hand, a mere proposal to reduce judicial salaries might serve as an expressive signal by the legislature or the chief executive. But it is questionable whether we really intend to forbid such signals. Although there are strong norms against expressive signals from public officials regarding the outcome of a particular case, there are no such norms against expressions of general disapproval, as noted above. There are, moreover, valid reasons to grant elected officials the authority to reduce judicial salaries. Such salaries represent a higher proportion of state and local budgets than of the federal budget; if all government salaries are being reduced as part of a general economy effort, excluding judicial salaries might be burdensome.

A less commonly discussed, but perhaps more important set, of institutional protections for judges involves their job assignments and the resources that are available to them. In some cases, a judge's job assignment can be changed by a superior judge, by an elected official, or by an administrative official without restrictions on the basis of the reassignment. An official with this authority could readily compromise the fairness of the trial judge's adjudication. For a judge to be reassigned to an undesirable subject matter (exiled to family court, for example) or to an undesirable location (transferred from San Francisco to Fresno, or from Chicago to Cairo) or even an undesirable office (moved from a corner office with a sweeping view to a side office overlooking the air shaft) is a formidable sanction. Similarly, others judges or nonjudicial officials often determine whether the trial judge gets good furniture, a new computer, an extra clerk, a secretary, or a trip to the judicial training sessions at Lake Tahoe.

Unlike dismissals or salary reductions, these sanctions can be imposed on an individual basis and below the level of public scrutiny. Microanalysis suggests that they are a serious concern and, in contrast to the separation of powers concept, that this concern is equally serious when the authority to impose such sanctions is given to other judicial officers. The solution is that all important administrative decisions regarding an adjudicator's job assignment and job conditions should be made by an officer elected by the judges themselves, as in the federal system,[44] or by an independent officer or commission; it is also preferable if decisions are made according to articulated rules, such as seniority, credentials, or workload. This solution would be difficult to reach through the due process clause because an individual litigant could only raise it in the most egregious cases, and it is precisely the sub rosa subtlety of the sanction that constitutes its danger. The better approach, therefore, is to treat it as a matter of policy; legislators, who are the least likely to use such a sanction, should be willing to preclude its use by others.

The last issue that will be considered involves the role of the jury. It is relatively easy to preclude the transmission of performative, informative, or expressive signals from governmental units to a sitting jury; the prohibition of such signals is widely understood and violations of this prohibition can be met with severe punishment, including dismissal, or even imprisonment of the offending official. Performative signals from private parties can, of course, be prohibited as well, primarily by not authorizing any such signals and secondarily by declaring any effort to transmit these signals to be a criminal offense. As described above, however, it is extremely difficult to prevent all informative or expressive signals from private parties from reaching the jury. Informative signals are transmitted by media coverage of the case, which might range from a brief, and often inaccurate, story on the inside page of a local newspaper, to the media tsunami of the O.J. Simpson, Polly Klaas, Jon-Benet Ramsay, and Gary Condit cases. Expressive signals can be transmitted to jurors by any person to whom the juror describes the case ("Oh no, you can't acquit someone like that!"; or, "Those insurance companies are all crooks."). These signals, unlike the transmission of an informative signal from a person actually involved in the case, cannot be avoided by careful voir dire. To prohibit them by punishing their originators would be politically unacceptable and would, in some cases, constitute a violation of the First Amendment. Their effect on the decision maker cannot be drowned out by a bias because jurors are by definition ordinary citizens without legal training. The only solution would appear to be the current admonitions to the jurors or the extreme mechanism of sequestration.

This exposure of the jury to external information and opinion is not surprising once the origin of the jury is considered. The idea that juries should reach a decision on the basis of the facts and arguments presented in the trial is an afterthought, the product of an awkward adaptation of an institution that served an entirely different purposes for the first 500 years of its development. Juries were first used in the 13th century, when the prohibition of the ordeal by the Fourth Lateran Council (1215) had left the legal system without a means of resolving disputes between ordinary people (Holdsworth, 1931, pp. 77-78, 321-323; Landsman, 1983; Pollack & Maitland, 1898, pp. 641-650). They were themselves an adaptation of an earlier institution, the inquest, by which people from each area were called in to provide information to the king; this was the way, for example, that the Domesday Book was compiled (Maitland, 1908. pp. 111-125). As such, the jurors were supposed to have outside knowledge about the reputation of the parties, if not about the facts of the case, and they were supposed to reflect the moral sentiments of the community. In other words, juries did not arise because anyone thought they could be insulated from external information and opinion but because they were such an effective means of incorporating such matters into the decision. The idea that they could be insulated, and thus fulfill the functions of a decision maker in a trial based on contemporary concepts of fairness, is a product of sloppy institutional analysis. It is entirely understandable why this idea would develop in a practical situation in which changes occurred incrementally and, for the same reason, it is entirely understandable why the idea is incorrect.

Sometimes the problem can be satisfactorily resolved. Mere admonitions to the jury are probably sufficient in a significant number of cases. A dispute between two businesses about performance of an ordinary size commercial contract is unlikely to elicit any media coverage and will probably be so boring to the jurors' family and friends that they will tune out well before they are in a position to express an opinion. But in many other cases, these admonitions seem so ineffectual that they simply fail to satisfy our demand for fairness. If we really want the decision maker to be insulated from informative and expressive signals, sequestration would appear to be the only sincere option in any case that receives a modicum of attention from the media or that can generate a modicum of interest among the people with whom jurors speak in their daily lives. But sincerity of this sort would only exacerbate, to an extreme degree, the existing problems with the use of juries—that they are difficult to recruit and place unfair burdens on those who serve. Of course, juries, even more than judicial elections, are a well-established component of our judicial system that could not conceivably be regarded as a violation of due process and, at the federal level, they are required in certain kinds of cases by a constitutional provision of their own. Nonetheless, microanalysis reveals a major difficulty with the use of juries, a major compromise of our prevailing notion of fairness in adjudication. As a matter of policy, they should be avoided whenever possible.

᠑ᠣ Conclusion and Possibilities for Further Research

Modern epistemology indicates that research agendas are controlled by the researcher's preempirical premises; these premises determine the questions that the researcher will pursue, the choice of the methodology that the researcher will employ to gather data, and the interpretation that the researcher will impose on the data that have been gathered (Berger & Luckman, 1967; Bernstein, 1978; Damasio, 1994; Gadamer, 1975; Kuhn, 1962; Putnam, 1981; Rorty, 1979; Winch, 1958). The choice of these beliefs cannot be based on data because it is anterior to the collection of data, nor on some methodology because it is anterior to the choice of methodology. It can be guided only by one's intuition about what will yield interesting results and one's commitments about the kinds of questions that are important to answer. The proposal of this chapter is that our preempirical premises should be based on the reality of the modern state, the administrative state that has evolved during the course of the preceding centuries.

This chapter has argued that the administrative state is best conceived as a network of interacting units, rather than as a three-branch tree, and that judicial independence is best understood as a mechanism for restricting certain types of signals within that network, rather than as an inherent aspect of one of the three branches. Both networks and trees, being metaphors, are preempirical; one cannot prove that one particular metaphor is right and another is wrong. The question is whether the metaphor provides a mental framework for describing its referent and whether it helps generate recommendations that will enable us to achieve our goals in a more effective manner. The network metaphor possesses both these advantages; it facilitates microanalysis of independence as a mechanism used in modern government for the judiciary and for other units and, by doing so, it suggests a strategy for thinking about modifications to our existing approach.

This leads to some concluding suggestions for future research. When researchers begin with the mental image of three branches, they are likely to regard independence as unique, or at least particular to the judiciary, and they are likely to begin by focusing on formal institutional structures, such as judicial elections or salary protection. When the government is conceived as a network, and the problem is subjected to microanalysis, a different research agenda emerges. To begin with, research on the behavior of juries, generally considered a separate subject area, becomes relevant to the issue of independence. Second, the problem becomes generalized to include all the units of government in which the mechanism of independence is employed, such as independent agencies, or the super-independent central banks. In other words, the problem becomes contextualized. This not only provides a larger data base for the study of independence, but also opens this study to the kinds of survey research and institutional analysis that characterize studies of juries and of nonjudicial governmental agencies.

Focusing on the study of judges themselves, microanalyis will tend to reverse the perspective from which many studies of judicial independence are conducted. Instead of beginning with the institutional structure, it would encourage researchers to begin with the individual decision maker, in other words, the judge. What precisely are the signals that judges receive in various contexts? How do they respond to these signals? Which ones affect their decision-making process and which ones can be ignored? The point of framing the research program in this manner is that we should not assume that particular institutional structures are the most important or relevant determinants of judicial independence. For example, it may turn out that veiled threats from an administrator to delay construction of a new judicial office building produce a powerful impact, whereas ringing public condemnations by the legislature are shrugged off, even by elected judges, as empty rhetoric.

One way to pursue the research strategy suggested by the network model and the microanalytic method it facilitates is to interview judges and ask them about their perceptions. Interviewing has its limits as a research strategy of course—one cannot rely on criminals, for example, to identify the causes of crime—but independence is largely a subjective perception. If the judge genuinely feels that a particular event or statement has no effect on decision making, most people would be willing to say that the judge is independent of that statement or event. Of course, judges might not be fully aware of the effects that impinge on them, and they might misrepresent the actual situation from a desire to increase their sense of self-importance, or to express alarm at undesirable developments. Still, there is much to be gained by beginning with the phenomenological experience of judges themselves rather than from premodern assumptions about the nature of independence.

This approach can be expanded to include not only judges but all adjudicators, most significantly those in administrative agencies. The issue of whether ALJs perceive themselves as independent is important on its own terms; in addition, it can provide some additional data that can be compared with the data obtained from the judiciary. Is it more important to have life tenure or be separate from any particular agency, or is it more important to simply believe in independence, to think of oneself as a judge, the way the ALJs apparently have? Such questions bring us back to the three-branch metaphor that was discussed at the start. This metaphor, being outdated and inapplicable, is likely to distort our perceptions and our research agendas. By setting it aside, we can more effectively explore the phenomenon of independence in all parts of the government, that is, in all parts of the modern, administrative government in which we actually live.

ᘇᙆ Notes

1. For a general description, see Dorny, 1993; Hou, 1995, p. 14.

2. For an elaborate effort to model modern government in network terms, see Deutsch, 1963.

3. See Patterson, 2001, for a description of the president's immediate staff.

4. As Justice Rehnquist stated in *Laird*, "[p]roof that a Justice's mind was a tabula rasa in the area of constitutional adjudication would be evidence of lack of qualifications, not lack of bias"(*Laird v. Tatum*, 1927, p. 901). The standard is even less stringent with respect to administrative rule making. See *United Steelworkers of American v. Marshall*, 1980; Strauss, 1980. For an exception, where a breach of neutrality was found, see *Cinderella Career & Finishing Schools, Inc. v. FTC*, 1970. (Chair of the FTC gave a speech condemning the practices of proprietary vocational schools when a proceeding against one such school was pending before the Commission.)

5. Mixing signals in this manner is described, in mechanical engineering, as summing. See Dorny, 1993, p. 118.

6. Recognition of the policy-making role of courts does not necessarily lead to the conclusion that doctrine does not matter at all; one view is that the two factors are combined. See Epstein & Kobylka, 1992; Feeley & Rubin, 1998.

7. See, e.g., *Board of Regents v. Roth*, 1972 (property interests are only created by state law); *Meachum v. Fano*, 1976 (liberty interests are only created by state law); *Vitek v. Jones*, 1980 (liberty interests are created by the Constitution itself, as well as state law).

8. For criticisms of the Court's due process cases, see Ely, 1980, p. 19; Mashaw, 1985; Monaghan, 1977; Rubin, 1984; Van Alstyne,1977. Although the weight of scholarly opinion has been negative, the Court's position does have some defenders. See Simon, 1983; Smolla, 1982; Terrell, 1982.

9. This is essentially the theory of the famous "Footnote 4." *United States v. Carolene Products Co.*, 1938. For elaborations of this theory, see Ely, 1980; Balkin, 1989; Brilmayer, 1996; Rubin, 1984.

10. The administrative cases triggered a reconsideration of the necessary components of due process. See Mashaw, 1974, 1983.

11. Because the authors define the problem in terms of neutrality alone, rather than including the more common issue of a decision on the record, they discuss only prophylactic rules and the prohibition of financial interest, and do not consider performative, informative, or expressive signals.

12. Codified at 28 U.S.C. §§ 331, 332, 372, 604.

13. 28 U.S.C. § 332(d) & (e).

14. In the federal system, it is, of course, a crime to threaten a witness, 18 U.S.C. § 1503, but it is also a crime to attempt to influence a juror "upon any issue or matter pending before such juror . . . by writing or sending to him any written communication in relation to such issue or matter" (18 U.S.C. § 1504).

15. Each jurisdiction has its own rules regarding amicus briefs. For an example, see *Rules of the Supreme Court of the United States* (2001), Rule 37.

16. Federal Rule of Civil Procedure 24. For a discussion of the significance of intervention in administrative cases, see Stewart, 1975.

17. See, e.g., *Administrative Procedure Act*, 5 U.S.C. § 557(d) (A) ("no interested person outside the agency shall make or knowingly cause to be made . . . an ex parte communication relevant to the merits of the proceeding.") See *PATCO v. FLRA*, (1982). The same issue arises in the rule making context, but its resolution is substantially less clear. See *Home Box Office v. FCC*, 1977; Gellhorn & Robinson, 1981.

18. In fact, in some public interest litigation, such as enforcement of environmental statutes, no individual is even involved. The Supreme Court, getting confused between a case or controversy and the presence of individuals as litigants, has sometimes held that such cases must be dismissed for lack of standing. See, e.g., *Allen v. Wright*, 1984; *Lujan v. Defenders of Wildlife*, 1992.

19. With respect to the federal system, see *Federal Rules of Appellate Procedure*.

20. Federal Rule of Civil Procedure 52.

21. Model Code of Judicial Conduct (1990), see, e.g., Canon 2 (B) ("A judge shall not testify voluntarily as a character witness."); Canon 3 (B)(9) ("A judge shall not, while a proceeding is pending or impending in any court, make any public comment that might reasonably be expected to affect its outcome or impair its fairness, or make any nonpublic comment that might substantially interfere with a fair trial or hearing."); id. E(1) ("A judge shall disqualify himself or herself in a proceeding . . . where . . . the judge has . . . personal knowledge of disputed evidentiary facts concerning the proceeding".)

22. U.S. Const., Art. I, Sec. 9. cl. 3 ("No Bill of Attainder or ex post facto Law shall be passed."); id. Sec. 10, cl 1 ("No State shall . . . pass any Bill of Attainder). Thus, the provision applies to civil penalties, such as exclusion from pursuing a particular occupation, see *Cummings v. Missouri*, 1866 (individual may not be required to take an oath that he not aid the Confederacy before being allowed to be a clergyman); *Ex parte Garland*, (1866) (same, for attorney); *United States v. Lovett*, 1946 (legislature may not decide to deny payment of salary to designated employees on grounds of disloyalty). Because these sweeping provisions are concerned with fairness, and not efficiency, they do not apply to the legislative provision of benefits to particular people. Thus the legislature may give grants to specific individuals, or allow specific individuals to sue the government for breach of contract, without running afoul of the prohibition. The practice may be bad public policy, but it certainly does not mistreat any individual citizen.

23. Of course, the judiciary might not respond to the request and the legislator might not keep his or her promise. The point, however, is not that these signals are always effective, but simply that it is not considered improper to issue them.

24. 28 U.S.C. §§ 331, 2071-2075.

25. Although Congress is acting by legislation, it is in fact issuing a direct command to the Court to reverse a specific decision that it has made. This is not equivalent to legislation changing the substantive legal rules that the courts will then follow in a range of adjudications. Moreover, there is nothing in our political morality that would have prevented Congress from providing that the Supreme Court's proposal did not become effective in the case of Congressional inaction, that is, in the case where there was no legislation; the decision to reverse the presumption was based on expedience.

26. For the federal system, see 5 U.S.C. § 556(d) ("Any oral or documentary evidence may be received, but the agency as a matter of policy shall provide for the exclusion of irrelevant, immaterial or unduly repetitious evidence."). See Pierce, 1987.

27. 5 U.S.C. §§ 3105, 7521.

28. 5 U.S.C. § 5372.

29. 5 U.S.C. § 3105.

30. These are generally embodied in the rules against ex parte contact. 5 U.S.C. §§ 554(d), 557(d)(1).

31. This is generally the notice and comment procedure of the Administrative Procedure Act, 5 U.S.C. § 553, although Congress may specify other procedures if it chooses; see *Vermont Yankee Nuclear Power Corp. v. NRDC,* 1978. Duly adopted procedures constitute commands to courts as well as ALJs, of course.

32. 5 U.S.C. §§ 554(d), 557(d)(1).

33. 5 U.S.C. § 557(d)(1)(D).

34. The constitutionality of this mechanism was upheld in *Humprhey's Executor v. United States,* 1935; see also *Morrison v. Olson,* 1988. For commentary, see Strauss, 1988; Sunstein, 1987.

35. Originally established, at the federal level, by the *Pendleton Act,* 1883, now governed by the *Civil Service Reform Act of 1978.*

36. Under the Civil Service Reform Act, this function is implemented by the Office of Personnel Management

37. Under the Civil Service Reform Act, this function is implemented by the Merit Systems Protection Board. The protections afforded by the Act are essentially those provided by the due process clause. The Act does not specify, however, that the initial decision maker, that is, the person who dismisses or disciplines an employee, must be impartial. See *Arnett v. Kennedy,* (1975). In fact, this person is often the employee's superior, who is not impartial at all.

38. For general descriptions of the Fed's monetary control functions, see Bryant, 1983; Greider, 1987; Maisel, 1973; Mayer, 2001. The historical development of this mechanism is described in Wueschner, 1999.

39. It does so, in essence, because it generates enormous revenues from the securities it holds as part of its monetary control operation. It turns over the bulk of these revenues to the Treasury, but it keeps the change, and funds its operations from that source.

40. Pub. Law No. 101-510, 104 Stat 1808 (1990), codified as amended in 10 U.S.C. The Act, which was time-limited, has lapsed. It currently appears at 10 U.S.C. § 2687 note.

41. Although our independent judiciary has certainly played a role in these efforts through its general authority to interpret constitutional provisions, so has the legislature through civil rights legislation, and so have various agencies, including the nonindependent Justice Department.

42. It is rare for the Court to state a rule that goes beyond the practice of a group of states that are moving in that same direction (see Rosenberg, 1991) and particularly rare in the due process area. For example, by the time *Goldberg v. Kelly* (1970) was decided, New York

City's welfare department was already in compliance with virtually all its requirements. For a discussion of the relationship between Supreme Court decisions and national norms, see Feeley & Rubin, 1998, pp. 149-203.

43. As of 1981, only Massachusetts, New Hampshire, and Rhode Island provided life tenure for all their judges. See Berkson, Beller & Grimaldi, 1981.

44. See *Judicial Councils Reform & Judicial Conduct and Disability Act of 1980,* Pub. L. No. 96-458, 94 Stat. 2035 (1980), codified at 28 U.S.C. §§ 331, 332, 372, 604; 28 U.S.C. § 332(d) & (e).

∿ References

Adamany, D., & Dubois, P. (1976). Electing state judges. *Wisconsin Law Review, 731*-779.

Administrative Procedure Act, 5 U.S.C. § 557(d) (A).

Allen v. Wright, 468 U.S. 737 (1984).

Arnett v. Kennedy, 416 U.S. 134 (1975).

Association of Administrative Law Judges v. Heckler, 594 F. Supp. 1132 (D.D.C. 1984).

Austin, J. L. (1962). *How to do things with words* (2nd ed.). Cambridge, MA: Harvard University Press.

Austin, R. (1989). Sapphire bound! *Wisconsin Law Review, 539*-578.

Balkin, J. (1989). The Footnote. *Northwestern University Law Review, 83,* 275.

Baum, L. (1990). *American courts: Process and policy* (2nd ed.). Boston: Houghton Mifflin.

Berger, T., & Luckman, P. (1967). *The social construction of reality.* Garden City, NY: Doubleday.

Berkson, L., Beller, S., & Grimaldi, M. (1981). *Judicial selection in the United States: A compendium of provisions.* Chicago: American Judicature Society.

Bernstein, M. (1955). *Regulating business by independent commission.* Princeton, NJ: Princeton University Press.

Bernstein, R. (1978). *The restructuring of social and political theory.* Philadelphia: University of Pennsylvania Press.

Bickel, A. (1962). *The least dangerous branch: The Supreme Court at the bar of politics.* Indianapolis, IN: Bobbs-Merrill.

Bloch, M. (1961). *Feudal society: Social classes and political organization* (Vol. 2). Chicago: University of Chicago Press.

Board of Regents v. Roth, 408 U.S. 564 (1972).

Brilmayer, L. (1996). Carolene, conflicts and the fate of the "insider-outsider." *University of Pennsylvania Law Review, 134,* 1291-1334.

Brown v. Board of Education, 347 U.S. 483 (1954).

Brownlow Commission. (1937). *Report of the committee with studies of administrative management in the federal government.* Washington, DC: Brownlow Commission.

Bruff, H. (1987). On the constitutional status of administrative agencies. *American University Law Review, 36,* 491-517.

Bryant, R. (1983). *Controlling money: The Federal Reserve and its critics.* Washington, DC: Brookings Institution.

Burbank, S. (1982). The rules enabling Act of 1934. *University of Pennsylvania Law Review, 130,* 1015-1194.

Cargill, T. (1990). *Central bank independence and regulatory responsibilities: The Bank of Japan and the Federal Reserve.* New York: New York University Press.

Carp, R., & Rowland, C. K. (1983). *Policymaking and politics in the federal district courts.* Knoxville: University of Tennessee Press.

Carrington, P. (1998). Judicial independence and democratic accountability in the highest state courts. *Law & Contemporary Problems, 61,* 79-126.

Cinderella Career & Finishing Schools, Inc. v. FTC, 425 F.2d 583 (D.C. Cir. 1970).

Civil Service Reform Act of 1978, Pub. L. No. 95-454, 92 Stat. 1119, 5 U.S.C. § 7101 et seq.

Corder, J. K. (1998). *Central Bank autonomy: The Federal Reserve system in American politics.* New York: Garland.

Croly, S. (1995). The majoritarian difficulty: Elective judiciaries and the rule of law. *University of Chicago Law Review, 62,* 689-794.

Cummings v. Missouri, 71 U.S. (4 Wall.) 277 (1866).

Damasio, A. (1994). *Descartes' error: Emotion, reason and the human brain.* New York: G. P. Putnam.

Deleuze, G., & Guattari, F. (1987). *A thousand plateaus.* Minneapolis: University of Minnesota Press.

Deutsch, K. (1963). *The nerves of government: Models of political communication and control.* New York: Free Press.

Dorny, C. N. (1993). *Understanding dynamic systems: Approaches to modeling, analysis and design.* Engelwood Cliffs, NJ: Prentice Hall.

Dubois, P. (1980). *From ballot to bench: Judicial elections and the quest for accountability.* Austin: University of Texas Press.

Dworkin, R. (1977). *Hard cases, in taking rights seriously.* Cambridge, MA: Harvard University Press.

Dworkin, R. (1986). *Law's empire.* Cambridge, MA: Belknap.

Elliott, S. (1957). Judicial selection and tenure. *Wayne Law Review, 3,* 175-186.

Elster, J. (1984). *Ulysses and the sirens: Studies in rationality and irrationality.* New York: Cambridge University Press.

Ely, J. (1980). *Democracy and distrust: A theory of judicial review.* Cambridge, MA: Harvard University Press.

Epstein, L. & Kobylka, J. (1992). *The Supreme Court and legal change: Abortion and the death penalty.* Chapel Hill: University of North Carolina Press.

FTC v. Cement Institute, 333 U.S. 683 (1948).

Federal Reserve Bank of New York (1987). *Depository institutions and their regulators.* New York: Author.

Federal Rules of Criminal Procedure for the United States District Courts, Rule 21.

Feeley, M., & Rubin, E. (1998). *Judicial policy making and the modern state.* Cambridge, UK: Cambridge University Press.

Ferejohn, J. (1974). *Pork barrel politics: Rivers and harbors legislation, 1947-1968.* Stanford, CA: Stanford University Press.

Friedenthal, J. (1975). The rulemaking power of the Supreme Court: A contemporary crisis. *Stanford Law Review, 27,* 673-686.

Friedman v. Rogers, 440 U.S. 1 (1979).

Friendly, H. (1975). Some kind of hearing. *University of Pennsylvania Law Review, 123,* 1267-1317.

Gadamer, H.-G. (1975). *Truth and method.* New York: Crossroad Press.

Garland, 71 U.S. (4 Wall.) 333 (1866).

Gellhorn, E., & Robinson, G. (1981). Rulemaking "due process": An inconclusive dialogue. *University of Chicago Law Review, 48,* 201-262.

Gibson v. Berryhill, 411 U.S. 564 (1973).

Goldberg v. Kelly, 397 U.S. 254 (1970).

Greider, W. (1987). *Secrets of the temple: How the Federal Reserve runs the country.* New York: Simon and Schuster.

Gwyn, W. (1965). *The meaning of separation of powers: An analysis of the doctrine from its origin to the adoption of the United States Constitution.* New Orleans: Tulane University Press.

Habermas, J. (1984). *The theory of communicative action* (T. McCarthy, Trans., Vol. 1). Boston: Beacon Press.

Hart, H. L. A. (1961). *The concept of law*. Oxford: Clarendon.

Havrilesky, T. (1993). *The pressures on American monetary policy*. Boston: Kluwer Academic.

Holdsworth, W. S. (1931). *A history of English law* (Vol.1). London: Methuen & Co.

Home Box Office v. FCC, 567 F.2d 9 (D.D.C. Cir.), cert. denied, 434 U.S. 829 (1977).

Horwitz, M. (1977). *The transformation of American law, 1790–1860*. New York: Oxford University Press.

Hou, T.-H. (1995). Using neural networks for the automatic monitoring and recognition of signals in manufacturing processes. In H. Parsaei & M. Jamshidi (Eds.), *Design and implementation of intelligent manufacturing systems* (pp. 141-160). Engelwood Cliffs, NJ: Prentice Hall.

Howard, P. (1996). *The death of common sense*. New York: Warner Books.

Humprhey's Executor v. United States, 295 U.S. 602 (1935).

Jacoby, H. (1973). *The bureaucratization of the world*. Berkeley: University of California Press.

Johnson, R., & Libecap, G. (1994). *The federal civil service and the problem of bureaucracy: The economics and politics of institutional change*. Chicago: University of Chicago Press.

Judicial Councils Reform & Judicial Conduct and Disability Act of 1980, Pub. L. No. 96-458, 94 Stat. 2035 (1980).

Kuhn, T. (1962). *The structure of scientific revolutions*. Chicago: University of Chicago Press.

Laird v. Tatum, 409 U.S. 824 (1972).

Landsman, S. (1983). A brief survey of the development of the adversary system. *Ohio State Law Journal, 44*, 713-739.

Lesnick, H. (1975). The federal rule-making process: A time for re-examination. *American Bar Association Journal, 61*, 579-584.

Lubbers, J. (1981). Federal administrative law judges: A focus on our invisible judiciary. *Administrative Law Review, 33*, 109-131.

Lujan v. Defenders of Wildlife, 504 U.S. 555 (1992).

Maisel, S. (1973). *Managing the dollar*. New York: Norton.

Maitland, F. (1908). *The constitutional history of England*. Cambridge, UK: Cambridge University Press.

Malloy, M. (1988). *The corporate law of banks*. Boston: Little Brown.

Marshall v. Barlow's, 436 U.S. 307 (1978).

Marshall v. Jerrico, Inc., 446 U.S. 238 (1980).

Mashaw, J. (1974). The management side of due process: Some theoretical and litigation notes on the assurance of accuracy, fairness and timeliness in the adjudication of social welfare claims. *Cornell Law Review, 59*, 772-824.

Mashaw, J. (1981). Administrative due process: The quest for a dignitary theory, *Boston University Law Review, 61*, 885-931.

Mashaw, J. (1983). *Bureaucratic justice: Managing Social Security disability claims*. New Haven, CT: Yale University Press.

Mashaw, J. (1985). *Due process in the administrative state*. New Haven, CT: Yale University Press.

Mathews v. Eldridge, 424 U.S. 680 (1976).

Mayer, M. (2001). *The Fed: The inside story of how the world's most powerful financial institution drives the market*. New York: Free Press.

Meachum v. Fano, 427 U.S. 215 (1976).

Miller, G. (1986). Independent agencies. *Supreme Court Review*, 41-97.

Miller, G. (1998). An interest-group theory of Central Bank independence. *Journal of Legal Studies, 27*, 433-453.

Model Code of Judicial Conduct (1990).

Monaghan, H. (1977). Of "Liberty" and "Property." *Cornell Law Review, 62*, 405-444.

Morris, I. (2000). *Congress, the president, and the Federal Reserve: The politics of American monetary policy-making*. Ann Arbor: University of Michigan Press.

Morrison v. Olson, 487 U.S. 654 (1988).

Noonan, J. (1988). *Bribes.* Berkeley: University of California Press.

Occupational Safety and Health Act, § 8(a), 29 U.S.C. § 657(a).

PATCO v. FLRA, 685 F. 2 ed 547 (D.C. Cir. 1982).

Patterson, B. (2001). *The White House staff: Inside the West Wing and beyond.* Washington, DC: Brookings Institution.

Pendleton Act, 22 Stat. 403 (1883).

Pierce, R. (1987). Use of federal rules of evidence in federal agency adjudications. *Administrative Law Review, 39,* 1-26.

Pierce, R., Shapiro, S., & Verkuil, P. (1999). *Administrative law and process* (3rd ed.). New York: Foundation Press.

Pinello, D. (1995). *The impact of judicial selection method on state-supreme-court policy.* Westport, CT: Greenwood Press.

Pollack, F., & Maitland, F. (1898). *The history of English law before the time of Edward I* (Vol. 2). Cambridge, UK: Cambridge University Press.

Pub. Law No. 101-510, 104 Stat 1808 (1990).

Putnam, H. (1981). *Reason, truth and history.* New York: Cambridge University Press.

Redish, M., & Marshall, L. (1986). Adjudicatory independence and the value of procedural due process. *Yale Law Journal, 95,* 455-555.

Richardson, H. G., & Sayles, G. O. (1963). *The governance of mediaeval England from the Conquest to Magna Carta.* Edinburgh: University Press.

Rohr, J. (1986). *To run a constitution: The legitimacy of the administrative state.* Lawrence: University of Kansas Press.

Rorty, R. (1979). *Philosophy and the mirror of nature.* Princeton, NJ: Princeton University Press.

Rose-Ackerman, S. (1999). *Corruption and government: Causes, consequences, and reform.* Cambridge, UK: Cambridge University Press.

Rosenberg, G. (1991). *The hollow hope.* Chicago: University of Chicago Press.

Rubin, E. (1984). Due process and the administrative state. *California Law Review, 72,* 1044-1179.

Rubin, E. (1996). The new legal process, the synthesis of discourse, and the microanalysis of institutions, *Harvard Law Review, 109,* 1393-1438.

Rules of the Supreme Court of the United States (2001).

Saint Phalle, T. de. (1985). *The Federal Reserve: An intentional mystery.* New York: Praeger.

Schubert, G. (1974). *Judicial policy making: The political role of the courts.* Glenview, IL: Scott, Foresman.

Searle, J. (1969). *Speech acts.* London: Cambridge University Press.

Segaller, S. (1998). *Nerds 2.0.1: A brief history of the Internet.* New York: TV Books.

Senate Commission on Governmental Affairs. (1977). *Vol V—Regulatory Organization,* at 8, Sen. Doc. No. 95-91, 95th Cong., 2nd Sess.

Simon, P. (1983). Liberty and property in the Supreme Court: A defense of Roth and Perry. *California Law Review, 71,* 146-192.

Smolla, R. (1982). The displacement of federal due process claims by state tort remedies. *University of Illinois Law Forum,* 831-886.

Spurlin, P. (1969). *Montesquieu in America, 1760-1801.* New York: Octogon.

Stewart, R. (1975). The reformation of american administrative law. *Harvard Law Review, 88,* 1669-1813.

Strauss, P. (1980). Disqualifications of decisional officials in rulemaking. *Columbia Law Review, 80,* 990-1051.

Strauss, P. (1984). The place of agencies in government: Separation of powers and the fourth branch. *Columbia Law Review, 84,* 573-669.

Strauss, P. (1988). Formal and functional approaches to separation of powers questions—A foolish inconsistency? *Cornell Law Review, 72,* 488-526.

Strayer, J. (1970). *On the medieval origins of the modern state.* Princeton, NJ: Princeton University Press.

Struve, C. (in press). The paradox of delegation: Interpreting the federal rules of civil procedure. *University of Pennsylvania Law Review, 149.*

Stumpf, H. (1998). *American judicial politics* (2nd ed.). Upper Saddle River, NJ: Prentice Hall.

Sunstein, C. (1987). Constitutionalism after the new deal. *Harvard Law Review, 101,* 421-510.

Terrell, T. (1982). "Property," "due process"and the distinction between definition and theory in legal analysis. *Georgetown Law Journal, 70,* 861-941.

Tumey v. Ohio, 273 U.S. 510 (1927).

United States v. Carolene Products Co., 304 U.S. 144 (1938).

United States v. Lovett, 328 U.S. 303 (1946).

United Steelworkers of American v. Marshall, 647 F.2d 1189 (D.C. Cir. 1980).

Van Alstyne, W. (1977). Cracks in "the new property": Adjudicative due process in the administrative state. *Cornell Law Review, 62 ,* 445-493.

Vermont Yankee Nuclear Power Corp. v. NRDC, 435 U.S. 519 (1978).

Vile, M. J. C. (1967). *Constitutionalism and the separation of powers.* Oxford, UK: Clarendon.

Vitek v. Jones, 445 U.S. 480 (1980).

Ward v. Village of Monroeville, 409 U.S. 57 (1972).

Warren, W. L. (1973). *Henry II.* Berkeley: University of California Press.

Weber, M. (1978). *Economy and society* (G. Roth & C. Wittich, Eds.). Berkeley: University of California Press.

Webster, P. (1995). Selection and retention of judges: Is there one "best" method? *Florida State University Law Review, 23,* 1-42.

Welborn, D. (1977). *Governance of federal regulatory agencies.* Knoxville: University of Tennessee Press.

West, R. (1988). Jurisprudence and gender. *University of Chicago Law Review, 55,* 1-72.

Winch, P. (1958). *The idea of a social science.* London: Routledge & Kegan Paul.

Wooley, J. (1984). *Monetary politics: The Federal Reserve and the politics of monetary policy.* New York: Cambridge University Press.

Wueschner, S. A. (1999). *Charting twentieth-century monetary policy: Herbert Hoover and Benjamin Strong, 1917-1927.* Westport, CT: Greenwood Press.

Part III

THEORY AND EVIDENCE

Chapter 5

Does Judicial Independence Exist?

The Lessons of Social Science Research

Terri Jennings Peretti

J udicial independence is considered to be a norm of vital importance in our legal system. Its goal is impartial, "law-based" decision making by judges and, thus, the certain protection of text-based rights, even those unpopular with current majorities and powerful politicians. Impartiality is secured by freeing judges of popular and partisan pressures—in obtaining their positions, retaining their positions, and making their decisions. Because the people can be confident that judges made their decisions fairly and objectively, compliance with court rulings is thereby assured. High regard for courts continues, as then does their legitimacy, power, and unique ability to protect our treasured rights and liberties.

I am tempted to refer to this collection of claims as "the judicial independence myth." This is due to its proponents' tendency to present judicial independence as fact rather than as an ideal or set of normative values about courts. As this suggests, I am rather dubious about the existence of judicial independence. Unlike many scholars, however, I am not particularly troubled by this state of affairs. I have already defended that argument and need not do so here (Peretti, 1999). I will instead focus on the primary cause of my frustration with much of the scholarship on judicial independence: the lack of empirical grounding for its key claims. Whether one's goal is to protect judicial independence or to limit it, social science research regarding courts has much to offer and is ignored at the reformer's peril.

This chapter will examine several facts about courts that empirical research has consistently revealed and contrast them with the claims made about judicial independence, noting the wide gap between the two. I then conclude with a call for greater accuracy and less advocacy in our discussions about judicial independence and an appreciation of the virtues of limited judicial independence.

Before beginning, I must note that, for two reasons, my focus is almost exclusively on the federal courts, and the Supreme Court more particularly. First, this is where my expertise lies. Second, most agree that federal judges enjoy more independence than state judges; after all, many state judges are subject to popular election. Nonetheless, politics exerts a powerful influence even on federal judges, despite their tenure and salary protections.

∞ Judicial Selection

The norm of judicial independence has strong implications for the judicial selection process. As Neubauer explains, "[i]f judges are to be free to decide cases unfettered by the whims of the current regime, then they should be selected in ways that maximize their independence so they are free to follow the law as they see it" (1997, p. 158). Federal judges, however, are selected by the president and Senate, leaders of the current regime. This fact alone suggests a significant limitation on judicial independence. Although federal judges enjoy life tenure and protection against salary diminution, the inherent tension—between judicial independence and the selection of judges by politicians—remains. As a result, many scholars urge the president and Senate to ignore political considerations such as ideology in choosing judges. For example, former Supreme Court nominee Robert Bork, in rejecting calls to withdraw his nomination in the face of certain defeat in the Senate, argued that

> Federal judges are not appointed to decide cases according to the latest opinion polls. They are appointed to decide cases impartially according to law. But when judicial nominees are assessed and treated like political candidates the effect will be to chill the climate in which judicial deliberations take place, to erode public confidence in the impartiality of our judges, and to endanger the independence of the judiciary. (1990, pp. 313-314)

Professors Fein and Neuborne (2000) believe that judicial independence requires a ban on "case-specific questioning" of judicial nominees, in effect forbidding ideological screening because candidates could not be asked about their views on such key cases as *Roe v. Wade.* Along the same lines, Stephen Burbank has argued that "because ideologues of any political stripe are not truly independent, a conscious effort to secure their appointment to the federal bench would be an attack on judicial independence" (1996, p. 120). Although not forbidding "an assessment of an individual's general political attitudes and legal philosophy" (1999, p. 338), he urges the president and Senate to evaluate a nominee's "capacity for independence."[1]

Even assuming that we could figure out how to define merit and measure, in advance, a candidate's capacity to be independent, this suggestion flies in the face of all we know about the pervasive influence of politics in judicial selection. A multitude of studies confirm David O'Brien's conclusion that "partisan politics dominates the selection of judges," despite the "myth . . . that judges should be selected strictly on the basis of merit" (1988, p. 35; see also Abraham, 1999; Goldman, 1991, 1997). This should not be surprising given that the process is controlled by elected officials who see judgeships both as opportunities to influence judicial policy and as "grand political plums" (Murphy 1990, p. 218). Of course, the balance of power between the president and Senate in selecting judges varies considerably, with senatorial courtesy empowering home-state senators belonging to the president's party greatly with regard to district court judgeships, moderately for appellate court positions, and not at all in the selection of Supreme Court justices. Accordingly, partisanship and local political ties are critically important for district court nominees, whereas ideology and merit are more important for Supreme Court nominees. Nonetheless, the research consistently and convincingly demonstrates that political factors, particularly partisanship and ideology, dominate the selection of federal judges at all levels of the bench.

One clear measure of the critical nature of partisanship in judicial selection is the fact that at least 90% of nominees (and all Supreme Court nominees since 1975) have belonged to the president's party (Baum, 2001, p. 48; Carp & Stidham, 2001, p. 225). In fact, "[a]s often as not, a seat on the bench goes to a reasonably active or visible member of the party in power" (Carp & Stidham, 2001, p. 226). Of course, this should be expected when senators are granted a veto power over appointments to judicial vacancies in their state. Clearly, "judgeships are still considered part of the political patronage system," and political activity is necessary to bring the potential candidate to the attention of "judicial power brokers" (i.e., presidents, senators, and local party leaders) (Carp & Stidham, 2001).

With regard to the president's Supreme Court nomination decisions, Abraham's (1999) historical review reveals that "political and ideological compatibility . . . has arguably been *the* controlling factor," outweighing other considerations such as merit, personal friendship, and symbolic representation (pp. 2-3; Goldman, 1991; Hulbary & Walker, 1980). Professor Baum states it even more strongly, asserting that "all presidents seek to put on the Court individuals who share their views on important policy questions" (2001, p. 43). Further verifying the importance of ideology in presidential nomination decisions, Nemacheck (2001a) finds that presidents are more likely to choose "ideologically proximate nominees" when they enjoy the greatest freedom to do so (i.e., when the Senate is closely aligned with the president in terms of both partisanship and ideology).

Senate voting on judicial nominees is also strongly influenced by political factors, most notably ideology, partisanship, and presidential clout. A study by Cameron, Cover, and Segal (1990) analyzing more than 2000 Supreme Court confirmation votes concluded that "confirmation voting is decisively affected by the ideological distance between Senators and nominees" (p. 530; Felice & Weisberg, 1988/1989; Rohde & Spaeth, 1976; Segal, Cover, & Cameron, 1988/1989; Songer, 1979; Watson & Stookey, 1995). The influence of ideology can also be seen in the high correlations between senators' liberalism and their confirmation votes on several recent controversial nominations: Fortas (+.79), Haynsworth (-.84), Carswell (-.84), Bork (-.83), and Thomas (-.81) (Segal & Spaeth, 1993, pp. 135-137,138-142).

Partisanship is also a strong and consistent influence in Senate confirmation voting. Not surprisingly, Republican senators are much more likely than Democratic senators to vote to confirm Republican presidents' nominees (86% versus 44% for nine controversial Supreme Court nominations studied by Felice and Weisberg, 1988/1989). The partisan basis of Senate voting on the Bork and Thomas nominations is even more striking: 96% of Democrats opposed Bork whereas 87% percent of Republicans supported him, and 81% of Democrats voted to reject Thomas whereas 95% of Republicans voted to confirm him (Segal & Spaeth, 1993, pp. 139,142). Partisan influence is also revealed when the president attempts "opposite party replacement," in which a Democratic justice replaces a Republican justice and vice versa; under these circumstances, the Senate rejection rate doubles (Ruckman, 1993). A final example of the influence of party is the fact that the Senate confirmation rate is much lower when the Senate is controlled by the opposition party (59%) than when it is controlled by the president's party (89%) (Baum, 2001, p. 52; Segal, 1987, p. 1007).

The final political factor influencing Senate confirmation is presidential clout, a function of public popularity, party strength in the Senate, and lame-duck status. In other words, Senate opposition is far less likely if the nomination is made early in the president's term and if he enjoys strong public support and a partisan majority in the Senate (Cameron et al., 1990; Halper, 1972; Palmer, 1983; Segal et al., 1988/1989). For example, Palmer found that a "President whose party controls 60 percent of the Senate and who has three years left in his term has about a 90 percent chance of having his nominee confirmed. However, a President whose party controls 40 percent of the Senate and who has one year left in his term has about a 52 percent chance" (Palmer, 1983, p. 160). Segal similarly found that 88%

of the Supreme Court nominations occurring in the president's first three years of office were confirmed, compared to only 54% of the nominations occurring in the president's final year (1987, p. 1008).

As these last figures remind us, because the presidency and Senate are dominated by different constituencies and often by different parties, the judicial selection process has considerable potential to be contentious. An initial glance at the recent numbers, though, suggests otherwise. Although one third of Supreme Court nominees were rejected by the Senate in the 19th century, only 10% have been rejected since. In fact, only five nominations since 1900 failed to win Senate confirmation and only two successful nominees failed to win at least two-thirds Senate support (Baum, 2001, p. 50). These figures, however, tell only part of the story and are somewhat misleading. Although the president has enjoyed much greater success with the Senate since 1900, this is partly because of the reduced incidence of unfavorable confirmation conditions, with fewer nominations occurring in election years or during times of divided party control (Baum, 1989, p. 49; Segal, 1987, p. 1010). In any case, scholars agree that the Senate has become much more aggressive in scrutinizing judicial nominees in the last half of the 20th century, particularly since the late 1960s. For example, Baum notes that "[o]f the twenty-eight [Supreme Court] nominations considered by the Senate from 1949 through mid-2000, four were defeated, seven received more than ten negative votes, and others faced serious opposition" (2001, p. 50). In addition, the amount of time the Senate devotes to nomination hearings has increased substantially (Allison, 1996; Hartley & Holmes, 1997). For example, despite Clinton's conciliatory approach to judicial selection, the confirmation delay faced by his lower court nominees when Republicans gained control of the Senate was extraordinary. Although the Democratic Senate of the 103rd Congress waited an average of 59 days to hold hearings on Clinton's district court nominees, the three Republican Senates that followed waited an average of 76, 161, and 97 days respectively. Clinton's circuit court nominees fared even worse; although Bush's and Clinton's first term appellate court nominees waited an average of 77 to 81 days, the delay for Clinton's nominees in the 105th Congress jumped sharply to 231 days and in the 106th Congress to 247 days (Goldman, 1998; Goldman, Slotnick, Gryski, & Zuk, 2001, pp. 234-235). Goldman and his colleagues' well-supported conclusion is that the confirmation "process that once had been routine for most nominees turned into an obstacle course fueled by partisan and ideological divisions to which only a minority of nominees were immune" (Goldman et al., 2001, p. 231).

Although divided party control has played a critical role in making the confirmation process more contentious in recent years, the contribution of interest group pressure cannot be overlooked. Interest group activity in judicial nominations is certainly not new, but it is no longer episodic in nature. With hundreds of groups now devoted to participating in the judicial selection process, "organized group mobilization and pressure on controversial judicial nominations has become a permanent feature of our political landscape. . . . This conflict has become institutionalized"(Caldeira, 1988/1989, p. 538; Caldeira & Wright, 1995).

Political influence extends to two final facets of the judicial selection process—the creation of judgeships and judicial retirements. First, the creation of new judgeships is more likely if the president and the majority of members in Congress belong to the same party (Barrow, Zuk, & Gryski, 1996). A good example is the *Omnibus Judgeship Act of 1978,* in which a Democratic Congress created a record number of federal judgeships, contributing greatly to President Carter's judicial appointment opportunities. In the end, Carter appointed nearly 40% of the federal bench, exercising considerable influence on judicial policy making in the lower courts. DeFigueiredo and Tiller (1996) find that expansion of the judiciary is especially likely when a unified Congress follows a divided or opposite party Congress, suggesting that its goal is to regain partisan control of the courts. Presidential appointment opportunities can also be created by judges themselves, via retirement. Here the evidence shows that federal judges are more likely to retire when they share the president's partisan affiliation (Goldman, 1997).

The fact that partisanship and ideology dominate judicial selection does not necessarily mean that merit plays no role. Even for federal district court appointments, the candidate must demonstrate a modicum of professional competence and accomplishment. However, in referring to "the unwritten rule that potential judges be more than just warm bodies with a law degree," Carp and Stidham obviously regard this as a relatively low threshold requirement (2001, p. 225). Legal ability and professional competence are more important screening criteria for Supreme Court justices as compared to lower court judges. Supreme Court nominees with questionable qualifications are more likely to arouse Senate opposition and will in any case be less able to advance the president's policy agenda effectively. Nonetheless, screening for merit still leaves the president with a sizable pool of potential nominees; it does not rule out or even substantially constrain ideological or partisan selection. Most studies conclude that objective qualifications are also less important for the Senate as compared to such political factors as ideology and partisanship (Halper, 1972; Segal, 1987, p. 1010; Songer, 1979; but see Cameron et al., 1990). As Halper points out, Senate rejections due primarily to lack of qualifications are few in number (1972, p. 107). Finally, the participation of the American Bar Association's (ABA's) Standing Committee on Federal Judiciary does not guarantee the strong focus on objective qualifications that proponents of judicial independence desire. Its professional judgments and the process that produces them have been subject to considerable criticism. For example, its endorsement of Nixon nominees Clement Haynsworth and the "patently inferior" G. Harold Carswell (Abraham, 1999, p. 11) raised questions about the rigor of its investigations and the worth of a "qualified" recommendation. (In fact, the Committee has never given an "unqualified" rating to a Supreme Court nominee [Baum, 2001, p. 35].) The more persistent criticism alleges Committee bias. For example, Slotnick's (1983) study found that the most significant correlate of high ABA ratings was "the candidate's white male status" (p. 393). This was assumed to be a product of the fact that, until the ABA's deliberate efforts at diversification in the 1970s, "a relatively narrow segment of the legal establishment . . . dominated [the] Committee. . . . Its members tended to be characteristically men; successful lawyers; partners in large, big-city firms; veterans of local bar-association politics" (Abraham, 1999, p. 24). Since the 1980s, the Committee has been a target of conservatives who claim its recent evaluations, particularly of Reagan and Bush nominees, have been political and biased in a liberal direction. President George W. Bush, no doubt, pleased his conservative allies with his withdrawal in 2001 of the Committee's vetting role.

The evidence is overwhelming that politics pervades the judicial selection process. Exhorting presidents and senators to ignore political factors and instead select judges based on their objective qualifications and capacity for independence thus defies the historical pattern. More importantly, it defies logic. Politicians interested in reelection and policy success cannot reasonably be expected to ignore such splendid opportunities to please their constituents, help their party, and realize their policy goals. Until the selection process is radically altered, the call for merit and independence as selection criteria is futile; absent fundamental change, it is about as effective as urging the sun not to shine.

Judicial Decision Making

Independent judges are free of political pressure, whether from the public or politicians. They need not worry about how others will react to their decisions because no reprisals can be administered. Decisions can thus be made impartially, according to the law and the facts of the case. Central to judicial independence, then, is impartial decision making, free of the "taint" of personal preference, public opinion, or interbranch pressure. Social science research, once again, tells a different story. In fact, studies prove that each of these three political factors influences judicial decisions.

Personal Preference. Despite the hope for impartiality, an extensive body of research confirms that a judge's personal political attitudes strongly influence his or her decisions. This "attitudinal" model is widely accepted by social scientists who study the courts. As Professor Segal asserts, "[n]o serious scholar of the judiciary denies that the decisions of judges, especially at the Supreme Court level, are at least partially influenced by the judges' ideology" (1999, p. 237).

The attitudinal model posits that, in deciding cases, judges pursue their policy goals and consequently vote in accordance with their political attitudes and policy preferences. "Simply put, Rehnquist votes the way he does because he is extremely conservative, Marshall voted the way he did because he is extremely liberal" (Segal & Spaeth, 1993, p. 65). The empirical evidence in support of the attitudinal model is abundant and convincing. Numerous studies demonstrate that the justices' votes are ideologically driven (Hagle & Spaeth, 1993; Segal & Cover, 1989; Segal, Epstein, Cameron, & Spaeth, 1995; Segal & Spaeth, 1993). For example, Segal and Cover (1989) found a .80 correlation between the justices' reputed ideology and their civil liberties decisions from 1953 to 1987. Studies also reveal considerable ideological variation in voting among the justices. For example, 76% of Justice Stevens's votes in the 1998 term were liberal, compared to only 23% for Rehnquist (Baum, 2001, p. 147; O'Connor & Palmer, 2001, p. 267). In addition to ideological variability among justices, there is considerable ideological consistency in the voting patterns of individual justices, both across issues and over time. Patterns of agreement, with like-minded justices such as Scalia, Rehnquist, and Thomas voting together more than 90% of the time, also point to an ideological explanation of judicial decision making. The influence of ideology is additionally seen in the fact that membership change on the Court produces corresponding policy change (Baum, 1992, 1988). For example, the Court's support for civil liberties claims significantly declined, first, with Nixon's four appointees (Burger, Blackmun, Powell, and Rehnquist) and, second, when Souter and Thomas replaced Brennan and Marshall (Baum, 2001, p. 155). Other studies have verified that ideology and partisanship influence judicial decision making in the lower federal courts as well (Goldman 1966, 1975; Rowland & Carp, 1996; Segal, Songer, & Cameron, 1995; Smith 1990; Songer & Davis, 1990; Stidham, Carp, & Songer, 1982, 1996; Ulmer 1962; and more generally, Pinello, 1999).

The empirical evidence is compelling in proving the strong influence of political attitudes. They are not, however, the sole determinant of judicial decisions, as political scientists too often fail to acknowledge. If that were the case, we would never see unanimous decisions and judges with ideologically polarized views would never agree. However, even on the Supreme Court, 35% of its decisions in the 1998 term were unanimous (Baum, 2001, p. 134). Additionally, Justice Stevens, the Court's most liberal member, joined the opinions of Scalia and Thomas, the Court's most conservative members, in nearly half (46%) of the cases decided in the 1997 and 1998 terms (Baum 2001, p. 151). Obviously, influences that are not attitudinal in nature must be at work. One study that is particularly useful in characterizing the contribution of both legal and political factors in judicial decision making is Jon Gottschall's (1986) analysis of Reagan's appellate court appointees.

Gottschall's aim was to test the degree to which Reagan's judges were ideologically extreme and unusually uniform in their conservatism. (He concluded that, although they were indeed conservative, they were neither more conservative nor more uniformly conservative than the Nixon judges.) More directly relevant here, however, was his finding that despite their ideological differences, Carter and Reagan appointees agreed in 74% of the cases in which they participated jointly. In the 26% of cases in which they disagreed, however, ideology proved to be profoundly important, with Carter's judges voting the liberal outcome 95% of the time and Reagan's judges only 5% of the time. This study and others like it (Howard, 1977) consistently reveal that judges often agree with one another, no doubt because the law is clear and they follow it. However, when the law is unclear, when precedents are lacking or in conflict, political attitudes exert a powerful influence.[2] Of course, the law is more apt to be unclear or in conflict in cases heard by higher courts, explaining why the influence of political attitudes is more evident in Supreme Court decisions.

The assumption that independent judges use their freedom to decide impartially according to law is contradicted by the empirical evidence. Political attitudes exert a substantial influence on judicial decisions, especially on difficult issues decided by higher courts. As even a critic of this political science research admits, "in major cases with a significant policy component, judges are pretty clearly influenced by ideology, more than they are driven by neutral legal principles" (Cross, 2000, p. 18).

Interbranch Pressure. Whereas viewing judges as "single-minded seekers of legal policy" (George & Epstein 1992, p. 325) has proven to be a productive research assumption, recent studies employing a rational choice or institutionalist perspective suggest that strategic considerations play a decisive role as well. Judges do indeed pursue their policy goals but must do so strategically by taking into account various institutional restraints, both endogenous and exogenous (Clayton & Gillman, 1999; Epstein & Knight, 1998; Murphy 1964). For example, members of collegial courts who wish to see their policy preferences put into law must do more than simply vote those preferences; they must anticipate and accommodate the views of other judges, thereby securing enough votes to produce a majority decision (Maltzman, Spriggs, & Wahlbeck, 2000).

Judges who seek to maximize their policy goals must also consider external constraints, most notably the structural rules of separation of powers and checks and balances. The Court's decisions are not self-executing and instead require funding from the legislature and enforcement support from the executive branch. A policy-motivated justice will consequently include, in his or her decision-making calculus, the likely reactions of politicians who can implement, ignore, or undermine the Court's rulings. In *Brown,* for example, the Court gave serious con-

sideration to the potential for noncompliance with and nonenforcement of a ruling against racial segregation. Strategies were adopted to help promote compliance, including striving for unanimity and writing a short, nonlegalistic opinion
that could be printed in full in the nation's newspapers. As Rosenberg carefully
documents, desegregation in Southern schools did not in fact occur until Congress and the executive branch joined the battle by threatening to withhold federal educational funds (Rosenberg, 1991). Justices who care deeply about their
policy aims will consider the likelihood of, and adopt tactical measures designed
to increase, implementation support within the discretion of other political actors
to provide or withhold.

Judges who wish to see their decisions effectively implemented must not only
try to ensure policy support from the other branches; they must also be mindful of
potential sanctions imposed by the other branches. Congress, for example, can
express (and has expressed) its displeasure with the Court by withholding salary
increases and limiting its budget. More direct political attacks on the courts, such
as jurisdiction-stripping bills and impeachment efforts, are frequent but rarely
successful (B. Friedman, 1998) and mostly take the form of saber rattling. They do,
however, provide critical information to judges about whether they should forge
ahead or temporarily retreat, and they are not without their effects. For example,
Rosenberg found that intense Congressional hostility did in fact produce decisional reactions by the Supreme Court, even when court-curbing bills were not
successfully enacted (Rosenberg, 1992). Of course, the most well-known instance
of the Court responding to political opposition is its about-face in 1937 on the
issue of the government's economic regulatory powers. The potent combination
of, first, intense criticism and political pressure and, then, nine new appointments
by FDR led the Court in a dramatic turnaround to defer to rather than second-
guess and typically overrule the legislature's economic policy choices.

No account of interbranch influence would be complete without acknowledging the solicitor general's office. It represents the executive branch before the
Supreme Court and enjoys both extraordinary access and extraordinary success,
leading Caplan (1987) to label it "the Tenth Justice." For example, the Court
granted review to cases appealed by the federal government 70% of the time,
compared to only 8% for other parties (Segal, 1991). In addition, the solicitor general participated, often at the Court's invitation, as a party or amicus in 84% of the
cases in which the Court heard argument in the 1998 term (Baum, 2001, p. 99). The
federal government, in addition, wins about two thirds of its cases (Epstein, Segal,
Spaeth, & Walker, 1994, p. 569-572) and won more than 70% in the 1990s (Baum
2001, p. 175). Its success persists even when controlling for other factors, such as
case facts, ideological direction of the brief, strategic case selection by the solicitor
general's office, and presidential influence in appointments (Segal, 1990, 1991;

Segal & Reedy, 1988). Thus, "deference to the executive is a stronger explanation for the solicitor's succcess" (Segal, 1990, p. 149).

Whether the Court, because of strategic considerations, also accedes to the wishes of Congress in its statutory interpretation role has been the focus of much recent research. Because Congress can override the Court's interpretation of statutes by a simple majority vote, policy-motivated justices will, it is argued, play a "separation of powers game," in which "the Court takes a position that is as close to its ideal point as possible without being so far from Congress that it is overturned" (Ferejohn & Shipan, 1990; Maltzman, Spriggs, & Wahlbeck, 1999, p. 49; Spiller & Gely, 1992). For example, "a liberal Court facing a conservative Congress might moderate its views so as to avoid overrides that would leave the policy outcomes even further to the right" (Segal, 1999, p. 237).

A lively debate has ensued regarding the empirical validity of the separation-of-powers model. Strategic behavior by the Court is evident in some individual cases or policy areas (Epstein & Walker, 1995; Eskridge, 1991; Gely & Spiller, 1990) and some time periods (Baum, 2001, p. 176-177). Segal (1997, 1999), however, finds that aggregate voting data more closely fit the attitudinal rather than the separation-of-powers model, with justices usually voting their sincere preferences rather than accommodating congressional preferences. Baum has also observed that "strategic considerations do not move justices very far from their own favored positions" (2001, p. 146) and that the Court has in general "exhibited considerable resistance to congressional pressures" since the 1950s, standing firm on such unpopular constitutional policies as school prayer and flag burning (Baum, 2001, p. 177). The critics, in explaining the logic underlying these contrary findings, point out that the uncertainty and complexity characteristic of the legislative process give the Court considerable discretion; it need not always adjust its decisions because a legislative response is not always, or even often, likely (Baum, 1997; Segal, 1997; but see Bartels, 2001). In addition, attitudinalists have long emphasized that Supreme Court justices can freely express their political views in their decisions because they lack ambition for higher office, enjoy tenure and salary protections, exercise considerable control over their docket, and deal with legally ambiguous cases (Segal & Spaeth, 1993, p. 60).

The critical issue here is whether judges are constrained in their decision making by Congress and other political actors or whether they are free to vote their sincere preferences.[3] Of special interest here is the fact that neither behavioral model satisfies judicial independence norms.[4] If the strategic model is correct and the justices accommodate Congressional preferences, they are not deciding independently. If the attitudinal model is correct, then the justices are indeed independent but use their freedom to ignore the desires of powerful political actors and to favor their personal policy preferences instead, contrary to the requirement of judicial independence that decisions be impartial and strongly rooted in the law. In addition, the personal policy preferences that judges inject into the law are not "independent." They are, in a significant sense, exogenously determined by the president and Senate who have selected them, thus weakening the claim that judicial decisions are neutral, law bound, and independent of the ruling regime.

This point can be clarified by examining Suzanna Sherry's discussion of judicial independence as it relates to Justice Scalia. She argues that "whatever you might think of Justice Scalia's rulings . . . you cannot accuse him of bending to popular sentiment—nor can he be punished for his failure to do so. If his interpretation of the Constitution is wrong, it is not because the legislature is looking over his shoulder as he writes" (1998, p. 809). It is certainly true that, within rather broad limits, Scalia can decide as he wants and employ an interpretive approach of his choosing, without worry of immediate popular or congressional retaliation. Two important qualifications condition this initial assessment of substantial independence, however. First, Scalia is notorious for his combative style (particularly in opinion writing), his occasional alienation of other justices (especially O'Connor), and his unwillingness to participate in accommodation and coalition building. As a result, some have argued, Scalia has secured fewer victories for his conservative agenda (Smith & Beuger, 1993; Smith & Hensley, 1993; but see Kozinski, 1991). In other words, by failing to behave in a "sophisticated," strategic manner and instead voting his sincere preferences, Scalia has paid the price of reduced policy effectiveness. The second point is that Scalia would not be on the Court and thus, would not be free to pursue a conservative policy course if not for the electoral success of conservative politicians like Ronald Reagan.[5] Sherry is correct that Scalia does not decide the way he does because of interbranch pressure or the likely imposition of a postdecision punishment. If we regard judicial independence as freedom from this type of strong and direct political control, then Scalia, like most judges, is quite independent. If judicial independence is alternatively defined as freedom from political influence, then his decisions are not truly independent. Scalia does not, after all, evaluate each case, each challenge to government authority, with a clean slate. The ideological views anchoring and guiding his decisions were chosen by the elected politicians who selected him. President Reagan and a cooperative Senate knew precisely what they were getting with Scalia's appointment, and he has rarely surprised or disappointed them.[6]

As previously indicated, scholarly debate currently exists over the degree to which the Court accommodates the preferences of other political actors in its decisions. A strong consensus has long existed, however, regarding the exercise of interbranch influence through the vehicle of judicial selection. The personal values influencing judges' decisions have been actively and deliberately selected by the president and Senate in the process of screening and choosing appointees

(Peretti, 1999). Research has proven the strong influence of an appointing president on judicial decision making. Judges appointed by Democratic presidents render a significantly higher percentage of liberal decisions. For example, 52% of Carter's district court appointees' decisions were liberal, compared to only 37% for Reagan's district court judges (Carp & Stidham, 2001, pp. 244-248; see also Carp, Manning, & Stidham, 2001; Carp, Songer, Rowland, Stidham, Richey-Tracy, 1993; Gottschall 1986; Haire, Humphries, & Songer, 2001; Rowland & Carp, 1992; Rowland, Carp, & Songer, 1988; Stidham et al., 1996; Wenner & Ostberg, 1994). In addition, about 75% of Supreme Court justices have lived up to presidential expectations in their decisions, with the percentage increasing in modern times and for presidents who screen carefully (Peretti, 1999, p. 113-115; see also Lindquist, Yalof, & Clark, 2000). Politicians controlling the value bases of judicial decisions through the selection process must be regarded as a significant limitation on judicial independence, though a desirable one that promotes democratic accountability.

Public Opinion. Acknowledging the influence of elected officials in selecting judges necessarily means acknowledging the influence of public opinion, though its impact is largely indirect.[7] As Dahl (1957) explained nearly 50 years ago, the Court cannot hold out against majority sentiment for long, given that popularly elected officials regularly change the Court's membership. Though indirect, this democratic link between public opinion and the Court's decisions is nonetheless strong and has wide acceptance among social scientists, as Flemming and Wood (1997) acknowledge.

> To the extent the choices of presidents and voting decisions of senators reflect the public mood when new justices are nominated and confirmed, the elected branches adjust the Court's ideological makeup to bring it in line with the public's views. In this way, prevailing popular sentiment is filtered through the electoral process to shape the Supreme Court's policy direction. Empirical substantiation for this link is very strong . . . and is no longer a matter of controversy. (p. 492)

In selecting judges, in deciding how (or whether) to implement court rulings, and in seeking to curb courts, elected officials are expressing public preferences and group demands. Thus, it should not be surprising to see various studies proving a strong link between Court decisions and public opinion. Mishler and Sheehan's (1993) study of Supreme Court decisions and "the public mood" found that from 1956 to 1989 the Court was "highly responsive to majority opinion. Its decisions . . . have conformed closely to the aggregate policy opinions of the American public" (p. 97). Marshall (1989) found that 62% of the Court's decisions from 1935 to 1986 (on which there was comparable national poll data) were consistent with public opinion. In addition, the Court was more likely to uphold state or federal laws that were consistent with national opinion as compared to laws that were inconsistent with national opinion. Marshall and Ignagni (1994) also demonstrated that the Court's record in "rights claims" corresponded to public opinion. From 1953 to 1962, the Court ruled in favor of a civil rights, civil liberties, or equality claims 73% of the time when it was supported by the public, compared to only 40% of the time when the public opposed the claim. Another important empirical study by Stimson, Mackuen, and Erikson (1995) concluded that "court decisions do, in fact vary in accord with current public preferences," although less strongly and less quickly than for Congress and the president (p. 555). Particularly interesting are studies showing a more direct causal link between public opinion and judicial decisions. For example, sentencing by federal judges in draft evasion cases became more lenient as public opposition to the Vietnam War increased, and sentencing severity in marijuana cases by California judges changed in response to a public referendum on the issue (Carp & Stidham, 1983, p. 282). Whether the causal link is direct or indirect, it is clear that the Court has "seldom lagged far behind or forged far ahead" of public opinion (McCloskey, 1960, p. 225).

The central requirement of judicial independence that judges decide impartially, free of political influences, has not been met. Social science research finds instead that judges, especially at the Supreme Court level, pursue their policy goals primarily by voting their preferences, but when necessary, accommodating those who can limit policy success, including Congress. Additionally, elected officials substantially direct the judiciary both by the laws they write and the judges they select.

∽ Public Confidence in Courts

Yet another claim asserted by proponents of judicial independence is that compliance with court rulings and high regard for courts, their primary source of power, are dependent on the guarantee to the public of judicial independence. The public must believe that judges are deciding impartially, not out of bias or fear of political reprisal. Fein and Neuborne (2000), for example, argue that it is the judicial "culture that treasures intellectual honesty and principles that rise above the political moment" that "inspires the public to comply voluntarily with the countless judicial decisions rendered daily" (p. 60). They further assert that "judicial decrees tend to be accepted ungrudgingly as legitimate and fair because of the openness and impartiality of the judicial process and because of the reasoned analyses that are the signature of judicial opinion" (2000, p. 61). Research shows that, at least with regard to the U.S. Supreme Court, none of these claims is valid. In fact, compliance with the Court's rulings is uneven, public awareness and understanding of them are minimal, and public evaluations are neither exceptionally high nor rooted in beliefs about the Court's impartiality.

Compliance. Numerous judicial impact studies have proven that compliance with the Court's decisions is neither automatic nor complete (Bowen, 1995; Canon, 1991; Canon & Johnson, 1999; Fisher, 1993; Orfield, 1987; Reid, 1988; Rosenberg, 1991). "Consumers" may refuse to alter their behavior or take steps to undermine the Court's policies. For example, public schools may continue to permit (and may even require) school prayer, hospitals may continue to refuse to provide abortion services, and parents may evade school busing orders by placing their children in private schools. Officials charged with implementation may refuse to assist the Court, Congress with funding, and the executive branch with enforcement. State and local officials can take advantage of many opportunities to ignore or hinder the Court's policies. Gerald Rosenberg's study (1991) demonstrated that many of the Court's social reform efforts, for example regarding school desegregation, abortion, and rights of the accused, were largely unsuccessful, primarily due to a lack of implementation support. For example, *Brown* had virtually no impact in the South until Congress enacted and the executive branch vigorously enforced the Civil Rights Act of 1964. Similarly, the number of abortions increased more substantially before the Court's *Roe v. Wade* ruling than after, and women's access to abortion remains limited and widely uneven. Even the issue of school prayer remains unsettled, with legislative responses frequent and some noncompliance still evident.

Of course, most court decisions do not involve issues that are as salient or divisive as abortion and school prayer. Nonetheless, enforcing "run-of-the-mill" lower court judgements is neither simple nor automatic. Award collection can be difficult and uncertain, with payment especially unlikely for small claims judgments. Noncompliance is also a common problem in divorce and child custody cases. Even if evidence could be provided that compliance with court decisions is nearly automatic and uniform, an additional claim remains to be proven—that unthinking compliance is due to the public's high regard for courts and its belief in judicial neutrality and independence.

Public Awareness of the Court. Few political institutions operate with as much secrecy or receive as little media attention as the Supreme Court. It is, thus, not surprising that public awareness and knowledge of the Court, its members, and its decisions are quite limited. A variety of surveys conducted over the last 40 years (summarized in Peretti, 1999, p. 164-167) reveal that: A majority of Americans admit that they pay no attention to the Court or have insufficient information to form an opinion of it; fewer than half can name a Supreme Court decision they like or dislike; a majority of Americans are not aware that federal judges enjoy life tenure; there is considerable misunderstanding of decisions, even in such well-publicized areas as abortion and school prayer;[8] and from one half to more than two thirds of Americans have at various times been unable to identify a single Supreme Court justice. In fact, more Americans can name all three Stooges than can name a single Supreme Court justice (Morin, 1995, p. C5).[9] Clearly the Court, its members, and its decisions lack salience for most Americans (Adamany & Grossman, 1983; Caldeira, 1991; Dolbeare, 1976; Franklin & Kosaki, 1995; Kessel 1966; Marshall, 1989; Murphy & Tanenhaus, 1968a, 1968b).

Public Evaluations of the Court. The fact that Americans have limited knowledge of the Court does not keep them from expressing opinions about it. The public, at least in recent years, has been more positive in its evaluations of the Court than other political institutions, though the evidence is more mixed than is generally acknowledged (Peretti, 1999, pp. 167-173). For example, a 1998 national poll reported that 50% of Americans expressed a high level of confidence in the Court compared to 26% for the executive branch and only 18% for Congress (Baum, 2001, p. 21). A Gallup poll conducted in 2000 similarly found that fewer Americans have "a great deal" or "quite a lot" of confidence in Congress (26%) compared to the Supreme Court (49%); however, Americans are equally confident in the president and the Court (both at 49%) and more confident in the military (68%) and police (57%) (Fiorina & Peterson, in press). Even though the Court usually fares better than Congress, it is clear that the Court is not held in unusually high regard. As Marshall notes, national polls have consistently revealed that "only a third to a half of Americans have held clearly favorable views of the Court" (1989, p. 141; Peretti, 1999, pp. 167-170). In addition, the public's views toward specific Court decisions are considerably more negative than positive. As Caldeira (1986) puts it, "On the visible issues of the day however one couches the issues, most people find fault with the choices the Court makes" (p. 1211; Peretti, 1999, p. 170).

The evidence also fails to support the claim that support for the Court is dependent on the public's belief in judicial impartiality and independence. It is rare to find even a majority of Americans agreeing that the Court is unbiased or that it simply follows the law (Adamany, 1973, p. 811; Casey, 1974, pp. 392-393). In fact, in a study by Murphy and Tanenhaus (1968b), only 12.8% of respondents thought that the Supreme Court carried out its constitutional role "in an impartial and competent fashion." A 1991 survey found that 47% of Americans believed that the Court's decisions are based on political pressure or the justices' political beliefs, with 44% believing that they are based on facts and law (Wasby, 1993, p. 355). Survey results from 1946 suggest that this "realism" about the Court is not new: 43%

of respondents then agreed that the Supreme Court "decides many questions largely on the basis of politics" (Marshall, 1989, p. 139). Hensler's (1999) review of statewide opinion surveys similarly finds no support for the claim of public faith in judicial impartiality. Far more commonly expressed is the public's belief that "politics influence court decisions" and "courts treat whites and minorities differently" and "the rich and poor differently" (Hensler, 1999).

The modest public support that exists for the Court appears not to be dependent on a belief in its neutrality or independence. Instead, scholars agree that the dynamics of public support for the Court "bear a remarkable resemblance to those for Congress and the presidency" (Caldeira, 1986, p. 1224; Franklin & Kosaki, 1995). Research reveals that public approval of the Court, at both the individual and the aggregate level, is strongly tied to ideology, with evaluations dependent on political agreement with the substance of the Court's decisions (Caldeira, 1986, 1991; Casey 1976; Dolbeare & Hammond, 1968; Jaros & Roper, 1980; Murphy & Tanenhaus, 1968a, 1968b; Murphy, Tanenhaus, & Kastner, 1973; Tanenhaus & Murphy, 1981). For example, Franklin and Kosaki (1995) found that "evaluations of the Court are closely tied to the respondents' ideological preferences and to the shifting nature of the Court," with conservatives, especially those most knowledgeable about the Court's recent conservative shift, expressing more positive feelings about it than liberals (p. 373). In addition, there is "a strong connection between approval or disapproval of decisions and diffuse support for the Court [i.e., legitimacy]; those who, on balance, favor the Court's decisions will, over time, accord it high levels of diffuse support" (Caldeira & Gibson, 1995, pp. 359-360; but see Caldeira & Gibson, 1992).

Bush v. Gore (2000) will likely supply a good test of the concern that a Court displaying partisan bias loses its legitimacy. In fact, the Court has fared much worse in the eyes of legal scholars than the public (Kritzer, 2001). According to survey data collected by Gibson, Caldeira, and Spence (2001), a majority of Americans thought the Court "acted fairly in the dispute" and decided the case "on the legal merits" rather than on the justices' desire for Bush to become president. Not surprisingly, evaluations of the decision were strongly related to partisan affiliation, with Democrats (and black Democrats in particular) much less likely than Republicans to approve of the decision and to regard it as a legal rather than a partisan decision. Similarly, Yoo (2001) reports that *Bush v. Gore* (2000) had virtually no effect on the Court's overall approval ratings, with 59% in January 2001 approving of the way it is handling its job, only 3% less than in August 2000. This minimal change, however, hides a significant jump in approval by Republicans (from 60% to 80% in the same time) and a considerable drop in approval among Democrats (from 70% to 42%) (Kritzer, 2001; Yoo, 2001).

The conventional wisdom that the Court is viewed in exalted terms and enjoys substantial support and unthinking compliance due to the public's belief that it is impartial and independent is flatly contradicted by the evidence. Compliance with the Court's rulings is uneven. Public support is neither unusually high nor rooted in beliefs about judicial neutrality. Finally, support for the Court is contingent on substantive agreement with its policy choices. The public's evaluations are driven by partisanship and ideology, not mythic expectations of impartiality.

∾ Judicial Independence and the Rights Guarantee

As Professor Burbank (1996) notes, "[j]udicial independence is a means to an end rather than an end in itself" (p. 117). Judicial independence not only enables impartial decision making but is assumed to accomplish a variety of other noble ends. Fein and Neuborne (2000) claim that it "strengthens ordered liberty, domestic tranquility, the rule of law and democratic ideals" (p. 63). California Superior Court Judge Terry Friedman (1998) maintains that attacks on judicial independence "imperil . . . our fundamental rights and freedoms as Americans, especially free speech and equal opportunity, which historically the courts have protected, sometimes even when contrary to majority will" (p. 7). The central claim here is that independent judges can ensure the certain protection of our rights and liberties, particularly those of powerless minorities, even when doing so arouses the opposition of majorities or powerful politicians.

The empirical evidence, again, does not support these expectations. First, as would be expected when elected officials (and, in many states, voters) choose judges, American courts do not frequently issue unpopular, countermajoritarian rulings. As previously noted, Supreme Court decisions are consistent with public opinion more than 60% of the time and nearly as often as Congress's policy decisions, making the Court's "countermajoritarian reputation" greatly exaggerated (Barnum, 1985; Marshall, 1989).

The Warren Court and its egalitarian activism and protection of powerless minorities looms large in popular (and even scholarly) conceptions of the Court. A quick glance at history, however, fails to confirm that the Court has served as a reliable defender of constitutional rights and liberties. Decisions like *Schenck v. US.* (1919), *Dennis v. U.S* (1951), *Barenblatt v. U.S.* (1959), and *Uphaus v. Wyman* (1959) demonstrate the Court's failure to protect free speech during wartime and the McCarthy era. Racial minorities have not fared well (*Dred Scott v. Sandford*, 1851; *Korematsu v. U.S.*, 1944; *Plessy v. Ferguson*, 1896), nor have powerless workers (*Hammer v. Dagenhart*, 1918; *Lochner v. New York*, 1905), the poor (*James v. Valtierra*,

1971; *San Antonio Independent School District v. Rodriguez*, 1973) or homosexuals (*Bowers v. Hardwick*, 1986). Nor should we expect a change in this historical pattern with the election of George W. Bush, who has expressed his desire to appoint judges similar in outlook to Scalia and Thomas, two justices with very low civil liberties support scores (O'Connor & Palmer, 2001, p. 267). Advocates of judicial independence must acknowledge that independent courts may choose not to use their freedom to challenge government authority and protect civil rights and civil liberties. They must also admit that the Supreme Court's record in this regard is checkered at best.

∽ A Call for Empirical and Theoretical Rigor

For many, the account provided here of the pervasive influence of politics on courts necessarily leads to a call for reforms that will eliminate those influences and restore judicial independence to its rightful place. I would prefer instead that the revelations of social science be put to better use: helping us become more realistic and moderate in our discussions of judicial independence. More specifically, I urge greater empirical rigor, more attention to theoretical development, and more empirically informed normative analysis of judicial power and independence.

Too much of the scholarship on judicial independence is polemical rather than empirical, and it is often shockingly in error. For example, Fein and Neuborne (2000) have argued that

> Most Americans respect the courts and the rule of law in large part because they believe in judicial independence. Deeply controversial decisions in highly polarizing areas like abortion, prayer in school, affirmative action, and the death penalty are widely obeyed because the outcomes are not "rigged" but are the result of a principled process in which independent judges do their best to interpret the law in accordance with their understanding of the correct interpretive philosophy. (p. 59)

These assertions are presented by scholars as fact, yet they are flatly contradicted by the evidence. Judges are not independent, impartial decision makers guided by legal principle; instead, the political views for which they were chosen strongly influence their decisions. Americans do not strongly or uniformly believe in judicial independence. Court decisions are not widely obeyed. And compliance is not dependent on public confidence in judicial impartiality. These sorts of unsubstantiated, if not false, claims appear far too frequently in this field. We should find it unacceptable as scholarship and ineffectual (if not pointless) as advocacy.

Extremism also characterizes too much of what is written about judicial independence. Conservative critics attack "the imperial judiciary" and call for new and often radical checks on courts, such as easing impeachment requirements, urging the aggressive use of Congress's power of jurisdictional control, and allowing Congress to reverse Supreme Court decisions by a simple majority vote (Bork, 1996; George & Ponnuru, 2000; Meese & DeHart, 1997; Taylor, 1998). Court defenders are not immune. They characterize recent political attacks as a "virus . . . [that] increasingly infects the branch of government intended to be nonpolitical, the judiciary" (T. B. Friedman, 1998) and warn that, because of this "cancer . . . [s]omeday we may wake up to find a very different United States" (Goldman, 1998). Judicial independence, they further assert, "is the backbone of the American democracy" and "essential to preserving our nation" (White, 1996, p. 3). Without it, "[p]oll taxes, literacy tests, loyalty oaths, political gerrymandering, segregated public accommodations, and lynchings would all have survived" (White, 1996, p. 5). Judges influenced by ideology "decide cases according to personal whim," and those influenced by popular opinion are "mere mouthpieces of popular sentiment," leading "cherished constitutional limitations [to] largely vanish" (Fein & Neuborne, 2000, pp. 59, 60). This tendency toward hyperbole is perhaps the product of the intrusion of political advocacy into the domain of scholarship, itself a product of having lawyers and judges, including those under attack, frequently contribute to judicial independence scholarship. Although their participation is not illegitimate, greater care must be used in how we treat their contributions. Political advocacy is not social science. But, particularly when it appears in scholarly journals, it should not ignore or contradict available empirical knowledge.

Political scientists, of course, have their blind spots as well. We have traditionally focused too strongly on appellate courts, highly controversial issues, and nonunanimous decisions. These offer the requisite variation and opportunity to discover attitudinal influences. However, factors that impel judges to consensus are too often ignored, as are the mass of routine decisions made daily by lower court judges.

My primary complaint here is that too much of the judicial independence literature disregards or defies social scientific knowledge about courts. An additional concern is the inattention to critical empirical questions directly relating to judicial independence. We need precise measures of judicial independence[10] and research that then tests its causes and consequences. For example, we cannot sim-

underlying a system of judicial independence is not obvious and it must be carefully explicated. At a minimum, the theoretical foundation of judicial independence arguments is weak and unclear; at worst, it is faulty and illogical.

My final suggestion is that scholars do a better job of normatively reconciling their desire for judicial independence with both the democratic demand for political accountability and the reality that judicial decision making is largely attitudinally based. They must explain why, in a democracy, unelected and life-tenured judges should be free of political restraints imposed by the people or their elected representatives, particularly with such weak evidence that judicial independence promotes human rights. They must also explain why we should tolerate an independent judiciary that uses its freedom to advance the personal policy agenda of its members. A response is needed and neither the perpetual (and perpetually ineffective) call for neutrality and self-restraint nor the empty insistence that legal influences in fact dominate but are simply too subtle or difficult to measure will suffice.

One such alternative I have already offered (Peretti, 1999) asserts that "value-voting" by Supreme Court justices is defensible to the degree that those values have been consciously selected by elected officials, interest-representation is improved, and political stability is enhanced. According to this view, the appointment of a Supreme Court justice can be seen as a victory for a particular set of values and groups. Those that win sufficient support in presidential and Senate elections are granted long-term representation on the Court. Justices who vote their values are satisfying the expectations of those who selected them and are therefore fulfilling their democratic obligation. Value-voting can also enhance political stability by protecting past political bargains from being voided by a single election or short-term political trends. Winners are not easily or quickly transformed into losers and new directions in policy must win widespread and long-term approval. In this view, the Court in the early 1930s correctly used its modest independence to resist the federal government's dramatic economic policy shift. Fortunately, the Court is not so independent that it could continue to impose its economic policy preferences unilaterally or permanently. It gave in (or was forced to give in) only when those values and past political bargains were decisively rejected by the people. The New Deal coalition in the end justifiably earned formal, long-term representation on the Court. With electoral domination came nine appointments and a new constitutional policy course.

This account oversimplifies my argument, and I am aware of some of its weaknesses.[11] My point is not that I have provided the best or only way to reconcile judicial power, attitudinally based decision making, and democratic values. Rather, I simply urge scholars to make their own attempt, developing a normative argument about judicial power and democratic values that is strongly rooted in our empirical knowledge about courts (e.g., see Friedman, 2001).

ply assume that tenure and salary protections guarantee judicial independence. In fact, Stephenson (2001) reports that "a great deal of research has found that formal constitutional protections" like those regarding judicial selection, tenure, salary, and budget, "are no guarantee of a truly independent judiciary" (p. 5, citing Rosenn 1987; Domingo 1999; Vyas 1992; Widner 1999). His own research finds that "support for independent judicial review is sustainable only when the political system is sufficiently competitive, the judiciary is sufficiently moderate, and the political competitors themselves are sufficiently risk-averse and concerned with future payoffs" (Stephenson, 2001, p. 4). Thus, the traditional focus on formal structural protections as the primary vehicle for judicial independence appears to be misplaced.

The assumed causal link between judicial independence and civil liberties must also be tested. Although some support for that connection is provided by Brickman (2001), the evidence in general, in Cameron's (2001) view, is "skimpy, unsatisfactory, and incomplete" (p. 1). In addition to measuring the contribution of judicial independence, alternative explanations must be tested. For example, the evidence regarding the voting tendencies of judges selected by Democratic presidents suggests that electing Democrats to office may be a more effective strategy for protecting civil rights and civil liberties than strengthening judicial independence. We must also examine and seek to explain the effectiveness of rights protection in countries whose courts are not independent. As Rosenberg (2001) points out, the United States did less well in protecting political dissent in the Cold War as compared to countries lacking constitutionally independent courts, such as England, France, and Australia.

More research on judicial independence—its measures, causes, and consequences—is needed. It is especially important that greater care be used in our discussions of judicial independence. We must acknowledge current limits on our knowledge and not contradict the knowledge that does exist.

The weak empirical grounding of much of the scholarship on judicial independence is, in part, a product of the failure to elaborate its theoretical underpinnings carefully and persuasively. For example, why would judicial independence lead to greater protection of civil liberties? Does it do so inevitably or only under certain conditions? Does judicial independence ensure the protection of rights because judges are more benevolent and enlightened (Cameron, 2001)? And, if they are, why allow politicians to select them? Scholars must also confront the fact that judicial independence is, in reality, a rather odd, counterintuitive phenomenon. Why would politicians grant power to an institution that it is not allowed to control? Or, as Stephenson (2001) cleverly puts it, "why would people with money and guns ever submit to people armed only with gavels?" (p. 4). The logic

恥 Valuing Limited Judicial Independence

Clearly, American judges are not subject to intimidation and violence, as has been the case with judges in such countries as Colombia, Peru, and Italy. American judges are neither completely independent nor subject to direct and constant control by the public and other branches of government. As the social science evidence indicates and as legal scholars need to accept, judges have a limited amount of independence. In our system of separation of powers and checks and balances, that is precisely what is intended.

Congress has some independence to pursue its goals and interests, but of course not complete, unbridled authority to do so. So too for the president, whose constituency is certain to be and intended to be different from that of the Congress. The president can pursue his agenda and his constituents' interests, but only so far as Congress is willing to allow (and vice versa). Why not grant the judiciary the same modest role and autonomy of a similar type and degree? Judges have some independence to advance values and principles to which they are devoted but can do so only so far as the other branches will allow. Judges are free to use a variety of tools to advance their causes—persuasive opinion writing, public speeches, careful timing in issuing their decisions, a temporary retreat in the face of strong opposition, or an appeal to their allies in the legal profession—and they may win some victories. But thankfully, because the judiciary has no monopoly on virtue or truth, political controls limit the ability of judges merely to impose their views and policies on a nation that is in turn powerless to reverse them. As Fisher and Devins (2001) argue, "Just because the Court issues its judgment does not mean that we must suspend ours. The courts are an important element but not the only element, in maintaining a constitutional order. That task is necessarily shared with Congress, the President, the states, and the general public" (p. 15).

Our pluralist system of governance provides for an ongoing and often messy political dialogue over our nation's values and ideals. All three branches are granted a voice in that dialogue and each brings to the table a different perspective, a different set of interests, a different set of strengths. The genius of our system is that, through limits on the power of each branch, those strengths are pooled. Thus, a modest degree of independence for all three branches—legislative, executive, *and* judicial—is intended and should be valued.

Advocates of judicial independence seek to alter this carefully balanced system. They argue for an unhealthy expansion of judicial power, justifying it only with illogical and empirically unsupported speculation that human rights and freedom will be more effectively realized. Fortunately, the empirical evidence suggests that their hope for judicial independence is, as yet, unrealized.

~~ Notes

1. To Burbank, a judge lacking the capacity for independence is one whose pre-commitment to a particular ideology is so strong as to "subvert the judicial process" and "render the fruits of the judicial process irrelevant" (1996, p. 120). My initial reaction was that excluding nominees for whom particular case facts would have no relevance is not much of a screening device and would disqualify very few nominees. On the other hand, many judges can be regarded as ideologues and their votes in cases were quite predictable. Justices Brennan, Marshall, and Douglas come to mind, as does ousted California Supreme Court Chief Justice Rose Bird, at least with regard to the death penalty. Burbank (1999) suggests elsewhere that Robert Bork qualifies, though apparently because of the Reagan Administration's rigorous scrutiny of the judge's views on particular legal issues. However, such a standard would disqualify many nominees and not only those during the Reagan years (Nemacheck, 2001b). In addition, Bork presents, in his own defense, a strong though not flawless case that he was not a conservative ideologue who always voted against racial minorities and civil liberties claims, regardless of the law and case facts (Bork, 1990, pp. 323-336).

2. My mantra to students in describing (non-Supreme Court) judicial decision making is "ideology matters a lot, a minority of the time."

3. The attitudinal and strategic model can, of course, be viewed as complementary rather than contradictory. For example, the attitudinal model may better explain votes on the merits, and strategic behavior may be more evident at other stages, such as agenda setting, opinion assignment, and opinion writing. Decision making may also be attudinally driven in constitutional cases, but more strategic in statutory cases. Finally, sophisticated voting may also be more likely when the president and Congress are ideologically united and ideologically distant from the Court (Pacelle & Marshall, 2001).

4. Of course, the persuasiveness of this claim depends on one's definition of judicial independence. Does judicial independence require that judges be free of all political influences? Or must independent judges only be free from formal reprisals executed by the people or politicians in response to their decisions? The latter, I would argue, is not a terribly difficult standard for federal judges (and many state judges) to satisfy. Even House incumbents, who have enjoyed extraordinary reelection success since the mid-1960s, would be considered independent of the people according to this standard. For the point that, with regard to judicial independence, "influence is not control," see Burbank (1999, p. 328).

5. After all, had Democrats won more elections in the 1980s, I would perhaps be discussing whether Justice Laurence Tribe is independent.

6. Scalia's libertarian streak has revealed itself in some First Amendment cases. Probably topping the list of disappointments for conservatives are his opinions in the flag-burning cases.

7. Whether public opinion has a direct impact, in addition to its indirect influence via the selection process, is subject to dispute. [See Mishler and Sheehan (1993); Norpoth and Segal (1994); Mishler and Sheehan (1994); Flemming and Wood (1997).]

8. For example, only 41% of respondents in a 1982 poll correctly understood that *Roe v. Wade* banned restrictions on first-trimester abortions, 10% believed that *Roe* banned such abortions, and nearly half offered no opinion as to its meaning. In the same poll, 43% of Americans did not know that the Court's rulings prohibited school prayer (Marshall, 1989, p. 145). Some research suggests that public awareness of Court decisions is not uniformly low; it may be higher for some cases, some individuals, and shortly after the decision

(Franklin & Kosaki, 1995; Kosaki, 1991). Caldeira's study (1986) also suggests that the public does recognize and respond to trends in Supreme Court decision making; for example, public evaluations became more negative in response to Warren Court decisions protecting the rights of the accused.

    9. In a well-known 1989 survey, former People's Court Judge Joseph Wapner was identified by 54% of Americans, compared to only 23% for Justice O'Connor (the most frequently recognized justice) and 9% for Chief Justice Rehnquist (Epstein, Segal, Spaeth, & Walker, 1996, p. 609).

    10. I am reminded of Judge Kozinski's practical definition that "[j]udges I like and agree with are independent, and the ones that I disagree with are not independent. Those judges are governed by mob rule" (1998, p. 863-864).

    11. For example, ideology is not always the dominant consideration for the president (Yalof, 1999), or the Senate may not play a sufficiently aggressive role (Peretti, 1992). In addition, there are instances of justices who fail to fulfill presidential expectations (for example, Blackmun and Souter), a president's appointees may not vote cohesively (Lindquist et al., 2000), and appointees may drift from presidential desires over time (Segal, Timpone, & Howard, 2000).

⤜ References

Abraham, H. J. (1999). *Justices, presidents, and senators.* Lanham, MD: Rowman & Littlefield.

Adamany, D. W. (1973). Legitimacy, realigning elections, and the supreme court. *Wisconsin Law Review, 1973*(3), 790-846.

Adamany, D. W., & Grossman, J. B. (1983). Support for the Supreme Court as a national policymaker. *Law and Policy Quarterly, 5,* 405-437.

Allison, G. (1996). Delay in Senate confirmation of federal judicial nominees. *Judicature, 80,* 8-15.

Barenblatt v. U.S., 360 U.S. 109 (1959).

Barnum, D. G. (1985). The Supreme Court and public opinion: Judicial decision-making in the post-New Deal period. *Journal of Politics, 47,* 652-666.

Barrow, D. J., Zuk, G., & Gryski, G. S. (1996). *The federal judiciary and institutional change.* Ann Arbor: University of Michigan Press.

Bartels, B. (2001, April). *Supreme Court outputs and the political environment: A neo-institutional macro-analytic perspective.* Paper presented at the annual meeting of the Midwest Political Science Association, Chicago, IL.

Baum, L. (1988). Measuring policy change in the U.S. Supreme Court. *American Political Science Review, 82*(3), 905-912.

Baum, L. (1989). *The Supreme Court* (3rd ed.). Washington, DC: Congressional Quarterly Press.

Baum, L. (1992). Membership change and collective voting change in the United States Supreme Court. *Journal of Politics, 54*(1), 3-24.

Baum, L. (1997). *The puzzle of judicial behavior.* Ann Arbor: University of Michigan Press.

Baum, L. (2001). *The Supreme Court* (7th ed.). Washington, DC: Congressional Quarterly Press.

Bork, R. H. (1990). *The tempting of America: The political seduction of the law.* New York: Free Press.

Bork, R. H. (1996). *Slouching toward Gomorrah: Modern liberalism and American decline.* New York: Regan Books.

Bowen, L. (1995). Do Court decisions matter? In L. Epstein (Ed.), *Contemplating Courts.* Washington, DC: Congressional Quarterly Press.

Bowers v. Hardwick, 478 U.S. 186 (1986).

Brickman, D. (2001, August/September). *Judicial independence and the protection of civil liberties: A cross-national empirical analysis.* Paper presented at the annual meeting of the American Political Science Association, San Francisco, CA.

Burbank, S. B. (1996). The past and present of judicial independence. *Judicature, 80*(3), 117-122.

Burbank, S. B. (1999). The architecture of judicial independence. *Southern California Law Review, 72,* 315-351.

Bush v. Gore, 000 U.S. 00-949 (2000).

Caldeira, G. A. (1986). Neither the purse nor the sword: Dynamics of public confidence in the Supreme Court. *American Political Science Review, 80,* 1209-1026.

Caldeira, G. A. (1988/1989). Commentary on Senate confirmation of Supreme Court justices: The roles of organized and unorganized interests. *Kentucky Law Journal, 77,* 531-544.

Caldeira, G. A. (1991). Courts and public opinion. In J. B. Gates & C. A. Johnson (Eds.), *The American courts: A critical assessment.* Washington, DC: Congressional Quarterly Press.

Caldeira, G. A., & Gibson, J. L. (1992) The etiology of public support for the Supreme Court. *American Journal of Political Science, 36,* 635-664.

Caldeira, G. A., & Gibson, J. L. (1995). The legitimacy of the Court of Justice in the European Union: Models of institutional support. *American Political Science Review, 89,* 356-376.

Caldeira, G. A., & Wright, J. R. (1995). Lobbying for justice: The rise of organized conflict in the politics of federal judgeships. In L. Epstein (Ed.), *Contemplating courts.* Washington, DC: Congressional Quarterly Press.

Cameron, C. (2001, March/April). *Judicial independence: What is it good for? Theory and evidence.* Paper presented at a conference sponsored by the American Judicature Society and the Brennan Center for Justice, University of Pennsylvania, Philadelphia, PA.

Cameron, C. M., Cover, A. D., & Segal, J. A. (1990). Senate voting on Supreme Court nominees: A neoinstitutional model. *American Political Science Review, 84,* 525-534.

Canon, B. C. (1991). Courts and policy: Compliance, implementation, and impact. In J. B. Gates & C. A. Johnson (Eds.), *The American courts: A critical assessment.* Washington, DC: Congressional Quarterly Press.

Canon, B. C., & Johnson, C. A. (1999). *Judicial policies: Implementation and impact* (2nd ed.). Washington, DC: Congressional Quarterly Press.

Caplan, L. (1987). *The tenth justice.* New York: Knopf.

Carp, R., Songer, D., Rowland, C. K., Stidham, R., & Richey-Tracy, L. (1993). The voting behavior of judges appointed by President Bush. *Judicature, 76,* 298-302.

Carp, R. A., Manning, K. L., & Stidham, R. (2001). President Clinton's district judges: "Extreme liberals" or just plain moderates? *Judicature, 84,* 282-288.

Carp, R. A., & Stidham, R. (1983). *Judicial process in America.* Washington, DC: Congressional Quarterly Press.

Carp, R. A., & Stidham, R. (2001). *Judicial process in America* (5th ed.). Washington DC: Congressional Quarterly Press.

Casey, G. (1974). The Supreme Court and myth: An empirical investigation. *Law and Society Review, 8,* 385-419.

Casey, G. (1976). Popular perceptions of Supreme Court rulings. *American Politics Quarterly, 4*(1), 3-45.

Clayton, C. W., & Gillman, H. (Ed.). (1999). *Supreme Court decision-making: New institutionalist approaches.* Chicago: University of Chicago Press.

Cross, F. B. (2000). The politics of judges. *Court Review, 37*(2), 18-19.

DeFigueiredo, J., & Tiller, E. (1996). Congressional control of the courts: A theoretical and empirical analysis of the expansion of the federal judiciary. *Journal of Law and Economics, 39,* 435-462.

Dennis v. U.S., 341 U.S. 494 (1951).

Dolbeare, K. (1976). The public views the Supreme Court. In H. Jacob (Ed.), *Law, politics, and the federal courts*. Boston: Little, Brown.

Dolbeare, K. M., & Hammond, P. E. (1968). The political party basis of attitudes toward the Supreme Court. *Public Opinion Quarterly, 32*(1), 16-30.

Domingo, P. (1999). Judicial independence and judicial reform in Latin America. In A. Schedler, L. Diamond, & M. F. Plattner (Eds.), *The self-restraining state: Power and accountability in new democracies*. Boulder, CO: Lynne Rienner.

Dred Scott v. Sandford, 60 U.S. (19 How.) 393 (1851).

Epstein, L., & Knight, J. (1998). *The choices justices make*. Washington, DC: Congressional Quarterly Press.

Epstein, L., Segal, J. A., Spaeth, H. J., & Walker, T. G. (1994). *The Supreme Court compendium*. Washington, DC: Congressional Quarterly Press.

Epstein, L., Segal, J. A., Spaeth, H. J., & Walker, T. G. (1996). *The Supreme Court compendium* (2nd ed.). Washington, DC: Congressional Quarterly Press.

Epstein, L., & Walker, T. G. (1995). The role of the Supreme Court in American society: Playing the reconstruction game. In L. Epstein (Ed.), *Contemplating courts*. Washington, DC: Congressional Quarterly Press.

Eskridge, W. (1991). Reneging on history? Playing the Court/Congress/president civil rights game. *California Law Review, 79,* 613-684.

Fein, B., & Neuborne, B. (2000). Why should we care about independent and accountable judges? *Judicature, 84*(2), 58-63.

Felice, J. D., & Weisberg, H. F. (1988/1989). The changing importance of ideology, party, and region in confirmation of Supreme Court nominees, 1953-1988. *Kentucky Law Journal, 77,* 509-530.

Ferejohn, J., & Shipan, C. (1990). Congressional influence on bureaucracy. *Journal of Law Economics and Organization, 6*(1), 1-20.

Fiorina, M. P., & Peterson, P. E. (Eds.). (in press). *The new American democracy* (2nd ed., election update). New York: Longman.

Fisher, L. (1993). The legislative veto: Invalidated, it survives. *Law and Contemporary Problems, 56,* 273-292.

Fisher, L., & Devins, N. (2001). *Political dynamics of constitutional law* (3rd ed.). St. Paul, MN: West.

Flemming, R. B., & Wood, B. D. (1997) The public and the Supreme Court: Individual justice responsiveness to American policy moods. *American Journal of Political Science, 41,* 468-498.

Franklin, C. H., & Kosaki, L. (1995). Media, knowledge and public evaluations of the Supreme Court. In L. Epstein (Ed.), *Contemplating courts*. Washington, DC: Congressional Quarterly Press.

Friedman, B. (1998). Attacks on judges: Why they fail. *Judicature, 81*(4), 150-157.

Friedman, B. (2001). *Modeling judicial review*. Unpublished manuscript.

Friedman, T. B. (1998). The politicization of the judiciary. *Judicature, 82,* 6-7.

Gely, R., & Spiller, P. T. (1990). A rational choice theory of the Supreme Court with applications to the *State Farm* and *Grove City* cases. *Journal of Law, Economics, and Organizations, 6,* 263-300.

Gely, R., & Spiller, P. T. (1992). The political economy of Supreme Court Constitutional decisions: The case of Roosevelt's court-packing plan. *International Review of Law and Economics, 12,* 45-67.

George, R. P., & Ponnuru, R. (2000). Courting trouble: Only a frontal assault on the power of the courts can restore America's constitutional balance. In G. M. Scott & L. Gatch (Eds.), *21 debated issues in American politics*. Upper Saddle River, NJ: Prentice-Hall.

George, T. E., & Epstein, L. (1992). On the nature of Supreme Court decision making. *American Political Science Review, 86,* 323-337.

Gibson, J. L., Caldeira, G. A., & Spence, L. K. (2001, March/April). *The Supreme Court and the 2000 presidential election*. Paper presented at a conference sponsored by the American Judicature Society and the Brennan Center for Justice, Philadelphia, PA.

Goldman, S. (1966). Voting behavior in the United States Courts of Appeals, 1961-1964. *American Political Science Review, 60*(2), 374-83.

Goldman, S. (1975). Voting behavior on the United States Courts of Appeals revisited. *American Political Science Review, 69*(2), 491-506.

Goldman, S. (1991). Federal judicial recruitment. In J. B. Gates & C. A. Johnson (Eds.), *The American courts: A critical assessment.* Washington, DC: Congressional Quarterly Press.

Goldman, S. (1998). The judicial confirmation crisis and the Clinton Presidency. *Presidential Studies Quarterly, 28,* 838-844.

Goldman, S. (1997). *Picking federal judges.* New Haven,CT: Yale University Press.

Goldman, S., Slotnick, E., Gryski, G., & Zuk, G. (2001). Clinton's judges: Summing up the legacy. *Judicature, 84,* 228-254.

Gottschall, J. (1986). Reagan's appointments to the U.S. Courts of Appeals: The continuation of a judicial revolution. *Judicature, 70*(1), 48-54.

Haire, S. B., Humphries, M. A., & Songer, D. R. (2001). The voting behavior of Clinton's Courts of Appeals appointees. *Judicature, 84,* 274-281.

Halper, T. (1972). Senate rejection of Supreme Court nominees. *Drake Law Review, 22,* 102-113.

Hammer v. Dagenhart, 247 U.S. 251 (1918).

Hartley, R. E., & Holmes, L. M. (1997). Increasing Senate scrutiny of lower federal court nominees. *Judicature, 80,* 274-278.

Hensler, D. R. (1999). Do we need an empirical research agenda on judicial independence? *Southern California Law Review, 72,* 707-721.

Hulbary, W. E., & Walker, T. G. (1980). The Supreme Court selection process: Presidential motivations and judicial performance. *Western Political Quarterly, 33,* 185-196.

James v. Valtierra, 402 U.S. 137 (1971).

Jaros, D., & Roper, R. (1980). The Supreme Court, myth, diffuse support, specific support and legitimacy. *American Politics Quarterly, 8,* 85-105.

Kessel, J. (1966). Public perceptions of the Supreme Court. *Midwest Journal of Political Science, 10,* 167-191.

Korematsu v. U.S., 323 U.S. 214 (1944).

Kosaki, L. C. (1991, August/September). Public awareness of Supreme Court decisions. Paper presented at the annual meeting of the American Political Science Association, Washington, DC.

Kozinski, A. (1991). My pizza with Nino. *Cardozo Law Review, 12,* 1583-1591.

Kozinski, A. (1998). The many faces of judicial independence. *Georgia State University Law Review, 14,* 861-873.

Kritzer, H. M. (2001). The impact of *Bush v. Gore* on public perceptions and knowledge of the Supreme Court. *Judicature, 85*(1), 26-31.

Lindquist, S. A., Yalof, D. A., & Clark, J. A. (2000). The impact of presidential appointments to the U.S. Supreme Court: Cohesive and divisive voting within presidential blocs. *Political Research Quarterly, 53,* 795-814.

Lochner v. New York, 198 U.S. 45 (1905).

Maltzman, F., Spriggs, J., & Wahlbeck, P. (1999). Strategy and judicial choice: New Instituionalist approaches to Supreme Court decision-making. In C. W. Clayton & H. Gillman (Eds.), *Supreme Court decision-making: New Institutionalist approaches.* Chicago: University of Chicago Press.

Maltzman, F., Spriggs, J., & Wahlbeck, P. (2000). *Creating law on the Supreme Court: The collegial game.* New York: Cambridge University Press.

Marshall, T. R. (1989). *Public opinion and the Supreme Court.* Boston: Unwin Hyman.

Marshall, T. R., & Ignagni, J. (1994). Supreme Court and public support for rights claims. *Judicature, 78,* 146-151.

McCloskey, R. G. (1960). *The American Supreme Court.* Chicago: University of Chicago Press.

Meese, E., III, & DeHart, R. (1997). Reining in the federal judiciary. *Judicature, 80,* 178-183.

Mishler, W., & Sheehan, R. S. (1993). The Supreme Court as a countermajoritarian institution? The impact of public opinion on Supreme Court decisions. *American Political Science Review, 87*(1), 87-101.

Mishler, W., & Sheehan, R. S. (1994). Popular influence on Supreme Court Decisions: A response to Helmut Norpoth and Jeffrey A. Segal. *American Political Science Review, 88,* 716-724.

Morin, R. (1995, October 8). A nation of stooges. *The Washington Post,* C5.

Murphy, W. F. (1964). *Elements of judicial strategy.* Chicago: University of Chicago Press.

Murphy, W. F. (1990). Reagan's judicial strategy. In L. Berman (Ed.), *Looking back on the Reagan presidency.* Baltimore: Johns Hopkins University Press.

Murphy, W. F., & Tanenhaus, J. (1968a). Public opinion and the Supreme Court: The Goldwater campaign. *Public Opinion Quarterly, 32*(1), 31-50.

Murphy, W. F., & Tanenhaus, J. (1968b). Public opinion and the United States Supreme Court: A preliminary mapping of some prerequisites for court legitimation of regime change. *Law and Society Review, 2,* 357-384.

Murphy, W., Tanenhaus, J., & Kastner, D. (1973). *Public evaluations of constitutional courts: Alternative explanations.* Beverly Hills, CA: Sage.

Nemacheck, C. L. (2001a, August/September). *Justice confirmed: Ideology and the selection of Supreme Court nominees.* Paper presented at the annual meeting of the American Political Science Association, San Francisco, CA.

Nemacheck, C. L. (2001b). *Strategic selection: Presidential selection of Supreme Court justices from Hoover through Reagan.* Unpublished doctoral dissertation, George Washington University, Washington, DC.

Neubauer, D. W. (1997). *Judicial process: Law, courts, and politics in the United States* (2nd ed.). Fort Worth, TX: Harcourt Brace.

Norpoth, H., & Segal, J. A. (1994). Popular influence on Supreme Court decisions: Comment. *American Political Science Review, 88,* 711-716.

O'Brien, D. M. (1988). *Judicial roulette: Report of the Twentieth Century Fund Task Force on judicial selection.* New York: Priority Press.

O'Connor, K., & Palmer, B. (2001). The Clinton clones: Ginsburg, Breyer, and the Clinton legacy. *Judicature, 84,* 262-273.

Orfield, M. W., Jr. (1987). The exclusionary rule and deterrence: An empirical study of Chicago narcotics officers. *University of Chicago Law Review, 54,* 1024-1049.

Pacelle, R., & Marshall, B. W. (2001, August/September). *Strategic or sincere? The Supreme Court in constitutional decisions.* Paper presented at the annual meeting of the American Political Science Association, San Francisco, CA.

Palmer, J. (1983). Senate confirmation of appointments to the U.S. Supreme Court. *Review of Social Economy, 41,* 152-162.

Peretti, T. J. (1992.) Restoring the balance of power: The struggle for control of the Supreme Court. *Hastings Constitutional Law Quarterly, 20*(1), 69-103.

Peretti, T. J. (1999.) *In defense of a political court.* Princeton, NJ: Princeton University Press.

Plessy v. Ferguson, 163 U.S. 537 (1896).

Reid, T. V. (1988.) Judicial policy-making and implementation: An empirical examination. *Western Political Quarterly, 41,* 509-527.

Rohde, D., & Spaeth, H. (1976.) *Supreme Court decision making.* San Francisco: Freeman.

Rosenberg, G. N. (1991). *The hollow hope.* Chicago: University of Chicago Press.

Rosenberg, G. N. (1992). Judicial independence and the reality of political power. *Review of Politics, 54,* 369-398.

Rosenberg, G. N. (2001, March/April). *Thinking about judicial independence.* Paper presented at a conference sponsored by the American Judicature Society and the Brennan Center for Justice, University of Pennsylvania, Philadelphia.

Rosenn, K. S. (1987). The protection of judicial independence in Latin America. *University of Miami Inter-American Law Review, 19*(1), 1-35.

Rowland, C. K., & Carp, R. A. (1992). *Political appointments and political jurisprudence in the federal district courts.* Lawrence: University Press of Kansas.

Rowland, C. K., & Carp, R. A. (1996.) *Politics and judgment in federal district courts.* Lawrence: University Press of Kansas.

Rowland, C. K., Carp, R. A., & Songer, D. (1988). Presidential effects on criminal justice policy in the lower federal courts: The Reagan judges. *Law and Society Review, 22*(1), 191-200.

Ruckman, P. S., Jr. (1993). The Supreme Court, critical nominations, and the Senate confirmation process. *Journal of Politics, 55,* 793-805.

San Antonio Independent School District v. Rodriguez, 411 U.S. 1 (1973).

Schenck v. U.S., 249 U.S. 47 (1919).

Segal, J. A. (1987). Senate confirmation of Supreme Court justices: Partisan and institutional politics. *Journal of Politics, 49,* 998-1015.

Segal, J. A. (1990). Supreme Court support for the solicitor general: The effect of presidential appointments. *Western Political Quarterly, 43,* 137-152.

Segal, J. A. (1991). Courts, executives, and legislatures. In J. B. Gates & C. A. Johnson (Eds.), *The American courts: A critical assessment.* Washington, DC: Congressional Quarterly Press.

Segal, J. A. (1997). Separation-of-powers games in the positive theory of law and courts. *American Political Science Review, 91*(1), 28-44.

Segal, J. A. (1999). Supreme Court deference to Congress: An examination of the Marksist model. In C. W. Clayton & H. Gillman (Eds.), *Supreme Court decision-making: New institutionalist approaches.* Chicago: University of Chicago Press.

Segal, J. A., & Cover, A. D. (1989). Ideological values and the votes of U.S. Supreme Court justices. *American Political Science Review, 83,* 557-565.

Segal, J. A., Cover, A. D., & Cameron, C. M. (1988/1989). The role of ideology in Senate confirmation of Supreme Court justices. *Kentucky Law Journal, 77,* 485-507.

Segal, J. A., Epstein, L., Cameron, C. M., & Spaeth, H. J. (1995). Ideological values and the votes of U.S. Supreme Court justices revisited. *Journal of Politics, 57,* 812-823.

Segal, J. A., & Reedy, C. D. (1988). The Supreme Court and sex discrimination: The role of the solicitor general. *Western Political Quarterly, 41,* 553-568.

Segal, J., Songer, D., & Cameron, C. (1995). Decision-making on the U.S. Courts of Appeals. In L. Epstein (Ed.), *Contemplating courts.* Washington, DC: Congressional Quarterly Press.

Segal, J. A., & Spaeth, H. J. (1993). *The Supreme Court and the attitudinal model.* New York: Cambridge University Press.

Segal, J. A., Timpone, R. J., & Howard, R. M. (2000). Buyer beware? Presidential success through Supreme Court apointments. *Political Research Quarterly, 53,* 557-573.

Sherry, S. (1998). Judicial independence: Playing politics with the Constitution. *George State University Law Review, 14,* 795-815.

Slotnick, E. E. (1983). The ABA's standing committee on federal judiciary: A contemporary assessment. *Judicature, 66,* 349-362.

Smith, C. E. (1990). Polarization and change in the federal courts: *En Banc* decisions in the U.S. Courts of Appeals. *Judicature, 74*(3), 133-137.

Smith, C. E., & Beuger, K. A. (1993). Clouds in the crystal ball: Presidential expectations and the unpredictable behavior of Supreme Court appointees. *Akron Law Review, 27*(2), 115-39.

Smith, C. E., & Hensley, T. R. (1993). Assessing the conservatism of the Rehnquist court. *Judicature, 77*(2), 83-89.

Spiller, P. T., & Gely, R. (1992). Congressional control or judicial independence: The determinants of U.S. Supreme Court labor-relations decisions 1949-1988. *RAND Journal of Economics, 23,* 463-492.

Stephenson, M. C. (2001, August/September). *When the devil turns . . . : The political foundations of independent judicial review.* Paper presented at the annual meeting of the American Political Science Association, San Francisco, CA.

Stidham, R., Carp, R. A., & Songer, D. (1996). The voting behavior of President Clinton's judicial appointments. *Judicature, 80*(1), 16-20.

Stimson, J. A., Mackuen, M. B., & Erikson, R. S. (1995). Dynamic representation. *American Political Science Review, 89,* 543-565.

Tanenhaus, J., & Murphy, W. F. (1981). Patterns of public support for the Supreme Court: A panel study. *Journal of Politics, 43*(1), 24-39.

Taylor, C. (1998). The judiciary is too powerful. *Judicature, 82*(1), 28-34.

Uphaus v. Wyman, 360 U.S. 72 (1959).

Vyas, Y. (1992). The independence of the judiciary: A Third World perspective. *Third World Legal Studies,* 127-77.

Wasby, S. L. (1993). *The Supreme Court in the federal judicial system* (4th ed.). Chicago: Nelson-Hall.

Watson, G. L., & Stookey, J. A. (1995). *Shaping America: The politics of Supreme Court appointments.* New York: Harper Collins.

Wenner, L., & Ostberg, C. (1994). Restraint in environmental cases by Reagan-Bush judicial appointees. *Judicature, 77,* 217-220.

White, P. J. (1996). It's a wonderful life, or is it? America without judicial independence. *University of Memphis Law Review, 27*(1), 1-12.

Widner, J. (1999). Building judicial independence in common law Africa. In A. Schedler, L. Diamond, & M. F. Plattner (Eds.), *The self-restraining state: Power and accountability in new democracies.* Boulder, CO: Lynne Rienner.

Yalof, D. A. (1999). *Pursuit of justices.* Chicago: University of Chicago Press.

Yoo, J. C. (2001). In defense of the court's legitimacy. In C. R. Sunstein & R. A. Epstein (Eds.), *The vote: Bush, Gore & the Supreme Court.* Chicago: University of Chicago Press.

Chapter 6

Judicial Independence

How Can You Tell It When You See It? And, Who Cares?

Charles M. Cameron

∽ Introduction

Throughout this volume, two clusters of questions arise repeatedly:

1. Is "judicial independence" such an ambiguous, amorphous, or confused concept that it is useless analytically? Or does it actually mean something? If so, what?

2. If "judicial independence" refers to something real, is it actually good for anything? As Lewis Kornhauser stresses in his contribution to this volume, judicial independence is not an end in itself. It is purely instrumental, a *means* to an end. But, what end or ends? And, how well does judicial independence serve those ends?

In this brief chapter, I sketch some answers to these questions, in enough detail (I hope) to suggest that judicial independence is more than a slogan and worth study.

To answer the first question, I draw on a long and well-developed tradition of power analysis in political science. From a power perspective, judicial independence is synonymous with judicial autonomy, and autonomy can be defined fairly precisely. In principle, we can measure autonomy, empirically and, in fact, some scholars have tried to do so, at least in a few special contexts. Given measurement of judicial independence between countries or states, or over time within one jurisdiction, one could ask what factors lead to greater or lesser independence. In other words, judicial independence, defined this way, becomes a respectable "dependent variable" that we can study.

To answer the second question, I draw on modern political economy. The work I invoke links economic growth to efficient property rights and credible contracting, devices that facilitate economic exchange and economic growth. I outline an argument—not terribly original—why well-functioning courts might support economic growth. I review some empirical studies that try to assess the evidence on this score as well as other studies that examine links between human rights and judicial systems. We don't have as much evidence as we want, but even so it appears that in some cases judicial independence matters.

⤳ A Power Analysis of Judicial Independence

What do we mean by an independent judiciary? There is a somewhat tendentious literature on this question, but a straightforward answer flows from the political scientific analysis of power (Dahl, 1963; Nagel, 1975). In this line of analysis, power is defined as a *causal relationship between preferences and outcomes.*[1] In other words, an actor has power when a particular outcome is desired and causes that outcome to transpire. By extension, an actor (like a judge) has independence or autonomy when he or she consistently has power over the relevant outcome (Nordlinger, 1981).

A (reasonably) simple example may make this type of analysis much clearer. Consider Figure 6.1. In the figure, there are three actors: A, B, and a judge, J. Actor A might be, say, an interest group and Actor B might be a wealthy individual. Or, A might be the median floor member of the House of Representatives and B might be the president. In any event, each actor, including the judge, has preferences about an outcome.[2] In this example, the outcome can be either (and only) Outcome 1 or Outcome 2. The arrows indicate potential causal relationships. For example, path AO indicates direct power of A over the outcome. Path AJ indicates that A might cause J's preferences, which in turn affect the outcome via path JO. Now suppose we observe preferences and outcomes according to Table 6.1.

TABLE 6.1   An Example of Power Analysis

Observation	A wants —	B wants —	J wants —	Outcome
1.	1	1	1	1
2.	1	2	1	1
3.	2	1	2	2
4.	1	2	2	2

Suppose we have seen only Observation 1—what can we infer? Very little. The problem is what statisticians call "multicollinearity"—too much intercorrelation between the preferences of A, B, and J to disentangle their separate influences. But now suppose we obtain Observation 2. In this case, actors A and J desire Outcome 1 whereas B desires Outcome 2; Outcome 1 prevails. In this case, it is clear that Actor B did not have power. However, the evidence is equally compatible with several other inferences, as shown in Figure 6.2. For example, A's preferences may have driven the outcome directly; J's preference may have driven the outcome; A's preferences may have determined J's preferences, which then determined the outcome; or, J's preferences may have determined A's preferences, which then caused the outcome.

Suppose we then see Observation 3. But Observation 3 (as constructed) is really the same as Observation 2 and thus does not eliminate further paths of influence. However, Observation 4 is much more helpful. In this observation, the Actor A's preferences diverge from the Judge's and the outcome follows the Judge's preferences. Taken in tandem with Observation 2 (or 3), Observation 4 leaves only one path of influence, that from the Judge (alone) to the outcome. If additional observations consistently confirm this inference, we can conclude that J has power over the outcome—and the judge acts autonomously and hence independently.

Pure autonomy is, of course, an extreme case. But even with only Observation 2 at our disposal, we might conclude that the judge acts independently of Actor B. This approach defines independence in an actor-specific way: Judicial independence is defined relative to the executive, the legislature, interest groups, firms, wealthy individuals, or other actors and not in absolute terms.

This example illustrates the basic ideas but real implementation is often more subtle. In practice, the analysis turns on comparative static tests, albeit of a particularly simple form: Vary Actor A's preferences while holding others constant and see if outcomes vary in a similar fashion (Calvert, Moran, & Weingast, 1987). If not, Actor A has no power over the outcome.[3] But if preferences and outcomes covary systematically and there is a theoretical reason to believe the covariation is causal in nature, then we should conclude (tentatively, at any rate) that A does have

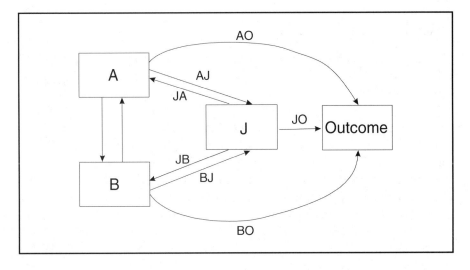

Figure 6.1

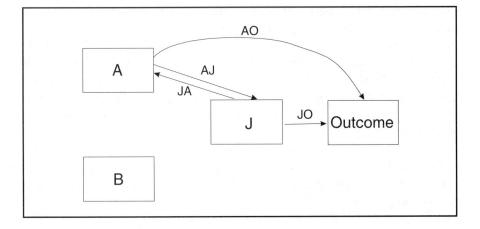

Figure 6.2

power. Measurement difficulties and statistical problems, such as inadequate independent variation in the preferences of different actors, often make it difficult to execute the comparative static test in practice. But this approach puts the study of judicial independence on a firm conceptual footing.

As a concrete example, consider the well-known Ferejohn-Shipan model of courts in the American separation of powers system (Ferejohn & Shipan, 1990). This game theoretic model makes clear predictions about the relationship between policy outcomes and the preferences of specific actors, such as judges and congressional committee chairs. In other words, the model makes predictions about who should have power and when. It also makes clear predictions about the relationship between judicial outcomes and the preferences of nonjudicial actors. Thus, it makes predictions about judicial independence relative to specific actors. A cottage industry has sprung up in which scholars attempt to empirically execute the key comparative static tests and determine whether the model's predictions are actually borne out (see, e.g., Spiller & Gely 1992; Segal, 1998). Another example from judicial politics is offered by Moraski and Shipan's excellent paper on Supreme Court nominations, which uses a power analysis to study who has influence in determining the ideology of nominees, the president or the Senate (Moraski & Shipan, 1992). In short, power analysis is practical though often difficult and data intensive.

Structural Protections Versus Norms

A power analysis separates the operational fact of independence (or the lack thereof) from structural features of a judicial system such as life tenure and protected salaries. Thus, one can meaningfully examine the relationship between the latter and the former. For example, Salzberger and Fenn (1999) show that judges on the English Court of Appeals who consistently take antigovernment positions are less likely to be promoted to the Judicial Committee of the House of Lords, the highest judicial venue in England, than lord justices of appeal who are less antigovernment. Similarly, Ramseyer (1994) and Ramseyer and Rasmusen (1997) show that antigovernment judges in Japan suffer less successful and less pleasant careers than do progovernment judges. The resulting incentive systems no doubt discourage antigovernment behavior by judges—which is to say, they diminish judicial independence from the government. But, this fact needs to be established empirically rather than assumed by *defining* judicial independence in terms of structural features like life tenure or protected salaries.

Moreover, one can imagine relatively independent judiciaries even in the absence of extensive structural protections. For example, within certain limits, legislatures or executives may afford a degree of independence to a judiciary that is "trustworthy." This argument follows straightforwardly from the standard logic of delegation in political settings (Epstein & O'Halloran, 1999). Here, the basic idea is that Congress will not find it worthwhile to exercise close control over an ideologically proximate judiciary because such judges will not take actions too disparate from congressional wishes even absent close control.

An important part of the logic of delegation is that Congress will not grant much independence to an ideologically distant judiciary. Somewhat piquantly, then, the judiciary can have independence but only so long as it won't use it to the disadvantage of Congress—or, at least, a Congress capable of defending its interests.

Extending this principal-agent logic, Ferejohn (1999) suggests that the greatest danger to the independence of the American judiciary occurs when Congress and the president are ideologically unified and the judiciary is comprised of judges with a different ideology. Under these conditions, the president and Congress will be willing and able to rein in an assertive judiciary. Surveys of the historical evidence support this view (Nagel, 1965; Rosenberg, 1992) as do case studies of specific episodes (Murphy, 1962; Pritchett, 1961). A more systematic quantitative analysis would be welcome but DeFigueiredo and Tiller (1996) is suggestive. In this study, the authors show that unified-party Congresses that follow other-party Congresses or divided-party Congresses have repeatedly expanded the size of the federal judiciary. These expansions allow the incoming unified-party Congresses to "repack" the judiciary with copartisans, thereby bringing the judiciary into closer ideological alignment with Congress.

A quite distinct line of reasoning also suggests that judicial independence can exist absent structural protections. According to this view, a folk-theorem-friendly environment can yield a set of cultural norms that support the rule of law. This logic is explored in a recent paper by Weingast (1997).[4] But the same idea, without the game theoretic trappings, is standard in the literature on the English constitutional system (Dicey, 1915). Many commentators also invoke this line of reasoning to explain the failure of FDR's court-packing scheme and Truman's acquiescence in the steel seizure case.

Conversely, explicit structural protections may prove to be but parchment barriers to an aggressive executive or legislature unconstrained by voters who value judicial independence. The sad experience of the Argentinean judiciary demonstrates this fact very clearly (Helmke, 1999; Spiller & Tomasi, in press). There, strong executives have fired high court justices at will, despite legal prohibitions to the contrary.

The Argentina example suggests that nominal protections like "life tenure" probably require backing by a political norm, in which other actors—especially voters—punish an executive who tramples on the judiciary's formal protections. Absent such a norm, an executive who comes into conflict with the judiciary is apt to "mug" the judiciary regardless of constitutional or statutory protections. The real value of explicit structural features like salary protection and "life tenure under good behavior" is that they establish bright lines for determining when the executive or legislature violates a societal or political convention supporting judicial independence. Kaushik Basu (1997) applies this logic to laws in general; Russell Hardin (1989) analyzes constitutions from the same perspective.

This norm- or convention-based line of reasoning soon leads to questions about the emergence, maintenance, and breakdown of social norms and conventions. This topic has proved fascinating to proponents of the "new Chicago school" of law and economics. But to my taste, the ratio of insight-to-ink-spilled is distressingly low. This is not so much a criticism of the "new Chicago" scholars as an unavoidable reality imposed by fundamental limits in the current social scientific understanding of conventions. Recent advances in evolutionary game theory seem to hold some promise for improving our understanding of the emergence and breakdown of norms and social conventions (see, e.g., Young, 1998). But it is apt to be some time before this very abstract material proves useful in understanding highly applied phenomena, like judicial independence—though I would love to proven wrong about this.

Let me summarize so that I can move on. At least within a power analysis, the idea of judicial independence is meaningful. Within this framework, current studies suggest that formal, structural protections are neither necessary nor sufficient to ensure judicial independence. Probably more critical is a basic congruence between the values of judges and other powerful political actors. Still, it would be surprising if there were *no* relationship between formal protections and actual judicial independence because formal protections are so useful in sustaining social conventions by providing "bright line" demarcations. From one perspective, it is ultimately those conventions, rather than the formal protections per se, that are the foundation for judicial independence. Unfortunately, our ability to investigate the emergence, maintenance, and breakdown of social conventions protecting judicial independence is severely limited by our sketchy understanding of the basic social mechanisms at work. And this is not apt to change soon.

⚭ Theory: Judicial Independence and Liberal Democracy

Why should limiting the power of the executive, legislature, and politically powerful actors over judicial decisions facilitate economic growth, the preservation of human rights, and the maintenance of democracy?

One answer might be that judges themselves value economic growth, human rights, and democracy and act positively to support them. Limiting the power of the executive, legislature, and plutocrats over judicial outcomes thus allows benevolent judges to advance good ends without unwholesome interference from potentially predatory actors. Call this the "strong view" of judicial independence. The Fuller Court might stand as the poster child for the strong view, particularly the 1895 term in which the Court struck down the income tax and other progressive reforms that majorities on that Court believed were assaults on a well-ordered economy.

In a series of interesting papers, David Scott Yamanishi (1999, 2000a, 2000b) mounts a sharp attack on the strong view of judicial independence. His argument is worth reproducing at length.

> If we accept that people hold a variety of beliefs across countries and cultures about such matters [as the protection of property rights], and we accept that judicial selection processes don't *necessarily* favor candidates in the former category, then it seems that there's nothing in the very nature of being a judge that compels judges to favor strictly individualistic and capitalistic property rights. . . . If independent judges are more free to exercise their preferences, and if there's no reason to believe that judges will hold any particular economic belief, it's evident that judicial independence is not a precondition of the protection of property rights for investors. (2000a, pp. 4-5)

His argument extends easily to the protection of human rights and democracy.[5]

This attack on the strong view seems hard to rebut—but there is a weak argument for judicial independence that Yamanishi tends to underplay. This argument has two parts. First, within a liberal democratic order, a well-functioning set of courts is apt to enhance economic growth and civil liberties. The argument invokes advantages from the division of labor: Courts are good devices for settling economic disputes and enforcing contracts and protecting citizens from mild encroachments by errant policemen and bullying bureaucrats. And, *within* a liberal democratic order, courts *are* apt to be staffed with people who have the right values—they will want to do the right thing.

Second, within a liberal democratic order, a degree of judicial independence is apt to confer some dynamic stability to the system. This argument is essentially the familiar checks-and-balances view. Random perturbations may yield a bad executive or legislature (or for that matter, judiciary). But cross-checking vetoes from the other branches will allow the system to weather the bad draw. There are severe limits to the argument: The judiciary will not have much restraining power in the face of a military coup and it's silly to hope otherwise. But a somewhat independent judiciary may temporarily check a merely overweening executive or legislature and this temporary check will often prove sufficient to gain the day.

⟳ Judicial Independence and Economic Growth

A recent study of Russia provides some support for the weak argument for judicial independence. Frye and Zhuravskaya (2001) study the operation of small shops in Moscow, Ulyanovsk, and Smolensk. In 1996, Ulyanovsk had seen little economic reform and Communist party figures retained political power. In contrast, Smolensk had seen extensive economic reform and considerable turnover in government personnel. Moscow was intermediate between these two extremes. Shopkeepers in Ulyanovsk faced an intense regulatory burden (as measured by the length of time needed to open a shop, the number of permits needed, the number of inspections, and so on), those in Smolensk a much lighter burden, and those in Moscow an intermediate burden.

Frye and Zhuravskaya investigate the propensity of shop owners to contact the "racket" to obtain private protection services and the likelihood shopkeepers would use legal services in the face of a perceived need. They show that the likelihood of contacting the racket was directly related to regulatory burden. And the likelihood of using the courts was directly related to their perceived efficacy in protecting the shopkeepers' rights against the government and against other businessmen. Finally, they show a negative relationship between regulatory burden and perceived court efficacy.

Frye and Zhuravskaya make sense of these findings in the following way: Differences in the level of regulation should produce two stable equilibria. In one equilibrium, the local government levies comparatively low levels of regulation and provides comparatively competent and accessible legal institutions. These policies encourage shopkeepers to operate in the official economy, rely on the state to enforce property rights, and shun private protection organizations. In the other equilibrium, the local government levies extensive regulation and provides weak legal institutions. This mix of state policies compels shopkeepers to operate in the unofficial economy and turn to a private protection racket to enforce their unofficial economic activity.

Finally, the authors suggest that these alternative political arrangements have consequences for economic activity. The low-burden/efficacious court environment in Smolensk was associated with greater employment in the small business sector than in the high-burden/inefficacious court environment of Ulyanovsk.

This one study is, at best, suggestive but it is compatible with the weak argument for judicial independence: A set of somewhat independent courts complements the other branches in a liberal democratic order, so that all the institutions hang together in a way that has good economic consequences. Of course, economic activity can still take place in the face of a rapacious executive and weak, ineffective courts, partly because private organizations spring up to provide protection services. But this social arrangement carries a cost in economic growth.

Micro-oriented studies like this one are impractical to conduct over many countries but one can examine aggregate evidence in search of broad, systematic patterns. Barro (2000) examines economic growth in 100 countries during the 1960s, 1970s, and 1980s. He finds a positive, statistically significant, and substantively important link between economic growth and "rule of law values" as measured by surveys and reported in the *International Country Risk Guide.* "A rise of one category (among the seven used) in the Political Risk Services Index is estimated to raise the growth rate on impact by 0.5 percent per year. A change from the worst rule of law (0.0) to the best (1.0) would contribute an enormous 3.0 percent per year to the growth rate" (Barro, 2000, p. 222).

Sala-i-Martin (1997) examines the robustness of Barro's growth equations and confirms that the ICRG "rule of law" variable continues to exert a palpable impact on growth across many different specifications.

If the Barro results are believable—and one must be inclined to accord at least agnosticism to results from one of the leading students of economic growth—then an important issue is the determinants of "rule of law values." Barro studies this question, and shows that increases in per capita GDP lead to higher rule of law scores, as do increased levels of education and decreased levels of economic inequality. Countries' colonial heritage apparently affects rule of law scores—former colonies do worse than noncolonies, with Portuguese colonies suffering the worst legacy and British colonies the least-bad legacy. Democracy, as measured by an electoral rights index, does not predict rule of law values (nor does it have much influence on economic growth). Barro (2000) suggests that "the evolution of electoral rights and the rule of law are largely independent," once one controls for the way in which economic development raises both measures. He argues that an increase in rule of law values increases growth, which in turn leads to greater electoral rights as well as further strengthening of rule of law.

Unfortunately, Barro does not investigate whether judicial independence furthers rule of law values. However, Yamanishi (2000b) does look at structural features of the judiciary, using data from Humana on judicial independence. In his analysis, he finds no impact of judicial independence on rule of law values. Nor does he find a link between judicial independence and economic growth. However, the statistical analysis in this convention paper is clearly rather preliminary and the results rather tentative.

This area needs a much closer and more careful look, one that is sensitive to the arguments about norms and formal protections made earlier and the sort of micro-mechanisms suggested by the Frye-Zhuravskaya study. As doubtless occurred to the reader, sensitivity to measurement issues is vital.

~ Judicial Independence and Human Rights and Liberties

This area has been studied by Yamanishi (2000b) and by Brickman (2000). Both use data from Humana on human rights and civil liberties scores from the 1980s and 1990s. The Humana data contain many different indicators related to civil liberties and human rights. Brickman focuses on ten indicators that seem more closely related to civil liberties. Rather sensibly, she factor analyzes the measures and shows that a single factor seems to underlie the ten indicators. The calculated principal component score then acts as her dependent variable. In contrast, Yamanishi analyzes 49 different Humana scores, each treated separately. He also groups them into four broad categories and considers patterns within and across the categories.

Brickman finds a strong, statistically significant and substantively important relationship between civil liberties and judicial independence. Yamanishi's results are difficult to summarize succinctly. However, in many cases, judicial independence appears to facilitate a human right or civil liberty.

These studies are an impressive beginning, but much remains to be done.

~ Judicial Independence and the Stability of Democracy

Until recently, data did not allow systematic investigation of the stability of democracies; new data sets now allow such analyses (see particularly Przeworski, Alverez, Cheibub, & Limongi, 2000). But no one has yet investigated the impact of judicial independence on democratic stability. Thus, this is a completely open area for study. Again, one should have modest expectations about the likely results, but any finding would be interesting.

~ Conclusion

In my view, we care about judicial independence because it supplies part of the institutional matrix supporting economic freedom and opportunity, governmental accountability, and a decent, humane society. Or so the story goes: This is hardly an original argument. In fact, this claim is virtually a cliché in legal writings.[6] But there is at least some evidence that goes beyond cliché. The stakes matter: If there is a discernable link between an independent judiciary and a liberal, humane order, then we stand on firm ground when we argue for independent judiciaries. But if the purported link does not exist, or is so weak as to be practically indiscernible, then a defense of judicial independence must rest on other grounds. Or perhaps judicial independence is not as important as we had thought.

What is judicial independence good for? Somewhat tentatively, judicial independence appears to be good for civil liberties. "Rule of law values" appear to be good for economic growth but it is unclear what relationship (if any) might exist between judicial independence and those values. We seem to know nothing about the impact of the judiciary on democratic stability. In each of these areas, we could know much more than we do. It seems worth taking the trouble to find out.

✑ Notes

1. There are very good reasons for preferring this definition over others; for example, it correctly attributes power to actors even in the absence of actions (the "second face of power").

2. During the conference discussion of this chapter, Professor Geoffrey Hazard questioned whether it makes sense to think of judges as having preferences, in the sense that the law may be clear and a judge's desire may be simply to decide the case in accordance with law. In this case, one can consider the clear command of the law as the judge's preference. Then the question becomes, Can the judge carry out the law? Who has power—a litigant, an affected party, a legislator, or the judge?

3. The controls are usually statistical, typically via multiple regression.

4. The analysis supplies a game theoretic rendering of "culture." The basic idea is that social groups "hang together" and punish governments that act in a predatory fashion toward any one of them, rather than "hang separately" by failing to punish predations suffered by another group. In a repeated game, hanging together can be an equilibrium—but so can hanging separately.

5. He argues, however, that many judges might support some rights that enhance their prestige and power.

6. Brickman (2000) supplies many citations.

✑ References

Barro, R. (2000). Democracy and the rule of law. In B. Bueno de Mesquita & H. Root (Eds.), *Governing for prosperity* (pp. 209-231). New Haven, CT: Yale University Press.

Basu, K. (1997, May). *The role of norms in law and economics: An essay on political economy.* Paper presented at the conference sponsored by Institute for Advanced Study, Princeton, NJ.

Brickman, D. (2000, August/September). *Judicial independence and the protection of civil liberties: A cross-national empirical analysis.* Paper presented at the annual meeting of the American Political Science Association, Washington, DC.

Calvert, R. L., Moran, M. J., & Weingast, B. R. (1987). Congressional influence over policy making: The case of the FTC. In M. D. McCubbins & T. Sullivan (Eds.), *Congress: Structure and policy* (pp. 493-522). Cambridge, UK: Cambridge University Press.

Dahl, R. (1963). *Modern political analysis.* Englewood Cliffs, NJ: Prentice-Hall.

DeFigueiredo, J., & Tiller, E. (1996). Congressional control of the courts: A Theoretical and empirical analysis of the expansion of the federal judiciary. *Journal of Law and Economics, 39,* 435-462.

Dicey, A.V. (1915). *Introduction to the study of the law of the Constitution.* Indianapolis, IN: Liberty Fund.

Epstein, D., & O'Halloran, S. (1999). *Delegating powers: A transaction cost politics approach to policy making under separate powers.* Cambridge, UK: Cambridge University Press.

Ferejohn, J. (1999). Independent judges, dependent judiciary: Explaining judicial independence. *Southern California Law Review, 72,* 353-384.

Ferejohn, J., & Shipan, C. (1990). Control of the bureacracy [Special issue]. *Journal of Law, Economics, and Organization.*

Frye, T., & Zhuravskaya, E. (2001). Rackets, regulation, and the rule of law. *Journal of Law, Economics, and Organization, 16*(2), 478-502.

Hardin, R. (1989). Constitutions as conventions. In B. Grofman & D. Wittman (Eds.), *The Federalist Papers and the new institutionalism.* New York: Agathon.

Helmke, G. (1999). *Ruling against the rulers: Insecure tenure and judicial independence in Argentina, 1976-1995.* Unpublished manuscript.

Moraski, B., & Shipan, C. (1992). The politics of Supreme Court nominations: A theory of institutional constraints and choices. *American Journal of Political Science, 43,*1069-1095.

Murphy, W. (1962). *Congress and the Court: A case study in the American political process.* Chicago: University of Chicago Press.

Nagel, J. (1975). *The descriptive analysis of power.* New Haven, CT: Yale University Press.

Nagel, S. (1965). Court-curbing periods in American history. *Vanderbilt Law Review, 18,* 925-943.

Nordlinger, E. (1981). *On the autonomy of the democratic state.* Cambridge, MA: Harvard University Press.

Pritchett, C. H. 1961. *Congress versus the Supreme Court, 1957-1960.* Minneapolis: University of Minnesota Press.

Przeworski, A., Alverez, M., Cheibub, J. A., & Limongi, F. (2000). *Democracy and development: Political institutions and well-being in the world, 1950-1990.* New York: Cambridge University Press.

Ramseyer, J. M. (1994). The puzzling (in)dependence of courts: A comparative approach. *Journal of Legal Studies, 23,* 721-747.

Ramseyer, J. M., & Rasmusen, E. B. (1997). Judicial independence in a civil law regime: The evidence from Japan. *Journal of Law, Economics, and Organization, 13,* 259-286.

Rosenberg, G. (1992). Judicial independence and the reality of political power. *Review of Politics, 54,* 369-398.

Sala-i-Martin, X. (1997). I just ran two million regressions. *American Economic Review, 87*(2), 178-183.

Salzberger, E., & Fenn, P. (1999). Judicial independence: Some evidence from the English Court of Appeals. *Journal of Law and Economics, 42,* 831-847.

Segal, J. (1998). Separation-of-powers games in the positive theory of Congress and courts. *American Political Science Review, 91,* 28-44.

Spiller, P., & Gely, R. (1992). Congressional control or judicial independence: The determinants of U.S. Supreme Court labor-relations decisions, 1949-1988. *RAND Journal of Economics, 23,* 463-492.

Spiller, P., & Tomasi, M. (in press). Judicial decision making in unstable environments, Argentina 1935-1998. *American Journal of Political Science.*

Weingast, B. (1997, June). The political foundations of democracy and the rule of law. *American Political Science Review, 91,* 245-263.

Yamanishi, D. S. (1999, August/September). *Judicial independence and the rule of law: The ineffectiveness of judicial independence alone as a path to development.* Paper presented at the annual meeting of the American Political Science Association, Atlanta, GA

Yamanishi, D. S. (2000a, August/September). *Rule of law, property rights, and human rights: An informal theory of the effects (and non-effects) of legal institutions.* Paper presented at the annual meeting of the American Political Science Association, Washington, DC.

Yamanishi, D. S. (2000b, August/September). *Rule of law, property rights, and human rights: An empirical study of the effects (and non-effects) of legal institutions.* Paper presented at the annual meeting of the American Political Science Association, Washington, DC.

Young, P. (1998). *Individual strategy and social structure: An evolutionary theory of institutions.* Princeton, NJ: Princeton University Press.

∽ Chapter 7

Behavioral Factors Affecting Judicial Independence

Charles H. Franklin

In considerable measure, judicial independence is a function of institutional structures. The Constitution creates a federal judiciary as a separate and co-equal branch, not as the servant of the president or Congress. The power of judicial review provides a basis for the third branch to critique and invalidate actions of the elected branches. And the lifetime appointment of federal judges (along with protection against salary reduction) insulates the federal judiciary from personal retribution by Congress or the president. This is well known and widely considered in the literature.

Yet as Ferejohn (1999) points out, these institutional features seem insufficient to prevent a determined Congress and president from severely undermining the judiciary. The control over jurisdiction, appointment and possible impeachment of judges, enforcement of court rulings, appropriations for the operation of the courts, and indeed the writing of laws and redrafting of legislation found wanting by the courts, all provide the other branches wide avenues to influence the judiciary. At the state level, the opportunities for political influence are all the greater in systems that make tenure in office subject to the choices of voters or appointment by governors. A wise judiciary knows its vulnerability well and must act to protect its autonomy even as it asserts that independence.

This interplay of institutional actors rests substantially on behavioral considerations rather than solely institutional ones. My aim here is to point to some behavioral features of the judiciary, at both state and federal levels, and suggest that we pay attention to how these features affect the extent and the limits of judicial independence.

Proponents of judicial independence are particularly concerned with the problem of arbitrary judicial decisions based on the demands of other political actors. The specter of "telephone justice" determining who is convicted and who freed, whose rights are upheld and whose denied, is given primacy in this view. In contrast, in this chapter I am most concerned with the flip side of the independence issue, the problem of a responsive judiciary in a democracy. Although judicial reform efforts have focused attention for many years on how to insulate the judiciary from political pressures, I want to argue that the electoral institutions' reformers have chosen to rely too heavily on incorrect understandings of the nature of voting behavior. In an effort to insulate the judiciary, these institutions make elected judges *more* subject to capricious voters, *more* vulnerable to attacks by interest groups, and *not responsive enough* to the values voters wish to see embodied in their judges.

There is an inherent struggle between independent judges and the democratic demand for a responsive judiciary. In this chapter I outline how this struggle takes place in the behaviors of voters, interest groups, presidents, members of Congress, and the judges themselves. The interaction of institutions and behaviors are key to the character of judicial independence and responsiveness. The excessive focus on institutions has failed to understand the ability of behaviors to modify intended institutional effects.

A core element of my argument is the observation that judges differ in their views of the law. This is a mundane observation in political science, which takes the existence of judicial ideology for granted and assumes that judges act to achieve their policy aims (Segal & Spaeth, 1993). The empirical evidence that judges have consistent patterns of decision is overwhelming. Among law faculty and judges themselves, the use of "ideology" may have more negative connotations than intended by the common usage in political science. "Judicial philosophy" may be more acceptable as a description of the fact that judges differ in their reading of the law. Whether we call it "ideology" or "philosophy," it is a necessary part of my argument that judges differ in systematic and consistent ways that reflect their views of the law. In what follows, I will use the two terms interchangeably to mean that judges are somewhat predictable in how they will view legal issues. I believe these differences are entirely legitimate and, indeed, are a foundation for ensuring the balance of independence and responsiveness of the judiciary.

ஒ Independent Judges, Responsive Judiciary

There are many senses of "judicial independence" but what it must *not* mean is that the courts are completely unresponsive to the demands of citizens or of the other branches. To say that judges should be independent, that they should base their decisions on the facts of individual cases rather than in response to outside pressure is one thing. But to say that courts in general should not be held accountable by the public and by the other branches is to ask for a protection no democratic society should grant.

At the most basic level, when Congress or state legislatures make new law or amend old law, we rightly expect the courts to base their decisions on the new law. We expect this even if it reverses the basis of past decisions. Even judicial review of legislation is a form of judicial responsiveness, for it requires that the courts enter into a dialogue with the elected branches over the limitations of the statute, not that the courts merely ignore laws they dislike.

But beyond responding to new statutes, the courts adjust to changes in how the society views particular issues. Consider, for example, the behavior of the courts in response to public opinion shifts on topics such as drunk driving, spouse abuse, gay bashing, sentencing practices, and the death penalty. To a great extent, courts have shifted their approach to such issues as public opinion changed, rather than only as the law has changed.[1] Spouse abuse is now much more likely to be treated as a serious crime rather than a private matter. Drunk driving is more likely to result in jail time rather than a fine. Violence against gays is no longer routinely seen as justified. Victim impact statements before sentencing are common. And courts are far less reluctant to impose the death penalty.

This responsiveness means that judges do change their behavior and that this necessarily influences their decisions on the cases they hear.[2] To the extent these changes in views of the law are applied equally across all cases, we do not view them as unacceptable instances of "telephone justice," even though they do represent judicial responsiveness to broad shifts of public opinion. In adjusting to public preferences, the judiciary maintains its legitimacy without losing its independence in particular cases.

So how do we balance the protection of judges from public pressure in individual cases with the desire for courts to be responsive to changes in public views of what is justice? The evolution of this balance has moved away from partisan election of state judges toward nonpartisan elections or noncompetitive retention elections or even an appointed judiciary. How does electoral behavior affect efforts to insulate an elected judiciary?

∾ Mob Justice: Electing Judges Based on Next to No Information

An elected judiciary promotes democratic responsiveness but risks mob justice by proxy. Making judges subject to popular election enforces limits on judicial discretion so long as judges care about remaining judges and so long as voters sometimes respond to judicial decisions in casting their ballots. If judges couldn't care less about retaining their office, the threat of future electoral sanctions would be empty. If voters never learned of judicial decisions, then their votes could not discipline those decisions (even defeating an incumbent judge would be unrelated to decisions on the bench, an odd independence but independence nonetheless.)

Although it seems quite likely that the first of these conditions is met because most state judges regularly seek reelection (or stand in retention elections), the second condition is far more tenuous. If we consider the realities of public information about judges, it is likely that most ballots cast in judicial elections are based only on the most fragmentary knowledge. To what extent this insulates judges depends critically on which fragments of information voters have.

The fundamental fact of mass electoral politics is that most voters most of the time rely only on information they receive through the most casual attention to politics. Decades of studies of the mass public have documented the low levels of information about politics held by ordinary citizens. This lack of knowledge may be attributed to "rational ignorance," given the low instrumental value of political information (Downs, 1957) or to simple lack of citizen interest in politics (Delli Carpini & Keeter, 1996). The behavioral reality that low levels of citizen information create is that votes are cast based on easy shortcuts, such as partisan cues and incumbency, or whatever information is sufficiently prominent to be noticed by voters who are not actively seeking political information but who receive it as a byproduct of their normal activities, such as being exposed to a political advertisement while watching television.

Zaller's (1992) model of public opinion provides a good explanation for the dynamics of information and voting in judicial elections (see his Chapter 3 for the details of the model). A small number of highly interested voters are able to receive and evaluate campaign information in light of their underlying partisan and ideological preferences and link these to candidates. In judicial elections, these preferences may also include specific issues such as abortion rights or the death penalty. Such highly involved citizens are likely to accept information consistent with their preferences while recognizing and rejecting messages that run counter to their preferences. These voters are therefore very likely to cast ballots for the candidates who match their political predispositions rather than to be much influenced by campaign information.

For many more citizens, political information is in such short supply that it is difficult for them to recognize a message as either consistent or inconsistent with their predispositions. Because few citizens possess well-developed views of legal issues and because judicial campaigns often avoid debating substantive issues of law due to the restrictions on campaigning in the ABA Canon of Judicial Ethics, it is especially difficult for most citizens to match their basic preferences with judges' judicial philosophy or ideology. In such cases, any information that happens to be received is likely to be uncritically accepted and added to the storehouse of considerations relevant to a vote choice. In low visibility judicial elections, especially those stripped of partisan cues, it is likely that many voters fall into this category. These voters are therefore likely to cast ballots consistent with the balance of campaign messages they have received, giving a substantial advantage to the candidate best able to get his or her message out to voters.

Finally, a significant additional fraction of the public simply lacks sufficient interest in judicial elections to develop any perceptions of the race at all and are therefore most likely not to vote. The relatively high rates of nonvoting in judicial elections, even when held during a general election, shows the difficulty the public has in developing strong preferences for judicial candidates.

Because the most informed voters are also those least likely to be persuaded to vote counter to their underlying preferences, the key dynamic in low visibility elections is the second group of voters. For these people, the important question is whether they link their political preferences to the candidates in a way that allows their ballots to reflect their preferences, or whether they are more likely to cast ballots based on the net balance of messages alone. In higher visibility elections, with a clear partisan or ideological content, it is possible for these modestly informed voters to make such connections. Without such cues, it becomes much more difficult for these voters to interpret the messages they receive in light of their preferences and hence their votes are much less anchored to preferences.

Given this limited amount of information among voters, how likely is it that election of judges promotes either democratic responsiveness or judicial independence? Reform efforts have generally favored mechanisms to insulate judges from partisan politics.[3] The adoption of nonpartisan judicial elections in 13 states and noncompetitive retention elections in 16 states now far exceeds the use of partisan contests in eight states.[4] Unfortunately, given the likely information available to voters in these nonpartisan election contexts, it is unlikely that such contests provide efficient mechanisms for democratic responsiveness and, paradoxically, may produce situations in which judges are particularly vulnerable to electoral challenges based on narrow issues that arouse particular interest groups rather than the broad quality of their performance on the bench.

If ordinary citizens are almost always unaware of judges' decisions on the bench, interest groups are keenly aware of the details of those decisions and their impact on the groups' concerns. This informational asymmetry allows groups to select candidates for support or opposition based on the groups' preferences and the judge's rulings. Thus the ability to promote interest representation for groups is much higher than for ordinary citizens. This asymmetry is, of course, not limited to judicial elections but because of the low visibility of such contests and because citizens have much more trouble translating their issue and ideological preferences into a candidate choice in judicial contests, organized interests have a much greater opportunity to influence judicial elections than they do in more information rich and more clearly partisan elections. Partisan contests mute the effects of interest groups simply because candidates are much more obviously linked to party, providing ideological cues that even modestly informed citizens are able to decode and thus reach the correct candidate choice given their preferences.

Given this asymmetry between groups and individual citizens, it is paradoxical that "reform" efforts have created a system of judicial elections that maximizes the ability of interest groups to affect elections while minimizing the ability of citizens to vote for candidates who reflect their preferences. Although judges may not be forced to run under partisan banners in most states, they have a hard time communicating with voters about the substance of their judicial philosophies. As a result, voters become especially susceptible to messages from independent groups who sponsor "issue advertising" in judicial campaigns.

Judicial elections, both partisan and nonpartisan, are further complicated by the reluctance of sitting judges to discuss specific cases or legal issues. In Wisconsin, for example, a recent report recommended that "the rules should prohibit campaign rhetoric that commits or appears to commit a candidate for judicial office with respect to particular cases, controversies, or issues likely to come before the court" (Commission on Judicial Elections and Ethics, 1999). As the report notes

> At least since the 1924 ABA Canons of Judicial Ethics, campaign promises by judicial candidates have been considered problematic. The 1924 Canons proscribed promises appealing to "cupidity or prejudices of the appointing or electing power" and forbade a candidate's announcing in advance "his conclusions of law on disputed issues to secure class support."

Although most would agree that discussion of a specific future case is suspect, the restriction against discussion of "issues likely to come before the court" is so broad as to virtually prohibit judicial candidates from discussing anything that matters. This ethical canon provides cover for judicial candidates to avoid taking positions on issues that are of general public concern, yet it in no way prevents the judge from actually having a position on such issues. Refusing to state a position on *Roe v. Wade* before the Senate judiciary committee has not meant that Justices lack such positions. Nor does the avoidance of campaign discussion of similar legal issues ensure that elected judges "just apply the law."

The problem with this limitation on judicial campaign speech is that it limits the ability of voters to translate their preferences into choices at the ballot box. From the voter's point of view, so long as judges actually differ in their interpretation of the law, it is important to vote for the one who will apply the death penalty or who will protect a woman's right to choose. To say otherwise is to deny the purpose of democratic elections. To say that only impartiality and competence matter is to deny the reality that judges differ in their reading of the law.

When judges are restricted in discussing the issues that actually matter, the voter is left to guess which candidate takes which positions. There are numerous cues to this, even in nonpartisan elections. For example, lists of supporters almost always includes partisan elected officials who provide good cues. Likewise, interest group support may convey information to those politically aware enough to decode it: Knowing which candidate is supported by Wisconsin Right to Life is a pretty good cue. Yet the absence of open discussion between the candidates means that voters will be less well-informed than they could be and that the role of campaigns in educating voters is reduced. It also maintains the fiction that judges just apply the law rather than admit the reality of legal interpretation.

Voters who are more uncertain about their true preferences between judicial candidates are therefore much more likely to respond to spurious elements of the campaign. This results in electoral outcomes that are less constrained by substance and more driven by television ads or campaign gaffes. In the search for judicial independence, it is not clear that making election outcomes more random is an improvement over voters with real preferences making informed choices.

Paradoxically, partisan election leads to a more policy-relevant voting pattern but to *less* voting in response to specific decisions, which in turn results in a judiciary that better reflects partisan and perhaps ideological preferences of citizens yet that is also more effectively insulated from campaign attacks based on specific decisions (a classic case of judicial nonindependence). The anchoring cue of party makes it easier for marginally informed citizens to link their preferences to particular judges and to resist the influence of campaign messages that are not consonant with their preferences. Thus partisan elections both provide a policy preference relevant cue and a measure of resistance to campaign messages from independent groups.

Nonpartisan judicial elections make it harder for voters to anchor their vote choice to their preferences and make it more likely they will cast votes in response to messages sent during the campaign, often from independent groups. This means the link between voter ideology and judicial philosophy is made more tenuous, whereas the ability of interest groups to influence the campaign is maximized. In view of the ban on judicial candidates speaking openly about their judicial philosophies, this makes it more likely that substantive differences between candidates will be hidden from voters who will have to rely on subtle cues (such as who endorses the candidates) or what issue ads are run by independent groups. In these situations, judges may win by substantial margins when faced with weak opponents yet find their margin dramatically altered when stronger candidates enter and independent groups become mobilized. As a result, the dynamic swings of votes from election to election may be much greater for nonpartisan elections and the potential role of specific decisions is enhanced because the anchoring effects of partisanship in the electorate are removed.

Thus partisan elections produce a judiciary that is more likely to reflect partisan and ideological divisions yet which is less likely to have its decisions effectively questioned at the ballot box. Nonpartisan elections produce judges who are less aligned with partisan and ideological conflicts yet who may be more subject to punishment for specific decisions. Such punishment, however, is likely to occur sporadically and unpredictably, making judges potentially even *less* independent because they can't predict which issues are likely to get them into trouble—hence they have to be careful all the time. Similarly, without a partisan base it is more difficult for nonpartisan judges to assure themselves that their electoral base continues to support them.

The desire to insulate the judiciary from partisan hacks and from the most base partisan decisions has given considerable impetus for nonpartisan elections in preference to partisan contests. Yet it is not clear that elections that are the most devoid of clear signals to voters can accomplish the goal of an impartial and qualified judiciary. It may make the judiciary all the more sensitive to the possibility of electoral challenge rather than making them more independent. It clearly cannot strip judges of their differences in reading the law. Of course, lifetime tenure cannot ensure that partisan patterns of decisions will not emerge either. The issue is whether, when we choose judges, voters are allowed to consider the likely pattern of future decisions or whether they choose in ignorance.

The conflict between the values of democratic responsiveness and judicial independence play themselves out in partisan and nonpartisan electoral institutions. Counter to the notion that nonpartisan elections are more insulated from mob pressures, partisan election provides both a measure of popular control and independence from the mob's reaction to particular decisions. Nonpartisan institutions are inherently more fragile bulwarks of judicial independence than is commonly assumed.

扶 Judicial Turnover and Congressional Control

At the federal level, lifetime tenure of Article III judges ensures an institutional independence of the judiciary from Congress. Yet as Ferejohn (1999) argues, Congress has broad powers to affect the operations of the courts and to make independence costly. Despite this possibility, overt congressional action to limit the courts is rare. Ferejohn suggests that the political basis for judicial independence rests on the tendency of the federal courts and the popular bodies to settle into long-term stability that provides acceptable policy agreement. Disagreements tend to arise when the popular bodies experience sudden change while the judiciary remains stable. Such an argument rests on the actual dynamics of judicial turnover.

Imagine a world in which every federal judge serves 20 years and then retires. Assume that appointments are uniformly distributed over time. Then the president gets to nominate and the Senate confirm 1/20th of the judiciary each year and it takes five years to change a quarter of the judges, 10 years to replace a majority. Will such a system provide an equilibrating dynamic that brings congressional and judicial policy views into accord?

If one party controls both the presidency and the Senate for long enough, and if that party's policy views remain stable, then clearly the judiciary will be responsive to the preferences of the elected institutions thanks to mere population replacement. But the time frame for changing the policy preferences of the judiciary is not just the 10 years it takes to replace half the judges. Much depends on who appointed judges 20 years earlier. Imagine the dominant party was in power for 20 years, out of power for 10 years and is now back in power. For the first 10 years of its new reign, it is replacing judges it appointed 20 years earlier. It takes 10 years before it gets to replace the first judge appointed by the hated opposition. Thus the judiciary changes with painful slowness. (Note that the hated opposition got to affect the tenor of the judiciary from its first appointment, thanks to the previous long stay of the dominant party.) Thus the speed with which a new electoral majority can affect the makeup of the judiciary depends on the past history of government control and on the pattern of alternating party control of government. Minority parties are actually advantaged when in power because more of the judges they replace were appointed by the majority party.

If judges don't retire after a fixed term but retire at random, then much the same story holds and the judiciary is remade at a pace that depends on the average length of judicial service. Again, the policy effects of a new majority party depends primarily on past history of control of judicial appointments.

But what if judges have policy preferences and their retirement decisions are partially guided by their desire to see those policies continued? In this case, retirement is not randomly distributed with respect to the president and Senate majority. Evidence suggests (Spriggs & Wahlbeck, 1995) that federal judges are more likely to retire when they expect to be replaced by judges who share their preferences. From the perspective of presidential and Senatorial control over the judiciary, this "support" for a congenial party has paradoxical consequences. It means that a new majority party is more likely to be faced with retirements from judges close to its preferences, whereas judges far from those preferences linger. The result is that new appointments are more likely to maintain the balance of judicial policy views rather than sharply alter that balance. Thus the judiciary will equilibrate more slowly than it would with random retirements. Of course, no one can linger forever, so over very long periods of one party dominance, the electoral institutions can indeed work their way on the judiciary. But if party competition is sufficient to provide frequent changes in party control, then the lingering behavior of opposition judges serves to *further* insulate the judiciary.

So what is an elected official to do? Control of the composition of the judiciary is the one constitutional power the president and Senate have over the personnel of the courts. In order to maximize that control, vacancies must occur. One approach has been to increase the number of judges. In part, this is simply an administrative matter to deal with increased case loads. However, expansion of the judiciary inevitably means the appointment of judges by the party then in power and resulting long-term influence. Whether expansion of the judiciary can be explained as an effort to secure greater partisan control of the courts is an important empirical question.

A second way to exert control is to appoint judges who can be expected to serve lengthy terms on the bench. Thus the appointment of younger judges allows a party to extend its influence. This race for younger appointments is limited to some extent by the qualifications of judges, but given the opportunity to nominate two equally qualified candidates, a president seeking to extend his influence should pick the younger one.

A third way of increasing control over the composition of the judiciary is to increase the retirement rate or, equivalently, lower the average length of service. Especially if parties cannot be sure of long periods of control of the presidency or the Senate, they have an incentive to encourage shorter judicial careers. The higher turnover that results means more assured influence through appointments over shorter periods in office. How might this incentive manifest itself? Low pay, heavy workload, good retirement benefits. Chief Justice Rehnquist complains "I consider the need to increase judicial salaries to be the most pressing issue facing the federal judiciary today" (Howe, 2001). The American Bar Association (2001) reports that 52 district and circuit court judges resigned in the last decade, the most in history, and attributes this to salary shortfalls relative to what is available in private practice.

One might attribute this perennial problem to the reluctance of congress to increase federal budgets. Or, one might see the hand of congressional control. Although the chief justice, and certainly all federal judges, would prefer to see comfortable salaries in order to encourage well-qualified judges to serve as long as possible, the interests of the Congress (and the president) are decidedly on the other side. Whereas good public policy does require a relatively stable judiciary, Congress and the president benefit from turnover of judges. We should not see the Congress rush to improve the financial condition of the judiciary.

The length of judicial service, the appointment of judges to fill vacancies, and the expansion of the judiciary are all very much subject to the influence of Congress and the president. By taking steps to ensure ample opportunities to influence the courts through appointments, the elected branches exert their control over the judiciary. The countervailing behavior on the part of judges is a reluctance to leave the bench when the opposition party controls the presidency and Senate. Thus the judiciary's behavior with respect to retirement serves to dampen the influence of the president and the Senate. How long it takes for elected institutions and the judiciary to reach equilibrium depends a great deal on the behaviors of each.

൦ᕞ A Brief Agenda

Institutional analysis can only take us so far in understanding judicial independence. At both state and federal levels, important elements of independence are functions of the behaviors of judges, voters, interest groups, members of the Congress, and the president. Viewed in this light, judicial independence is maintained or eroded as much by choices and behaviors as by institutions and laws. We should work to improve our understanding of these behavioral factors in judicial independence.

൦ᕞ Notes

1. To be sure, the law has also changed in these arenas as elected officials have responded to these same shifts of public opinion.

2. Alternatively, turnover of members of the bench may provide the same responsiveness of the *judiciary* if not among individual judges.

3. An additional insulating mechanism used in many states is long terms of office, though I do not consider this further here. The use of "Missouri Plan" style nominating commissions is also intended to reduce partisan influence in initial appointments.

4. Twelve states use judicial selection mechanisms that avoid direct reliance on voters altogether, usually by gubernatorial appointment with legislative approval. New Mexico uses a mixed system in which initial appointment is followed by a partisan contest that in turn is followed by subsequent retention elections.

❧ References

American Bar Association, & Federal Bar Association. (2001, February). *Federal judicial pay erosion: A report on the need for reform* [On-line]. Available: http://www.abanet.org/poladv/fedjudreport.pdf

Commission on Judicial Elections and Ethics. (1999, June). *Final report of the commission on judicial elections and ethics.* Madison, WI: Wisconsin Court System.

Delli Carpini, M. X., & Keeter, S. (1996). *What Americans know about politics and why it matters.* New Haven, CT: Yale University Press.

Downs, A. (1957). *An economic theory of democracy.* New York: Harper.

Ferejohn, J. (1999). Independent judges, dependent judiciary: Explaining judicial independence. *Southern California Law Review, 72,* 353-384.

Howe, K. (2001, February 14). Pay for federal judges must be increased, Rehnquist says. *Los Angeles Times.* A5.

Segal, J. A., & Spaeth, H. J. (1993). *The Supreme Court and the attitudinal model.* New York: Cambridge University Press.

Spriggs, J. F., II, & Wahlbeck, P. J. (1995). Calling it quits: Strategic retirement on the Federal Courts of Appeals, 1893-1991. *Political Research Quarterly, 48,* 573-598.

Zaller, J. R. (1992). *The nature and origins of mass opinion.* New York: Cambridge University Press.

Customary Independence

Charles Gardner Geyh

When a conference attended largely by political scientists devotes itself to developing a "research agenda," it creates the unspoken assumption that the research solicited for inclusion on such an agenda will be empirical in character and lean heavily on data collection and statistical analysis. As an academic lawyer who has no business opining on—let alone conducting—that sort of research, I must look elsewhere to earn my keep and in this chapter I have developed an agenda line item that has one foot in history and the other in law.

Be it a date-night dispute over whether Certs is a candy mint or a breath mint, a quarrel between beer drinkers over whether Lite beer tastes great or is less filling, or a tiff between a consumer and his oleo dish as to whether Parkay is butter or margarine, no one beats Madison Avenue when it comes to crafting arguments that linger and lead nowhere. Judges and legislators nonetheless deserve an honorable mention for their continuing debate over the relative priority of judicial independence and accountability—a debate that may be less vacuous but is considerably more intractable than its commercial advertising corollaries. In the world according to Madison Avenue, arguments are easily resolved by resort to a disembodied voice who cheerfully explains that each disputant is right: Certs is a candy *and* a breath mint; Lite tastes great *and* is less filling; Parkay is margarine *and*

I'd like to thank Steve Burbank, Lauren Robel, Emily Van Tassel, and Carl Tobias for their comments and suggestions on earlier drafts of this chapter.

tastes like butter. By the same token, demonstrating that judges should be independent *and* accountable ought to resolve the matter and return us to regularly scheduled programming.

The problem is that independence and accountability are, at least in absolute terms, incompatible. An absolutely independent judge is—by definition—dependant on no one. If you make that judge accountable to anyone, you have reduced his or her independence to the extent of his or her accountability. Of course, those who profess to support independence and accountability are not speaking in absolutes; rather, they favor some of each. The critical inquiry thus becomes *how much* of each? Where should independence end and accountability begin?

Suppose, for example, that Congress removed (or threatened to remove) a judge by impeachment because the decisions were unpopular, or stripped (or proposed to strip) the district courts of jurisdiction to hear a category of cases the courts have decided in unpopular ways. What if the Senate rejected (or threatened to reject) a judicial nominee because of a refusal to commit to deciding a particular case a particular way? Or if Congress sought to control the outcomes of judicial decisions by manipulating (or at least trying to manipulate) court size, or holding the judiciary's budget hostage? Would these actions pose an illegitimate threat to judicial independence or represent a legitimate effort to promote accountability? Definitive answers to such seemingly elemental questions remain elusive, more than two centuries after those who drafted and ratified the United States Constitution ostensibly provided for an independent judiciary.

Why? Sometimes the problem lies in a disagreement over factual questions that an empirical research agenda might conceivably address, such as whether (essentially idle?) threats of impeachment impair or otherwise affect judicial decision making.[1] More often, however, such questions are irrelevant, for even if we found that a given kind of threat tended to interfere with judicial decision making, it would only beg the question of whether such interference represented an assault on independence from which judges should be protected, or a simple side effect of ensuring judicial accountability that judges must endure.

In this chapter, I will first recharacterize judicial independence in terms of its sources, to the end of suggesting that our continuing inability to resolve judicial independence issues is often attributable to the disputants' failure to look to the right source for answers—the search has traditionally been limited to constitutional doctrine infrequently developed by courts, and has largely excluded the constitutional customs or norms that Congress employs in deciding whether and how to regulate the third branch. Second, I will propose a research agenda to explore customary independence more fully. Third, I will illustrate the utility of exploring customary independence through the example of court packing, which court doctrine has left largely untouched but which Congress has rejected as a matter of custom.

怀 Customary Independence Described

I propose that we reanalyze judicial independence by differentiating between three sources of independence: doctrinal independence derived from judicial interpretation, functional independence derived from nonregulation, and customary independence derived from congressional interpretation.

Doctrinal independence refers to that slender band of issues resolved by the text of Article III and court interpretations of that text, which together comprise a body of judicial independence doctrine that the political branches *must* respect. Doctrinal independence thus declares, for example, that Congress may not reduce judicial salaries directly or indirectly; may not remove individual judges during good behavior; and may not usurp the judicial power by disturbing final court judgments.

Functional independence, in contrast, refers to the freedom from interference that flows naturally from the judicial office in the absence of regulation or that is a serendipitous biproduct of a congressional delegation of authority to the courts. Put another way, in the absence of congressional or intrajudicial regulation, judges have the functional independence to do whatever they are not prohibited from doing; conversely, if for reasons unrelated to judicial independence, Congress gives the judiciary a measure of responsibility or control over a subject that it would not otherwise possess, the judiciary's functional independence is increased commensurately. By definition, functional independence is extra-constitutional in nature and exists solely as a matter of congressional and intrajudicial sufferance. Thus, for example, judges retained the functional independence to employ their own standards for recusal until the federal disqualification statute was enacted; by the same token, judges lacked the functional independence to make procedural rules governing the appealability of district court decisions until Congress gave them that power.

Customary independence refers to the zone of independence that Congress respects as a matter of custom when exercising its constitutional powers over courts and judges. It differs from functional independence in that customary independence—like doctrinal independence—is a product of constitutional interpretation. Unlike doctrinal independence, however, customary independence concerns political or quasi-political constitutional questions in which the interpreter of primary, if not final, resort is Congress rather than the courts. By way of example, the Senate has historically excluded unpopular judicial decisions from the ambit of "high crimes and misdemeanors" that will subject a judge to removal by impeachment, not out of fear that the courts would or could so hold but out of an evolved understanding—a constitutional custom—that removing judges for making wrongheaded decisions is unduly antithetical to judicial independence.

Recharacterizing judicial independence in this way is important for two related reasons. First, it underscores the important role that Congress plays in defining the contours of judicial independence—despite the fact that legal scholarship to date has focused almost exclusively on court-fashioned, doctrinal independence. Second, if we shift some of our focus from doctrinal to customary independence, we may find that many of the questions that the former leaves unanswered are addressed and sometimes resolved by the latter, which may help to loosen if not break the deadlock over some of the issues in the independence-accountability debate.

This second point warrants elaboration. From the perspective of many accountability afficionados, the independence imponderables raised earlier are easy enough to resolve: It does not threaten judicial independence for Congress to impeach and remove "activist" judges, subject "activist" judicial nominees to litmus tests, strip the courts of jurisdiction to make decisions with which Congress disagrees, and so on because the courts have not held that Article III stands in the way of Congress doing so. Insofar as courts would not hold that such actions run afoul of doctrinal independence, the independence Congress constrains must be functional only and may therefore be freely regulated. The rejoinder from independence advocates is typically a rather whiney one, to the effect that such actions violate the spirit but (implicitly) not the letter of Article III independence.

If, however, we acknowledge customary independence and take it seriously, the analysis changes. Less ephemeral than the "spirit" of independence, customary independence embodies the constitutional balance struck by the political branches over time between judicial independence and accountability. The political branches have the power to alter that balance, just as the courts have the power to alter the scope of doctrinal independence. Unlike functional independence, however, which existence turns on the vagaries of any given day's public policy, customary independence—like its doctrinal counterpart—is tethered to constitutional principle. To the extent that Congress has, as a matter of "constitutional custom," declined to impeach unpopular judges, to impose litmus tests on judicial nominees, or to court pack or jurisdiction strip because it has long regarded such practices as antithetical to Article III independence, the stature and stability of Congress's self-restraint is logically enhanced. Although Congress remains free to overlook or override its customs and precedents, decisions to do so must first overcome the presumption that such action is contrary to the Constitution as Congress has traditionally construed it.

◦◦ A Customary Independence Research Agenda

To recognize and realize the potential for customary independence to reorient the independence-accountability debate, if not break the impasse, a multiphase research agenda might logically be pursued.

First, the existence of customary independence must be adequately established and accepted. Making the case for customary independence is relatively easy with true "political questions," in which the business of interpreting constitutional text has been delegated wholesale to the political branches. In cases of judicial removal or appointment, for example, Congress's chronic resort to constitutional text, original intent, and its own precedent as means to circumscribe and define its role in impeachment and confirmation proceedings leaves little room for doubt that Congress is interpreting the Constitution and that such interpretations are thought to operate as limiting principles on congressional prerogatives (how "limiting" Congress actually finds these principles to be is a separate question that I address in the fourth point, that follows). Less clear are cases in which Congress is acting in its traditional capacity as lawmaker and the courts retain the final word on the constitutionality of its actions. Even then, however, the case can (and should) be made that congressional discretion to implement the constitutional framework by establishing, regulating, and appropriating monies to the courts (or not) is so vast that for the most part Congress has only itself to consult when deciding whether court packing, jurisdiction stripping, or budget slashing is consistent with the independent judiciary that the Constitution assigned it to create.

Second, once the existence and relevance of customary independence is accepted as a general proposition, we need to know a constitutional custom when we see one. At what point does an isolated constitutional interpretation establish a "custom"? When it is accepted as a conclusive reading of the Constitution at the time? When it is undisturbed for a sufficiently long duration? When it is alluded to frequently? Or at regular intervals?

Third, after the definition of a constitutional custom is clarified, specific customs need to be identified. This is admittedly a difficult—and some would say an impossible—undertaking. Courts articulate their interpretations of the Constitution in formal written opinions; Congress does not. Individual members of Congress opine on the Constitution in hearings, mark-up sessions, and floor debates; legislative committees express their views in reports, and inferences may be drawn from legislation Congress passes or other actions it takes as to whose interpretations were accepted. Resort to legislative history as a means to ascertain congressional intent in statutory interpretation has often been criticized, and such criticism applies with equal force to using those same sources to divine congressional constitutional understanding. One needs look no further than the Clinton impeachment to appreciate that legislative "precedent"—there, on the meaning of "high crimes and misdemeanors"—is subject to manipulation and conflicting interpretations. By the same token, the use of legislative history in statutory interpretation remains an accepted practice, detractors notwithstanding, and turning to congressional hearings, debates, and reports for the purpose of isolating constitutional customs can be defended on similar grounds: The fact that legislative materials are subject to misuse and conflicting interpretation means only that they should be used with caution and not that they should not be used at all.

Fourth, the circumstances under which Congress will or should overturn constitutional customs ought to be explored. Those who subscribe to a public choice vision of congressional decision making may well regard much of my proposed research agenda as a waste of time. From their vantage point, members of Congress will spin the Constitution to best serve their personal or partisan ends and it is hopelessly naive to suppose that they would ever let constitutional principle stand in the way of naked self interest. Hence, when retention of a constitutional custom furthers their reelection agenda, members of Congress will argue in its favor and, when it does not, they will argue against its retention, dispute its existence, or ignore it altogether.

Congress is admittedly less likely to adhere to its interpretive precedent than are courts (who are not exactly stalwart guardians of constitutional stare decisis themselves). Legislators are subject to the vagaries of fickle majoritarian influence in ways that courts are not, and punctuate their disconnection from past decision making by assigning Congress a new name and number every other year, whereas judges seek to preserve continuity by maintaining the appearance of a seamless connection to their predecessors. This is as it should be—by denominating the constitutional questions at issue here "political" or "quasi-political," we *want* the answers Congress provides to be subject to political, which is to say majoritarian, influence. If, for example, officials are subject to impeachment for "political" offenses manifesting "the abuse or violation of some public trust," as Hamilton argued, then the meaning of "high crimes and misdemeanors" ought to evolve in tandem with the public's changing perception of when its trust is violated.

Conceding that customary independence is more malleable than its doctrinal counterpart, however, is not to concede it out of existence. As my proposed research agenda is designed to verify and document, such customs exist and are respected for a variety of reasons: Adhering to established practices that preserve the longstanding balance between judicial independence and accountability saves time and energy by avoiding protracted digressions to reinvent the wheel, if not the flat tire; it enhances the legitimacy of Congress, by adding a measure of stability and consistency to its constitutional decision making; it protects the settled expectations of "interest groups," for want of a better phrase—judges, lawyers, and litigation "consumers"; and (with a curtsy to Pollyanna) it's the right thing to do for legislators who take their oath to uphold the Constitution seriously, insofar as it respects the permanence and durability of the constitutional text that Congress is interpreting.

To be sure, Congress has disregarded or manipulated its precedent in times of political crisis, as has the Supreme Court its precedent. For Congress and Court alike, this may demonstrate that hard cases make bad law but does not refute the point that precedent matters most of the time. The burden of this fourth proposed research agenda item, then, is to identify the circumstances in which the benefits of adhering to the tenets of customary independence will be overcome by the substantive or political costs of doing so, as a consequence of which Congress is likely to modify or disregard the custom in question.

Fifth, the study of customary independence could be extended to state systems. Episodes of judge bashing and attempted jurisdiction stripping and budget slashing are increasingly common in some states and all but completely absent in others. Variations between the states in their approaches to judicial independence and accountability are sometimes attributable to differences in constitutional structure, but often such variations exist where constitutional structures are similar, if not identical. Quasi-historical studies of state customary independence may pinpoint differences in legal or constitutional culture that can help to explain how states with formally identical constitutions strike the independence-accountability balance in fundamentally different ways.

❧ Customary Independence Illustrated: The Norm Against Court Packing

Having described customary independence and scoped out a research agenda through which the contours of customary independence can be more fully explored, in this final section of the chapter I will illustrate the utility of customary independence as an explanatory device in an effort to convince you that this proposed research agenda is indeed worth pursuing on a larger scale. To do that, I will first adopt a working definition of custom that I will then employ to explain one isolated thread in the richly textured weave of customary independence: the *de facto* prohibition on congressional court packing and unpacking.

In an article by Michael Glennon (1984) that explores when "the inaction of one branch in the face of an established practice of another branch, may properly be deemed to authorize the actions of the latter" in separation of powers adjudication, Professor Glennon identifies six attributes of established interbranch practices or "customs": (a) consistency—the similarity of the unrelated events that purportedly constitute a custom; (b) numerosity—the number of times a "custom" has been followed; (c) duration—the length of time during which a "custom" has been respected; (d) density—how frequently the "custom" has been followed relative to its duration; (e) continuity—the regularity with which the "custom" is followed; and (f) normalcy—the extent to which the "custom" cuts across different Congresses to exist independent of the personalities or political agendas of particular decision makers. Although all six attributes support the finding of a custom, Professor Glennon argues that among them, only consistency is indispensable (Glennon, p. 133).

This is a useful point of departure for discussion here. At bottom, we are looking for a series of factually comparable but otherwise unrelated historical events spanning a significant period, giving rise to recurring constitutional questions that different Congresses have resolved in similar ways with reference to a common understanding. I would, however, retool Professor Glennon's analysis in one particular way to meet the special needs of our situation. Whereas Professor Glennon speaks of customs in terms of *practices* the branches of government follow, I am more focused here on the *interpretations* that Congress employs. Adherence to *custom* in constitutional interpretation might be better characterized as adherence to *precedent,* and the role of precedent in constitutional analysis is decidedly dynamic. In the context of constitutional interpretation, then, the need for "consistency" must coexist with the recognition that custom or precedent of this kind is fluid and evolves without destroying its essential character as custom or precedent.[2]

Having defined custom for purposes of this exercise, it remains to define court packing before turning to an examination of the historical record. By court "packing" and "unpacking" generally, I mean congressional adjustments in court size or shape, for reasons unrelated to improving judicial administration—which thus excludes from its scope upward or downward adjustments to accommodate geographical expansion, changes in caseload, subject matter jurisdiction, litigation practice, demographics, and so forth. This definition is still overly broad for my purposes insofar as it technically captures legislation that has no particular relevance to judicial independence—such as a judgeships bill that adds unnecessary judgeships in the states of influential legislators to win their support. Rather, the subset of court packing and unpacking of relevance here is limited to those situations in which congressional manipulation of court size is potentially inimical to the institutional or decision-making autonomy of the judiciary, as would be the case if Congress were to increase the size of a court to shift the fulcrum of its decision-making majority, obliterate a court altogether in retaliation for an unpopular decision, or make a casualty of the judiciary's structural integrity in a political branch war with the president.

Professor Stephen Burbank (1998) observes that when it comes to the size of the Supreme Court, "the number nine sticks in our brains not so much as a function of current legal awareness but as a number that has assumed the proportion of a constitutional understanding." A similar statement can be made with respect to the lower courts: Although the size of the lower courts is not similarly fixed and Congress is more inclined to add judgeships when the president's political party affiliation coincides with that of the congressional majority, it is difficult to imagine that Congress would act to "unpack" or abolish the offices of unpopular judges.

Court Building and the Constitution at the Time of the Founding

The text of the Constitution offers no obvious explanation for our current court-packing taboo. As to the size of the Supreme Court, the Constitution tells us that there shall be one Court but implicitly leaves it to Congress to determine its size.[3] As to the lower courts, by vesting "the judicial power" in the Supreme Court and "such inferior courts as Congress *may* from time to time ordain and establish," the Constitution would seem to give Congress the authority to establish the lower courts or not, and, by implication, to disestablish courts it had previously established.[4] It is clear from James Madison's (1787/1911) notes of the Constitutional Convention that the decision to make the creation of inferior federal courts discretionary with Congress was a compromise that he negotiated in the teeth of a Convention vote against establishing such courts in the Constitution itself.[5] This meant that the Constitution left the size of the Supreme and lower courts indeterminate, which, defenders of the Constitution argued at the time, was as it should be. As one pseudonymous commentator (1788/1990) opined, "to have entered minutely into the subject . . . would have spun out the work to a tedious length," and "in that case the Constitution must have ascertained the number of inferior courts necessary, the number of judges and other offices . . . the introduction of which would have made a strange appearance." For that reason, the delegates "properly left to Congress the power of organizing by law the Federal Court."

By speaking in terms of the Constitution leaving to Congress the power to decide "the number of inferior courts necessary," the above-quoted writer appears to assume that establishment of inferior federal courts was a *fait accompli*. Indeed, the compromise that Madison fashioned—which clearly contemplated a congressional prerogative *not* to establish inferior courts—was not common knowledge outside of the Constitutional Convention (Collins, 1995). It thus became possible for a new textual twist of Article III to gain influence during the debates on the Judiciary Act of 1789 just two years later: Because the Constitution dictated that Article III judicial power "shall" be vested in such inferior courts as Congress may establish, the argument went, and because Congress could not vest Article III power in non-Article III state courts, Congress *must* establish inferior federal courts (Geyh & Van Tassel, 1998).[6]

This spin on the lower courts' institutional independence is at odds with current thinking, which posits that Congress possesses complete discretion over whether to establish or not establish lower courts. It is, however, indicative of the depth of the founding generation's commitment (at least in principle) to implementing an independent judicial branch, which was expressed in terms of a need for the three branches of government "to be made as independ[en]t as possible" (Madison, 1787/1911, pp. 79, 86),[7] in which the judges, by virtue of the "independent spirit" that permanent tenure instilled, were to serve as "bulwarks of a limited Constitution against legislative encroachments" (Hamilton, 1787/1961).

To implement their vision of an independent judicial branch, the first Congress established a tier of district courts with original jurisdiction—one to a state, with one judge per district. The judicial districts were grouped into three regional circuits and the circuit courts, which possessed a combination of original and appellate jurisdiction, were to be staffed by ex officio district judges and Supreme Court justices. At the apex of the new court system was the Supreme Court, the size of which was set at six justices to make two justices available to ride each of the three circuits. In short, the size of the various courts was dictated by the logic of the court structure Congress had created.

Logical though the structure may have been, Congress did not emerge from this process to the sound of huzzahs and champagne corks. "We are in our house totally incompetent to such a business," complained Representative Thomas FitzSimons (Marcus, 1992, p. 400),[8] and legislators made it clear that the number and configuration of the courts it had established in 1789 were likely to change. "It is pregnant with difficulties," said Madison of the Act, and "the most that can be said in its favor is that it is the first essay, and in practice will surely be an experiment" (Marcus, 1992, p. 491).[9]

The "Midnight Judges Act" of 1801, and Its Repeal in 1802

Madison's "experiment" went ka-blam in 1801. It was then that outgoing President John Adams appeared to create an opportunity to pack the federal courts with lame-duck Federalist partisans and thereby avoid relinquishing all federal power to the incoming Jeffersonian Republicans, who had captured the White House and both houses of Congress in the election of 1800. The 1801 legislation, which had in fact been under serious consideration well before the Federalists' fall from power was imminent, had a number of features that, in retrospect, seem quite sensible.[10] Chief among the legislation's virtues was its prescience in recognizing that circuit riding would become increasingly onerous for the Supreme Court as the nation expanded westward and that the staffing needs of the circuit courts were better served by a separate tier of permanently assigned circuit court judges armed with appellate jurisdiction.

Unfortunately, the race to pass the legislation after the Federalists had lost the election and fill judgeships the Act created before they left office made the partisan motivations underlying the legislation seem transparent. Jeffersonian Republicans did not look smilingly on these developments and pressed for repeal of the 1801 Act soon after they took office. Federalist legislators challenged the constitutionality of such a move. "Can you repeal a law establishing an inferior court under the Constitution?" inquired Senator Uriah Tracy. "Will it be said that although you cannot remove the judge from office, yet you can remove his office from him?" In Tracy's view, "we can, with propriety, model our judiciary system, so that we always leave the judges independent," but "if we can, by repealing a law, remove them, they are in the worst state of dependence" (History of Congress, 1802, January 12, p. 57). Jeffersonian Republicans, of course, thought differently. Senator George Mason observed that Article III gave Congress discretionary power to establish inferior courts but not the Supreme Court because "the Supreme Court was considered by the framers of the Constitution, as established by the Constitution, while they considered the inferior courts as dependent upon the will of the Legislature." Analogizing the lower courts to a bridge that Congress is authorized to build and dismantle, Mason likened an inferior court judge to a bridge toll-taker "who receives the promise of an annual payment as long as he discharges his duties faithfully." "If a flood comes and sweeps away the bridge," Mason asked with rhetorical flourish, "will the toll-taker, like the judge, contend that though the bridge is gone . . . he shall, notwithstanding, receive his compensation for life, though he cannot continue those services for which his annual stipend was to be the compensation and reward?" (History of Congress, January 12, 1802, pp. 59, 62).

Angry Jeffersonians seized the day and repealed the Act. In *Stuart v. Laird* (1803), a seemingly intimidated Supreme Court approved the 1802 Act's reintroduction of circuit riding on the grounds that 12 years of acquiescence to the practice prior to 1801 validated it as a matter of custom and pretended that the constitutionality of removing judges by means other than impeachment had never been briefed, ignoring the issue altogether (see also Geyh & Van Tassel, 1998, pp. 84-85).

When sorting through the rubble of the events of 1801 and 1802 in search of threats to judicial independence, latter day analyses have naturally tended to focus on the 1802 repeal. The repeal, after all, effected a partisan-motivated, constitutionally suspect removal of judges, and emboldened a victorious Senator William Giles to claim in the aftermath of the repeal that "the theory of three distinct departments is . . . not critically correct . . . although it is obvious that the framers of our Constitution proceeded upon this theory in its formation." As far as he was concerned, "the word *independent* as applied to the judiciary . . . is not . . . justified by the Constitution" because the judiciary lacked the power "to organize itself and to execute the peculiar functions assigned to it without aid, or in other words, independent of any other department" (Annals of Congress, 1808, pp. 114-115). Observers at the time, however, tended to take a winner's view of history and pointed to the partisan court packing of the Midnight Judges Act as the independence-threatening catalyst for the 1802 repeal, which merely restored equilibrium and reinstated the structure of the 1789 Act, that for its part, gradually came to be revered as an almost holy document.

Expanding the Circuit System Westward in the 1820s and 1830s

By demonizing the Midnight Judges Act, Congress created a precedent against precipitous reform of the judiciary, including but not limited to court packing, that would influence the future of court reform from that point forward. Even though the geographical expanse of the western states made riding the circuits that embraced those states increasingly impracticable, the lesson of 1801 made Congress unwilling to deviate significantly from the road paved by the 1789 Act. Over the course of the 1820s and 1830s, Congress rejected alternative proposals to create a tier of intermediate appellate courts, or to staff the western circuits differently than the eastern, ultimately opting in favor of simply extending the existing circuit system westward. Senator Martin Van Buren offered a widely shared explanation as to why.

If there be a case in which, more than any other, the hand of innovation should be watched with lynx-eyed jealousy, this is surely that case. A total change was made in 1801, but the measure met with a total overthrow in one short year. Strong as the feelings then produced were, time and experience have demonstrated the wisdom of the Act of 1802, by which the system of 1789 was restored and improved. (Register of Debates, 1826, p. 414)

Understanding the gradual emergence of a precedent against court packing in the aftermath of the 1801 and 1802 fiasco requires an appreciation for the relationship between this relatively discrete precedent and a much broader one that eschewed precipitous, short-sighted court reform in favor of a conservative, sometimes timid, incrementalist approach born of founder worship and respect for the enterprise of implementing constitutional structure. For it was the development of this broader custom of reverence for longstanding structural stability, from which a rejection of ends-justifies-the-means court reform followed naturally, that made politically motivated court packing increasingly untenable. Representative Thomas Crawford's (Register of Debates, 1830) almost lyrical denunciation of experimental court reform in 1830 captured the early essence of this emerging theme.

When, therefore a plan has been happily laid in our land, which, in its execution commands the public confidence, and so ensures obedience to its decrees, will prudence, will the careful watchfulness that belongs to our stations allow us to leave that road that we have found so smooth and fragrant from the flowers that have bloomed along its sides, and to enter upon an unbeaten way that may lead us into miry and swampy ground? (p. 571)

Reducing the Size of the Supreme Court in 1866

From 1789 to 1866, the Supreme Court's size remained firmly soldered to the number of regional circuits Congress created: Having started with six, in 1807 Congress added a seventh justice to ride a circuit comprised of the recently admitted western states; in 1837, it added two more circuits and two more justices, for a total of nine; and in 1863, a tenth justice was added to ride a tenth circuit. Then, in 1866, Congress enacted legislation that would reduce the number of circuits from ten to nine and decrease the size of the Supreme Court to seven. In so doing, it did not ham-handedly obliterate judicial offices and with them the office holders, as its predecessor Congress had done in 1802 with the newly appointed circuit judges; rather, it provided for reduction to seven by attrition.

Even so, a reduction to seven, just three years after the number had been increased to ten, raises the specter of court unpacking. Opinions differ as to whether this was in fact the case. Frankfurter and Landis (1928) say yes: The move was designed by an overwhelmingly Republican Congress to deprive Democratic President Andrew Johnson of the opportunity to make appointments that could influence the balance of power on the Supreme Court (p. 172). Charles Fairman (1971) concludes no: The reduction was made at the behest of Chief Justice Salmon Chase, who hoped to trade a drop in Supreme Court workforce for an increase in the remaining justices' salaries (pp. 167-168).

The essential point for purposes here, however, is that speculation is so open because the legislative record is so spare. Senator Lyman Trumbull introduced the measure on the Senate floor as an amendment to legislation on configuration of the circuits that had originated in the House. The Senate approved the amendment with literally no explanation for the reduction and no debate of its merits (Congressional Globe, 1866, pp. 3698-3699). When the bill returned to the House and the Senate amendment was considered, Representative John Wentworth inquired as to whether it would eliminate a vacancy on the Court for which a nomination was then pending and Representative Wilson replied in the affirmative, adding that "I know that a number of the members of the Supreme Court think it will be a vast improvement" (Fairman, 1971, p. 169). And that is about it. The House accepted the amendment and President Johnson signed the legislation into law.

Unlike every other piece of legislation discussed in this chapter, deliberation preceding adoption of the amendment to reduce the size of the Court from nine to seven was so truncated that no conclusive inferences can be drawn as to Congress's underlying motivations. Although Trumbull must have had his reasons, he proposed the amendment to his colleagues for adoption sans rationale, and given the paucity of discussion, it is altogether likely that they obligingly approved it as proposed—sans rationale. The 1866 Supreme Court reduction may thus be better characterized as an example of "sneak legislation" akin to the 1875 creation of general federal question jurisdiction, which was likewise insinuated into a court improvements bill as an unexplained, undebated 11th hour amendment, rather than as an example of court-packing legislation akin to the Midnight Judges Act (Chadbourn & Levin, 1942).

Increasing the Size of the Supreme Court and Establishing Nine Permanent Circuit Court Judgeships in 1869

Like Ravel's *Bolero,* the docket of the Supreme Court experienced a relentless crescendo throughout the 19th century that gradually made circuit riding in the justices' "spare time" a virtual impossibility. Even so, Congress's inherent conservatism on the issue of judicial reform remained entrenched and when Senate Judiciary Committee Chairman Lyman Trumbull reintroduced legislation to create an intermediate court of appeals in the 1860s, the proposal went nowhere (Frankfurter & Landis, 1928, pp. 70-71).[11] Senator Eugene Casserly explained Congress's persistent unwillingness to pursue significant reform in terms of its reluctance to abandon "a system under which the country has grown up and under which its jurisprudence has been formed"; given "the remarkable growth of the nation," Casserly conceded that "an accession to the judicial workforce of the Union is required," but argued that "such accession should be made at the expense of as little disturbance as possible to the existing system" (Congressional Globe, 1869, March 23, p. 213). Representative Michael Kerr linked Congress's institutional conservatism vis-à-vis the courts to its constitutional duty to preserve judicial independence. Maintaining the judiciary's "absolute purity and independence," he asserted, "is the surest anchorarge of our system of government against the encroachments of the other departments," for which reason "we should look with distrust upon any proposition materially to alter it" (Congressional Globe, 1869, March 29, p. 341).

Against this backdrop, Trumbull introduced a measure that, as ultimately adopted, would create one permanent circuit judgeship for each of the nine circuits but leave circuit court jurisdiction otherwise unchanged; restore the historical parity that had existed between the size of the Supreme Court and the number of circuits, by increasing the number of justices on the Court from seven to nine; and reduce but not eliminate the justices' circuit-riding obligations. He defended this proposal on the grounds that it "leaves the judiciary system of the United States just as we found it" (Congressional Globe, 1869, March 23, p. 208). Even then, some were concerned. The customary respect for an independent judiciary that had long counseled against precipitous court packing of the kind undertaken in 1801 would likewise foreclose precipitous court unpacking of the sort employed in 1802 and thereby render the pending legislation irreversible, once enacted. "After these judges are once appointed," declared Senator Charles Buckalew, "you cannot reduce the number. Their tenure of office is during good behavior," he noted. "[Y]ou cannot reduce the number, and thus retrace the steps which you have taken. Therefore an increase in the number of these judges ought to be made upon great deliberation" (Congressional Globe, 1869, February 23, p. 1487). Supporters and opponents of the 1869 legislation agreed that when it came to restructuring the courts, Congress was engaged in the semipermanent exercise of retooling the constitutional framework—an exercise members of Congress understood to demand a unique measure of restraint (Congressional Globe, 1869, March 23, p. 208).[12] When Trumbull suggested somewhat defensively that Congress could later abolish the circuit courts if they turned out to be a bad idea, Senator George Edmunds replied that reducing the size of the federal bench "by the operation of nature" was the only acceptable method of attrition, which in Edmunds view provided the means by which his own proposal to double the size of the Supreme Court to 18 (with one half at any given time sitting qua Court and the other half riding circuit) could be remedied if it proved unworkable. Trumbull, doubtful that the "operation of nature" would work swiftly enough, asked Edmunds, "Do they die daily?" to which Edmunds retorted, "It is much better to diminish the number of judges by letting them die daily, or as often as they get an opportunity," than to "undertake a legislative revolution, and fly in the face of the substance and spirit of the Constitution by legislating bodily out of existence nine men whom you have appointed and who the Constitution declares shall hold their offices during good behavior" (Congressional Globe, 1869, March 23, p. 216).

Although Trumbull was handed his hat for suggesting that Congress was at liberty to abolish the judgeships his proposal would create, at the end of the day, Trumbull's bill proved to be the least disruptive of the plans designed to alleviate the workload of the Supreme Court. And a preference for nondisruptive, incremental reform remained an enduring legacy of the debacle of 1801-1802. Edmunds' alternative was rejected, precisely because it smacked of radical change and raised the troubling issue of whether Congress had the constitutional power to prevent half the justices of the Supreme Court from sitting on the Court at any given time. Senators such as Casserly were unwilling to "vex posterity" in "so delicate a matter as the construction of the highest tribunal in the country," by "leav[ing] a fundamental question of constitutional power to be a trouble and an obstruction to the members of that court and to the validity of its decisions for all time" (Congressional Globe, 1869, March 23, p. 214).

At the conference that gave rise to the chapters in this volume, Professor Barry Friedman (2001) commented that "if you go back to Reconstruction, they . . . packed the courts . . . and had a gay old time with the judiciary." As to the relative gaiety of the moment, I defer to Professor Friedman's assessment; his observation with respect to court packing, however, is in tension with the point I have sought to make here, for which reason it is worth a second look. In a superb draft article on countermajoritarian criticism during Reconstruction, Professor Friedman identifies four events in support of his court-packing point. Three are enactments previously mentioned: the 1863 Act increasing membership on the Court to ten; the 1866 Act decreasing membership on the Court to seven; and the 1869 Act establishing permanent circuit judgeships and increasing membership on the Supreme Court to nine. The fourth is President Grant's appointment of two Supreme Court justices to fill vacancies created by the 1869 Act, for the purpose of overturning the unpopular decisions that the Court had rendered in the so-called legal tender cases.[13]

With respect to the three enactments, Professor Friedman's draft offers a finely nuanced analysis that readily concedes the viability of claims that these various adjustments to court size and structure were bona fide reforms, but simply points out that they can likewise be explained in terms of their consonance with the political agenda of the Reconstruction Congress. If court packing was its dominant motivation, however, Congress took great pains to conceal it behind alternating veneers of silence or professed commitment to incremental, apolitical court improvement. Given the Reconstruction Republicans' penchant for threatening the Supreme Court with annihilation whenever it suited their mood—a point Professor Friedman underscores—I find it curious that they would feel constrained to conceal their court-packing motives. Either court packing was not their dominant motivation or they recognized that their plans to court pack ran counter to established norms against such a practice and so needed to be obscured. If Reconstruction legislators did indeed pack and unpack the courts—and Professor Friedman presents a persuasive case that the unparalleled chutzpah of the Reconstruction Congress makes that conceivable—it may be better characterized as an exception to an evolving rule that would become increasingly manifest in the years to come.

With respect to Grant's two appointments to the Supreme Court in the legal tender cases, Harvard law professor Erwin Griswold made a critical point when assessing the precedential value of the event in the context of a congressional hearing on Franklin Roosevelt's court-packing plan, in 1937. "Modern research has tended to show that Grant knew the views of these two men on the legal tender question when he appointed them," he noted, which is "the basis for the assertion that President Grant 'packed' the Court." Critical to Griswold's analysis, however, was that "the vacancies were not created for the purpose of enabling Grant to appoint men whose views would affect the decision of a pending controversy," and "it is not 'packing' the Court to use Presidential judgment in filling vacancies which occur in due course" (*Reorganization of the Federal Judiciary*, 1937). A President's manipulation of judicial appointments may be at least as destructive of the Court's decisional independence as court packing, but as Griswold argued, that is *not* court packing—a point which Professor Friedman ultimately acknowledges. This is no small distinction. This chapter seeks to document the long-standing norm, custom, or precedent against congressional court packing. No comparable norm constrains presidents from filling (and in that sense "packing") the courts with ideological soul mates whom the president hopes will unravel infelicitous precedent.

Creating the Court of Appeals in 1891

Superficially, at least, Congress's time-honored custom of restrained, incremental court reform ended in 1891, when Congress jettisoned the circuit court system that had been in place, more or less, since 1789, replaced it with a comprehensive court of appeals structure, and infused the courts with additional judges. Incremental efforts to relieve the Supreme Court's docket throughout the 19th century had been a dismal failure: The 636 cases languishing on the Supreme Court's calendar in 1870—which the 1869 legislation had been calculated to address—had ballooned to 1,202 cases by 1880 (Congresional Record, 1882, May 1, p. 3464). More drastic reform was needed.

Even so, three qualifications are in order. First, despite the path-breaking character of the 1891 legislation, Frankfurter and Landis (1928, pp. 99-100) rightly credit Senator William Evarts, the Act's namesake, for making passage possible by amending the House bill in ways that "satisfied traditionalists": He kept the geographical configuration of the district and circuit courts as they were; kept the accretion of new circuit courts of appeals judges to a minimum; and instead of pulling the plug, left the moribund practice of circuit riding on life support.

Second, legislation sponsors took pains to emphasize that although the judicial structure created by the bill may have departed significantly from that which had been in place since the founding, the bill would nonetheless have received the blessings of the founders and remained, in that sense, a conservative reform. Representative William Culbertson, for example, observed that the founders "foresaw the coming greatness and grandeur of the United States," and conferred the authority to regulate the courts on Congress "for the purpose of enabling Congress to adapt the appellate jurisdiction of the court to the varying demands of the business . . . of the country, and to protect and shield that great tribunal from conditions which exist today."

Third, the Evarts Act was passed in the early stages of an escalating period of court-directed hostility that saturated floor debates on the bill. Although radical proposals to end life tenure, permit judicial recall, circumscribe judicial review, and strip the court of subject matter jurisdiction swirled about in the speeches of populists, progressives, unionists, and the popular press, Congress stayed a fundamentally conservative course. The court of appeals proposal won passage in part because it was sold as a means to end the "despotism" of the district courts decried by numerous legislators. As contrasted to other, independence-threatening means of promoting judicial accountability then being bandied about, the Evarts Act was independence *enhancing,* in that it made judges more accountable to each other by improving the judiciary's capacity to correct its own mistakes, thereby strengthening the independence of the judiciary as an institution.

In short, the watershed Evarts Act was adopted without Congress abandoning its long-standing reverence for structural stability and its preference for conservative court reform. To the contrary, the Evarts Act should be credited for taking the first step down a new path of incremental court reform that would dominate the 20th century. It was a path in which Congress sought to enhance judicial accountability not by undermining judicial autonomy but by systematically establishing an independent, self-regulating judiciary that, in 1922, would be authorized to govern itself with a conference of senior circuit judges; in 1934, would be authorized to promulgate its own procedural rules; in 1939, would be handed control of its budget and administration; in 1966, would be given a Federal Judicial Center to educate its judges and study its own problems; and in 1980, would be given explicit authority to administer discipline for judicial misbehavior. It was likewise a path that would leave increasingly little room for court packing.

Abolition of the Commerce Court in 1913

In 1910, the Taft administration urged the adoption of legislation that would create a Commerce Court comprised of five Article III judges with circuit court jurisdiction to hear appeals from railroad rate decisions of the Interstate Commerce Commission (ICC). The theory was that a single, specialized appellate court would be better able than the regional circuit courts to decide ICC appeals expeditiously, expertly, and without risk of intercircuit conflicts (Carpenter, 1918, p. 81). Congress complied unenthusiastically. Indeed, Representative William Adamson later explained that "[t]he creation of this Commerce Court was a great mistake . . . caused by the absence of our colleagues at a baseball game," whose presence on the House floor would have broken a tie vote on an amendment to delete the Commerce Court proposal from the President's legislative package to which it was affixed.

In the inaugural year of its nasty, brutish, and short existence, the Commerce Court lost what minimal support it once had: The general public was offended by the frequency with which it reversed decisions of the popular ICC (Dix, 1964, pp. 251-252); shippers lost interest when the Supreme Court declared that the Commerce Court lacked jurisdiction to hear their appeals from "negative" ICC orders dismissing ratemaking petitions (Dix, p. 248); and the railroads, which had developed a working relationship with the ICC, were indifferent to the intercession of a new, unfamiliar court (Dix, pp. 244-245).[14] And so Congress passed legislation to abolish the court. Taft vetoed the bill, with the explanation that he could not find "a single reason why the court should be abolished except that those who propose to abolish it object to certain of its decisions," which he likened to "a recall of the judiciary" that he "utterly opposed" (Congressional Record, 62nd Congress, p. 11908).

Representative Adamson took offense at President Taft's veto message and "emphatically . . . dissent[ed] from any statement . . . that the only argument urged against this court is that some of the decisions of the judges are wrong" (Congressional Record, 1913, September 3, p. 1208). To support his point, Adamson republished his original remarks in opposition to creation of the Commerce Court. Among his earlier arguments: (a) there were "so few cases in the past as to create no necessity for the court"; (b) the special expertise of the court is overstated because "it is not insisted by anybody that circuit judges will know any more while sitting in Commerce Court than when presiding on circuit"; and (c) if judges are appointed with an eye to their special expertise, it will be "men who know more about . . . consolidation of railroads, destruction of competition, and disregard of public right through long training as corporation lawyers. . . . If anybody doubts this, let him wait and see" (Congressional Record, 1913, September 3, pp. 4208-4209).

In the minds of Commerce Court critics, experience with the court in operation validated these three concerns. As to the court's inconsequential docket, "Decisions of the Supreme Court [depriving the Commerce Court of jurisdiction to hear appeals from "negative" ICC orders, for example] . . . have clarified the situation," Adamson noted, which ensured that "business of that character will be much less in the future than in the past" (Congressional Record-House, 1913, Sept. 13, p. 4208). Skepticism of the Commerce Court's special expertise was heightened by Supreme Court reversals in 10 of its first 12 cases on appeal from the Commerce Court, which prompted Representative Thetus Sims (Congressional Record, 1913, June 24) to observe derisively that "they have had uniformity of decision, I am ready to admit, but it is uniformity of error" (p. 2147). And as to the prediction that the Commerce Court would be biased in favor of the railroads, the suspicion appeared to be confirmed by a 1911 ICC report finding that "out of 27 cases passed upon by the Commerce Court, preliminary restraining orders or final decrees have been issued in favor of the railroads in all but seven cases, and of these only three are of any magnitude" (p. 59). These developments—occurring as they did against the backdrop of an ongoing impeachment investigation of Commerce Court Judge Robert Archbald on corruption charges—served to verify preexisting congressional concern that the court was, by its very nature, less than impartial. By 1913, Taft was gone from the White House, Congress acted to abolish the Commerce Court a second time, and President Wilson signed the bill into law.

Although one could argue that Congress unpacked the Commerce Court in much the same way as the Jeffersonian Republicans unpacked the circuit courts in 1802, there are three significant differences. First, there was more to the explanation for eliminating the Commerce Court than the political reality that the balance of decision-making power in Congress had shifted. Unlike the circuit courts of 1801, which never heard a case, it was the Commerce Court's performance on the job that confirmed preexisting suspicions and sealed its fate. Although one could argue that this difference simply makes the obliteration of the Commerce Court all the more independence threatening, such a conclusion needs to be qualified: Yes, the court was, in some sense, ended because its decisions were unpopular. But the reasons offered to abolish the court (with its decisions being introduced as evidence) were that the court was unnecessary, that it lacked the special expertise that was its raison d'etre, and that a specialized tribunal designed to second-guess the ICC would possess an inherent antiregulatory bias—reasons that linked abolition directly to improving judicial administration and arguably removed it from the definitional scope of court unpacking altogether.

Second, unlike the circuit courts of 1801, Congress never really conceptualized the Commerce Court as integral to the Article III judiciary. Historian George Dix (1964) argues persuasively that Congress thought of it instead as a sort of adjunct to the Interstate Commerce Commission that could be regulated out of existence without regard to the congressional ethic of restraint that the federal judiciary generally had come to enjoy over the course of the preceding century. Insofar as abolition of the Commerce Court politicized federal court disestablishment in ways unprecedented since 1802, it was not because Congress abandoned well-developed norms against politicizing federal court structure and size but because those norms were deemed less than fully applicable to this new, hybrid tribunal.

Third, and most important of all, despite the hybrid status of the Commerce Court itself, Congress recognized that the court was constituted of Article III judges, and unlike its 1802 predecessor, resisted the temptation to decommission the court's officeholders when it closed down the court. In the House, momentum to abolish the judgeships along with the court was considerable. "If the creation of these judgeships was a mistake, their continuance now will be equally a mistake," declared Representative Melville Kelly (Congressional Record-House, 1913, Sept. 8, p. 4540), who quoted Thomas Jefferson for the proposition that "The judiciary is a subtle corps of sappers and miners, constantly working to undermine the foundations of our confederated fabric," who "consider themselves secure" after "having found from experience that impeachment is an impracticable thing, a mere scarecrow" (Congressional Record-House, 1913, Sept. 8, p. 4541).

With the exception of this oblique reference, the relationship between the push to abolish judgeships in 1913 and 1802 went unappreciated in the House, which voted to expel the judges along with the Commerce Court. The Senate debates, however, were a different matter. Senator Hoke Smith, like Kelly in the House, favored elimination of the excess judges caused by abolition of the Commerce Court and saw no constitutional impediment to doing so: Congress "was given the power to say what inferior courts we should have and how many judges should be upon them . . . decreasing the number if Congress saw fit" (Congressional Record-Senate, 1913, October 3, p. 5410). Senator William Borah disagreed, suggesting that if Smith were right, legislators searching for an easy way to remove judges could bypass impeachment and simply abolish their stations. Smith denied that a legislator could "vote simply for the abolition of a particular circuit or of a particular district because his object was in that way simply to remove a judge," because "such conduct would be highly improper" and "would be violative of the spirit of the Constitution," although he stuck by his guns that Congress had the power to eliminate judgeships at will. "Exactly," Borah retorted. "Then we come back to the proposition . . . that the country will be glad to know, in view of this urgent propaganda for the recall of judges, that they need not wait for the slow process of impeachment or recall, but that they can call upon their Senators and Representatives to eliminate any man from the bench that they want off the bench. They can simply abolish his circuit, get him out, and recreate the circuit" (Congressional Record-Senate, 1913, October 3, pp. 5411-5412).

The debate then took a turn for the historical. For the framers, observed Senator Thomas Walsh, "independence of the judges was something which all parties at that time deemed of the very first consequence," which led him to conclude that "the legality of . . . this method of getting rid of obnoxious judges is open to the most serious doubt on constitutional grounds" (Congressional Record-Senate, 1913, October 3, p. 5414). In defense of abolishing the judgeships, Senator Smith pointed to the 1802 repeal of the Midnight Judges Act as precedent, noting that "Congress proceeded to abolish . . . those inferior courts that had been established, and with their abolition went out of office the men who had filled them. . . . So it is clear that power is with Congress" (Congressional Record-Senate, 1913, October 3, p. 5410).[15] Senator John Shields, however, regarded the 1802 Act as an exception to a different rule of considerably longer standing: "with [the 1802 Act] exception, for more than 100 years until this Act was introduced and passed by the House, it was never attempted to substitute a statute for the mode pointed out by the Constitution of removing judges by impeachment" (Congressional Record-Senate, 1913, October 3, p. 5415). Walsh agreed, adopting Justice Story's analysis of the 1802 Act as his own.

> The act may be asserted, without fear of contradiction, to have been against the opinion of a great majority of the ablest lawyers at the time; and probably now, when the passions of the day have subsided, few lawyers will be found to maintain the constitutionality of the act. No one can doubt the perfect authority of Congress to remodel their courts, or to confer or withdraw their jurisdiction at their pleasure, but the question is whether they can deprive judges of the tenure of their office and their salaries after they have once become constitutionally vested in them. (p. 5415)

The Senate voted against elimination of the judgeships. The House concurred, the Commerce Court was abolished, its judges were assigned to the circuit courts of appeal, and the norm against court unpacking was respected.

The Roosevelt Court-Packing Plan of 1937

Although rejection of President Roosevelt's court-packing plan is sometimes identified as the event that set a precedent against politically motivated adjustments to Court size, the preceding discussion would suggest that it is better characterized as the culminating development in a series of precedents spanning the previous 150 years. The story of the court-packing plan is sufficiently familiar to all that a thumbnail sketch should suffice.[16] The President was unhappy that the Supreme Court had invalidated New Deal legislation. On the disingenuous pretext that many federal judges were old and falling behind in their work, Roosevelt lit on a proposal originally developed in 1913 by then-Attorney General James McReynolds, who a quarter of a century later—as an aging Supreme Court justice who often voted against New Deal legislation—would be hoisted on the petard of his own invention. Roosevelt proposed that whenever a federal judge remained on the bench past the age of 70, the President be authorized to make an additional appointment. With respect to the Supreme Court, that would have enabled FDR to nominate six new justices. Congress held hearings. Justice Roberts, who had been one of the Court's 5-member majority that invalidated New Deal legislation, switched sides. Congress dropped the plan, and Justice Robert's change of heart was dubbed the "switch in time that saved nine."

Without disputing that the court-packing plan may have influenced Justice Roberts' epiphany (even though Roberts denied it to his grave), which in turn made implementation of the plan unnecessary, it is misleading to suggest that the plan would have been enacted had it not been for Roberts' change in vote. "The switch in time that saved the President a humiliating defeat in Congress" may be less memorable, but what it lacks in pithiness it makes up for in accuracy. Despite Roosevelt's popularity and the Supreme Court's unpopularity, the court-packing plan lacked majority public approval (Ross, 1994), won the support of surprisingly few Court critics (Ross, p. 309), and received a tepid welcome in Congress. Fellow conference participant and Professor William Ross, in his excellent study of populist and progressive court reform failures, offers an explanation for the demise of the court-packing plan that resonates nicely with the theme of this chapter.

> [The court-packing plan] ultimately failed because it contravened the respect for the judiciary so deeply engrained in the American character. . . . Roosevelt's calm and frequently repeated assertion that "the people are

with me"underestimated the profound esteem that "the people"accord to the Supreme Court as long as its decisions do not diverge too radically from popular opinion. As an Idaho farmer wrote to Roosevelt, the Supreme Court "is a judicial body . . . and is not a plow horse for or with anyone."

The incompatibility of the plan with what were by then well-established norms against court packing specifically and precipitous, independence-threatening court reform generally was recognized at the time by scholars who testified before Congress in opposition to the plan. Professor Erwin Griswold began his testimony with the "dull but instructive subject of precedents"and after surveying the history of Congressional adjustments to the size of the Supreme Court, concluded that

at their most they do not hold a candle to the present proposal. No one of them added more than two judges, and only once have as many as two places been added to the Court. And it cannot be shown that the dominant purpose in increasing the size of the Court was ever the desire to influence or control the results of its decisions. (*Reorganization of the Federal Judiciary,* 1937)

Even more striking were the extraordinary remarks of Raymond Moley, Newsweek editor and professor of public law at Columbia University. By opposing the court-packing plan in terms of its incompatibility with a constitutional custom of interbranch restraint, Moley's observation serves as an appropriate ending for this chapter, and an equally appropriate beginning for a more comprehensive exploration of customary independence.

A deliberate attempt by one branch of Government to weaken another has very few parallels in our history. And none of them is creditable. . . .

That way has always been open to the purposes of any dominant Executive and congressional majority. But the very fact that it has not been employed, except in one or two cases of which we are not very proud, has established an inhibition upon the use of this method—an inhibition based upon custom and tradition. In other words, a custom has been established that fundamental changes should not be so attained—a custom of the Constitution, or a doctrine of political stare decisis, if you will, which is as binding upon public officials as a written provision of the Constitution itself. . . . The maintenance of the custom of the Constitution is essential to the preservation of a stable Government under which people are able to plan their lives and direct their actions. It is true that the custom of the Constitution changes, but it changes slowly and its existence is an indispensable element in a democratic government. (*Reorganization of the Federal Judiciary*, 1937)

Conclusion

In this chapter I have attempted to explain why and how we should devote more time to customary independence. The discussion of the emergence and development of norms against court packing and unpacking is illustrative of the kind of work that might profitably be done. By giving the understudied subject of customary independence the attention it deserves, we will improve our understanding of judicial independence and in so doing may create an opportunity to refocus the independence-accountability debate for those involved. For me, that's more than enough to make it worth our time to pursue.

In advocating further research into customary independence, however, I need to be careful not to overstate my case. First, unless Congress revises its rules to require that its constitutional customs be articulated explicitly and authoritatively (which is unlikely to happen anytime soon), customary independence will remain inherently indistinct at some level, and when that level is reached, efforts to make it otherwise will be as messy and futile as undertaking to tattoo soap bubbles. We thus cannot hope to make customary independence *perfectly* distinct; we can only make it more so. Second, the disputants in the independence-accountability debate may remain utterly unmoved by efforts to clarify the role that customary independence ought to play. By elevating the profile of customary independence through intensified study, we can only provide the water. The rest is up to the horse.

Exporting these caveats into the court-packing context, I must be careful not to suggest that norms against court-packing proposals have become so entrenched as to prevent them from gaining a purchase. For example, legislation to split the Ninth Circuit has been introduced in recent years by legislators from the Pacific Northwest who have no history of interest in judicial administration but whose constituents would benefit by a gerrymandering of their states into a separate circuit populated by judges more sympathetic to the timber industry. Even so, it is noteworthy that the sponsors' timber industry sympathies have been used as a weapon by bill opponents to condemn the legislation as invidious court re-packing, while doe-eyed sponsors have protested that sound judicial administration is their only goal (Banks, 2000; Tobias, 1995). The norm against court packing thus remains an 800-pound gorilla in the court reform arena that legislators may enlist as an ally, struggle to avoid, but cannot ignore.

∽ Notes

1. I say that an empirical study might "conceivably"address such an issue because I am frankly hopeful that the number of victimized judges remains insufficient to form an adequate study sample. For a discussion of past episodes in which threats of impeachment influenced judges' decisions to resign or retire, see Van Tassel (1993).

2. I do not pretend to suggest that this initial swipe at defining constitutional custom is adequate to the long-term task of fully exploring customary independence. To develop the definitional contours of custom more completely, at least two analogs might logically be pursued: the use of custom in international law and in the law of Great Britain. See Janis, 1988 (discussing the definition and role of custom in international law); and Wilson, 1992 (describing constitutional conventions in Great Britain, and arguing for their application in the United States).

3. U.S. Constitution, Art. III, §1.

4. Ibid.

5. Specifically, "they observed that there was a distinction between establishing such tribunals absolutely and giving a discretion to the Legislature to establish or not establish them."

6. Quoting members of Congress.

7. Notes of observation made by Delegate John Dickinson.

8. Letter from Thomas FitzSimons to Benjamin Rush (June 2, 1789).

9. Letter from James Madison to Samuel Johnson (July 31, 1789).

10. Indeed, it is not at all clear that the 1801 Act would have encountered a similar fate had it been acted upon earlier.

11. Characterizing the Trumbull bill as "premature."

12. According to a statement by Senator Williams, "In amending the judiciary system of the United States it is necessary . . . to proceed with great deliberation, for the reason that whenever we do agree to any amendment, the system which that amendment establishes is fastened upon the country and is entirely beyond our reach"); in a statement by Senator Conkling, "this bill becoming law, during the lifetime of men now living no great change is likely to occur in the judicial system and the judicial staff of the United States. Therefore, it is, in the present and in the future, a subject of very grave importance"(id. p. 211); in statement by Senator Edmunds, "We ought not make haste to adopt this new method, this new system, but rather, if there be a difference of opinion upon it, take time to reflect, so that a system when adopted under our constitution is a final one, at least for many years, may be thoroughly considered before it is put into operation"(id. p. 214).

13. For a brief, but published analysis, leading a different author to similar conclusions, see White, 1996.

14. "Faced with the inevitability of restrictions of some sort, the roads seemed to have accepted regulation by the Commission as preferable to regulation by the individual states or the federal judiciary."

15. Senator Williams concurred with Smith to the extent of adding that Chief Justice Marshall himself conceded the validity of the repeal in private conversations. Williams was more cautious than Smith, however, noting that Congress's authority to abolish judgeships derived from its power to abolish the court to which the judges were appointed; in this case the judges had technically been appointed as circuit judges, not Commerce Court judges per se, which led Williams to doubt whether Congress could eliminate a circuit judgeship without abolishing the circuit court. Id. pp. 5410-5411.

16. For an exhaustive discussion of the events leading up to the court-packing plan, including those summarized below, see Kline, 1999.

⟳ References

17 Annals of Congress, 114-115 (1808).

A native of Virginia, observations upon the proposed plan of federal government. (1990). In J. P. Kaminski & G. J. Saladino (Eds.), *The documentary history of the ratification of the Constitution* (pp. 655, 686-687). Madison: State Historical Society of Wisconsin. (Original published 1788, May 17)

Banks, C. (2000, July/August). The politics of court reform in the U.S. Court of Appeals. *Judicature, 84,* 34-43.

Burbank, S. (1998). The architecture of judicial independence. *Southern California Law Review, 72,* 315-351.

Carpenter, W. S. (1918). *Judicial tenure in the United States, with special reference to the tenure of federal judges.* p. 81. New Haven, CT: Yale University Press.

Chadbourn, J., & Levin, A. L. (1942). Original jurisdiction of federal questions. *University of Pennsylvania Law Review, 90,* 639-674.

Collins, M. (1995). Article III cases, state court duties, and the Madisonian compromise. *Wisconsin Law Review,* 39-197.

Congressional Globe, July 10, 1866.

Congressional Globe, February 23, 1869.

Congressional Globe, March 23, 1869.

Congressional Globe, March 29, 1869.

Congressional Record, 62d Congress.

Congressional Record, May 1, 1882.

Congressional Record, June 24, 1913.

Congressional Record, September 3, 1913.

Congressional Record-House, September 13, 1913.

Congressional Record-Senate, October 3, 1913 at 5410.

ICC Report, 1911.

Dix, G. (1964). Death of the commerce court: A study in institutional weakness. *American Journal of Legal History, 8,* 238-260.

Fairman, C. (1971). VI History of the Supreme Court of the United States: Reconstruction and reunion, 1864-88.

Frankfurter, F., & Landis, J. (1928). *The business of the Supreme Court.* New York: Macmillan.

Geyh, C. G., & Van Tassel, E. F. (1998).The independence of the judicial branch in the new republic. *Chicago-Kent Law Review, 74,* 31-89.

Glennon, M. J. (1984). The use of custom in resolving separation of powers disputes. *Boston University Law Review, 64,* 109-148.

Hamilton, A. (1961). *The Federalist No. 78.* (C. Rossiter, Ed.). (Original published, June 14, 1788)

History of Congress, January 12, 1802.

History of Congress, January 13, 1802.

Janis, M. (1988). *An introduction to international law, 3rd Ed.* 35-46. Boston: Aspen.

Kline, S. O. (1999). Revisiting FDR's court packing plan: Are the current attacks on judicial independence so bad? *McGeorge Law Review, 30,* 863-954.

Madison, J. (1911). Notes. In Max Farrand (Ed.), *2 Records of the Federal Convention of 1787*. (Original published 1787, June 5).

Marcus, M. (Ed.). (1992). *4 Documentary History of the Supreme Court of the United States, 1789-1800*.

Register of Debates, April 17, 1826, p. 414.

Register of Debates, February 17, 1830, p. 571.

Reorganization of the Federal Judiciary: Hearings on S. 1392 Before the Comm. On the Judiciary of the U.S. Senate, 75th Cong. 760, 763 (1937).

Ross, W. (1994). *A muted fury: Populists, progressives, and labor unions confront the courts, 1890-1937*. Princeton, NJ: Princeton University Press.

Stuart v. Laird, 5 U.S. (1 Cranch) 299, 309 (1803).

Tobias, C. (1995). The impoverished idea of circuit-splitting. *Emory Law Journal, 44*, 1357-1416.

Van Tassel, E. F. (1993). Resignations and removals: A history of federal judicial service—and disservice—1789-1992. *University of Pennsylvania Law Review, 142*, 333-430.

White, G. W. (1996). Salmon Portand Chase and the judicial culture of the Supreme Court in the Civil War Era. In J. M. Lowe (Ed.), *The Supreme Court and the Civil War*. Washington, DC: Supreme Court Historical Society.

Wilson, J. G. (1992). American constitutional conventions: The judicially enforceable rules that combine with judicial doctrine and public opinion to regulate political behavior. *Buffalo Law Review, 40*, 645-738.

Part IV

COMPARATIVE DIMENSIONS

Selecting
Selection Systems

Lee Epstein
Jack Knight
Olga Shvetsova

෬ Introduction

Of all the difficult choices confronting societies when they go about designing legal systems, among the most controversial are those pertaining to judicial selection and retention: How ought a nation select its judges and for how long ought those jurists serve? Indeed, some of the most fervent constitutional debates—whether they transpired in Philadelphia in 1787 (Epstein & Walker, 2000; Farber & Sherry, 1990) or in Moscow in 1993 to 1994 (Blankenagel, 1994; Hausmaninger,

This is a revised version of a paper written for the conference on Judicial Independence at the Crossroads: Developing an Interdisciplinary Research Agenda, Philadelphia, PA, March 31-April 1, 2001. We thank the Center for New Institutional Social Science for supporting our research on judicial selection. We also are grateful to Larry Baum, Greg Caldeira, Jim Gibson, Micheal Giles, and Thomas G. Walker for counsel tendered at the early stages of this project; to Jeff Staton for research assistance; and to Gary King for his technical suggestions. Please email comments to Epstein at epstein@artsci.wustl. edu. We used SPSS and STATA to analyze the data. http://www.artsci.wustl.edu/~polisci/epstein/research houses all data and documentation necessary for replication.

1995)—over the institutional design of the judicial branch implicated not its power or competencies; they involved who would select and retain its members.[1]

Why institutions governing selection and retention engender such controversy is an interesting question, with no shortage of answers.[2] But surely a principal one is that political actors and the public alike believe these institutions will affect the types of men and women who will serve and, in turn, the choices they, as judges, will make (e.g., Brace & Hall, 1993; Bright & Kennan, 1995; Goldman, 1997; Gryski, Main, & Dixon, 1986; Hall, 1984a; Hall, 1987; Hall & Brace, 1992; Langer, 1998; Levin, 1977; Peltason, 1955; Pinello, 1995; Sheldon & Maule, 1997; Tabarrok & Helland, 1999; Vines, 1962; Volcansek & Lafon, 1988). Some commentators, for example, assert that providing judges with life tenure leads to a more independent judiciary—one that places itself above the fray of ordinary politics (e.g., Croly, 1995; Segal & Spaeth, 1993; Stevens, 1995; Wiener, 1996)—whereas those subjecting justices to periodic checks conducted by the public or its elected officials leads to a more accountable one. Seen in this way, not only are institutions governing the selection of judges fundamental to discussions of judicial independence, they also convey important information about the values societies wish to foster (Gavison, 1988; Grossman & Sarat, 1971; Haynes, 1944).

And possibilities for choice abound. To be sure, many nations, typically those using the civil law system, have developed similar methods for training and "choosing" ordinary judges. But they depart from one another rather dramatically when it comes to the selection of constitutional court justices. In Germany, for example, justices are selected by Parliament, though 6 of the 16 must be chosen from among professional judges; in Bulgaria, one third of the justices are selected by Parliament, one third by the president, and one third by judges sitting on other courts. Moreover, in some countries with centralized judicial review, justices serve for a limited time. In South Africa, for instance, they hold office for a single 12-year term, in Italy a single 9-year term. In others, including the Czech and both Korean Republics, justices serve for a set, albeit renewable, term.

Variation is even present in societies that grew out of similar legal traditions and created their court structures at roughly the same historical moment. Table 9.1, which depicts the *formal* institutions governing the selection of constitutional court judges in the former republics of the Soviet Union, makes this clear: The republics took at least 5 different approaches: (a) executive-legislative parity (each able to appoint a specified number of judges); (b) executive-judicial (along with, in some instances, legislative) parity; (c) executive nomination (usually) with legislative confirmation; (d) executive-legislative-judicial parity in nomination with parliamentary confirmation; (e) judicial appointment.

Variation is not, of course, limited to societies elsewhere. Although the president nominates and the Senate confirms all federal U.S. judges, who then go on to serve during good behavior, institutions governing the selection of U.S. state

TABLE 9.1.   Selection Systems Used in the Former Republics of the Soviet Union

Lithuania	*Latvia*	*Estonia*
Parity in nomination: president, the chairs of Parliament and Supreme Court. Appointed by Parliament. * * * * Nonrenewable 9-year term	3 nominated by Parliament; two each by the Cabinet of Ministers and Supreme Court. Appointed by Parliament. * * * * Nonrenewable 10-year term	Nominated by the chief justice of Supreme Court. Appointed by Parliament. * * * * Life tenure
Russia	*Belorussia*	*Ukraine*
Nominated by president. Appointed by upper chamber of Parliament. * * * * Was life tenure; changed to nonrenewable 12-year term	Parity in appointment. President and upper chamber of Parliament. * * * * 11-year renewable terms	Parity in appointment: Parliament, the president, an assembly of judges. * * * * Nonrenewable 9-year term
Georgia	*Armenia*	*Azerbaijan*
Parity in appointment. President, Parliament, Supreme Court. * * * * Nonrenewable 10-year term	Parity in appointment. Parliament and president. * * * * Life tenure	Nominated by president. Appointed by Parliament. * * * * 10-year renewable terms (a)
Moldova	*Kazakhstan*	*Uzbekistan*
Parity in appointment. Parliament, the president, and Magistracy. * * * * 6-year renewable terms (a)	Parity in appointment. President, chairs of Upper and Lower Houses. * * * * Nonrenewable 6-year term but half members must be renewed every 3 years	Nominated by president. Appointed by Parliament. * * * * Nonrenewable 5-year term
Tajikistan	*Turkmenistan*	*Kyrgyzstan*
Nominated by president. Appointed by Parliament. * * * * Nonrenewable 5-year term	Nominated and appointed by president. * * * * 5-year term but president can remove before completion	Nominated by president. Appointed by Parliament. * * * * Nonrenewable 15-year term

NOTES: This table displays countries via a (very rough) geographical mapping.

(a) Different procedures may be used for nomination and appointment of the chief justice.

judges differ from each other and usually from those for federal jurists. Today, the states follow one of five basic plans—partisan elections, nonpartisan elections, gubernatorial appointment, legislative appointment, the merit plan[3]—though the intraplan differences (especially the terms of office) may be as great as those among them.

Not only do practices in the U.S. states shore up the degree of variation in selection and retention institutions but they also demonstrate the malleability of those institutions: Virtually every state in the Union has altered its selection system at one time or another.[4] And the same could be said of many countries. In some cases, change has come after decades of experimentation with a particular mechanism; in others, it has occurred with all deliberate speed. Such was Russia, where constitutional court justices appointed in 1991 could expect to hold their jobs for life, but those selected after the adoption of the new constitution in 1993 were granted only a single, limited term.

And yet, despite all this variation in selection and retention systems and their apparent malleability, scholars have (with the critical exception noted in the section dealing with the current literature below) devoted almost no time to addressing questions associated with institutional choice: Why do societies choose particular selection and retention institutions? Why do they formally alter those choices? Rather, literature on judicial selection is "imbalanced"—and, interestingly enough, in much the same way as is scholarship on electoral rules (Boix, 1999). Just as research on electoral laws tends to focus on their impact on political stability, voting behavior, and party systems (e.g., Duverger, 1954; Hermens, 1941; Rae, 1971), analyses of judicial selection systems center on whether the various institutions produce different kinds of judges (e.g., Alozie, 1990; Berg, Green, Schmidhauser, & Schneider, 1975; Canon, 1972; Champagne, 1986; Dubois, 1983; Flango & Ducat, 1979; Fund for Modern Courts, 1985; Glick, 1978; Glick & Emmert, 1987; Graham, 1990; Hall, 1984b; Jacob, 1964; Lanford, 1992; Nagel, 1973; O'Callaghan, 1991; Scheb, 1988; Tokarz ,1986; Watson & Downing, 1969) or lead judges to behave in different ways (e.g., Atkins & Glick, 1974; Brace & Hall, 1993; Bright & Kennan, 1995; Canon & Jaros, 1970; Domino, 1988; Gryski et al., 1986; Hall, 1984a; Hall, 1987, 1992; Hall & Brace, 1989, 1992; Langer, 1998; Lee, 1970; Levin, 1977; Nagel, 1973; O'Callaghan, 1991; Pinello, 1995; Schneider & Maughan, 1979; Stevens, 1995; Tabarrok & Helland, 1999; Vines, 1962). In other words, scholarship both on electoral laws and judicial selection mechanisms usually focuses on effects of the institution and not on the processes and causes of institutional creation and change.

To be sure, we understand the importance of investigating institutional effects; indeed, just as literature on electoral laws has uncovered regularities of consequence, so has scholarship on selection systems. In the case of electoral rules, as Boix (1999) writes, "the higher the entry barrier (or threshold) set by the electoral law, the more extensive strategic (or, more precisely, sophisticated) behavior will be" among voters and elites (p. 609). In the case of judicial selection and retention institutions, the greater the accountability established in the institution, the higher the opportunity costs for judges to act sincerely and thus, the more extensive strategic behavior will be (see, generally, Brace & Hall, 1993, 1997; Bright & Kennan, 1995; Croly, 1995; Gryski et al., 1986; Hall, 1984a; Levin, 1977; Pinello, 1995; Stevens, 1995; Tabarrok & Helland, 1999).[5]

But it is exactly these sorts of findings that underscore the need to address questions associated with the causes of institutional choice and change. For if social scientists and legal academics believe that institutions affect the behavior of actors, then surely the designers of those institutions believe the same. More to the point, they anticipate institutional effects and adopt those rules that conform best with their preferences.

In this chapter, we attempt to give these questions the attention they merit, first by evaluating what we take to be the primary reason why this research area has lain so dormant. The existence of the standard story of institutional adoption and change—a story that, as we explain below, scholars have told decade after decade without seriously questioning its conceptual and empirical underpinnings.

The results of this evaluation lead us to conclude that a new account is necessary and, in the second part of the chapter, we offer one. On our account, the creation of and changes in the institutions used to select justices serving on (constitutional) courts of last resort must be analyzed as a bargaining process between relevant political actors, with their decisions reflecting their relative influence, preferences, and beliefs at the moment when the new institution is introduced— along with (and critically so) their level of uncertainty about future political circumstances.

Among the interesting results our account yields is the following: As uncertainty increases, the probability of adopting (or changing to) institutions that lower the opportunity costs of justices (again, the political and other costs justices may incur when they act sincerely) also increases. In other words, political uncertainty produces selection mechanisms that many scholars associate with judicial independence (e.g., life tenure or long terms of office). Under certain conditions, the converse also holds: As uncertainty decreases, regimes may be more inclined to devise (or change) their institutions to increase judicial opportunity costs. This follows from the fact that the designers believe they will remain in power and, thus, hope to inculcate a beholden judiciary.

⌒ Current State of the Literature: The Standard Story of Judicial Selection Systems

Although the notion that institutional designers anticipate the effect of various rules and adopt those that serve their goals seems patently obvious, scholars have all but ignored it. In fact, as we suggest above, they have all but ignored virtually every important question associated with the choice of judicial selection and retention systems. Explaining this void is not difficult. For decades now, scholars—at least those studying practices in the United States[6]—have accepted what we can only call the standard story of judicial selection systems. On this explanation, the initial choice of judicial selection mechanisms (and alterations in that choice) comes about through changes in the tide of history, that is, of states "responding to popular ideas at different historical periods" (Glick & Vines, 1973, p. 40). More specifically, the standard story unfolds in four chapters or "phases" of change, during each of which groups of reformers sought to supplant one selection system with another with the supposed goal of creating a "better" judiciary (e.g., Berkson, 1980; Berkson, Beller, & Grimaldi, 1980; Brown, 1998; Bryce, 1921; Carbon & Berkson, 1980; Carrington, 1998; Champagne & Haydel, 1993; Elliott, 1954; Escovitz, Kurland, & Gold, 1975; Friedman, 1973; Glick & Vines, 1973; Goldschmidt, 1994; Grimes, 1998; Haynes, 1944; Hurst, 1950; Noe, 1997/1998; Roll, 1990; Scheuerman, 1993; Sheldon & Maule, 1997; Shuman & Champagne, 1997; Stumpf & Culver, 1992; Volcansek & Lafon, 1988; Watson & Downing, 1969; Webster, 1995; Winters, 1966, 1968; Witte, 1995)—with the term "better," although defined differently across time, always standing for some general societal benefit.

Chapter 1: The Revolutionary Period and Appointed Judiciaries

The standard story begins with the Revolutionary period, when—in response to a call in 1776 issued by the Continental Congress—many of the states turned to the task of drafting constitutions. Most of their knowledge about legal systems, of course, came from England, where for centuries judges held their positions at the pleasure of the king and their terms of office expired on the death of the sovereign who had appointed them. This dependence on royal favor frequently made for judicial subservience. But not until 1701 did the English Act of Settlement provide that judges should serve during good behavior, with removal contingent on parliamentary approval. And it was not until 1760 that judges' commissions did not expire on the death of the king who had appointed them.

The British belief in the value of an independent judiciary was transplanted to America and royal abuse of this principle was one of the grievances that gave a moral tinge to the Revolutionary cause. The Declaration of Independence accused George III of having "made Judges dependent on his Will alone, for the Tenure of their Offices, and the Amount and Payment of their Salaries."

It was the hostility toward any system enabling one individual to select and retain judges, on the standard story, that permeated constitution-drafting sessions in the states and in Philadelphia (e.g., Champagne & Haydel, 1993; Goldschmidt, 1994; Sheldon & Maule, 1997; Smith, 1976; Webster, 1995). Following this predilection could have led the states to adopt provisions calling for the election of judges. But none did[7]—at least not for members of their highest benches. Rather, in the aftermath of the Revolution, they all retained some form of appointment though, according to standard-story chroniclers, they attempted to diffuse power by giving legislatures either sole responsibility for judicial appointments (7 or 8 of the original 13 states)[8] or some role in them (5 or 6 of the 13); "most" also attempted to ensure judicial independence by guaranteeing judges virtual life tenure (see Elliott, 1954; Grimes, 1998; Sheldon & Maule, 1997; Volcansek & Lafon, 1988).

At the Philadelphia Constitutional Convention in 1787, the framers were presented with several plans for choosing federal judges. Those delegates (e.g., George Mason, Elbridge Gerry, and Oliver Ellsworth) who opposed a strong executive, wanted to follow the dominant state practice and vest appointing authority in Congress. Others (e.g., Alexander Hamilton, James Madison, and Gouverneur Morris) wanted the executive to appoint judges. It was Hamilton who first suggested that the president nominate and the Senate confirm *all* federal judges, but the Convention twice rejected this compromise before finally adopting it. Following British practice and that emerging in the states, the new Constitution provided that federal judges should serve during good behavior.

Chapter 2: Jacksonian Democracy and Elected Judiciaries

On the standard story, then, the design of the original selection and retention systems involved little more than common applications of procedures about which the designers believed they had knowledge of institutional effects. A similar perspective informs the story's explanation of the three key instances of institutional change.

Depending on the particular version of this story, the first change—a move toward the popular election of judges—came about as a result of Jefferson's charges in the early 1800s of a runaway, aristocratic, and unaccountable judiciary (Croly, 1995; Roll, 1990), Jackson's emphasis several decades later on the importance of broad popular participation in government (along with his hostility toward elitist judges produced by appointed systems) (e.g., Brown, 1998; Bryce, 1921; Escovitz et al., 1975; Webster, 1995), or both (Haynes, 1944; Hurst, 1950; Volcansek & Lafon, 1988). Mississippi was, in 1832, the first state to select all of its judges via partisan elections and from there "a democratic spirit swept the young nation"(Roll, 1990, p. 841)—one designed to force greater accountability of judges by broadening the base from which they would have to garner support.

Regardless of whether this "spirit" was "based on emotion rather than on a deliberative evaluation of experience under the appointive system"(Hurst, 1950, p. 140), it indeed seems to have engulfed the country. As standard-story chroniclers like to point out, (a) 19 of the 21 constitutional conventions held between 1846 and 1860 approved documents that adopted popular election for (at least some of) their judges; (b) by the time of the Civil War, 19 of the 34 states (Carpenter, 1918, p. 181) or 21 of 30 states (Hall, 1984a) or 21 of 34 (Grimes, 1998) or 22 of 34 (Elliott, 1954) or 24 of 34 (Escovitz et al., 1975; also see Note 8) had adopted elections (though not necessarily for all judges); and (c) every new state admitted to the Union between 1846 and 1912 provided for the election of (again, at least some) judges (Roll, 1990).

Chapter 3: Machine Politics and the Move to Nonpartisan Elections

Despite this apparently ringing endorsement of electoral mechanisms for judicial selection and retention, it was not long before a new tide began to rise. This one, according to the standard account, probably appeared as early as 1853 (Berkson et al., 1980), gained in strength right before the turn of the century (Noe, 1997/1998), and reached its zenith during the progressive movement (Carrington, 1998; Grimes, 1998; Webster, 1995). Such is hardly surprising because this new response took the form of a growing disdain for partisan judicial campaigns and all the politics those entailed. Especially distasteful to reformers and members of newly emerging local bar associations was the control political machines in many major cities exerted over the judicial selection process. Machine politics, they alleged, was causing citizens to view the judiciary as "corrupt, incompetent, and controlled by special interests" (Grimes, 1998, p. 2273).

According to the standard story, the states were quick to respond to this latest selection-mechanism backlash: In an effort to take "the judge out of politics," they began invoking nonpartisan ballots for judges. Cook County in Illinois was the first but states followed suit such that by 1927, 12 placed judges on the ballot without reference to their party affiliation (Carbon & Berkson, 1980).

Chapter 4: Legal Progressives and the Merit Plan

Although some reformers continued to push states to adopt nonpartisan ballots, others began deriding elections altogether. As early as 1906, in an oft cited speech before the American Bar Association, Roscoe Pound (1962) proclaimed that "putting courts into politics, and compelling judges to become politicians, in many jurisdictions has almost destroyed the traditional respect for the bench."[9] To Pound (joined several years later by William Howard Taft), not even nonpartisan elections satisfactorily removed judges from politics because they still had to campaign to attain and retain office. Others, too, became disenchanted with nonpartisan elections but for a different reason; namely, "candidates for judgeships [continued to be] regularly selected by party leaders and thrust upon an unknowledgeable electorate which, unguided by party labels, was not able to make reasoned choices" (Berkson et al., 1980; see also Belknap, 1992; Brown, 1998; Grimes, 1998; Webster, 1995; Winters, 1968).

A response to these concerns came in 1914, when Northwestern Law School professor and director of the newly formed American Judicature Society's research wing, Albert M. Kales (1914), offered what he called a "non-partisan court plan" (now often termed the merit or Missouri plan)—a compromise of sorts between post-Revolutionary mechanisms that stressed judicial independence and those of Jacksonian democracy that emphasized accountability (e.g., Champagne & Haydel, 1993; Sheldon & Lovrich, 1991). Under Kales's proposal, states create a judicial commission that nominates candidates solely on the basis of merit. From the commission's list, the state's chief justice (the only elected judicial office under the plan) selects judges, who later run in noncompetitive, nonpartisan retention elections (Belknap, 1992; Carbon & Berkson, 1980; Roll, 1990; Winters, 1968). A decade or so later, social scientist Harold Laski (1926) chimed in, suggesting various modifications to the Kales plan. He argued that the governor rather than the chief justice ought make the appointments from the commission's list. (Laski also opposed retention elections; he believed judges should have life tenure.)

In 1934, California became the first state to adopt a merit plan, though it differed rather markedly from the ones offered by Kales and Laski. Under California's adaptation, judges were to be appointed by the governor with the consent of a three-person commission (consisting of the chief justice, the presiding judge of a district court of appeal, and the attorney general)—in other words, a sort of merit plan in reverse. Three years later, the American Bar Association endorsed the more traditional version of merit selection,[10] which Missouri adopted in 1940. Under Missouri's scheme, a seven-member judicial commission sends a list of three candidates to the governor. After the governor makes a selection from the list, the judge's name appears on the ballot (unopposed) in the first general election after appointment; thereafter, at the end of each 12-year term, the judge runs unopposed on a nonpartisan retention ballot (see Note 3).

Over the next few decades, most states that changed their selection system moved toward to the merit plan.[11] They did so, at least according to the standard story, out of a belief that merit selection would transform "the general level of the judiciary, in terms of intelligence, integrity, legal ability and quality in performance" (Winters, 1968, p. 780).[12]

☙ An Evaluation of the Standard Account

The standard story has been told and retold so many times that to call it conventional wisdom is to undercharacterize its place in the sociolegal literature. It appears, in one version or another, in virtually every scholarly study of judicial selection (e.g., Brown, 1998; Carrington, 1998; Champagne & Haydel, 1993; Glick & Vines, 1973; Goldschmidt, 1994; Grimes, 1998; Haynes, 1944; Noe, 1997/1998; Roll, 1990; Scheuerman, 1993; Sheldon & Maule, 1997; Shuman & Champagne, 1997; Volcansek & Lafon, 1988; Watson & Downing, 1969; Webster, 1995; Witte, 1995); it forms the centerpiece of discussions of selection in nearly all contemporary judicial process texts (e.g., Carp & Stidham, 1998; Stumpf, 1998; Tarr, 1999); and it has even been repeated by judges in court opinions (e.g., *Smith v. Higinbothom*, 1946). It also is remarkably thin and, in many ways, remarkably misleading.

We are certainly not the first to level such charges. Despite the standard story's place in the literature, it has been the target of criticism—though much of it has come from studies of particular chapters in the story. Hall (1984a), for example, takes issue with the conclusion that "that broadened base of popular political power associated with Jacksonian Democratic party prompted [the] sweeping" move toward partisan elections (p. 347; see also Hall, 1983). Rather, he gives the credit (or blame) to the nation's lawyers, who believed that elections would maximize the prestige of judges (and, by implication, of themselves).[13] Likewise, Puro and her colleagues (1985)—implicitly taking issue with the standard story—argue that we must look toward diffusion "theory" to account for the "widespread" adoption of the Missouri plan. As they explain it, policy diffusion occurs between states that share common features. And though it was not clear to them from the onset which features would be relevant to the adoption of merit selection, they eventually learned that states with nonprofessional legislatures and relatively large urban populations found it most attractive.

These and other particular critiques may not be especially compelling but they do have the virtue of shoring up various gaps and weaknesses in the standard story. To us, the key shortcomings boil down to three: the omission of politics, the failure to consider political motives, and the lack of systematic empirical support.

Where's the Politics?

Despite scholarly recognition that the choice of judicial selection and retention mechanisms is inherently a political choice with political implications—or as Friedman (1985) puts it, "American statesmen were not naïve; they knew it mattered what judges believed and who they were. How judges were to be chosen and how they were to act was a political issue in the Revolutionary generation, at a pitch of intensity rarely reached before" (p. 124)—the standard account is notably devoid of politics. Rather, it views the choice of institutions (and changes in that choice) as a simple, nearly reflexive, response to some prevailing social sentiment that something is amiss in the judiciary.

Nothing could be further from political reality, as various accounts of debates in the states and, of course, in Philadelphia shore up. Earlier, we mentioned that, despite their experience with British practice, some of the framers wanted the executive to retain control of the judicial appointments. Debates in various states may have been more acrimonious (see, e.g., Ziskind, 1969); even the idea of life tenure was the cause of serious controversy in some. If Constitution drafters were merely responding to social conditions, it is hard to explain ensuing disagreements at the founding period as well as at virtually all other points in history when states considered amending their institutions (e.g., Averill, 1995; Brinkley, 2000; Grimes, 1998; Noe, 1997/1998; Orth, 1992; Pelander, 1998; Roll, 1990; Smith, 1951; Wooster, 1975).

And such debates continue today. So, for example, as Champagne (1988) tells us, when the chief justice of Texas proposed that his state move from partisan elections toward a merit plan (which would have included Senate confirmation of candidates), opposition came from all quarters, including minorities and women, who thought it would lead to the appointment of white, male judges; plaintiffs' attorneys, who wanted to continue to contribute to the coffers of judicial candidates; and both political parties, though for different reasons. The proposal, almost needless to write, was a nonstarter.

Where Are the Political Motives?

Champagne's account, along with many others (e.g., Averill, 1995; Grimes, 1998; Noe, 1997/1998; Orth, 1992; Pelander, 1998; Roll, 1990; Smith, 1951; Wooster, 1975), suggests another, perhaps even more important (though related) weakness in the standard story: It assumes that, at each point in history, the relevant actors all held rather noble goals, whether to create (a) an independent judiciary (our nation's founders), (b) a more accountable judiciary (Jefferson, Jackson, and state governors and legislators), (c) a less politicized judiciary (the Progressives and state governors and legislators), (d) a more meritorious one (Pound and state governors and legislators), or (e) some combination thereof. No one in this story, or so it seems, is out for their own individual political gain.

Again, specific accounts of the various relevant actors work to undermine this rather naïve picture. Consider Thomas Jefferson, who, under the standard story, pushes for an elected judiciary (or at least a system in which judges must be reappointed every six years by the president and both houses of Congress) to further democratic principles. To support this view, standard-story tellers often point to a letter Jefferson wrote in 1820: "Our judges are as honest as other men, and not more so. They have, with others, the same passions for party, for power, and the privilege of their corps. Their maxim is *boni judicis est ampliare jursidctionem,* and their power the more dangerous as they are in office for life, and not responsible, as the other functionaries, to the elective control" (Lipscomb, 1903, p. 276). And yet, Jefferson never expressed such democratic fervor prior to his presidency; in fact, until 1803, he was an ardent supporter of life tenure for judges: "The judges .. . should not be dependent upon any man or body of men. To these ends they should hold their estates for life in their offices, or, in other words, their commissions during good behavior" (quoted in Haynes, 1944, pp. 93-94). Why the conversion? A principled change of heart? Hardly. Jefferson only discovered democracy and accountability for judges after learning of the U.S. Supreme Court's decision in *Marbury v. Madison,* 1803 (Haynes, 1944; Volcansek & Lafon, 1988). If he could not control policy produced by appointed, life-tenured judges, at least he could give control of their tenure to a group that did support his views: the electorate.

TABLE 9.2. Patterns of State Adoption of the Various Judicial Selection Systems

Selection System	1776-1831	1832-1885	1886-1933	1934-1968
Legislature	48.5%	6.7%	0.0%	0.0%
Governor	42.4	20.0	10.7	5.6
Partisan Election	9.1	73.3	25.0	11.1
Nonpartisan	—	—	64.3	11.1
Merit	—	—	—	72.2

SOURCE: Glick & Vines (1973, p. 41).

We could go on and offer similar accounts of so many others involved in the choice of judicial selection and retention institutions. For surely various state legislators, at least when debating elective judiciaries, "had more on their mind than merely applying democratic principles" (Nelson, 1993, p. 192); they were just as interested, if not more so, in packing the bench with partisan supporters (Carrington, 1998). So, too, progressive groups—what with their contempt for the laissez-faire jurisprudence endorsed by particular political parties—were not merely interested in cleaning up the machines. And, following Hall's (1983) logic, not even Pound was above pursuing policy ends. But it is the more general point that should not be missed: The standard story's failure to recognize political motivations on the part of key actors is near fatal. Not only does it run counter to the historical evidence (not to mention defy good sense and logic); it also is at odds with virtually every important theoretical account of institutional choice and change in the political science literature (see, e.g., Boix, 1999; Knight, 1992; Knight & Sened, 1995).

Where's the Empirical Support?

Our critique, up to this point, has been primarily theoretical and anecdotal but systematic empirical analysis both is possible and necessary. For to many scholars, the standard story is on its strongest ground when it is pitted against real-world observations. Often-cited facts and figures are the ones we already have provided in the text—such as, "every new state admitted to the Union between 1846 and 1912 provided for the election of [at least some] judges"—as well as those depicted in Table 9.2. Advocates of the standard account suggest that such data provide conclusive evidence that the design and change of selection and retention systems is primarily a series of responses to broad societal concerns.

Unfortunately, the data in Table 9.2 are anything but conclusive. Quite the opposite: They suffer from two relatively minor (though irritating) problems and two more important ones. Turning to the former first, we note that so much of the data scholars cite come not from primary sources (e.g., state constitutions, state laws) but rather from secondary fonts (especially *The Book of the States,* 1937-present; Berkson et al., 1980; Haynes, 1944)—many of which are imprecise (e.g., they do not always specify whether elections are partisan or not), commit sins of omission (e.g., they do not report all changes in judicial term length) and commission (e.g., they all contain downright errors in dates and facts), or all of the above. But because the errors have gone unnoticed or uncorrected, scholars simply transmit them from one piece of research to the next—with the effect of occasionally stating and restating questionable conclusions. So for example, we are often led to believe, in accord with Chapter 1 of the standard story, that "virtually all" constitutional documents of the 18th century provided life tenure for justices. As Champagne and Haydel (1993) put it: "During the Revolutionary War period the colonists . . . greatly resented King George III's power to appoint and remove judges. . . . Although they resented the King's control over judicial selection, the colonists still believed that judges should be appointed, not elected. They thought lifetime judicial appointments would ensure independence"(pp. 2-3). Yet, a check of the documents themselves (in Thorpe, 1909) and a multitude of other sources (Dunn, 1993; Elliott, 1954; Escovitz et al., 1975; Felice, Kilwein, & Slotnick, 1993; Grimes, 1998; Haynes, 1944; Smith, 1976; Taft, 1893; Witte, 1995; Wooster, 1969; Ziskind, 1969) reveals that, prior to *Marbury v. Madison* (1803), fully 41% ($n = 7$) of the 17 states did *not* guarantee life tenure to the justices of their highest courts; and 1 of the 10 that did (New York) qualified the guarantee with the proviso that justices retire at age 60.

A second rather minor concern is that scholars rarely define their selection categories. This is not a serious issue for institutions such as partisan elections, the meaning of which seems clear, but it is for some of the other mechanisms. Does California qualify as a "merit selection" state because it is the governor, not a commission, who nominates candidates? To Abraham (1998), it does indeed; but to Carp and Stidham (1998), it does not. What about New York, where the governor appoints judges (subject to legislative confirmation) from lists provided by judicial commissions, but judges do not run for retention; rather they are reappointed by the governor and legislature? Is New York a "merit" state? Tarr (1999) says yes; Carp and Stidham (1998) say no.

Although some may see these as minor categorical differences, little doubt exists that the ways in which scholars categorize state institutions significantly affect the conclusions they reach; for example, many point to the states' initial refusal to give governors the power of appointment as Exhibit #1 in their defense of the standard story. To be sure, prior to *Marbury,* 9 of the 17 states gave exclusive power to the legislature but in the remaining eight the governor, other members of the executive branch, or both played a significant role—either as the nominator or appointer. Indeed, today most scholars would classify all, if not most, of the eight as "gubernatorial" states.

Now let us consider the more serious problems. The first centers on the literature's insistence on categorizing states by their *selection* system and, then, lumping into one category all states that use a particular system (e.g., all those that invoke partisan elections, legislative selection, and so on; see Table 9.2). This procedure ignores two facts. First, even under the standard story (i.e., even putting aside political motivations), *reformers were generally less interested in how judges got to the bench than they were in how they retained their seats* (Carpenter, 1918; Hasen, 1997). Second, when states adopted even a particular kind of selection and retention system, say, partisan elections, they did not do so *homogeneously;* rather some specified renewable terms of, say, 6 or 10 years, whereas others were nonrenewable terms.

If we believe that the choice of judicial-selection/retention mechanism affects the choices justices make—as even the standard account suggests—then these gross categorizations are a mistake. To see why, assume, as the extant literature suggests, that elections increase the opportunity costs for justices to act sincerely (or, in the parlance of the existing literature, that elections will induce greater accountability) (Brace & Hall, 1993; Vines, 1962; Watson & Downing, 1969) and lead them to reach decisions that reflect popular sentiment (Croly, 1995; Gryski et al., 1986; Hall, 1987; Pinello, 1995; Stevens, 1995; Tabarrok & Helland, 1999). If elections are held on a regular basis, we would agree. But what about states that adopt 20-plus-year terms? Is it sensible to equate partisan elections every 20 years with those held every two? Surely not. Rather, we must be attentive both to selection-retention mechanisms *and* the terms of office.

Finally, the sorts of data typically invoked (e.g., the data displayed in Table 9.2) are insufficiently developed and too gross to assess what we take to be the standard story's central propositions; namely, (a) societies (e.g., the U.S. states) adopt selection-retention mechanisms in response to "popular ideas at different historical periods" (Glick & Vines, 1973, p. 40) and (b) entities within a society (e.g., the U.S. states), because they are responding to the same pressures, should possess roughly the same selection-retention systems at any given historical moment.

To see why existing data are not particularly useful in assessing these propositions, consider Figure 9.1. There we provide a visual depiction of the propositions along with the specific form the standard story takes. Assume that the Y-axis represents a scale of the opportunity costs that the various selection-retention mechanisms (including whatever term length they specify) exact on justices, such that

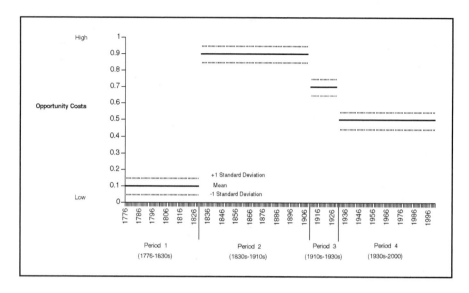

Figure 9.1. Visual Depiction of the Standard Story's Propositions (I)

institutions on the very low end—say appointment with life tenure—provide justices with the highest degree of independence to act on their sincere preferences—and those on the very high end—say partisan elections every two years—with the lowest. What the standard story suggests is that the mean of this opportunity cost measure, across all the entities in a given society (e.g., the mean score of all U.S. states), should stay constant until the entities respond to the next change in societal sentiment. What is more, because all entities are responding at roughly the same time, the standard deviation from that mean should be relatively low.

In other words and to be more concrete, if we were able to create a measure of costs—one based on the dimensions of retention and the terms of office—we would expect very low mean scores across all existing states during Period 1 (Chapter 1 of the standard story) (see Figure 9.1). That is because state constitution drafters, in response to English practice, sought to create independent judiciaries, those in which judges would enjoy life tenure and thus, presumably pay the lowest opportunity costs for acting sincerely. As we move toward the Jacksonian era, we would expect to see a dramatic increase in the opportunity cost measure, what with states moving toward partisan elections and shorter terms of office. Finally, Chapters 3 and 4 of the standard story suggest that opportunity costs would decrease as states began to invoke nonpartisan and retention elections.[14]

Putting this together into one cohesive story (that is, connecting the lines in Figure 9.1) suggests the intriguing pattern depicted in Figure 9.2: an inverted U,

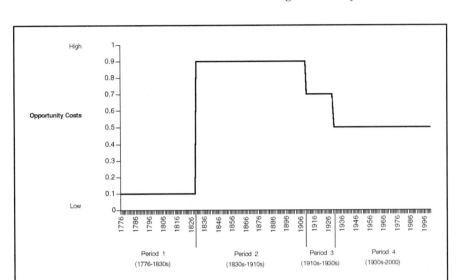

Figure 9.2. Visual Depiction of the Standard Story's Propositions (II)

with low opportunity costs at the onset, far higher ones during most of the 1800s, and lower costs yet again during the 20th century. And though we do not depict the standard deviations here, we would, once again, anticipate rather low ones as states move together in response to societal forces.

Assessing these propositions obviously requires much finer (and more reliable) data than scholars typically invoke. Moreover, data-collection efforts ought be attentive to critiques we offer above, especially to the need to emphasize retention mechanisms and the terms of office.

Developing a Measure to Assess Empirically the Standard Story

It is with these points in mind that we approach the task of testing the standard story's core propositions. The most important part of that task entails developing a measure of opportunity costs—one that incorporates the two dimensions of retention and the length of tenure. Let us begin with retention and note that previous efforts have attempted to place *selection* systems on an ordinal scale tapping judicial independence (accountability) (see, e.g., Sheldon & Lovrich, 1991). Typically such scales move from partisan elections (highest accountability) to judicial appointment by the governor (lowest accountability) (e.g., Champagne & Haydel, 1993). We prefer, first, to reconceptualize the underlying scale as one of opportunity costs, that is, the costs that judges will incur if they always act sincerely (see Note 5) and, second, to focus on retention, rather than selection.[15]

Low Opportunity Costs					High Opportunity Costs
Life Retention Tenure	commission Non-partisan reappoints	Governor Partisan and Commission reappoint	2 Houses reappoint election	Governor and election Legislature reappoint	Governor, Legislature, election and Commission reappoint

Figure 9.3. Opportunity-Cost Scale: The Retention Dimension

These preferences lead us to the scale depicted in Figure 9.3, which arrays all retention mechanisms used in the U.S. states between 1776 and 2000. Underlying it is a straightforward-enough assumption: The more players involved in reappointment, the higher the opportunity costs (see, generally, Sheldon & Lovrich, 1991; Sheldon & Maule, 1997).[16]

Most of the placements are obvious, but those on elections may require some justification. Partisan races are at the very high end of the scale because voter turnout is greater and roll-off is less in those than in judicial retention (Dubois, 1979, 1980; Hall, 1999) or in nonpartisan elections (Adamany & Dubois, 1976; Dubois, 1979, 1980; Hall, 1984a; Hall 1999); in other words, more players participate in the reappointment decision when ballots list the party affiliation of judges. The distinction between retention and nonpartisan elections is finer. Though Hall (1999) finds virtually no difference in voter participation between the two, Dubois (1979, 1980) demonstrates monotonic declines in turnout and monotonic increases in roll-off from partisan to nonpartisan to retention elections (see Table 9.3). Given that Dubois's research covers a longer time span than Hall's (1948 to 1974 vs. 1980 to 1995) and that his results sit comfortably with other studies (e.g., Aspin, 1999; Griffin & Horan, 1979, 1982; Jenkins, 1977; Luskin, Bratcher, Renner, Seago, & Jordan, 1994) and with conventional wisdom (e.g., Webster, 1995, p. 34, noting "voter drop-off has been more significant in retention elections than in either partisan or non-partisan judicial elections"; see also Slotnick, 1988), we place retention elections to the left of nonpartisan contests.[17]

To animate this retention dimension, we collected data on the institutions used in the states to retain justices serving on courts of last resort since 1776 (for our sources, see Figure 9.4) and coded them from 1 (life tenure) through 9 (partisan elections) (see Figure 9.3). We then standardized the codes on a 0 to 1 scale, such that scores closer to 0 represent low-opportunity cost retention systems (e.g., life tenure) and those moving toward 1, high-cost systems (e.g., partisan elections).

TABLE 9.3.   Mean Turnout and Mean Roll-Off in State Judicial Elections

Election Type	Presidential Election Years		Mid-Term Election Years	
	Mean Turnout	Mean Roll-Off	Mean Turnout	Mean Roll-Off
Partisan Ballot	62.4%	8.5%	50.3%	8.4%
Nonpartisan Ballot	45.0	32.4	38.7	28.3
Merit Retention Ballot	38.2	40.2	32.4	36.1

SOURCE: Dubois (1980, pp. 46, 48).

Finally, we generated the yearly mean of the retention scores across states.[18] Figure 9.4 plots this measure over time.

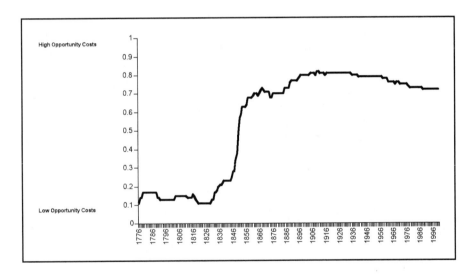

Figure 9.4. Mean (Standardized) Retention Scores in the U.S. States, 1776-2000
SOURCES: State codes, state constitutions available in, among other places, Thorpe (1909); *The Book of the States* (various years); Official Manual of the State of [Name of State] (various years); e-mail correspondence with various experts (state officials and scholars); official court web sites; American Judicature Society (1995); Atkins and Gertz (1982); Aumann and Walker (1956); Benson (1993); Berkson et al., (1980); Brown (1998); Carbon & Berkson (1980); Cooper (1995); Coyle (1972); Dealey (1915); Diggers (1998); Dubois (1980); Dunn (1993); Elliott (1954); Escovitz et al., (1975); Felice et al., (1993); Friedman (1999); Goldschmidt (1994); Hall (1983); Hall (1999); Haynes (1944); Heffernan (1997); Herndon (1962); May (1996); Pelander (1998); Pinello (1995); Puro et al., (1985); Richman (1998); Robinson (1941); Roll (1990); Sacks (1956); Sait (1927); Sheldon & Maule (1997); Smith (1951); Smith (1976); Smith (1998); Stephens (1989); Swackhamer (1974); Taft (1893); Vaughan (1917); Webster (1995); Winslow (1912); Winters (1966); Witte (1995); Wooster (1969); Ziskind (1969).

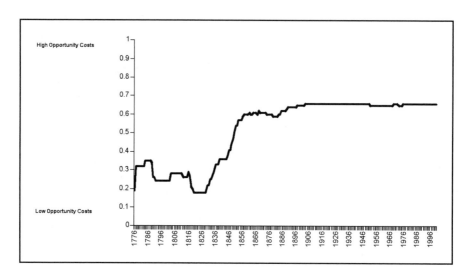

Figure 9.5. Mean (Standardized) Term-Length Scores in the U.S. States, 1776-2000
SOURCES: See Figure 9.4.

Quite clearly, state retention systems have, over time, increased the opportunity costs for justices.[19] But such data tell only half the story. Because "term length is a key component in determining the balance between judicial independence and judicial accountability" (See, 1998; see also Smithey & Ishiyama, 1999), we also must be attentive to judicial tenure—that is, our ultimate measure of opportunity costs ought take account of the length of the terms of office (with the primary assumption being that as the length increases, opportunity costs decrease).

To incorporate this dimension, we standardized judicial terms (which have ranged in the U.S. states from life tenure to reappointment every year) to fall along a 0 to 1 scale such that scores closer to 0 represent life tenure or very long terms and those closer to 1, very short terms.[20] Figure 9.5 displays the results of this transformation.

Given that the means displayed in Figures 9.4 and 9.5 seem to move together (see Figure 9.6), we added the two scores to arrive at a final measure of opportunity costs. Figure 9.7 depicts the results of this set of calculations.

Assessing the Standard Story

With our measure now in hand, we can begin to assess the key propositions of the standard story. We start with the account's emphasis on the notion that societies merely respond to "popular ideas at different historical periods" (Glick & Vines, 1973, p. 40)—and, more specifically, that the U.S. states reacted to four such

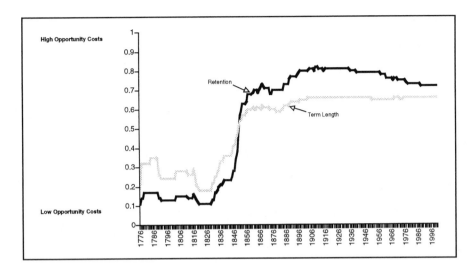

Figure 9.6. Mean (Standardized) Term-Length and Retention Scores in the U.S. States, 1776-2000
SOURCES: See Figure 9.4.

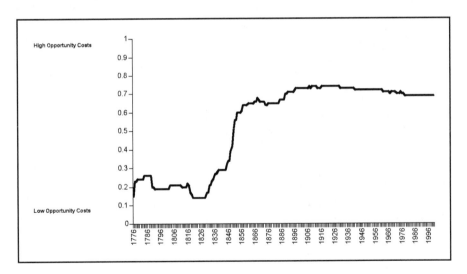

Figure 9.7. A Measure of Opportunity Costs Associated With State Retention Mechanisms and Term Lengths, 1776-2000
SOURCES: See Figure 9.4.

ideas. Linking those together, the standard story suggests that judicial opportunity costs moved from very low to very high to a more moderate position.

Figure 9.8, in which we map our measure against a visual depiction of the standard account (initially displayed in Figure 9.2), however, suggests quite a different

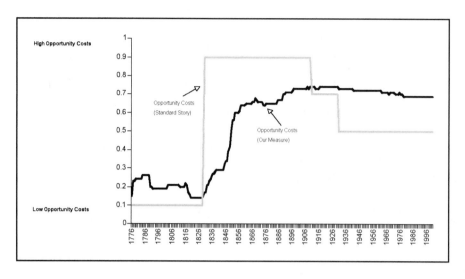

Figure 9.8. Judicial Opportunity Costs and the Standard Story, 1776-2000

story. *Judicial opportunity costs induced by the retention and term-length components of selection systems have—nearly monotonically—increased overtime.* In other words and to use more standard language, states have moved to hold their justices more and more accountable; no downward trend appears to exist.

These data may serve to undermine one aspect of the standard story—the form of changes in U.S. judicial selection systems—but they do not assess its other central proposition. Because states are responding to the same societal pressures, little variation should exist in these systems at any given moment. To consider this, we plot +1 and –1 standard deviations from the mean of our opportunity cost measure. Figure 9.9 displays the results.

Certainly some of the (large) observed deviation during the first 100 years or so may be due to the small number of states relative to the contemporary period. But we are hard pressed to explain, at least under the standard story, why deviation remains so high into the tail end of the 20th century.

The Standard Story: One Last Look

Based on logic, history, and empirical evidence, we are now prepared to reject the standard story of judicial selection in the United States. We understand, though, that some may criticize at least our empirical assessment on the grounds that we have distorted the standard story by considering retention mechanisms *and* the terms of office—rather than simply the system for appointing judges. The

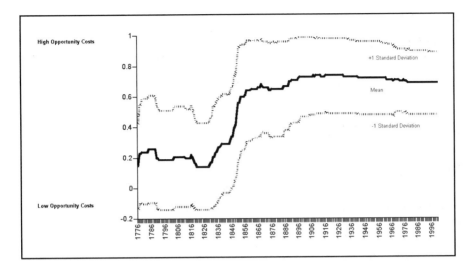

Figure 9.9. Our Opportunity Cost Measure: The Means and Standard Deviations Over Time, 1776-2000

standard story, they might argue, speaks not to specifics but rather to general selection mechanisms.

For the reasons we offer above—for example, institutional designers were equally concerned, if not more so, with retention than they were with appointment—we disagree. Nonetheless, in the interest of thoroughness, let us write what surely would be the easiest test for the standard story to pass; namely, societies emerging from the same legal, political, and historical experience should adopt, at least at the onset of their development, the same general mechanisms for the selection of judges.

Unfortunately for its proponents, the standard story cannot pass even this simple exam. As Table 9.1 makes clear, the former republics of the Soviet Union that established constitutional courts took at least five different approaches to the appointment of judges. Given that these republics operated under the same "legal" system and, more generally, under the same political regime for nearly eight decades, it is discouraging, to say the least, that they are all over the map with regard to judicial selection systems.

Even more disturbing is that the standard story does not hold up against the cases it was designed to explain: The 17 states creating high courts between 1776 and 1803 also invoked five different appointment mechanisms: legislature alone ($n = 9$), governor alone ($n = 1$), governor and legislature ($n = 2$), governor and council ($n = 4$), and council alone ($n = 1$).

ᘒ An Alternative Account of the Selection of Selection Systems

This last bit of evidence, at least to us, clinches the case. The standard story does not provide a particularly satisfying account of judicial selection systems. So the questions we raised at the onset remain: Why do societies choose particular selection and retention institutions? Why do they formally alter those choices?

In a larger project on constitutional courts, we (Epstein, Knight, & Shvetsova, 2001) advance the following proposition, which we believe has bearing on these questions. The creation of and changes in constitutional courts come about through a process of political bargaining that occurs within a preexisting political system. Decisions about these courts are the strategic choices of the relevant political actors and reflect those actors' relative influence, preferences, and beliefs at the moment when the new institution is introduced. It is the variation in influence, preferences, and beliefs that leads to the creation of distinct courts; and it is these resulting formal institutional distinctions that influence the performance of the judicial branch *and* the level of independence that it can attain in the long run.

To apply this general framework to explain the choice of selection and retention systems for judges, we begin with the basic assumption that designers of constitutional courts prefer institutional rules that will best serve their long-term political goals. But, because attaining this goal requires them to determine the relationship between their present political preferences and the long-term effects of the rules governing constitutional courts, their preferences over judicial selection and retention mechanisms will vary depending on their beliefs about present and future political conditions. So, for example, the more uncertain those conditions—in the fundamental sense that the actors do not know the political circumstances they will face in the future—the less the designers of the court will be able to constrain (with confidence) the court and, thus, the greater the independence the institutional rules will provide the justices.

The effect of this uncertainty—and a causal effect at that—necessarily directs our attention to the types of information available to political actors at the time they are establishing beliefs about the long-term effects of institutional rules. Particularly relevant to our analysis are two general types of information: (a) information regarding the designers' personal political futures and (b) information about popular preferences (the polity) that will affect future political outcomes, such as elections and plebiscites. We would expect an increase in uncertainty along each dimension to affect positively the independence (i.e., decrease the opportunity costs) of resulting courts.

As for the first dimension—the personal career expectations of individuals involved in the design of judicial institutions—we can characterize it as a continuum between the following information states. At one extreme is an environment in which even the most immediate political outcomes (at least from an individual's point of view) are highly uncertain. This could represent an environment characterized by an on-going constitutional conflict between branches (or levels) of government such that any of the competing groups of actors can hope to prevail; or it may be one in which there is the potential for considerable mobility of individual politicians to other branches or levels of government such that it would be difficult for politicians to decide exactly what they wanted with regard to the court. At the other extreme, uncertainty is low. This environment could result either from a complete dominance by one of the government branches or, if separation of powers is preserved, from the absence of an explicit constitutional conflict and, thus, the establishment of fixed institutional identities for the decisive political actors.

We can characterize the second dimension, dealing with the makeup of the electorate, by the following extreme information states. At one extreme, we place conditions creating high uncertainty. These might occur when the electorate is fairly homogenous, making it difficult to identify sizeable groups with clear and conflicting preferences that would present obvious targets for political mobilization. Alternatively, the electorate could be highly fragmented, consisting of numerous small groups. In such circumstances, as long as no clear and fixed lines for coalition building are observable, the likelihood of success of political mobilization remains unknown. The opposite extreme is one of low uncertainty with regard to the polity, which may occur when the electorate is polarized. Although bases for polarization can vary, deep societal cleavages (in particular, those of the ascriptive nature) are the most likely ones to incite political mobilization and shape future policies.

Table 9.4 summarizes these ideas. There we place the two dimensions and the outcomes particular combinations yield.

Each of the predicted outcomes requires a few words of explanation. At least on our theory, designers will select institutions meant to induce a high degree of independence when their uncertainty levels are the highest on both of the relevant dimensions (Case I). At no other information states would they be willing to devise retention and selection mechanisms that lower the opportunity costs to the same extent. By the same logic, combined low uncertainty on both dimensions will lead to the most accountable (dependent) courts, with selection-retention systems generating the highest opportunity costs for the judges (Case IV).

The two intermediate cases are those in which there is high uncertainty on one dimension and low uncertainty on the other. If there are differences in the types of

TABLE 9.4.   Summary of Predicted Outcomes

		Dimension 2. The Polity	
		High Uncertainty *(e.g., homogeneous polity or divided polity with no pre-determined outcome)*	**Low Uncertainty** *(e.g., polarized polity with predetermined outcome)*
Dimension 1. Personal Political Future	**High Uncertainty** *(e.g., high personal political risks)*	Selection-retention systems are designed for maximal court independence (create lowest opportunity costs) (I)	Selection-retention is controlled but not to the extreme (III)
	Low Uncertainty *(e.g., stable personal political risks)*	Selection-retention is more controlled by the other branches of government or by the electorate (II)	Selection-retention systems are designed for minimal court independence (create highest opportunity costs) (IV)

courts established in these two cases, they will be a function of how the designers weigh the relative importance of the two dimensions. For purposes of this discussion, we have assumed in Table 9.4 that uncertainty on the polity dimension will have a greater effect on the independence of courts than will uncertainty on the personal political dimension. If this is the case, then it leads to the following preferences over judicial institutions. In a situation of low uncertainty on the personal dimension but high uncertainty on the polity dimension, relatively independent courts with selection mechanisms bestowing authority on either the other branches of government or the electorate will be preferred (Case II); in a situation of high personal uncertainty but low uncertainty about future politics, greater institutional constraints through intermediate controls on judicial retention will be preferred (Case III).

With this, we can now state our main hypothesis: In general, as the combined index of political uncertainty increases, the likelihood that the design of the court's selection-retention system will lower opportunity costs for judges also increases. As a secondary hypothesis, we expect that, as the overall level of political uncertainty in a given society and for the relevant actors declines, any changes in selection-retention systems will serve to raise opportunity costs for the judges. We plan to assess both predictions against data collected on selection systems in the U.S. states and those in all countries with constitutional courts.

✑ Conclusion

Finding the standard story of judicial selection severely wanting, we sketched a new approach—one that we believe provides a more realistic and generalizable picture of institutional development and change.

On the surface, the data we presented on state selection systems *appear* consistent with our account. In the aggregate, as political uncertainty in the United States has declined, selection mechanisms designed to induce greater accountability (i.e., raise judicial opportunity costs) have increased.

We stress "appear" because, almost needless to write, much work remains before we can fully support this claim both as it pertains to the U.S. states and to other societies. We must consider, for example, whether our opportunity cost measure—the measure that will eventually serve as the key dependent variable in the test of our central hypotheses—and any adjustments necessary to accommodate various nations should include dimensions other than retention and term length. A few (e.g., mandatory retirement ages or limits on the number of terms) readily come to mind. But there are undoubtedly others. Finally, we must develop measures of the concepts contained in our independent variables, the two dimensions of political uncertainty: personal political future and the polity. We have some ideas along these lines but welcome any suggestions readers are able to supply.

✑ Notes

1. Haynes (1944, p. 4) actually traces controversies over judicial selection and tenure back to the 4th century B.C. For examples and discussions of particular debates, see Carrington, 1998; Champagne, 1988; Champagne & Haydel, 1993; Friedman, 1973; Grimes, 1998; Noe, 1997/1998; Pelander, 1998; Roll, 1990; Smith, 1951; Smith, 1976; Webster, 1995; Wooster, 1969; Ziskind, 1969.

Haynes also points to immense scholarly and public interest in the subject. In the "United States alone," he notes, "whole shelves could be filled with the speeches, debates, books and articles that have been produced . . . dealing with the choice and tenure of judges." Writing nearly 40 years later, Dubois (1986, p. 31) claims that "It is fairly certain that no single subject has consumed as many pages in law reviews and law-related publications over the past 50 years as the subject of judicial selection."

2. We adapt some of the language in this and the next paragraph from Murphy, Pritchett, & Epstein (2001).

3. Merit plans differ from state to state but usually they call for a screening committee, which may be comprised of the state's chief justice, attorneys elected by the state's bar

association, and lay people appointed by the governor to nominate several candidates for each judicial vacancy. The governor makes the final selection but is typically bound to choose from among the committee's candidates. At the first election after a year or two of service, the name of each new judge is put on the ballot with the question whether he or she should be retained in office. If the voters reject an incumbent, he or she is replaced by another "merit"candidate. If elected, the judge then serves a set term, at the end of which he or she is eligible for reelection.

4. Based on data reported in the section "An Evaluation of the Standard Account" of this chapter, between 1776 and 2000 the average state changed its method for the retention of state supreme court justices or the terms of office (i.e., the length of time a justice holds his or her position before he or she must stand for reappointment) 4.8 times. Only six states made no changes either in retention or terms.

5. We should offer three caveats to this statement. First, judicial specialists tend to speak in far more specific terms than do we. So, for example, rather than make claims about opportunity costs associated with particular selection institutions, they argue that popularly elected justices are more likely to suppress dissents (Brace & Hall, 1993; Vines, 1962; Watson & Downing, 1969) and reach decisions that reflect popular sentiment (Croly, 1995; Gryski et al., 1986; Hall, 1987; Pinello, 1995; Stevens, 1995; Tabarrok & Helland, 1999) than are their appointed counterparts. To us, these are merely examples of the more general phenomenon; namely, the greater the accountability established in the institution, the higher the opportunity costs for judges to act sincerely.

Second, there is probably less agreement about the effect of selection mechanisms than about the impact of electoral rules—with some studies, albeit typically older ones, arguing that selection mechanisms do not affect dissent rates (Canon & Jaros, 1970; Flango & Ducat, 1979; Lee, 1970) or other types of judicial behavior (Atkins & Glick, 1974; Crynes, 1995; Domino, 1988; Schneider & Maughan, 1979). Scholars are in greater accord over whether various selection systems produce more minority and women judges, those who are more professionally qualified, and so on. The vast majority agree with Flango and Ducat (1979, p. 31) "it appears that neither educational, legal, local, prior experience, sex, race, non-role characteristics clearly distinguish among judges appointed under each of the five types of selection systems" (see, e.g., Alozie 1990; Berg et al., 1975; Canon, 1972; Champagne, 1986; Dubois, 1983; Glick, 1978; Glick & Emmert, 1987; Watson & Downing, 1969; but see Graham, 1990; Scheb, 1988; Tokarz, 1986; Uhlmann, 1977).

Finally (and again, in contradistinction to literature on electoral rules), almost all conclusions about the effect of judicial selection and retention mechanisms emanate from studies on the United States; comparative work is virtually nonexistent. (The exceptions include Anenson, 1997; Atkins, 1989; Bell 1988; Danelski, 1969; Gadbois, 1969; Meador, 1983; Morrison, 1969; Volcansek & Lafon, 1988). Some argue that the near-exclusive focus on the United States is highly problematic because differences between the state judicial selection systems are so trivial as to create distinctions without meaning (Baum, 1995). We, of course, agree that incorporating cases abroad is highly advantageous. At the same time, we take issue with the general claim that differences between the states are negligible; we believe instead that the way scholars have approached those differences—by lumping states into broad *selection*-system categories (e.g., partisan elections, nonpartisan elections, and so on) without considering the dimensions of retention and terms of office—fails to exploit them, either theoretically or empirically. We offer a corrective in our section "An Evaluation of the Standard Account."

6. U.S. practices are the only ones that have attracted serious scholarly attention. See Note 5.

7. And not because "direct election of judges was unknown" (Orth, 1992); indeed, quite early on Vermont (1777), Georgia (1812), and Indiana (1816) provided for the election of some lower court judges (Croly, 1995, p. 714; Hurst, 1950). Rather, most probably eschewed elections out of a belief that "the electorate was not capable of evaluating the professional qualities of judicial candidates" (Grimes, 1998).

As an aside, here and throughout the rest of the chapter, we place emphasis on the selection and retention of judges serving on state courts of last resort (usually called state supreme courts). We highlight these courts because we are interested in developing a theory of judicial selection that we can invoke to study (constitutional) courts of last resort here and abroad.

8. The figure of 7 (e.g., Elliott, 1954; Volcansek & Lafon, 1988) or 8 (e.g., Grimes, 1998; Sheldon & Maule, 1997) depends on who is doing the chronicling. That scholars disagree on even basic facts about judicial selection systems shores up a problem that plagues much of this research: Analysts tend to rely on a few (flawed) secondary sources—especially *The Book of the States,* Berkson et al. (1980), and Haynes (1944)—and thus transmit errors from one piece of research to the next. In this section, we rely on those "flawed" data since they have become a part of the standard story; in the next, we present analyses based on "corrected" data.

9. Actually criticisms of elections came nearly a century before Pound's speech. In 1821, Justice Joseph Story expressed concern about the trend toward elections. And in 1835, Alexis de Tocqueville (1954, p. 289) wrote: "Some other state constitutions make the members of the judiciary elective, and they are even subjected to frequent re-elections. We venture to predict that these innovations will sooner or later be attended with fatal consequences; and that it will be found out at some future period that by thus lessening the independence of the judiciary they have attacked not only the judicial power, but the democratic republic itself."

10. The plan the ABA endorsed, though vague, was something of a cross between Kales's and Laski's. It called for the executive or another elected officer to select a judge from a list presented by an unelected agency. It endorsed retention elections, as well as the possibility of legislative confirmation of the governor's choice.

11. As Sheldon and Maule (1997) put it: "The trend now favors the Missouri plan."

12. Over the next decade or so, scholars may be adding a fifth chapter to the standard story, as the merit plan "has come under increasing fire from the left and the right, with liberals arguing that minorities are underrepresented on the bench and conservatives viewing it as undemocratic" (Pelander, 1998, p. 668).

13. For a critique of Hall's argument and yet more conjecture over why the states moved to elections, see Nelson (1993).

14. The literature would justify this claim by pointing to lower levels of competition (or no competition at all) in these sorts of elections. Such, in turn, results in less threat to incumbent justices and, thus, lowers judicial accountability. We offer a somewhat different justification in the text.

15. In addition to the reasons already offered, focusing on retention eliminates a problem inherent in many studies of judicial selection: Perhaps as many as 60% of all "elected" state supreme court justices were not initially elected but rather appointed to office (as interim appointees) (see, e.g., Herndon 1962).

16. We acknowledge a potential problem with this assumption, namely, the converse is possible: the fewer the actors monitoring the justices, the higher the opportunity costs. This possibility flows from principal-agent models that suggest that as the number of principals increase, the opportunity costs for the agent decrease because he or she can play the

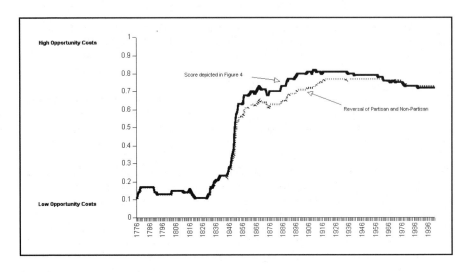

Figure N.1.

principals off one another—if those principals have heterogeneous preferences. We plan to consider this possibility in future work.

17. We have empirically assessed the degree to which this decision affects the resulting measure. Because Note 19 displays the results, suffice it to write here that reversing partisan and nonpartisan elections has no appreciable effect on the measure.

18. All data and documentation necessary to replicate the measures displayed in Figures 9.4 through 9.7 are available at: http://www.artsci.wustl.edu/~polisci/epstein/research.

19. Given potential concerns over the placement of partisan and nonpartisan elections on the retention dimension (see Figure 9.3), we reversed their order. As Figure N.1 shows, so doing leads to no appreciable change in interpretation. Accordingly (and for the reasons described in the text), we stick with our original ordering.

20. For purposes of animating this measure, life terms are the equivalent of 25 years. We base this on (the admittedly unverified but seemingly plausible) assumption that the average age of appointment is about 50.

⏎ References

Abraham, H. J. (1998). *The judicial process: An introductory analysis of the courts of the United States, England, and France* (7th ed.). New York: Oxford University Press.

Adamany, D., & Dubois, P. (1976). Electing state judges. *Wisconsin Law Review, 1976,* 731-779.

Alozie, N. A. (1990). Distribution of women and minority judges: The effects of judicial selection methods. *Social Science Quarterly, 71,* 315.

American Judicature Society. (1995). *Judicial merit selection: Current status.* Chicago: American Judicature Society.

Anenson, T. L. (1997, Fall). "For whom the bell tolls . . . Judicial selection by election in Latin America." *Southwestern Journal of Law and Trade in the Americas, 4,* 261-299.

Aspin, L. (1999). Trends in judicial retention elections, 1964-1998. *Judicature, 83*(2), 79-81.

Atkins, B. (1989). Judicial selection in context: The American and English experience. *Kentucky Law Journal, 77,* 577-617.

Atkins, B., & Gertz, M. G. (1982). The local politics of judicial selection: Some views of law enforcement officials. *Judicature, 66*(1), 39-44.

Atkins, B. M., & Glick H. R. (1974). Formal judicial recruitment and state supreme court decisions. *American Politics Quarterly, 2,* 427-449.

Aumann, F. R., & Walker, H. (1956). *The government and administration of Ohio.* New York: Crowell.

Averill, L. H., Jr. (1995). Observations on the Wyoming experience with merit selection of judges: A model for Arkansas. *University of Arkansas at Little Rock Law Journal,* 281-327.

Baum, L. (1995). Electing judges. In L. Epstein (Ed.), *Contemplating courts.* Washington, DC: CQ Press.

Belknap, M. R. (1992). *To improve the administration of justice: A history of the American Judicature Society.* Chicago: American Judicature Society.

Bell, J. (1988). Principles and methods of judicial selection in France. *Southern California Law Review, 61,* 1757-1794.

Benson, L. (1993). The Minnesota judicial selection process: Rejecting judicial elections in favor of a merit plan. *William Mitchell Law Review, 19,* 765-785.

Berg, L. L., Green, J. J., Schmidhauser, J. P., & Schneider, R. S. (1975). The consequences of judicial reform: A comparative analysis of California and Iowa appellate systems. *Western Political Quarterly, 28,* 263-280.

Berkson, L., Beller, S., & Grimaldi, M. (1980). *Judicial selection in the United States: A compendium of proposals.* Chicago: American Judicature Society.

Berkson, L. C. (1980). Judicial selection in the United States: A special report. *Judicature, 64,* 176-193.

Blankenagel, Alexander. (1994, Summer/Fall). The court writes its own law. *Eastern European Constitutional Review, 74.*

Boix, C. (1999). Setting the rules of the game: The choice of electoral systems in advanced democracies. *American Political Science Review, 93,* 609-624.

The Book of the States. (1937-present). Lexington, KY: Council of State Governments.

Brace, P., & Hall, M. G. (1993). Integrated models of dissent. *Journal of Politics, 55,* 919-935.

Brace, P., & Hall, M. G. (1997). The interplay of preferences, case facts, context, and rules in the politics of judicial choice. *Journal of Politics, 59,* 1206-1231.

Bright, S. B., &. Kennan, P. J. (1995). Judges and the politics of death: Deciding between the Bill of Rights and the next election in capital cases. *Boston University Law Review, 75,* 760-835.

Brinkley, M. H. (2000). *The Supreme Court of North Carolina: A brief history* [On-line]. Retrieved April 1, 2000. Available:http://www.aoc.state.nc.us/www/copyright/sc/facts.html

Brown, R. L. (1998). From whence cometh our state appellate judges: Popular election versus the Missouri Plan. *University of Arkansas at Little Rock Law Journal, 20,* 313-325.

Bryce, J. (1921). *Modern democracies.* New York: Macmillan.

Canon, B. C. (1972). The impact of formal selection process on the characteristics of judges—reconsidered. *Law and Society Review, 6,* 579-593.

Canon, B. C., & Jaros, D. (1970). External variables, institutional structure and dissent on state supreme courts. *Polity, 3,* 175-200.

Carbon, S. B., & Berkson, L. C. (1980). *Judicial retention elections in the United States.* Chicago: American Judicature Society.

Carp, R. A., & Stidham, R. (1998). *Judicial process in America* (4th ed.). Washington, DC: CQ Press.

Carpenter, W. S. (1918). *Judicial tenure in the United States.* New Haven, CT: Yale University Press.

Carrington, P. D. (1998). Judicial independence and democratic accountability in highest state courts. *Law & Contemporary Problems, 61*(3), 79-126.

Champagne, A. (1986). The selection and retention of judges in Texas. *Southwestern Law Journal, 40,* 53-117.

Champagne, A. (1988). Judicial reform in Texas. *Judicature, 72,* 146-159.

Champagne, A., & Haydel, J. (1993). Introduction. In A. Champagne & J. Haydel (Eds.), *Judicial reform in the states.* Lanham, MD: University Press of America.

Cooper, L. A. (1995). An historical overview of judicial selection in Texas. *Texas Wesleyan Law Review, 2,* 317-333.

Coyle, A. B. (1972). Judicial selection and tenure in Mississippi. *Mississippi Law Journal, 43*(1) 90-107.

Croly, S. P. (1995). The majoritarian difficulty: Elective judiciaries and the rule of law. *University of Chicago Law Review, 62,* 689-791.

Crynes, D. A. (1995). The electoral connection and the pace of litigation in Kansas. *Judicature, 78,* 242-246.

Danelski, D. J. (1969). The people and the court in Japan. In J. B. Grossman & J. Tanenhaus (Eds.), *Frontiers of judicial research.* New York: Wiley.

Dealey, J. Q. (1915). *Growth of American state constitutions.* Boston: Binn.

Diggers, M. S. (1998). South Carolina's experiment: Legislative control of judicial merit selection. *South Carolina Law Review, 49,* 1217-1235.

Domino, J. C. (1988). *State supreme court innovation and the development of the right to privacy: A comparative analysis.* Unpublished doctoral dissertation, Miami University, Oxford, OH.

Dubois, P. (1986). Accountability, independence, and the selection of state judges: The role of popular judicial elections. *Southwestern Law Journal, 40,* 31-52.

Dubois, P. L. (1979). Voter turnout in state judicial elections: An analysis of the tail on the electoral kite. *Journal of Politics, 41,* 865-887.

Dubois, P. L. (1980). *From ballot to bench: Judicial elections and the quest for accountability.* Austin: University of Texas Press.

Dubois, P. L. (1983, Spring). The influence of selection system and region on the characteristics of a trial court bench: The case of California. *Justice System Journal, 8,* 59-87.

Dunn, V. (1993). Judicial reform in Pennsylvania. In A. Champagne & J. Haydel (Eds.), *Judicial reform in the States.* Lanham, MD: University Press of America.

Duverger, M. (1954). *Political parties.* New York: Wiley.

Elliott, S. D. (1954). *Safeguards of judicial independence.* Paper presented at the annual meeting of the Fourth International Congress of Comparative Law, Paris, France.

Epstein, L., Knight, J., & Shvetsova, O. (2001). The role of constitutional courts in the establishment and maintenance of democratic systems of government. *Law & Society Review, 35,* 117-164. .

Epstein, L., & Walker, T. G. (2000). *Constitutional law for a changing America* (4th ed.). Washington, DC: CQ Press.

Escovitz, S. S., Kurland, F., & Gold, N. (1975). *Judicial selection and tenure.* Chicago: American Judicature Society.

Felice, J. D., Kilwein, J. C., & Slotnick, E. E. (1993). Judicial reform in Ohio. In A. Champagne & J. Haydel (Eds.), *Judicial reform in the states.* Lanham, MD: University Press of America.

Flango, V. E., & Ducat, C. R. (1979, Fall). What difference does method of judicial selection make? Selection procedures in state courts of last resort. *Justice System Journal, 5,* 25-44.

Friedman, D. (1999). Magnificent failure revisited: Modern Maryland constitutional law from 1967 to 1998. *Maryland Law Review, 58,* 528-598.

Friedman, L. M. (1973). *A history of American law.* New York: Simon & Schuster.

Friedman, L. M. (1985). *A history of American law* (2nd ed.). New York: Simon & Schuster.

Fund for Modern Courts. (1985). *The success of women and minorities in achieving judicial office: The selection process.* New York: Author.

Gadbois, G. H., Jr. (1969). Selection, background characteristics, and voting behavior of Indian supreme court judges, 1950-1959. In G. Schubert & D. J. Danelski (Eds.), *Comparative judicial behavior.* New York: Oxford University Press.

Gavison, R. (1988). The implications of jurisprudential theories for judicial election, selection, and accountability. *Southern California Law Review, 61,* 1617-1662.

Glick, H. R. (1978). The promise and performance of the Missouri Plan: Judicial selection in the fifty states. *University of Miami Law Review, 32,* 509-541.

Glick, H. R., & Emmert, C. F. (1987). Selection systems and judicial characteristics: The recruitment of state supreme court judges. *Judicature, 70,* 228-235.

Glick, H. R., & Vines, K. N. (1973). *State court systems.* Englewood Cliffs, NJ: Prentice Hall.

Goldman, S. (1997). *Picking federal judges.* New Haven, CT: Yale University Press.

Goldschmidt, J. (1994). Merit selection. *University of Miami Law Review, 49*(1), 1-78.

Graham, B. L. (1990). Judicial recruitment and racial diversity on state courts: An overview. *Judicature, 74*(1), 28-34.

Griffin, K. N., & Horan, M. J. (1979). Merit retention elections: What influences the voters? *Judicature, 63*(2), 78-88.

Griffin, K. N., & Horan, M. J. (1982). Patterns of voting behavior in judicial retention elections for supreme court justices in Wyoming. *Judicature, 67*(2), 68-77.

Grimes, S. L. (1998). Without favor, denial, or delay: Will North Carolina Finally adopt the merit selection of judges? *North Carolina Law Review, 76,* 2266-2329.

Grossman, J. B., & Sarat, A. (1971, Spring). Political culture and judicial research. *Washington University Law Quarterly,* (2), 177-207.

Gryski, G. S., Main, E. C., & Dixon, W. J. (1986). Models of state high court decision making in sex discrimination cases. *Journal of Politics, 48,* 143-155.

Hall, K. L. (1983, May). The judiciary on trial: State constitutional reform and the rise of an elected judiciary, 1846-1860. *The Historian, 45,* 337-354.

Hall, K. L. (1984a). Progressive reform and the decline of democratic accountability: The popular election of state supreme court judges, 1850-1920. *American Bar Foundation Research Journal, 1984*(2), 345-369.

Hall, K. L. (1984b). The "route to hell" retraced: The impact of popular election on the southern appellate judiciary, 1832-1920. In D. J. Bodenhamer & J. W. Ely Jr. (Eds.), *Ambivalent legacy: A legal history of the south.* Jackson: University Press of Mississippi.

Hall, M. G. (1987). Constituent influence in state supreme court: Conceptual notes and a case study. *Journal of Politics, 49,* 1117-1124.

Hall, M. G. (1992). Electoral politics and strategic voting in state supreme court. *Journal of Politics, 54,* 427-446.

Hall, M. G. (1999, August/September). *Ballot roll-off in judicial elections: Contextual and institutional influences on voter participation in the American states.* Paper presented at the annual meeting of the American Political Science Association, Atlanta, GA.

Hall, M. G., & Brace, P. (1989). Order in the court: A neo-institutional approach to judicial consensus. *Western Political Quarterly, 42,* 391-407.

Hall, M. G., & Brace, P. (1992). Toward an integrated model of judicial voting behavior. *American Politics Quarterly, 20,* 147-168.

Hasen, R. L. (1997). High court wrongly elected: A public choice model of judging and its implications for the voting rights act. *North Carolina Law Review, 75,* 1305-1367.

Hausmaninger, H. (1995). Towards a "new" Russian constitutional court. *Cornell International Law Journal, 28,* 349-386.

Haynes, E. (1944). *The selection and tenure of judges.* Newark, NJ: National Conference of Judicial Councils.

Heffernan, N. S. (1997). Judicial responsibility, judicial independence, and the election of judges. *Marquette Law Review, 80,* 1031.

Hermens, F. A. (1941). *Democracy or anarchy? A study of proportional representation.* Notre Dame, IN: Notre Dame University Press.

Herndon, J. (1962). Appointment as a means of initial accession to elective state courts of last resort. *North Dakota Law Review, 38*(1), 60-73.

Hurst, J. W. (1950). *The growth of American law.* Boston: Little, Brown.

Jacob, H. C. (1964). The effect of institutional differences in the recruitment process: The case of state judges. *Journal of Public Law, 13*(1), 104-119.

Jenkins, W. (1977). Retention elections: Who wins when no one loses. *Judicature, 61,* 79-86.

Kales, A. M. (1914). *Unpopular government in the United States.* Chicago: University of Chicago Press.

Knight, J. (1992). *Institutions and social conflict.* Cambridge, UK: Cambridge University Press.

Knight, J., & Sened, I. (Eds.). (1995). *Explaining social institutions.* Ann Arbor: University of Michigan Press.

Lanford, N. E. (1992). *The influence of selection process and urbanization on the Texas District Court.* Unpublished doctoral dissertation, University of Nevada, Reno.

Langer, L. L. (1998). *State supreme courts and countermajoritarian behavior.* Unpublished doctoral dissertation, Florida State University, Tallahassee.

Laski, H. (1926). The technique of judicial appointments. *Michigan Law Review, 24,* 529.

Lee, F. G. (1970). *An explanatory variable of judicial behavior on bi-partisan state supreme courts.* Unpublished doctoral dissertation, University of Pennsylvania, PA.

Levin, M. A. (1977). *Urban politics and criminal courts.* Chicago: University of Chicago Press.

Lipscomb, Andrew A. (Ed.). (1903). *The writings of Thomas Jefferson.* Washington, DC: Thomas Jefferson Memorial Association.

Luskin, R. C., Bratcher, C. N., Renner, T. K., Seago, K. S., & Jordan, C. J. (1994). How minority judges fare in retention elections. *Judicature, 77,* 316-321.

Marbury v. Madison, 1 Cr. (5 U.S.) 137 (1803).

May, J. C. (1996). *The Texas State Constitution.* Westport, CT: Greenwood.

Meador, D. J. (1983). German appellate judges: Career patterns and American-English comparisons. *Judicature, 67*(1), 16-27.

Morrison, F. L. (1969). The Swiss federal court: Judicial decision making and recruitment. In J. B. Grossman & J. Tanenhaus (Eds.), *Frontiers of judicial research.* New York: Wiley.

Murphy, W. F., Pritchett, C. H., & Epstein, L. (2001). *Courts, judges, and politics* (5th ed.). New York: McGraw-Hill.

Nagel, S. S. (1973). *Comparing elected and appointed judicial systems.* Beverly Hills, CA: Sage.

Nelson, C. (1993). A re-evaluation of scholarly explanations for the rise of the elective judiciary in antebellum America. *American Journal of Legal History, 37,* 190-224.

Noe, G. C. (1997/1998). Alabama judicial selection reform: A skunk in tort hell. *Cumberland Law Review, 28,* 215-243.

O'Callaghan, J. (1991). Another test for the merit plan. *Justice System Journal, 14,* 477-485.

Orth, J. V. (1992). The day North Carolina chose direct election of judges. *North Carolina Law Review, 70,* 1825-1851.

Pelander, A. J. (1998). Judicial performance in Arizona: Goals, practical effects and concerns. *Arizona State Law Journal, 30,* 643-726.

Peltason, J. (1955). *Federal courts in the political process.* New York: Random House.

Pinello, D. R. (1995). *The impact of judicial selection method on state-supreme-court policy.* Westport, CT: Greenwood.

Pound, R. (1962). The causes of popular dissatisfaction with the administration of justice. *Journal of the American Judicature Society, 46,* 55-66.

Puro, M., Bergerson, P. J., & Puro, S. (1985, Fall). An analysis of judicial diffusion: Adoption of the Missouri Plan in the American states. *Publius, 15,* 85-97.

Rae, D. W. (1971). *The political consequences of electoral laws.* New Haven, CT: Yale University Press.

Richman, G. F. (1998). The case for merit selection and retention of trial judges. *Florida Bar Journal, 72*(9), 71-76.

Robinson, W. M., Jr. (1941). *Justice in grey: A history of the judicial system of the Confederate States of America.* Cambridge, MA: Harvard University Press.

Roll, J. M. (1990). Merit selection: The Arizona experience. *Arizona State Law Journal, 22,* 837-894.

Sacks, L. (1956). *Selection, tenure and removal of judges in the 48 states, Alaska, Hawaii, and Puerto Rico.* New York: Institute of Judicial Administration.

Sait, E. M. (1927). *American parties and elections.* New York: Century.

Scheb, J. M. (1988). State appellate judges' attitudes toward judicial merit selection and retention: Results of a national survey. *Judicature, 72,* 170-174.

Scheuerman, K. E. (1993). Rethinking judicial election. *Oregon Law Review, 72,* 459-485.

Schneider, R., & Maughan, R. (1979). Does the appointment of judges lead to a more conservative bench? *Justice System Journal, 5,* 45-57.

See, H. (1998). Judicial selection and decisional independence. *Law and Contemporary Problems, 61,* 141-147.

Segal, J. A., & Spaeth, H. J. (1993). *The Supreme Court and the attitudinal model.* New York: Cambridge University Press.

Sheldon, C. H., & Lovrich, N. P., Jr. (1991). State judicial recruitment. In J. B. Gates & C. A. Johnson (Eds.), *The American courts: A critical assessment.* Washington, DC: CQ Press.

Sheldon, C. H., & Maule, L. S. (1997). *Choosing justice: The recruitment of state and federal judges.* Pullman: Washington State University Press.

Shuman, D. W., & Champagne, A. (1997). Removing the people from the legal process: The rhetoric and research on judicial selection and juries. *Psychology, Public Policy, and Law, 3,* 242-258.

Slotnick, E. E. (1988). Review essay on judicial recruitment. *Justice System Journal, 13*(1), 109-124.

Smith, G. B. (1998). Choosing judges for a state's highest court. *Syracuse Law Review, 48,* 1493-1498.

Smith, J. H. (1976). An independent judiciary: The colonial background. *University of Pennsylvania Law Review, 126,* 1104-1156.

Smith, M. (1951). The California method of selecting judges. *Stanford Law Review, 3,* 571-600.

Smith v. Higinbothom, 1946. 187 Md. 115.

Smithey, S. I., & Ishiyama, J. (1999, August/September). *Judicious choices: Designing courts in post-communist politics.* Paper presented at the annual meeting of the American Political Science Association, Atlanta, GA.

Stephens, R. F. (1989). Judicial election and appointment at the state level: Commentary on state selection of judges. *Kentucky Law Journal, 77,* 741-746.

Stevens, J. P. (1995). Dissenting opinion in *Harris v. Alabama.*

Stumpf, H. P. (1998). *American judicial politics* (2nd ed.). Upper Saddle River, NJ: Prentice Hall.

Stumpf, H. P., & Culver, J. H. (1992). *The politics of state courts.* New York: Longman.

Swackhamer, W. D. (1974). *Political history of Nevada.* Carson City: State of Nevada.

Tabarrok, A., & Helland, E. (1999). Court politics: The political economy of tort awards. *Journal of Law & Economics, 42,* 157-187.

Taft, R. S. (1893). The Supreme Court of Vermont. *The Greenbag, 5,* 553-564.

Tarr, G. A. (1999). *Judicial process and judicial policy making* (2nd ed.). Belmont, CA: West/Wadsworth.

Thorpe, F. N. (1909). *The federal and state constitutions, colonial charters, and other organic laws of the states, territories, and colonies.* Washington, DC: Government Printing Office.

Tocqueville, A. de. (1954). *Democracy in America.* New York: Vintage. (Original published 1835.)

Tokarz, K. L. (1986). Women judges and merit selection under the Missouri Plan. *Washington University Law Quarterly, 64,* 903-951.

Uhlmann, T. M. (1977). Race, recruitment, representation: Background differences between black and white trial court judges. *Western Political Quarterly, 30,* 457.

Vaughan, C. C. (1917). *Michigan official directory and legislative manual.* Lansing: State of Michigan.

Vines, K. N. (1962). Political functions on a state supreme court. In K. N. Vines & H. Jacob (Eds.), *Tulane studies in political science: Studies in judicial politics.* New Orleans: Tulane University.

Volcansek, M. L., & Lafon, J. L. (1988). *Judicial selection: The cross-evolution of French and American prac-*
tices. New York: Greenwood.

Watson, R. A., & Downing, R. G. (1969). *The politics of bench and bar: Judicial selection under the Missouri*
nonpartisan court plan. New York: Wiley.

Webster, P. D. (1995, Fall). Selection and retention of judges: Is there one "best" method? *Florida State*
University Law Review, 23, 1-42.

Wiener, S. D. (1996). Popular justice: State judicial elections and procedural due process. *Harvard Civil*
Rights-Civil Liberties Law Review, 31, 187-221.

Winslow, J. B. (1912). *The story of a great court: Being a sketch history of the supreme court of Wisconsin, its*
judges and their times from the admission of the state to the death of Chief Justice Ryan. Chicago: T. H.
Flood.

Winters, G. R. (1966). Selection of judges—introduction. *Texas Law Review, 44*(1), 1081-1087.

Winters, G. R. (1968). The merit plan for judicial selection and tenure—Its Historical development.
Duquesne Law Review, 7(1), 61-78.

Witte, H. L. (1995). Judicial selection in the People's Democratic Republic of Pennsylvania: Here the
people rule? *Temple Law Review, 68,* 1079-1149.

Wooster, R. A. (1969). *The people in power: Courthouse and statehouse in the Lower South, 1850-1860.*
Knoxville: University of Tennessee Press.

Wooster, R. A. (1975). *Politicians, planters and plain folk: Courthouse and statehouse in the Upper South,*
1850-1860. Knoxville: University of Tennessee Press.

Ziskind, M. A. (1969). Judicial tenure in the American Constitution: English and American precedents.
In P. B. Kurland (Ed.), *Supreme Court Review.* Chicago: University of Chicago Press.

Declarations of Independence

Judicial Reactions to Political Pressure

Kim Lane Scheppele

What does it mean for a judge to be independent?

This chapter will address that question in two stages. First, I will look at the paradigmatic case in which judges have been deemed *not* to be independent—that is, when judges receive instruction in the specific case—and I will contrast it with the case when judges are generally thought to be behaving appropriately—that is, when they are following the rules laid down in the law. I will argue that the two are less different than they look, if judges take a basically positivist attitude toward law. If judges are under pressure to decide a particular case in a particular way, it matters less whether those pressures come in the form of particular instructions or specific rules than whether judges have any possibility of finding some critical distance on statutes. Positivism as a judicial ideology discourages such distance. To explore this, I need to consider first whether there are some minimum criteria for judicial independence.

An earlier version of these ideas was prepared for the conference on Judicial Independence, held at the University of Pennsylvania Law School, March 31 to April 1, 2001. I would like to thank the participants of that conference for stimulating discussion that helped to shape the final product. I owe a special debt to Steve Burbank for his wise counsel, constant encouragement, and grammatical sensibility. And I would like to thank Serguei Ouskakine for his daily lessons on the surprises of soviet and post-soviet life.

Then I will examine the liberating effect on judges of the ever-increasing constitutionalization of politics. In a number of countries, new constitutions and expanded conceptions of judicial review have given extraordinary powers to judges to work around the positive law in the name of constitutional principles. If judges can use their constitutional role to gain a critical distance toward statutes, then judges will also have more independence relative to the executive and legislative branches of the government that enacts the laws. Empowered by constitutional principles, judges can (and some judges often) bend the positive law to a judicial conception of what the law should be, thereby challenging the political branches for the final word on what counts as law in the first place. That's the new face of judicial independence, perhaps more visible outside of the United States than in it, but there are important signs of this activism in the United States as well. The constitutionalization of politics raises the question: Is too much independence a good thing? In this second part, I will consider whether some maximum amount of judicial independence exists beyond which judging loses its special legitimacy.

In addressing these issues, I will consider both the standpoint of the judge who has a decision to make in a specific case and an institutional standpoint over the long run of cases in which the independence of the judiciary as a whole is in sharpest focus.[1] The individual judge is always embedded in an institutional context, which requires embedding the analysis of the individual judge's opinions and options in an institutional context as well. Judges may have institutionally permissible choices that they do not exercise in the individual case just as individual judges may deviate from institutionally normative practices. Without looking at both the concrete decisions of individual judges and the role of their courts in the broader scheme of things, it is hard to sketch a complete picture of judicial independence.

My approach will also be broadly comparative. Although an analysis of judicial independence must be sensitive to place and local detail, the broader view one can accomplish by looking at a number of different places in the same analysis argues in favor of comparative breadth over single-country depth. In the spirit of Tom Waits' lyrics, "Never saw my hometown 'til I stayed away too long," comparative analysis helps one to see things about one's own home territory that would otherwise fade into the background of the taken-for-granted. This chapter has something to say about American dilemmas of judicial independence, but by way of contrast and comparison.

Finally, this chapter calls attention to the specific devices and strategies through which judges have been constrained by the political branches as well as the specific devices and strategies through which judges have managed to slip the bonds of positive law in a growing number of countries. Among the former, I contend, one should count not just corruption, personal influence, and direct political pressure, but also positivism as a threat to core elements of the judicial role. On the latter, Americans are accustomed to having the debate about judicial power concentrate on basically interpretive practices in determining what the Constitution means, in which the familiar litany of framer's intent, plain meaning, and various forms of interpretivism form the relevant universe of concern. But judges elsewhere in the world have developed a more audacious set of constitutional tools, including activating preambles, threatening to declare constitutional amendments unconstitutional, finding that constitutional norms must be used to interpret other branches of law that are not—narrowly speaking—constitutional at all, invoking extralegal principles that go beyond the constitutional text altogether, and changing the ground rules of procedure, justiciability, and standing. Compared to traditional American practices (or at least the American academic discussions of these practices), these more audacious judicial tools raise new questions about what the role of judges should be in 21st-century democracies and what amount and type of judicial independence should be encouraged.

Normative questions are raised by this sort of analysis. Does formal independence from instruction in the concrete case mean that judicial independence is thereby guaranteed? Or are there (as I will suggest) other minimum criteria for judicial independence? Can judicial independence—a clear desideratum of most modern liberal democracies—ever be too much of a good thing? Or (as I will argue) should democracies accept as part and parcel of what it means to be a constitutional democracy that courts share important responsibilities for policy making?

The answers to the normative questions, however, rest crucially on empirical investigations into the actual practices of activist judging. In a deeply positivist legal order, for example, do judges in practice find ways to escape political pressures even though they are not supposed to go beyond the instructions that politicians give them? Or (as I will try to show) do judges need the authorization and constraint of a "higher law" in order to be able to confidently treat statutes with critical judgment? But then, if judges in fact need a higher law to be independent, what is to prevent judges from simply dismissing positive law altogether? Here, it is important to note whether courts try to evade the direct application of statutes only in special situations when lawmaking has broken down in critical ways (for example, when it has been captured by special interests to the exclusion of general ones) or whether judges bend the law to their sense of the right answer simply whenever their own political judgment tells them that the political branches got it wrong. The former is a check on democratic processes; the latter creates government by judiciary, which raises serious questions about the democratic accountability of policy. Surely, the nature and normative attractiveness of the stronger view of judicial independence rests on some analysis of the appropriate circumstances in which judges claim this power. As this chapter proceeds, it will be important to keep in view the broader effects of expanded judicial review on the sort of democracy that a country can have. How do judges, politicians, and the general public understand what judges are doing when they declare laws unconstitutional or declare actions of state officials to be in violation of the law? Do judges justify the exercise of their power to check politicians in the *name of* democratic values or as a *check on* democracy (or populism) run amok? Surely judicial independence, although clearly an important element of a democratic order, cannot be maximized to the complete exclusion of other voices and to the ruin of democracy itself.

The limits of the subject matter are now defined. Too little judicial independence can undermine the separation of powers; too much judicial independence can undermine the democratic basis of a political order. I start by exploring where the minimum standards for judicial independence should be and then proceed in later sections to probe the reasonable outer limit of judicial independence.

ᨄ Meditation #1. The Rule and the Case (Normative Explorations)

So, then, back to the beginning: What does it mean in common understanding for judges to be minimally independent? Surely, one must say, judges cannot be completely independent of the law—or at least it would be a novel approach to judging if they were. Judges are not free agents but take their place within a system of governance in which lawmakers make laws, executives enforce laws, and judges sort out the individual applications of the law. But statutes, and even regulations,[2] are often a partisan affair and so when a judge is dependent on "following the rules laid down," the judge is of course dependent (at least indirectly) on those who laid down the rules. But—dependent in what sense? I propose distinguishing first between *dependence at the level of the case* and *dependence at the level of the rule.*

At the level of the case, it is a commonplace in understandings of judicial independence that judges should be absolutely free to follow their best professional sense of what the law requires in a specific matter before their courts. A judge who had to take orders on what to do in individual cases would not have any meaningful independence. One can see that this is the common understanding by noting the canonical case of judicial *dependence:* when a politician or a party official calls the judge directly to suggest that the judge rule a particular way because of political connections of the plaintiff or because political officials have a special interest in the defendant. The clearest example of this is "telephone justice" in soviet states, when political officials telephoned judges to tell them what to do in concrete cases.[3] If the parties to the case or the subject matter of the dispute rose to the level of political attention, the judge would be instructed to follow the party line rather than the positive law. A judge who would follow such suggestions in a system of alleged judicial independence would be—at a minimum—corrupt. If judges felt that they *had* to take political orders at the level of the specific case as a condition of keeping their jobs, then surely these jobs involved no "judgment"per se. Being directly instructed in what to do in the specific case clearly destroys the independence of the judge.

But judges are not supposed to be legal free agents and it is generally accepted as part of the judicial territory that the independence of judges is not compromised if they are dependent on duly enacted statutes and regulations, even when those statutes and regulations are enacted by the very people whose instruction in the individual case would clearly violate judicial independence. At the level of the rule, then, judges are *supposed to be bound* by what they are told by political officials. But the instructions have to come in a very particular form—correctly enacted, publicly conveyed, leaving room for the judge's own interpretation of what they mean in the hard case.[4] If the rules meet these requirements, then a judge *is* supposed to take direction. This sort of direct political influence—in which political processes generate laws that judges must follow—is not generally considered to be a threat to judicial independence, however. In fact, the legitimacy of this sort of political influence goes even deeper: A judge who *ignored* the rules laid down would not be a suitable judge and perhaps even a candidate for impeachment, even though a judge who ignored particular political direction might be a model one. Judges, of all people, are supposed to follow the law, but they are not supposed to listen to the siren song of individual influence—political or otherwise—in the specific case.

That, I think, captures much of what scholars typically take for granted in discussions of judicial independence. But how solid is this absolutely consequential distinction between independence in the case and independence of the rules? I believe, heretically enough, that a judge bound by statute and a judge bound by the dictates of a party official are in many ways less different than they look.[5] To take the most obvious similarity, both the specific backstage instruction and the public statute are ways for politics and policy preferences to enter into the legal process. In both cases, as a result, the *legal* outcome is contingent on the specific policy preferences of those who are (at least temporarily) in charge of the *political* branches of government. The two forms of direction to a judge differ in method but not necessarily in substance. They do not necessarily produce different results. In both cases, those who hold political power extend that power to the legal realm. In both cases, the judge is expected to follow direction and not enter an intervening policy judgment. In both cases, the politician controls policy and the judge is supposed to follow along. This similarity requires some analysis. Let me elaborate.

Imagine World A where (a) a statute is duly enacted by a lawmaker following the procedures outlined in the country's constitution,[6] (b) the statute constitutes an exception to a previously enacted law so that it changes the treatment of a specific set of facts that were previously handled as part of a larger cluster under a previously enacted law, and (c) the exception created by the new rule could only apply in one sort of case (of which Case X is a clear example). The judge in World A gets Case X. It's quite clear to the judge what to do in this case because the law is quite clearly written and so the judge applies the law in the only way it can reasonably be applied in the specific circumstance. And this way amounts to creating an exception to the previous general rule because the law takes a type of case formerly covered by the old rule and puts it under a new one defining the exception. The judge has been a model judge, following the rules laid down, with all of their twists and turns. The judge is appropriately independent, though clearly highly constrained by the specificity of the statute.

Now imagine World B where (a) the general statute enacted in the appropriate way covers a range of cases, including Case X. But (b) the head of the governing political party who is also (not coincidentally) the head of the government (perhaps as the president or the prime minister) calls the judge to say that, in Case X, an exception should be made to the usual rule to reach an outcome different from the one that the general statute would usually require. Let us further suppose that this political official is (c) generally authorized to be the lawmaker in this particular regime because the official has the power to issue binding legal decrees but (d) this particular instruction in the particular case is not given in the form of a decree but instead through a phone call that the judge and the politician both know is supposed to be kept secret. In World B, unlike World A, the *outcome* in the one specific case is dictated directly by the caller *without reference to a legal norm*. But let us suppose that the judge in World B, like the judge in World A, does as instructed; Case X, which has specific political interest to the regime, is handled as an exception to the general rule. In World B, I submit, the judge has no independence and no moral credit left because the judge has caved in to direct political pressure.

But what exactly is the difference between World A and World B? In both worlds, the *result* is the same. This one particular case that came before the judge has been lifted out of the general run of cases to which a broader, more general rule applies and it has been handled as an exception. Moreover, it was the *specific instructions from someone in political power* that determined what happened in both cases. In World A, however, the instructions came in the form of legislation and in World B, the instructions were personally delivered without first being converted into a legal norm. In World A, the new norm was publicly announced whereas in World B, the instructions were secret. In World A, the judge was left alone to interpret the legal norm to determine its application in the particular case; in World B, the desired application of the instructions was specifically directed without any intervening judgment by the judge.

These three features—(1) proper procedure in making the law, (2) publicity in announcing the norms to be applied in the specific case, and (3) the discretionary space for judicial interpretation of those norms—make all the difference in whether the judge is independent or not. In fact, the loss of any one of the three would be sufficient to compromise judicial independence. In World A, the result in the specific case has been reached by application of a duly enacted rule to a specific case and the application process is conducted by the judge without further outside pressure. World A possesses (a) a notion of legitimate lawmaking procedures and allows the lawmaker to speak to the judge only in procedurally appropriate and public ways. The policy that the judge carries out in World A is (b) there for all the world to see because it has been converted into a legal norm. And, importantly, the judge retains (c) professional control over the process of applying the rule to the case. World A, then, has some crucial features of the "rule of law" in which the independence of the judge is ensured through procedural norms.

By contrast, World B doesn't have these rule-of-law guarantees. When the call comes to the World B judge, that judge has no way of knowing how widely shared or how public within the governing circles the specific desired outcome is; no one other than the judge and the politician would know that the outcome rested on the specific instructions in the specific case.[7] In World B, to separate the personal and official views of the official who calls is hard, but the judge understands nonetheless that the instructions of the official must be followed. The judge in World B would have every reason to suspect that what is really expected here is not an act of legal interpretation but instead an act of political acquiescence.

In both worlds, however, the politician and the judge are in a symbiotic relationship, in which the judge is dependent on the politician for instructions and the politician depends on the judge to carry them out. It is at least a notable fact that in World B, the politician feels that the decision cannot be made directly but must rely on the judge to pronounce the decision from the bench.[8] Regimes that bypass this elementary requirement of a separation of law and politics find themselves with no legal system at all.[9] Such regimes certainly exist. But regimes in which political orders are converted directly, without more, into legal orders have only a superficial resemblance to a real division of powers, which is the only sort of regime in which one can meaningfully talk about judicial independence. So instead, I will confine the discussion to situations in which the judge is not bypassed altogether. Some division of powers must exist to begin to discuss judicial independence. The politician must rely on the judge—but how much is the reverse true? This is what I consider next.

Because judicial independence relies on a strong form of division of powers, the sort of symbiosis that exists between politician and judge differs greatly between World A and World B.[10] In World A, the lawmaker lays out an abstract rule within officially authorized powers and the judge applies it without further intervention from the lawmaker to the specific case that comes within the ambit of

the judge's authorized responsibility. The powers of lawmaking and legal interpretation are divided between the politician and the judge. In World B, however,
the lawmaker intervenes directly at the level of the individual case, removing (or
compromising) the ability of the judge to enter an intervening interpretation of
law. The power to make the rule and the power to apply it are merged in the concrete political instruction to the judge. The only responsibility left to the judge is
the paperwork for recording the decision.

But if the law is so clear in World A, as I have constructed it to be in this hypothetical case, then don't the differences between World A and World B start to look
more formal than substantive? In World A, when the clear case comes,[11] there is
almost nothing for the judge to do, as is also true for the judge who receives the
direct instructions in World B. In World A, the law "clearly" applies and so the
judge, just following the law, does what "the law" requires. Is the judge independent? Or just following instructions, as the judge in World B does when given a
direct order?

It's hard, from looking at the behavior alone, to tell the two worlds apart. When,
at the end of the Burns and Allen television show, George Burns said to his partner
Gracie Allen, "Say good night, Gracie" and she obediently said "good night," was
she an independent actor exercising her own powers of interpretation or was she
just passing on a decision reached elsewhere?[12] When a politician tells a judge to
decide a case a particular way, and then the judge does so, the same question
arises. The clearer the instructions are from one to the other, the harder it is to tell
the difference between meaningful independence (the judge considered the
request and by independent judgment did what was suggested because the judge
thought it was the right thing to do under the circumstances as a matter of professional opinion) and having no mind of one's own (following orders). This indicates that distinguishing possible independence from almost certain dependence
itself depends crucially on what one takes to be subjective view of judges toward
their responsibilities as well as on the larger relationship between the "political
instructions" and the "decision." (And certainly just looking at the behavior of the
judge isn't enough.)[13]

But if the judge in World A were to do anything *other* than what the law requires
in a clear case, then would this judge be behaving appropriately as a judge? If the
rule clearly applies and the judge does *not* follow it, then perhaps this judge is not
engaged in proper judging at all. Instead, the judge has simply created a new policy in substitution for what the politician has said. So then, just *how* is the judge
independent to exercise judgment in the matter in which the rules are clear? Is the
judge simply saying "good night" on instruction, or is there a meaningful intermediate point at which the judge can review the options and, all things considered,
decide that this one possible outcome is really the best thing to say under the circumstances? Would a judge have independence at all if it weren't at least *possible*

to make the wrong decision without dire consequences?[14] Perhaps, just to preserve independence, the judge should be *encouraged* on occasion to make the wrong decision just to show *that* there is a possibility of independence? But doesn't that go too far? If it does, then one has to say that in the clear case, the judge just is dependent on the politician or otherwise the judge is not behaving properly. All the judge can do is say one thing—which happens to be the very thing that the politician wants said—or make a mistake. Dependence at the level of the case and dependence at the level of the rule seem to collapse into each other at this point.

If the judge considers the law and self-consciously decides to understand it in a different way from the politician, then this is the sort of thing one might mean by having judicial independence. But how does one distinguish (a) the free-spirited but self-consciously deviating judge in World A who considers the obvious interpretation, rejects it, and invents instead a less obvious interpretation *of the law* from (b) the judge who *disregards* the relevant law altogether? Surely, the latter would be completely independent but perhaps not a proper judge. And what should one say about the former? That this judge is independent but wrong? All one can say for certain is that a judge who *follows* the law exactly, using only the most obvious interpretations, may or may not be independent. One needs to know more.

That raises the next question: Is the important difference in the independence of the judge between World A and World B primarily the division of labor (or separation of powers) in who gets to say what to do in the individual case in *hard cases only*[15]—that is, for cases in which the proper application of the rule to the case is controversial or requires serious interpretive work, in which reasonable people would disagree about what the law requires? In clear cases under both the "level of the case" and the "level of the rule" analysis, the job of the judge is to directly carry out what the politician has requested. In hard cases, doing what the law requires itself requires judgment and reasonable people can disagree because the way the case fits under the law is open to argument. But that's true both in World A and in World B. Even if the politician gives the judge direct instructions about what to do in the specific case, as I hypothesized for World B, the judge might find that this could turn into a "hard case" if the judge can't figure out whether the case before her is the specific case that the politician had in mind, or if the instructions don't lead to a straightforward answer in the case that clearly is the one to which the instructions apply. For example, if the politician calls and says, "The case before you involving the child of a central committee member should be dismissed" and there happen to be two such cases, then the judge has a *hard case* determining which matter to dismiss even when there are direct instructions. Or if the politicians calls and says, "You should treat the case where the defendant applied for a foreign passport to live abroad in the harshest possible manner" and the evidence about the application for the foreign passport is contested, then what? The judge clearly has to do something beyond the instructions. Either the judge can "interpret" the instructions in order to get as close as possible to what the politician meant, or consider a broader frame in which what the politician meant is only one sort of guidance among others. (In the latter case, for example, the judge might consider that a defendant should not be convicted on the basis of insufficient evidence as a countervailing consideration.) But the judge could take the broader view if the case were hard in this sense in either World A or World B. Unclear instructions lead to the need for an intervening analysis by the judge. But then, are judges only independent (or only recognizably independent) in hard cases and then only partially so? (And is there any difference between World A and World B in this matter?)

The American poet John Ashbury once noted, "Everything is water if you look long enough." And perhaps that is also true of judicial (in)dependence. How could a judge following the law enacted by politicians be as dependent on politics as a judge who carries out directly what a politician instructs in the specific case?

۰&#x0; Meditation #2: Reality Checks

Of course, there is a clear difference between following the rules laid down and telephone justice. Isn't there? I have spent much of the last decade studying the legal systems of the former soviet world from which the example of telephone justice largely derives, and after that, the difference seems even less straightforward to me than it used to. Looking at "countries in transition," what I saw was both much better and much worse than I expected. Telephone justice was used more sparingly in the soviet time than I had imagined, but positivism was more rampant than I knew.

What is now becoming clear is that "the party" (the Communist Party, that is), however omnipotent, did not have the ability or perhaps even the desire to dictate the outcome of every legal case. The vast majority of routine cases decided by judges in soviet-style legal systems probably were decided on the merits (defined in a distinctively state socialist way, of course) and not on the basis of the particular political instructions in individual cases. In the vast majority of private law cases (for example, in family law), the party didn't typically care about particular outcomes and therefore did not usually engage in case-by-case oversight. Moreover, across the array of civil law cases, complete control was impossible on a case-by-case basis anyhow because the state didn't have the manpower. In most cases, telephone justice simply wasn't necessary because judges knew what was expected of them—and that was to follow the rules laid down. "Political cases" received special attention, but often special courts were set up to deal with them. That meant that ordinary judges were less likely to encounter the ringing telephone with specific instructions. Not that it didn't happen. But it was sufficiently rare that the ordinary judge still had to figure out to apply the law as written most of the time. Soviet judges, in other words, still had to know how to judge.

The best study of this to date is the extraordinary fieldwork done by Inge Markovits just as East Germany's legal system was being folded into West Germany's on unification. Of course, not all of the soviet-bloc countries were alike, but there were enough family resemblances to enable us to get some insight into soviet systems generally from an examination of one of the harshest regimes. One judge Markovits interviewed admitted that telephone justice was attempted some of the time, but "It was possible to fend that kind of thing off" (Markovits, 1996, p. 24). This same judge, however, remembered a prosecution for "unlawful crossing of the state border," a clearly political offense. Although she found telephone justice deeply insulting to her professional judgment, she had not the slightest problem applying the criminal code—even in such a political case— exactly as written. In one case where she had to apply this law, the defendant appeared to have been drunk at the time that he tried to cross the border, or at least so said the one arresting border guard who testified. The judge acquitted for lack of intent. The prosecutor appealed (again, a common feature of soviet-style systems) and the appeals court remanded for the judge to find more evidence. The judge called a second border guard who testified to the same effect as the first border guard, that the defendant had to be carried from the scene of the crime, because he was too drunk to walk on his own. Again, the judge acquitted. Still no intent. Again, on appeal, the regional court disagreed, this time registering a conviction (another universal possibility in soviet-style systems). The trial judge saw no problem with this either on the grounds of substantive law or on the grounds of judicial independence. As Markovits (1996) wrote

> I detect no criticism of a state that punishes its citizens for attempting to leave it, no outrage at the court of appeals for applying the punishment to people who pose no real threat to the system, and no self-righteousness on her part for having persisted in disagreeing with her superiors. (p. 24)

Markovits found that the judge took this latter sort of control of her judgments in stride and did not see it as a violation of her ability to make an independent judgment. The judge did her job and the appeals court did its job. She was an independent judge when she applied the rules as she saw them and she never caved in to direct instruction.

In fact, when asked about the relevant legal norms that she was supposed to apply to such cases, Markovits's judge went immediately to her shoebox of notes. These notes were taken in the meetings when valid interpretations of rules were announced orally by higher court judges because many of the rules ordinary judges were supposed to be applying were not published with the level of precision with which they were supposed to be applied. And Markovits's judge clearly believed that a good judge would find out all she could about the rules laid down so that she could conscientiously follow them. The Supreme Court in East Germany (as in other soviet-style states) generally promulgated more detailed directives to lower-court judges that specified how they were to interpret the more generally written laws (Markovits, 1996, p. 26).[16] No doubt the Supreme Court had been influenced by the Communist Party in formulating its directives (either because judges had to be party members or because the Supreme Court was itself under the supervision of the Justice Ministry), but as a formal matter, the directives came from judges at the top to judges at the bottom. This particular judge that Markovits interviewed, and other judges that made appearances in her book, showed great pride in keeping all of the various *rule-encapsulated* legal instructions they were given in good order so that they could do precisely what the law required of them. This judge, and other judges, clearly differentiated between telephone justice and more general rules, even if they did not always distinguish between legal norms that had been duly published and those that were conveyed in meetings for judges. Telephone justice was clearly a violation of the judge's professional status but following the precise and detailed rules laid down (from a variety of authoritative sources) was what the judge was supposed to do. After seeing how soviet judging worked close up, however, should one really want to hang an analysis of judicial independence on what turns out to be a relatively formal distinction between dependence at the level of the case and dependence at the level of the rule?

Although socialist legal theory announced its rejection of legal positivism in favor of a more instrumental and substantive conception of law, the conception of judging that came with that package was, strangely enough, heavily positivist.[17] Soviet legal theory harbored perhaps even more nervousness about judicial lawmaking than much of liberal legal theory does.[18] The arguments looked much the same as they do in liberal legal systems: The judge's job is to interpret the law, not to make it.[19]

So, were soviet-style judges independent? Perhaps they were at the level of the case much of the time, but they were certainly not free to improvise around the rules. Judges were specifically instructed to follow the law laid down in all of its detail, without question. Such a devotion to positive law meant that, as a routine matter, judges could not help but take direction in fairly literal ways, but they were taking direction *at the level of the rule.* According to one description of the way that judging was organized in the Soviet Union, from V.P. Radkov (1952):

> The Party agencies mobilize and direct judges to consistent realization of the demands of the law. However good the laws may be, they can provide nothing by themselves. Without extensive organizational work of the Communist Party of the Soviet Union, they would remain unenforced.... With its leadership, it provides tangible conditions for *subjection to law of the activity of all court organs* [italics added].... In exercising Party guidance over courts, the agencies and organizations of the Communist Party of the Soviet Union stop all activity violating the independence of judges in deciding concrete cases. (p. 152)

According to Radkov, judges failed to be independent when they were told specifically what to do in concrete cases, and political vigilance was necessary to ensure that judges remained independent of these sorts of corrosive influences. But judges still needed party oversight to ensure that law "subjugated" courts rather than the other way around. In short, judges were independent only insofar as they were free to strictly follow the rules laid down.

There was a reason why positivist approaches to judging were as popular in the soviet world as they are in some liberal democratic states. In both cases, positivism creates a certain sort of judicial accountability. Positivism accomplishes the political control of cases with more legitimacy than direct instruction can. If a government (or ruling party) can bind judges with rules together with a theory of judging that makes questioning the rules not a judge's job, then the government (or ruling party) can make judges do as they are told. What judges do in the individual case is then simply an extension of the political instructions they were given from elsewhere. A rational socialist government will therefore choose positivism over telephone justice to accomplish its goals because properly trained judges can carry out state policy at the level of the case perfectly well once they are instructed in the rules over which they have no say. If the government knows what the ideology of the law should be and therefore what the right answer is in every case, the judiciary should not have much to say about this but instead should be limited in its tasks to applying the instructions to specific cases. Positivism binds law to politics.

Liberal democratic governments single-mindedly devoted to republicanism will choose positivism also—but for reasons consistent with the principles of representative democracy. If law is to be crafted by representatives accountable to those who elected them, then judges are not supposed to be making the law. Judges are often not directly elected and even when they are, they are often invisible candidates who feel committed for professional reasons to not tell the voters what they would do in concrete cases. Given that judges in liberal democratic orders either do not have an electoral mandate or not a clear one that directs policy choices specifically, independent judges should, therefore, *not* be independent of the law in a representative democratic order either. Positivism ensures that judges are accountable to electoral majorities.

There are, therefore, political-theoretical reasons in both party states and electoral democracies to hold the judges strictly to following the rules. In both cases, the broader political rationale is that judges aren't the ones entitled to say what state policy should be. Only politicians can do that.

Soviet judges no doubt felt a strong difference between telephone justice and staying within the rules. But at some level, the two are interchangeable in terms of concrete outcomes in concrete cases. How are positivism and telephone justice interchangeable? In telephone justice, as in World B, the judge receives specific direction in the specific case. How much more efficient it is for the government (or the party) to put those specific instructions in a *rule* that covers the set of cases (or even single case) that the government (or party) wants decided in a particular way! In World A, the rule accomplishes the same thing, even making finely tuned exceptions to general rules. The problem, however, is that the rule has to be clear and the judge cannot deviate from it, or else the judge fails to come under the sway of the government (or the party). Under a positivist understanding of a judge's responsibility, following the rules laid down is all the judge can do. And under a positivist understanding of judging, making the relevant legal norms as specific as possible increases judicial accountability. The positivist judge is eager to take instruction for without black-letter law, there is nothing for the judge to apply in the concrete case. The law simply, in the language of Ronald Dworkin's (1978) critique of H.L.A. Hart, "runs out" (pp. 14-15). The positivist judge is instructed to ask only one thing about the law—and that is whether the norm to be applied is really the law. Positivist judges are therefore educated in pedigree tests; a norm is a *legal* norm if it has been approved in the requisite way by those in particular positions, regulated by a further norm about lawmaking procedure.[20] And if the norm is a legal norm, the judge must follow it.

A key survival skill of soviet-era judges was to keep their eyes on the law and not to deviate from it in any unpredictable or fancy ways. Of course, they expected special instruction in cases involving specific types of people—kids of party bosses, foreigners, dissidents. But those cases were often handed off to specialized courts or even more often handled (often dropped) in prosecutors' offices. In the stark positivism of soviet-style judging, when a case was brought and proof was presented, rules were rules. Law was supposed to be applied as written and without much regard to the softening circumstances of specific cases.[21] Judges wouldn't think (or if they thought, they wouldn't try) to challenge the rules. They were just following orders, orders in the form of rules.

The problem in soviet-style systems was not too little law. The problem, generally, was *too much.* Socialist systems typically regulated everything, down to the last detail. For one thing, the central plan for the economy had the status of law. The plan for a particular factory dictated how many tons of iron ore should produce how many tons of steel. A different ratio between inputs and outputs was a violation of the law because it was a violation of the plan. The rules regulating bakeries dictated how many ounces of flour (and which sort), how much butter, how much sugar, should be used in each different type of pastry. The plan did have its soft side; a certain amount was always calculated for waste (or—literally in the Russian word for this—*shriveling,* that is, private appropriation). But in the plan's intricate detail, it was hard for those regulated not to violate something.

One sees this reflected in the detective stories of the soviet period. In one series popular in the Soviet Union called *The Experts,* a team of three investigators tracked down evidence to show how crimes were committed.[22] But soviet detective novels did not start with the proverbial dead body on the floor; such things under socialism were not supposed to happen. Instead, detective novels showed how morally corrupt citizens failed their civic duties by trying to cheat on the plan. In one story, for example, the owners of a bakery used insufficient amounts of flour in their bread, hoarding it for another use, breaking the law. (They used the "stolen" flour to make pastry, which they could sell off the books for a higher price.) The experts came to investigate and through intricate examination of the bakery's books, through chemical analysis of the bakery's bread, and through scientific examination of other such tell-tale traces, they showed how the law was violated by those charged with baking bread according to the plan. The proof that could be presented to a court as a result of these investigations was hard to challenge, given the way that the methods of investigation were suited to the specificity of the crime. Chemical analysis showed that the bread had the wrong concentration of flour. Science didn't lie. *The Experts,* which also became a popular television series in the soviet time and which is still in reruns in the post-soviet period, showed (as did similar television series in the United States, albeit with different content) that crime did not pay. One difference between the typical American detective story and the typical soviet one, however, lies in what counts substantively as the criminal law whose violation needs such attention. But another difference was that the soviet law that was violated was far more, well, picky.

Commentators on the system of criminal law in the Soviet Union often note the detail, formality, and rigidity of the system. As Frits Gorlé (1987) observed

> Soviet criminal law has been endowed with a rigid dogmatic framework
> that leaves no doubt about the definition and contents of key principles of
> that branch of law. As for the various kinds of guilt, one can admit that such

an approach corresponds to a higher standard of formal legality; the reverse side of the coin is a greater rigidity. (pp. 265-266)

With the law defined so precisely and with official commentaries rather than a body of case law of unequal quality to fill in more detail, judges were rarely in doubt about what the law required. They could, and they did, just follow the rules.

In general, legal regulations were very detailed in socialist legal systems but that didn't mean that the rules taken together made any sense. Nor did it mean that it would be possible for someone to live an ordinary life without falling on the wrong side of one rule or another. Those who lived under the rules constantly complained about the Catch-22 quality of the legal order, in which you couldn't follow one rule unless you had obtained some certification that you had met some previous requirement, which of course you couldn't demonstrate without having to follow the first rule. Or two different rules applied to your intended action, each with contradictory consequences for guiding you in what you should do (Hankiss, 1990).

For example, in the Soviet Union, to be eligible for a *propiska* (residency permit) to live in a particular city, you had to show that you already had a flat there which counted as an official address to use in the application. But of course, you were not eligible to be assigned an apartment in that city from the centrally allocated stock of housing (and in most cities that was very nearly all that there was) unless you already had a job. And you couldn't get a job in that city unless you could go and stay there for long enough to look around. And to stay that long, you needed a propiska. Technically, it was possible to move; practically it was impossible. What was a judge to do with the person who was caught without a propiska? The law was clear; the propiska-less person would be forced to return to the place where he or she *did* have the propiska. End of case. And it wasn't a hard one. The judge was following the law, but the outcome was the same as if the judge had been told directly what to do by the local party boss who wanted to prevent people from moving around in an unauthorized fashion. It didn't work for the soviet citizen caught in the legal crossfire to point out the impossibility of the law in the first place.[23] Judges had no ability to listen to this, even if they too thought the rules were unfair. They might think that the rules were unfair only in their private lives; on the job, they had to follow the rules laid down. And soviet judges didn't just follow the rules because they were afraid of what would happen if they didn't. Soviet judges generally believed that it was their positive obligation as professionals to follow the rules. They were, after all, judges and this is what judges did.

The extraordinary positivism of the practice of judging was also revealed in what happened to a judge's decisions after they were made in the Soviet Union. Records were kept of all judgments, but the opinions giving the reasons for these judgments were not routinely published. If there was an appeal, then records were also kept of what happened to each trial judge's initial judgment when the next set of judges looked at what was done in the court below (and the same happened to the appeals judges' rulings when they were appealed to an even larger bench of judges). If the judgment of the appeals court differed from that of the trial judge, or if the outcome of a later appeal differed from an earlier one, the judgment overturned would be considered a "mistake" on the part of those judges who initially made it. And because the judges' opinions were not published, it was hard to tell the difference between the situation in which the judges took the law seriously but interpreted it differently and the situation in which judge failed to consider the law in the first place. The Justice Ministry in the Soviet Union didn't distinguish either; it just kept track of mistakes. If judges made too many mistakes, then their chances of promotion were nearly nil when they became eligible. And mistakes could also be the basis for disciplinary proceedings and dismissals in extreme cases.

Even though Russia in the post-soviet time has radically changed its legal system, this system of the supervision "mistakes" of lower court judges has remained the same. To this day, the system in which the overturned decisions of judges count against them is still in place and in fact, many Russian lawyers are astonished that any legal system could *fail* to keep track of whether the judges are doing their jobs adequately.[24] Doing one's job adequately means making few mistakes because if the law is written correctly, then it should have one and only one right answer which any professional judge should be able to determine.

The very idea of "a mistake" requires a sense that the law can only be read one way—the right way. And this extraordinary method of surveillance and supervision of judges feeds back into what it is permissible for a judge to do in the first place. What judges should do, then, is to guess what their superiors would do—and then do that. In some ways, American legal realism has no better follower than the soviet (perhaps even ex-soviet) judge. If judges are themselves judged according to the mistakes made, and mistakes are determined by what judges on appeal, in fact do, then it is rational for lower court judges to make decisions in light of a sober assessment of what the judges on appeal would say. Law becomes then simply "what judges do in fact," as Jerome Frank (1973) famously said. And the judge above is unlikely to give politically deviant interpretations of the law. Better, then, to read the law in the politically obvious way. That, of course, leaves less room for judges to do anything innovative.[25]

Insofar as soviet-style judges were compromised in their independence, it seems to me that it was far more by positivism than by being instructed what to do in the concrete case as a routine matter. Soviet-era judging left no room for the infusion of values, for a sense of the principles inherent in the law, for a sense that a legal subject caught in the cross-fire of conflicting legal regulations deserved relief. In short, soviet-era judges were not trained or rewarded for thinking about the broader point of law and the broader values that law should express. Statutes were statutes; law was law. The more detailed and precise, the better. The law in the soviet time embodied the dictatorship of the proletariat expressed through the unerring wisdom of the people's representatives who were the vanguard of the working class. Or it was at least what one found in the statute books.[26] Nothing more could be said.

Perhaps one reason why telephone justice was not more common was that a politically infused law, hardened by legal positivism and enforced by a rigid policing of disagreements among judges, made intervention in specific cases by and large unnecessary. Judges were to follow very detailed, very rigid, very specific laws in most cases. And records were kept of whether they had done it "correctly" or not. Such judges didn't have to be phoned up by party officials to be told what to do. But it would be hard to describe the judges living in soviet-world legal systems as independent. They weren't meaningfully independent even when they were following the rules laid down.

❧ Meditation #3: Constitutional Principle (Back to the Normative Argument)

So, then, what is wrong with this picture so far? Shouldn't advocates of good judging *want* judges to follow the rules laid down and, in doing so, to come as close as possible to the way that the lawmakers intended these rules to be applied?

Well, yes—and no. It seems to me that in general one should want judges to follow the rules laid down, except when the rules themselves have something wrong with them or when the rule is about to be applied to a case that doesn't seem to be the sort of case for which the rule was intended. One should want judges to think not only about how to apply the rules before them but whether it makes sense for them to do so. But, given that they are judges, there should be some broader constraints on the sort of "sense" that judges invoke. That "sense," I will argue, comes in the form of broader legal principles. In order to be independent of temporary politics in a satisfactory way, judges need to be *dependent at the level of the principle.*

What does that mean? Dependence at the level of the principle means that judges must be able to approach rules themselves with a critical attitude, an attitude that allows the judge to assess whether the rule is appropriately applied to the case at all and whether the rule itself is appropriately specified in the first place. But the judge can't just do this on an intuitionist basis because there should be something about judging that operates within an institutional constraint. Instead, there should be some not-entirely personal guidelines for carrying out this task too, so that judges can be held accountable to something besides their own consciences. There should be, in other words, a "higher law" that judges should follow to check their personal inclinations; judges can still follow this law but have some resources of their own to use to check what current politicians enact and then instruct the judges to follow. In short, judges need something that enables them to evaluate whether the politicians have acted correctly in creating new law, and that something is a higher law that outlasts particular politicians' terms. On this "higher law" model,[27] there should be some law with a source in something other than the one-time agreement of current politicians, something that gives some stability and predictability to the actions of government, something that both constrains the exercise of temporary power and enables citizens to whom the law applies to establish some boundaries on what can and cannot be done in their name. In most regimes that adopt this approach, that higher law is contained in a constitution,[28] but sometimes the principles that give judges the ability to gain some critical distance on statutory law are located somewhere else in the legal system, such as in the common law. Although I will focus here on con-stitutional issues, much of what I have to say can apply in many cases to the common law as well.

What having a judicially enforceable constitution amounts to, of course, is introducing to the model of judging some test besides that of a rule's pedigree (in which the pedigree test is the "is this a proper legal rule?" test). And this new test, famously explained by Ronald Dworkin (1978), is that the judge needs to be able to resort to principles to assess the rules.[29] If the judge has something beyond the statutes written by current politicians to use to assess those statutes, then the judge can gain substantial independence from the politician.[30] Judges can there-fore be independent both at the level of the case and at the level of the rule if they are *dependent instead on principles* and those principles are framed at some greater level of generality and at some temporal remove from the statutes that judges are called on to apply. The practice of writing constitutions in special constituent assemblies, although not followed everywhere, reveals how constitutional design is different from ordinary lawmaking. The greater persistence and entrenchment of a constitutional text helps it to become a critical background constraint on judg-ing. If judges were not dependent on something beyond their own personal views, then it would be hard to say that judges were applying law in the first place. The idea of a higher law, of a constitutional constraint on ordinary law, fulfills this purpose.

Some of the principles that judges will use to gain critical distance on statutes will be about lawmaking itself and the formal properties of statutes. Lon Fuller's famous discussion of the principles inherent in the idea of legality lists several of the most obvious ones. Laws should be nonretroactive and not contradictory. They should be made publicly, put in the form of rules comprehensible to those expected to follow them, and possible to follow. They should not be changed so frequently that those expected to follow them can't keep up. They should be applied as advertised (Fuller, 1964). Even when constitutions don't make these features explicit, some courts have taken them on as important legitimacy principles that statutes must follow.[31] For example, in the World A and World B example outlined in Meditation #1 above, one criticism of the rule in World A (where an appropriately enacted rule substitutes for the direct instruction to decide a case in a particular way) might be that the rule is insufficiently general or that the rule, because of the narrowness with which it is framed, in effect singles out particular cases. If a judge were convinced that a rule that he or she was asked to apply had the same actual effect as direct instructions in an individual case, then a sense of rule of law principles would enable the judge to avoid applying the law for the same reason that a judge should avoid following direct political instruction. The same would be true if the law were retroactive, or contradictory, or changing so fast that the subjects who were expected to follow the law didn't know how to orient their conduct toward it.

But many of the principles that a constitution provides will be substantive, growing either from actual agreements forged in moments of constitutional drafting about what a new polity will look like or from the flexibility of language in which a constitutional text is written. For example, Alec Stone Sweet (2000, pp. 42-43), in his comparison of the constitutions of France, Germany, Italy, and Spain, noted that all provide for public education, private property, political participation, and freedom of expression, but only France, Italy, and Spain provide by constitutional provision for public health care, old age pensions, vacation time, and unemployment compensation. Spain, alone among the four countries, also guarantees equitable distribution of resources and protection for consumers in its constitution. Germany alone elevates human dignity to the highest level of constitutional protection. The similarities and differences could be multiplied; suffice it to say that each constitution contains its own set of substantive provisions for different historical reasons. But whatever the constitutional specifics, a constitution provides a way for a judge to escape direct political influence, influence that comes with requiring the judge to follow the rules laid down. Not all constitutions provide explicitly for judicial review, but even those constitutions that do not give judges this power still represent some other source of law for judges to use in interpreting the rules that politicians enact. A history of judge-made law (for example, the common law) can do the same.

∞ Meditation #4: Constitutional Improvisations and Judicial Empowerment

Written constitutions became a commonplace of political life by the end of the 20th century, but it was not until the Second World War that judicial independence in the form of independent courts possessing at least some powers of judicial review became a routine part of those constitutions. It took even longer for judges, engaged in transnational borrowings, to hone a set of tools that could be used to establish at least a partial judicial independence from statutes within the context of judicial fidelity to constitutional principles. Because these tools are not used only for judicial review, strictly speaking, I will call the development of these mechanisms *judicial empowerment* instead. Judicial empowerment comprises all of those techniques that judges can use to gain critical distance on statutes. As judicial empowerment has come to new polities, the techniques through which independent judges assert their own power over statutory law have multiplied and spread. In many cases, this power has been exercised by constitutional courts that alone within a judicial system are empowered to exercise judicial review[32] rather than through a diffuse system of judicial review familiar in the United States. But even when constitutions do not explicitly provide for judicial review and, even among courts that do not have judicial review in systems where at least one court does, all courts can use their independent status to engage in judicial empowerment

Unlike the situation in the United States, judicial review is a principle that is explicitly adopted in the text of most modern constitutions, and it is adopted primarily with the goal of keeping the political branches within the bounds of the constitution. This gives judges substantial power over the understanding of what statutes mean and which statutes are allowed to exist, consistent with the constitutional text. In an increasing number of countries, judges seize this power eagerly and use it frequently. Even where judicial review is explicitly given, however, not all courts have it and not all courts that have it find it wise to use it frequently. Judges don't have to go so far as invalidating statutes to gain some critical distance on them. Instead, they can interpret statutes *in light of* constitutional principles, changing or limiting the statute's apparent meaning through infusing it with principles taken from elsewhere in the law. Whether they invalidate statutes or simply use the fact that principles beyond the rules can always be invoked to soften the statutes, judges who can appeal to principles that reach beyond the rules can engage in judicial empowerment.

In what follows, I will highlight some of the methods that judges have used to empower themselves, including (a) activating preambles, (b) developing a "core" set of principles in the legal order that cannot be amended or changed through positive legal enactments, (c) finding that legal norms developed in one part of the legal order must infuse the whole of the legal system, (d) invoking supra-positive (even metaconstitutional) principles, and (e) modifying judicial procedure, particularly through the expansion of justiciability and standing. These are not the only methods that judges use in self-empowerment, but they are among the most audacious.

Activating Preambles

In most constitutions, preambles spell out the ambitions as well as the rationale of the text. As a legal matter, it is generally accepted that preambles don't have the force of law. But some high courts have ruled that the preamble of their countries' constitutions provide a general framework within which the constitution operates, and through this, courts have expanded their powers substantially to find that statutes are unconstitutional.[33]

In France, the Constitutional Council had been given quite limited powers of review under the Gaullist Constitution of 1958. In fact, the Constitutional Council had been created in the first place merely to keep the Parliament from encroaching on the powers of the nearly almighty president. The tribunal's powers were also limited by virtue of the fact that the 1958 Constitution included no rights provisions in its text and referred to rights only sideways in the preamble. Until 1971, the Constitutional Council had limited its decisions to ensuring executive supremacy, as it was designed to do. But faced with a very real threat to a basic principle of the liberal constitutional order when the Parliament passed a series of amendments to the law on freedom of association,[34] the Constitutional Council rather stunningly announced in 1971 what amounted to a huge increase in its jurisdiction by claiming that the preamble of the 1958 Constitution was a legally enforceable provision.

The French constitutional preamble referred to the rights listed in the Declaration of the Rights of Man and the Citizen from 1789 and also to the rights mentioned in the preamble of the 1946 Constitution. Importing these rights into the 1958 Constitution through taking the preamble seriously, the Constitutional Council rewrote its role in the operation of French politics. If all of these rights were now to be considered part of the current Constitution and the Council was empowered to check new legislation for compliance with the whole Constitution, then the Council gave itself many new reasons to strike down legislation for failing to comply with the Constitution. Even with this expansion of powers, the

Constitutional Council has a limited ability to question laws because the Council is allowed to review statutes only in the brief space between the time that they are passed by the Parliament and the time that they are promulgated by the executive. Nonetheless, starting with the associations law, the Council declared a new statute unconstitutional in the name of (implied) constitutional rights.[35]

After the Council expanded its powers in this way, a constitutional amendment that came hard on the heels of that decision expanded standing to allow any 60 members of either house of the French parliament to refer a newly passed law to the Council for review. Before that time, only the President of the Republic, the prime minister, and the presidents of either house of the Parliament could refer a law to the Council. But the new constitutional amendment meant that the political opposition could always go to the Council as a last resort to prevent legislation from coming into effect. Since the mid-1970s, the parliamentary opposition has referred nearly one third of all legislation to the constitutional Council. And since 1981, more than half of all referrals have resulted in annulment of all or part of the referred laws.[36] As Alec Stone Sweet (2000) has noted, "the Council's intervention in the policy-making process can be characterized as systematic" (p. 63). In one rather dramatic case, for example, the Council found the socialist government's program to nationalize various industries in 1982 to be unconstitutional on the grounds that it violated Article 17 of the 1789 Declaration of the Rights of Man and the Citizen (the right to private property) (pp. 66-68). The only way that the 1789 Declaration was considered to be part of the Constitution at all was through a previous court decision. Activating the preamble has resulted in a much more activist court.

The Indian Supreme Court made a similar move to increase its powers relative to the Parliament. The Court found in *Kesavananda Bharati v. State of Kerala* (1973) that the preamble created a basic structure, identifying the most important elements of the Constitution. As one of the justices explained in *Kesavananda*, "The edifice of our Constitution is based upon the basic elements mentioned in the Preamble. If any of these elements are removed, the structure will not survive and it will not be the same Constitution or it cannot maintain its identity" (Kashyap, 1994, p. 53). This announcement that there was a basic structure of the constitutional order became entangled with the Court's elaboration of a doctrine of unconstitutional constitutional amendments because the case at hand occurred when Parliament was attempting to undermine previous Court decisions through constitutional amendment. About this, more later. But even without that connection, the activation of the preamble gave the Indian Supreme Court an interpretive framework that was quite broad and permitted the Court to have a great deal to say about political issues precisely because the Supreme Court was able to list a set of very general principles that could be used for whatever specific purposes the Court had in mind.[37]

Israel's active Supreme Court used a strategy very much like France and India, activating a basic text that was not, strictly speaking, part of the legally enforceable constitution. Israel does not have a single constitutional text, but instead has a series of twelve Basic Laws, each of which regulates in piecemeal fashion a part of Israel's constitutional order. Most of these laws are not entrenched and could be changed with a single act of any parliamentary majority. And until 1992, no Basic Laws were devoted to the subject of rights. Nor was there judicial review, strictly so called. But out of this ambiguous constitutional climate came a strong Supreme Court with many powers to hold government in check and, in particular, to radically alter the plain meaning of statutes through invoking Israel's equivalent to a preamble: the Declaration of Independence.

Israel's 1948 Declaration of Independence traces the history of the Jewish people in Palestine and proclaims the independence of the new state. It promised that Israel would enact a constitution within a year from date of the Declaration. This promise was broken, not least because there was a major disagreement over whether Israel was a Jewish or a secular state. And, as a result, the relevant parties could not agree on a constitution. But, most important for the Supreme Court, the Declaration included a paragraph announcing the basic principles of the state, principles that were to be used to guide further constitutional development. And that paragraph has much that the Supreme Court has been able to draw on as basic principles of the constitutional order:

> The State of Israel will be open to the immigration of Jews from all countries of their dispersion; will promote the development of the country for the benefit of all its inhabitants; will be based on the precepts of liberty, justice, and peace taught by the Hebrew Prophets; will uphold the full social and political equality of all its citizens, without distinction of race, creed, or sex; will guarantee full freedom of conscience, worship, education, and culture; will safeguard the sanctity and inviolability of the shrines and Holy Places of all religions; and will dedicate itself to the principles of the Charter of the United Nations. (Declaration of Independence of the State of Israel, 1948)

The Supreme Court found that this paragraph contained a number of general principles that the judges could use to guide and limit the meaning of statutes and to fill in what the missing parts of the Basic Law should say. The Court did this even though Israel had adopted parliamentary supremacy through one of the earliest Basic Laws, thus ensuring that the Court itself had a prominent place in the political order. For example, citing the "full social and political equality" clause of the Declaration, the Israeli Supreme Court required the government to provide gas masks to Palestinians in the Occupied Territories during the Gulf War in 1991 once it provided gas masks to Jews living there.[38] That was just one of many decisions in which the court, in the absence of either judicial review or a full written constitution, was able to use the Declaration as a legal document to give itself power to check the government.

Unconstitutional Constitutional Amendments

When a constitutional court becomes very active, the elected branches may want to reign it in by amending the constitution and removing the provisions that judges have used to thwart parliamentary plans. But the court may then claim that it has the power to declare constitutional amendments unconstitutional. A number of courts have taken the view that unconstitutional constitutional amendments are, theoretically at least, possible, even though no court has adopted a systematic strategy of declaring them to be so.

In its first decision striking down part of a law as unconstitutional, the Federal Constitutional Court in West Germany read the Basic Law (Germany's equivalent of a constitution) as containing an unamendable core and a more amendable periphery. Article 79(3) of the Basic Law explicitly puts limits on the amendment power by preventing the amendment of Article 1 (outlining the principle of human dignity and the right to life, and establishing Germany as a state based on respect for rights) and Article 20 (requiring federalism). In the *Southwest States Case* (1951) (Kommers, 1997, pp. 62-66), the Federal Constitutional Court quoted with approval the Bavarian Constitutional Court, which had said

> That a constitutional provision may itself be null and void is not conceptually impossible just because it is a part of the Constitution. There are constitutional principles that are so fundamental and so much an expression of a law that has precedence even over the Constitution that they also bind the framers of the Constitution, and other constitutional provisions that do not rank so high may be null and void because they contravene these principles. (Federal Constitutional Court, quoted in Kommers, 1997, p. 63)

Though the Federal Constitutional Court did not itself strike down a constitutional provision in the *Southwest States* case, it strongly hinted that a transitional constitutional provision that allowed specific state boundaries to be changed without going through the normal constitutional procedure was unconstitutional. But the Court stopped short of that conclusion and found instead that the transitional provision had to be interpreted in light of the more strongly embedded clause. That meant that some parts of the statute that the federal government had used to carry out its plans under the transitional provision were unconstitutional. The government went back, redesigned the procedure, and in the end came closer to the entrenched provision than to the transitional one in the way it handled the matter.

The Federal Constitutional Court elaborated this theory of unconstitutional constitutional amendments further in the *Klass Case* (1970), in which the dissenters were prepared to invalidate an amendment to Article 10 of the Basic Law. There, the amendment grew out of attempts to deal with domestic protest by limiting the privacy of communications under certain circumstances, a move that a substantial block of dissenters on the Court said would be unconstitutional.[39] In the end, the government backed down and withdrew the amendment even though the Court's majority did not say that the government had to do so. Though the Court has never actually invalidated a constitutional amendment to date, its persistent hints that it could do so remain an open threat. And from the way that the two cases using this threat have proceeded, the Court has pushed the government to back down and follow a more constitutional route without actually requiring it to do so.

Other courts, however, have not been so reticent about the possibility of declaring parts of a constitution to be unconstitutional, though it is clear that they do so only in exceptional cases. The South African constitutional transition that took place in the 1990s went forward only because the parties agreed that the newly founded Constitutional Court would have the power to declare parts of the new constitution to be inconsistent with general constitutional principles that had been established at the start of the transition process. The parties to the transition, particularly the National Party and the African National Congress, had been unable to agree to a final constitution when they started their negotiations. A potentially dangerous deadlock was broken as the parties adopted an Interim Constitution and a set of binding constitutional principles to be used by the Constituent Assembly in its work toward the final draft. But the Interim Constitution explicitly said that the South African Constitutional Court (an institution itself created by the Interim Constitution) would have the power to review the final constitution for consistency with the constitutional principles and this was, in fact, an important part of reaching the agreement in the first place (Klug, 2000). When the South African Constitutional Court received the final constitution for review, it in fact found certain provisions to be unconstitutional and required the Constituent Assembly to change them (*Certification of the Constitution*, 1996). The changes were made and the new constitution went into effect—and not coincidentally, the Constitutional Court established itself as a powerful new feature of the political landscape precisely because it had established that it had the power to say what the constitution could and could not say in the first place.

South Asia has seen more judicial activism declaring constitutional amendments to be unconstitutional than anywhere else. In India and Nepal, the Supreme Courts have taken the power to declare constitutional amendments to be unconstitutional, though in India the Court eventually backed off under serious political pressure.

Declaring constitutional amendments unconstitutional has been most controversial in India, where prolonged standoffs resulted in several attempts by Indira Gandhi's government to change the Constitution in the 1970s to neutralize an increasingly oppositional Supreme Court. But the Supreme Court had declared in dicta in the *Golak Nath* (1967) case that constitutional amendments could be unconstitutional. The showdown between the Court and the government occurred around the issue of property rights (and later also around charges that Indira Gandhi had corrupted an election). Indira Gandhi's government wanted to adopt a socialist approach to remedy India's extreme poverty, and that approach involved the nationalization of property. The Supreme Court felt that the right to private property in the Indian Constitution prohibited the methods that the government wanted to use and the Court had declared several laws attempting to do this unconstitutional. Increasingly frustrated with the Supreme Court's obstructionism, the Indian Parliament, at the urging of Prime Minister Gandhi, passed several constitutional amendments to accomplish the same purpose, amendments that were challenged in the *Kesavananda* case.[40]

Kesavananda Bharati v. State of Kerala (1973) is a confusing case by any measure. Its 800 published pages feature 11 opinions by 13 justices. Even in a country where seriatim opinions are routine and the apparent agreement of the majority constitutes the rule of the case, it is hard to figure out just what the case stands for. Moreover, while the case was under consideration, there were rumors of improper attempts by politicians to influence the justices and, as a result, a great deal of political tension was in the air. In the end, after the long and rambling seriatim opinions, 9 of the 13 justices signed a shorter and more direct statement that they claimed contained the holding of the case. Part of the confusion surrounding this case, however, stems from the fact that it is difficult to derive the result in that short statement from the longer published opinions. In the end, however, it appears that the Court backed off from its claim that it could declare constitutional amendments unconstitutional. At the same time, it said that the preamble to the Constitution provided the basic core of the constitution, which would remain the same regardless of amendments. Along the way in the specific case, the Court found an ordinary law that the Parliament passed along with the constitutional amendments to be unconstitutional because it violated the principles that were contained in the preamble.[41] Although the court upheld the amendments that the Parliament passed to restrict the right of private property, the court did preserve its apparent independence by reserving to itself the right to examine laws that the Parliament passed for their compliance with the basic principles of the constitution. By strategically backing off the extreme claim of power to declare amendments unconstitutional to the more defensible constitutional position that the Court would examine all laws for their consistency with the basic principles stated in the preamble, the Court extended its range while still leaving open the possibility that even constitutional amendments would be subordinate to principles contained in the preamble.

But even though the Court largely backed down, Indira Gandhi responded to its resistance to her plans by escalating the sense of crisis. The day after *Kesavananda* was announced, Gandhi appointed a new chief justice to replace the one who had previously announced his retirement. But instead of appointing the next most senior judge, as was the accepted convention, she took a justice out of sequence and named him head of the Court because he was most likely to support her views. Reaction from the bar was fierce; the popular press agreed that judicial independence had been attacked. With brewing objections to her imperious style, Indira Gandhi declared a state of emergency two months later. Her row with the Supreme Court was one of the major factors leading to this decision.

After the emergency was lifted two years later, the Supreme Court went back to being very activist, but this time in a leftward direction on behalf of India's poor. Resistance to the Court faded away as a result of the change of the Court's political direction. Activism in defense of the poor was more acceptable to India's political elite than activism in defense of property owners. The Court entirely changed its political leanings in part because the emergency government had amended the constitution to remove the property clause altogether, thereby depriving the Supreme Court of its textual basis for resistance. Although it may have been unconstitutional to add something to the Constitution under the Court's earlier decisions, the Supreme Court said nothing about whether it was constitutional to take something away.

Although the Indian Supreme Court seems to have foresworn the direct declaration of unconstitutional constitutional amendments, Nepal has apparently granted its Supreme Court this power in the 1990 Constitution, following from the Indian model.[42] Article 116(1) of the Nepalese Constitution provides

> A Bill to amend or repeal any Article of this Constitution, without prejudicing the spirit of the Preamble of this Constitution, may be introduced in either House of Parliament: Provided that this Article shall not be subject to amendment.

Arguably, the Nepalese Supreme Court is the institution given the power to determine whether an amendment "prejudic[es] the spirit of the preamble" because that Court has the power to interpret the text and to declare that laws are inconsistent with the Constitution. Commentator Richard Stith (1996) is a skeptic about this possibility, citing both Indian constitutional history, in which the Court ultimately refused the power to declare amendments unconstitutional, and the

Norwegian Constitution's explicit unconstitutional constitutional amendments provision, which gives the power to the legislature to make the determination about an amendment's compatibility with the "spirit of the constitution." But given the extraordinary powers of the Supreme Court in the Nepalese Constitution and the near-unanimous views of Nepalese lawyers reported by Stith, it seems at least plausible that the Court would legitimately feel that it could declare constitutional amendments unconstitutional.

One other place where the possibility of unconstitutional constitutional amendments surfaced briefly was in Argentina, where a district court held part of a constitutional amendment unconstitutional. Although the appeals court upheld the district court's judgment, it did so on the basis of a different theory avoiding the constitutional question (Gomez, 2000). As a result, it is hard to tell whether the Argentinian courts in general believe that they have this power.

Though no high court has routinely used the strategy of declaring constitutional amendments unconstitutional, enough courts have flirted with it to believe that the very assertion that the power exists may have some effect on what other constitutional actors do, even if courts don't actually use this power to strike down an actual amendment. A parliament or a government confronting a court that threatens to do just that might be well advised to seek some other resolution of the matter. Most, as has been demonstrated, have done so.

Pervasive and General Legal Norms

Courts also increase their powers through finding that the legal order does not just consist of sets of independent rules for specific problems but, instead, that it contains a set of general principles that must be used to interpret other laws regardless of whether they make explicit mention of the general principles or not. This is also called the problem of *horizontal application* and it can occur when a Court finds that a Constitution's general norms apply outside the area of constitutional law proper, or when a Court finds that the common law limits the broad application of statutes. In either case, principles derived from one area or type of law are held to apply to another area or type of law, thereby requiring that judges take account of the legal order as a whole instead of understanding the rules as applying in an all or nothing fashion, taken one by one.

The Federal Constitutional Court of Germany has cautiously led the way in this effort. In the *Lüth* case (1958) (Kommers, 1997, pp. 360 ff.), the Court elaborated the view that apparently private law matters could have constitutional significance if they touched on constitutional topics. *Lüth* involved the constitutional right of free speech of a local official in Hamburg who was outraged when a former Nazi film director issued a new film in postwar Germany. Though the new film had nothing overtly to do with the fascism of the director's earlier films, Lüth urged that the general public boycott the film anyway. The film's producers sued Lüth for interfering with their private law right to carry out their business without being harmed in pursuit of it, under Article 826 of the Civil Code, which provides for damages if someone "intentionally causes injury to another person in a manner contrary to good morals." A court of first instance had ruled against Lüth, finding that he had done just that.

Lüth appealed to the Constitutional Court, claiming that his constitutional right of free speech was implicated. The Court had to confront the question: Where were the edges of constitutional law? Did the Basic Law just regulate state action in the sense that a law could not be passed in direct violation of it? Or did it spill over into private law relations, as were at issue in *Lüth?* The Court found that the Basic Law had to be brought to bear in the interpretation of what the Civil Code could mean, even in areas that had been until that time outside of constitutional law proper. Because free speech was constitutionally protected, the Court found that the court of first instance had erred in failing to find that constitutional values have a "radiating effect" even into private law matters. To satisfy the state action requirement, the Court held that any court decision, regardless of the area of law in question, could trigger the relevant review because courts were state actors.

In the *Soraya Case,*[43] the Federal Constitutional Court made another foray into a strictly private law matter. The case involved a woman who had been the subject of a completely faked interview that was published in a major newspaper. She sued, claiming only dignitary harm but pointing to the irresponsibility of the newspaper, which had failed to conduct even the most elementary check of the story's reliability. The Civil Code, however, did not allow monetary damages unless the harm involved was to an economic or other concrete interest of the plaintiff. Dignitary harm, all that the plaintiff alleged, was not sufficient. Notwithstanding the clear language of the Civil Code, a trial court had awarded the plaintiff monetary damages and the newspaper appealed, claiming that the court below had acted in a legally unauthorized manner. The Constitutional Court, finding that constitutional interests of the plaintiff in the right to the development of her personality were implicated, allowed the extraordinary assessment of damages even in the face of plain contrary language in the Civil Code. Between *Lüth* and *Soraya,* it appears that the Federal Constitutional Court will find that even private law matters come under the Constitution's broad influence.

The Spanish Constitutional Tribunal, influenced by the German Constitutional Court, has also gone a long way toward requiring that private law be interpreted by ordinary courts in light of constitutional values. As in Germany, the development has been played out primarily in the area in which long-standing private law provisions come up against free speech norms from the Constitution. In a case that required a journalist to pay damages to a local mayor for violating the mayor's honor in a news story, both the trial court and the appeals court saw no violation of constitutional principles. But the Constitutional Tribunal in 1986 held that judges even in private law matters have to take into account constitutional values, with extra weight being given to a legal principle if it has constitutional status.[44] In the end, the journalist prevailed.

The South African Constitutional Court briefly followed the Canadian approach that makes a sharp separation between constitutional law and other fields of law.[45] But then the Court was explicitly authorized by the new South African Constitution to engage in horizontal application[46] and it started to do so even before the final Constitution with its explicit provision came into effect (Fitch, 1997, p. 1016). The South African Constitutional Court, in *Du Plessis v. De Klerk* (1996), was clearly ready to hold that constitutional values theoretically infused all law, even under the Interim Constitution, which did not say so explicitly. In the end, however, the South African Constitutional Court did not have to stretch the language of the new Constitution so far because the final text gave all courts in South Africa explicit power to interpret all laws in light of their compliance with constitutional principles.

Though it is by no means a commonplace that a court will find that the Constitution gives it power to interpret all laws in light of constitutional requirements, it is clear that there is an increasing trend for courts to take this view. Perhaps ironically, one of the best academic articles on the subject of whether constitutional values should infuse private law is written by Aharon Barak (1996), the Chief Justice of the Israeli Supreme Court.

Supralegal (Metaconstitutional) Principles

In addition to finding that constitutional principles have effect even in private law, courts sometimes find that principles having their primary source outside the formal legal order altogether justify their interpretations of what even the Constitution requires.

In South Africa, for example, the South African Constitutional Court, or at least a number of the individual justices of that Court, have called on the principle of *ubuntu,* a Zulu word variously translated as human nature, humaneness, or one's "real self." At the center of the idea of *ubuntu* is the recognition that a person can only be a person through connection with others and that the dignity of the individual is realized through community recognition.[47] The term does not appear in the constitutional text itself. But six of the justices in the Court's important death penalty case (*S. v. Makwanyane,* 1995) invoked the principle as a way of importing indigenous values into the understanding of what constitutional law required, agreeing that the death penalty violated *ubuntu.* In doing so, they indicated that important community principles would be used to understand what the Constitution means even when those principles are nowhere explicitly mentioned in the text. The justices of the Constitutional Court, despite having a very long Constitution full of general rights provisions, nonetheless felt it was important to reach beyond the text to anchor constitutional values in the community's sense of justice.

The Hungarian Constitutional Court did this same sort of thing also, but linked the court's jurisprudence to a different community. Instead of finding local community principles that the justices wanted to bring into formal law, the Hungarian Court went outside Hungarian state boundaries altogether to bring in as authoritative the "common constitutional law of Europe."[48] Court President László Sólyom led the way in doing this, and during his tenure from 1990-1998, the rest of the justices readily followed along. As a result of this, the Constitutional Court used the constitutional principles of France and Germany in ruling on the constitutionality of the personal identifier number, the legal practices of Denmark in the gay and lesbian domestic partnership case, and the constitutional innovations of the Italian Constitutional Court in deciding that "living law" (i.e., the case law of ordinary courts) could be reviewed even though the Constitutional Court Act said nothing about this. The examples could be multiplied.[49] In these cases, the Hungarian Court read the Hungarian Constitution in light of what other European countries had done, taking principles that other constitutional courts had developed as providing guidance on what the Hungarian Constitution should mean.

The Indian Supreme Court elaborated a theory of "natural justice" to go beyond their constitutional text, giving the justices more flexibility in understanding what the Constitution meant. In *Maneka Gandhi v. the Union of India* (1978), Justice Bhagwati's lead opinion noted,

> Natural justice is a great humanizing principle intended to invest law with fairness and to secure justice and over the years it has grown into a widely pervasive rule affecting large areas of administrative action. . . . [T]he soul of natural justice is "fair-play in action."

Going on from the elaboration of this very general metaconstitutional principle (and finding support for it also in the English common law), Justice Bhagwati derived from natural justice a general right of every citizen to be given a hearing when challenging an administrative ruling, another right that was nowhere in the Constitution itself.

Religiously inspired constitutions often present opportunities for the invocation of extraconstitutional principles. Islamic constitutions, for example, typically note that human rights are to be limited in a manner consistent with principles of the Shari'a, but nowhere in the Constitution does it specify what those principles are.[50] For example, the Cairo Declaration of Rights (copied in some Islamic constitutions) specifies in Article 12, as Ann Mayer (1994) notes:

[According to the Declaration,] 'every man (the neutral *insan* in Arabic) shall have the right, within the framework of the Shari'a, to free movement. . . .' This reference to the Shari'a as a framework opens the way to allowing re-strictions on women's movements, because according to conservative read-ings of Islamic requirements, wives cannot leave home without their hus-bands' permission and women cannot travel unless chaperoned by male relatives. (p. 322)

If Shari'a principles are to be taken from outside the Constitution and used to interpret constitutional provisions, then this is similar in methodology to the uses of "natural justice" by the Indian Supreme Court, the uses of the "common con-stitutional law of Europe" by the Hungarian Constitutional Court, and the uses of the principle of *ubuntu* by the South African Constitutional Court. The outcomes may be quite different, but the approach requires the same move outside the legal order for supralegal principles.

Changing Procedure and Expanding Standing

Courts are particularly attentive to legal procedure and, in many legal systems, courts participate actively and officially in lawmaking about procedure. It is not surprising, then, that courts can use their explicit or implied powers to develop rules of procedure through their decisions to give themselves more independence from the political branches.

An extreme case can again be found in the practices of the Indian Supreme Court, which changed court procedure radically without any input from the Indian Par-liament. Through radically weakening standing requirements, the Court opened up the whole area of public interest litigation (PIL). In *S.P. Gupta v. Union of India* (1982), lawyers filed several petitions with the Supreme Court claiming that the independence of judges in several different High Courts[51] had been compro-mised. The question was: What gave lawyers the right to bring to the Supreme Court issues of judicial independence? The lawyers could not show that they had been directly harmed by the conduct that they wanted to challenge. To the Supreme Court, the issues raised by the lawyers were sufficiently important that the court decided it should be able to reach them, even if the claims were not brought to the Court by parties who had standing in the narrow sense. So the Court simply expanded the concept of standing to cover the case. Holding that lawyers in general have a professional interest in the maintenance of judicial independence, Justice Bhagwati (*S.P. Gupta v. Union of India,* 1982) said whenever there is a public wrong or public injury caused by an act or omission of the State or a public authority which is *contrary* to the Constitution or the law, any member of the public acting *bona fide* and having sufficient interest can maintain an action for redressal of such public wrong or public injury (p. 190).... If public duties are to be enforced and social collective "diffused" rights and interests are to be protected, we have to utilize the initiative and zeal of public-minded persons and organizations by allowing them to move the Court and act for a general or group interest, even though they may not be directly injured in their own rights. (p. 192)

Starting with this case, a major era of judicial activism began.

The Indian Supreme Court was particularly concerned that the weak and the poor would not have the money or education to bring cases before the Court, so the Court specifically empowered nonpolitical and nonprofit organizations to bring cases on behalf of the poor. The opportunity soon arose to expand the definition of standing beyond what had been held in the *Gupta* case. In *People's Union for Democratic Rights v. Union of India* (1982, p. 1473), a public interest group formed solely for the purpose of vindicating the rights of the poor wrote to the Court complaining that the contractors building facilities for the Asian Games hired poor people to do the work without giving them the protections that Indian labor law required. The Court took the case even though the laborers themselves had not petitioned the Court. Justice Bhagwati, the mover behind public interest litigation, carried the Court with him when he argued

The Court has taken the view that, having regard to the peculiar socio-economic conditions prevailing in the country where there is considerable poverty, illiteracy and ignorance obstructing and impeding accessibility to the judicial process, it would result in closing the doors of justice to the poor and deprived sections of the community if the traditional rule of standing evolved by Anglo-Saxon jurisprudence that only a person wronged can sue for judicial redress were to be blindly adhered to and followed and it is therefore necessary to evolve a new strategy by relaxing this traditional rule of standing in order that justice may become easily available to the lowly and the lost. (pp. 1477-1478)

With this conception of standing, it is not surprising that public interest litigation became a signature innovation of the Indian Supreme Court. The long list of cases brought under these expanded standing rules in the 1980s and 1990s involved the Court in policy making and allowed the Court to put pressure on the political branches to take strong action on behalf of the poor.[52]

The Israeli Supreme Court also expanded standing provisions enormously, thereby putting themselves at the heart of political controversy. "The Basic Law:

Judiciary" divided the Supreme Court's jurisdiction into two types. When it sits as the Supreme Court, it is the highest court of appeal in the system of ordinary courts. But when it sits as the High Court of Justice, the Court has original jurisdiction to determine whether any state actor (or a private actor acting in a public capacity) has acted within legal mandate or has abused power. Here, too, the Supreme Court empowered itself to act as a general oversight body with respect to the national government by loosening traditional standing rules. Though the Israeli Court did not go as far as the Indian Court, it has said that anyone has standing to challenge state administrative action if "corruption, a constitutional violation, or another claim of outstanding public interest is alleged" (Gelpe, 1999).[53] By defining standing broadly, the Israeli Supreme Court has been able to closely monitor administrative activity.

Expanding standing is one device through which the Israeli Supreme Court has altered justiciability; seeing remediable harm almost everywhere is another. Israel's current chief justice, Aharon Barak, has made it clear that he sees few procedural barriers in the way of reaching political issues because the allegation of harm is enough to set the Court in motion toward reaching a substantive judgment. The Court simply does not worry too much about who brings the case or whether the harm alleged is a harm cognizable by a court. To Barak, virtually anything is justiciable. As he wrote

> The activist judge tends more than his non-activist colleague . . . to say: "I am ready to discuss and decide substantively." In line with this criteria, I am a radical activist. In my view, every problem is justiciable . . . and only in special and unusual incidents am I ready to view a controversy as unjusticiable. Therefore, I was ready in the past to discuss the legality of not drafting yeshiva students into the army and the legality of the Knesset's decisions. I was ready to decide the legality of a political agreement and the legality of a will that contradicts public opinion. In these cases and others, in the past judicial review had not been used, while in my opinion . . . there are no areas that law is not involved in them. (Barak, translated and quoted in Adam [2000], p. 498)

This view of justiciability has meant that, even in the absence of a definitive constitution and even in the absence of explicitly authorized judicial review, the Israeli Supreme Court takes an active part in virtually every political issue in the country.

The Hungarian Constitutional Court also expansively defined its own legitimate caseload in order to increase its power relative to the political branches. Given that the Court had the power to review all law for constitutionality, and given that the Constitution already said that "anyone" had the right to challenge the constitutionality of any law before the Court regardless of what that person's interest was in doing so, the only way that the Court could expand its powers in this area was to expand what was meant by "law." It could therefore make more cases justiciable before the Constitutional Court. The Court did this in two breath-taking ways. Early in the Court's life, it borrowed the idea of "living law" from the Italian Constitutional Court. *Living law* refers to the standardized practice of interpretation used by the ordinary courts, so that a pattern of court decisions could itself constitute law even in the absence of a written norm. Given that Hungary is a civil law system in which court decisions do not typically count as sources of law (except for the Constitutional Court decisions themselves), expanding the Court's jurisdiction to review how ordinary courts were interpreting the laws was a great leap. The Constitutional Court did not always feel comfortable with this much-criticized exercise of its jurisdiction, so it did not often use the power. But in 1997, the Court expanded its powers again, ruling that it could review treaties for their compatibility with the Constitution, even though the Constitutional Court Act did not explicitly give the Court this power. The Court reasoned that treaties had to be voted on by the Parliament and laws had to be voted on by the Parliament, making treaties like laws and therefore giving the Court judicial review over them.[54]

From this catalogue of tools, it is possible to see that judges can use their constitutional status to empower themselves relative to the political branches. This gives them a strong sense of independence, provided that the political branches go along. But it is always possible that a strong grab for political power on the part of a court will cause the political branches to defend their prerogatives against court interference. What determines whether courts can get away with judicial empowerment (even radical judicial empowerment) or not? To see this, our analysis returns to the former world of telephone justice, to the now-post-soviet states where judicial independence has a special meaning precisely because it was such a rare commodity in the soviet time.

∽ Meditation #5: A Tale of Two Courts: Institutions and Evasions in Constitutional Ethnography

Since the changes of 1989[55] and 1991[56] in the former soviet world, law has changed immensely in the countries formerly governed by socialist legality. Not only have new parliaments been passing laws at a fast and furious rate (and the speed often shows in the infelicities of draftsmanship), but also all of the former soviet-world countries have drafted new constitutions and created new constitutional courts.

Constitutional courts in the former soviet world have, by and large, not had an easy time of it. Some are still not able to oppose government on a regular basis, or even to get themselves established at all (see the central Asian states, Ukraine, Azerbaijan, Belarus and, so far, Yugoslavia).[57] Others have tried to oppose the government but have paid a price. The Bulgarian Constitutional Court challenged the neo-communist government in the mid-1990s and ran into fierce political opposition but survived;[58] the Russian Constitutional Court, as I will elaborate later, opened in 1991, but then it was shut down, reorganized, and reopened under new management between 1993 and 1995 (Hausmaninger, 1995). A few have been very active, garnering apparently deep legitimacy among the public as well as the recognition from the political branches of government that they are permanent features of the new political landscape (e.g., Hungary, Poland, Slovenia, Estonia) (Schwartz, 2000). Constitutional courts are enormously popular institutions in general wherever they are actually working throughout the former soviet world; citizens see in these courts a real hope for the rule of law. But sometimes this very popularity of the new constitutional courts is threatening to the new political forces in post-communist societies because, under the open access rules of many of these courts,[59] ordinary citizens can go to the constitutional courts in order to do an end-run around politics. The politicians don't always like this.

So—what do the politicians do now? The days of telephone justice are apparently over.[60] But the political and economic climates within which these courts operate make it very difficult for them to give birth to new constitutionally responsive regimes. Political instability, brought on by many splintering political parties, makes it hard to develop enduring expectations of what government will do. Economic constraints make it hard to realize rights. But the new governments are under enormous pressures to make things better for their citizens, to open up their markets (including markets in land) to outsiders, and to be fiscally responsible to the international financial institutions—and to do all of this while maintaining democratic legitimacy and the rule of law. Not surprisingly, when constitutional courts add things to the long lists that the politicians have to consider, the politicians resist.

So—can these new constitutional court judges be independent of the enormous political pressures that they are put under? Should they be?

I am going to suggest that they try to be, but not in the usual way. Courts in these difficult political circumstances find ways to evade certain political pressures while still upholding their sense that they are independently accountable to a population that expects them to ensure the realization of rights. The two countries I will discuss are Hungary and Russia.

The Hungarian Constitutional Court, through the 1990s, practically ran Hungary. In the book I am writing on this remarkable Court, I have called Hungary a "courtocracy"as a new regime type. Whatever the issue in Hungarian politics, the Hungarian Constitutional Court practically always had the last word. As a result, it was the strongest body of state through the 1990s.

The Hungarian Constitutional Court not only struck down about *one law out of every three* that came before it, but it developed a broad roaming jurisdiction under what I have called the "while we're at it"doctrine. If a statute were challenged for its constitutionality,[61] the Court had to undertake a review of it. But the Court wouldn't just review the directly challenged provisions. While they were "at it," they'd often review the whole law. The result was a far-reaching, far-ranging juris-prudence in which the Constitutional Court was constantly giving the Parliament homework assignments to revise laws to ensure their constitutionality. That, however, was not all the Court did.[62] The Court also had the power to declare that the Parliament was acting "unconstitutionally by omission,"which meant that, in the view of the Court, the Parliament had failed to regulate something it was con-stitutionally obliged to regulate. In this way, the Court required the Parliament to pass a new law on the rights of ethnic minorities and the rights of gay and lesbian couples to have their domestic partnerships recognized in law in the same way as the domestic partnerships of heterosexual couples were. Among other things. At its peak, the Hungarian Constitutional Court issued about 50 decisions a year finding constitutional omissions. More work for the Parliament.

And the Parliament nearly always complied. For those few situations in which the Parliament didn't, it was usually because the law required a two-thirds vote and there was simply not a two-thirds coalition able to agree on the specifics of the law. But everyone officially agreed on the proposition that the laws should be made constitutional and that it was emphatically the province of the Constitu-tional Court to say what the (constitutional) law was.

What is wrong with this picture? Well, it is accurate as far as it goes. But politi-cally speaking, the reality was a bit more complicated. The Hungarian Constitu-tional Court did in fact issue many sweeping decisions protecting rights and requiring changes in the laws to ensure that rights were protected. But if one were to look at the laws themselves several years later, the laws were positioned not at the point that the Constitutional Court said was required, but rather somewhere in between the initial law that the Parliament passed and the Constitutional Court's requirements. What happened?

Often, in the big cases, the first decision was the Court's shot over the bow of the Parliament. Parliament then got a chance to revise the laws in light of the Court's decisions, but the Parliament did not always do everything that the Court required. What then? The Court would issue a second decision, somewhat mod-erating its demands from the first case. And then the Parliament would go back and rewrite the law, again suggesting a compromise from the second decision. And so on. In a number of important areas, the Court and the Parliament went through several iterations of this process until they both settled on a constitutionally approved law. But it was often not the first constitutional opinion that settled the matter.

For example, a working majority in the first post-communist Parliament really wanted to root out communists and prosecute them for their soviet-era offenses against human rights. The law that was passed extended the statute of limitations for all crimes not prosecuted in the soviet time "for political reasons." The Constitutional Court, in a forceful opinion extolling the virtues of the rule of law, forbade this extension, claiming that it amounted to a retroactive application of the law, creating a crime after the fact. The Parliament, disappointed, reenacted something like that law again, but this time limiting themselves to particularly egregious crimes. This time, perhaps surprisingly, the Court agreed with the Parliament. The Court found its way clear to saying that war crimes would be an exception because under international law, war crimes have no statute of limitation, and international law rather than domestic law governed the crimes that were to be punished now. That was how it came to be that although the Court's first decision said that there were to be no prosecutions of offenses committed in the soviet time, there were nonetheless a number of trials of police who shot into the crowds in 1956 in places like Sálgotárjan.[63]

A similar negotiation took place with the Court's decisions on the IMF austerity program. When the Parliament passed this radical cutback in social welfare programs in 1995, the Court responded by saying that this was unconstitutional. The Court gave itself some wiggle room; they said in their first decision on the matter that the Parliament had erred by moving too fast and not giving people a time to adjust to the sudden loss of previously stable family payments. But the Court also found that there were at least some constitutionally entrenched social rights that had to be protected no matter how slow reform was.

Again—if you went back to Hungary several years later, you would have found that much of the social safety net was gone, despite that sweeping first decision. How was that possible? Parliament passed a series of targeted smaller changes, all of which the Constitutional Court approved. The changes were gradual and the program cuts were means-tested. So the Parliament's new laws were arguably within the boundaries set by the first opinion. But they were also clearly designed to accomplish what the Parliament had at first set out to do, cutting back Hungary's generous and universal welfare rights, a plan that the Court initially thwarted.

Were the Hungarian judges independent? The judges of the Sólyom Court had a reputation for being fiercely independent defenders of human rights, for not allowing the Parliament to compromise in its devotion to rights. That reputation was deserved in many ways. But it was also the case that, seeing the political landscape and particularly the economic costs realistically, the Court often declared victory and got out of an area where the justices had previously staked out a major claim, allowing something closer to the Parliament's vision to win in the end (with its initial edges softened by the application of some but not all constitutional constraints).

The Court was listening to politics when it backed off in the later cases.[64] Did the judges then call the constitutional questions as they saw them free of political influence? Yes, they clearly did at first, and then they allowed the possible to overcome the ideal. Is this a loss of judicial independence? Or is it a way of discovering that the judicial role is always dependent on forces outside legal control? Through this "two steps forward and then one step back" approach, the Court managed to remain on to fight another day and to improve rights protection at the same time.

In contrast, the Russian Constitutional Court has been far more embattled and far less successful in carving out a place for itself in Russian political life. But perhaps only the Hungarian Court was more audacious. In its first major decision, issued only a month after starting its work in 1991, the Russian Constitutional Court declared Boris Yeltsin's plan to merge the police and the internal security forces into a single ministry under Yeltsin's control unconstitutional because it violated the separation of powers. To a country that had not recognized separation of powers until just a few years before, this signaled a real change of system. The early Court, and particularly its visible president, Valerii Zorkin, went on to become involved in a series of highly charged political questions, ruling, for example, that Yeltsin's decrees banning the Communist Party and seizing its assets were at least in part unconstitutional. While President Zorkin went on to personally negotiate the proper relations between the legislative and executive branches, the Court officially determined that Yeltsin's decree granting himself emergency powers in 1993 to cope with a recalcitrant Parliament was unconstitutional. By the time that the battle literally erupted in the streets, with the communist-dominated Parliament refusing to cooperate with a stubborn state president, and with Yeltsin, as commander-in-chief, calling out the tanks, it was too late. On a confrontation course with the other major political institutions that ultimately resulted in the White House being bombed by tanks of its own government in October 1993, Yeltsin forcibly disbanded the Parliament, ousted its communist leadership, and suspended the operation of the Constitutional Court. The Court was closed for all of 1994 and resumed operations again only in 1995 under a new Constitution and a new Constitutional Court Act that added six new judges to the Court. Justice Zorkin is still on the Court, but no longer its president.

Since the court has been reconstituted, it has become much more modest in what it does. Faced with 10,000 to 15,000 petitions per year, the Court issues only 25 to 30 decisions annually. Many of these decisions feature long, heavily elaborated opinions that nonetheless reach politically cautious results. So why does anyone write to the court when the court, feeling itself politically vulnerable, does so little?

From a distance, it's hard to see why. But up close, it becomes clear that the Court has taken to handling cases in ways that fly under political radar. Instead of doing wholesale constitutional law in big published decisions, they do retail constitutional law through a massive correspondence department.[65] Every letter that comes into the Court receives an answer. This has massively burdened all of the employees of the general secretary's office, including nearly 100 staff attorneys, who spend huge amounts of their time answering these letters. The responses are not form letters telling petitioners to go away. Sometimes, letters from petitioners are answered by being forwarded to another state body (e.g., the regional duma, the local council, the social security office, an appeals court) with a note from the Constitutional Court saying what, in their opinion, this other state body should do to ensure that the petitioner's rights are realized. These letters are not published and they are by no means binding in any strict legal sense, but they seek informal constitutional control over the institutions of state by alerting them to the fact that the Constitutional Court is looking over their shoulders. This may or may not result in a substantive victory for the petitioner in this other body—and there are reasons to doubt that many of these other institutions pay attention—but the petitioners may well feel emboldened by knowing that a substantial state institution is on their side. The letters from the Court embody constitutional conceptions of the citizens' rights, and these letters constitute important elements of the growing constitutional consciousness, if not yet its formal doctrine.

The Russian Constitutional Court also issues what they call "dismissal definitions with positive content." This does not have an easy translation into English because the institution does not exist outside of Russia. Dismissal definitions with positive content are statements by the Court dismissing a petition. But the "positive content" means that the petitioner gets a written explanation of his or her rights and an interpretation of the challenged law (a "definition"). A dismissal definition with positive content defines the rights and relationships that are specified by the Constitution and applicable laws without reaching a judgment about a particular case. And these "definitions" are not only sent to the petitioners; they are also published by the Court. They do not have the force of binding decisions and they do not resolve concrete cases. But they do provide an important venue in which the Court can announce its view of the law short of making a formal decision with binding legal effect. This is another growing body of constitutional pronouncements that also does not yet rise to the level of doctrine but that provides evidence that the Russian Constitutional Court is trying its best to break out of the political box in which it finds itself.

The Russian Constitutional Court seems to be engaged in a sort of political evasion—being very active without actually resolving cases in a binding constitutional manner. They are trying to do constitutional law without coming to the attention of the political branches and without upsetting any particular political applecarts. By switching to a small scale advisory role instead of issuing, as they used to, large opinions on important political matters, the Court has bought itself some space for developing constitutional ideas.

The Russian and Hungarian Constitutional Courts, despite their radically different political fates, are actually closer than they look. Both courts had to learn how far they could push the political branches before the political branches shoved back. And both courts had to look for opportunities to bring the public along in the recognition of human rights while still keeping themselves out of (political) harm's way. Though the Hungarian Constitutional Court legislated out in the open, the Russian Constitutional Court is also very active, but just in one individual petition at a time. What is surprising, and hopeful, is that judges in both countries, once freed from the political constraints of positivism, immediately figured out strategies of judicial empowerment to give themselves some critical distance on what politicians were telling them to do.

∽ Meditation #6: Independence From What?

This chapter started by noting the difference between judges having to follow the rules laid down (good, or at least so I first thought, for judicial independence) and judges not being required to take orders from politicians in making decisions in individual cases (not good for judicial independence). The model was telephone justice, in which the judge would get a call with advice to make a particular sort of decision in a particular case—a clear violation of the independent role of the judge. But one can see now that the difference between taking orders directly and taking orders through very detailed statutes is not as striking as it appeared at first, at least in giving the judge any possibility of gaining some critical distance from statutes.

But can that be right? If a Democratic legislature in an American state passes a progressive law, conservative judges in that state are supposed to apply the law in the spirit in which it was written despite the fact that they would have written the law differently if they were in the state house. Allowing Republican judges to do what they prefer could mean canceling out the result of the last election. Judges are supposed to be independent in interpreting the law, but the judicial role is supposed to be characterized by legal interpretation and not legal invention.

Suppose, instead, that we move away from the two-party system in America to consider judicial independence in a different sort of regime. If a *fascist* government, operating in a state of emergency without going through a parliament to pass ordinary laws, were to issue perfectly valid decrees, then right-thinking judges should . . . well, one would *hope* that they would have the courage to refuse to apply such decrees in a deferential spirit. Any conception of judicial independence worth anything as a practical matter must have some way to understand what would happen if judges were to go off on their own at this point.

Just how much "on their own" can judges be, however? If ordinary law is embedded in a constitutional order, then those background constitutional norms can be invoked to give judges a way out. In a legal system with a hierarchy of norms, ordinary legal norms can be trumped by higher norms of a more general sort, which is precisely what a constitution does.

So then the question about meaningful judicial independence turns into one about the role of the judge in a constitutional order. It may be that the usual sense of judicial independence is hostage to preconstitutional, positivist ways of thinking about the law—in which the ability to apply law in the concrete circumstance of a particular case is the essence of what scholars have thought of as judicial independence. But in a constitutional order, in which judges have postpositivist obligations to ensure the constitutional coherence of the entire legal order, it may be too small a thing to ask for—that judges be able to make decisions in individual cases without interference.

The demand for resolving individual cases without interference is particularly poignant in the current Russian Constitutional Court. No one is telling the justices there to resolve individual cases in particular ways; telephone justice seems to be definitively gone. The Russian Constitutional Court can have its correspondence department send letters without interference to the thousands of petitioners who seek their advice and the Kremlin looks the other way. But the politicians get unhappy (less drastically but in similar ways in Hungary) when the courts try to establish constitutional principles that in fact constrain lawmaking. Parliaments resist constitutional imperatives; self-preserving judges try to push the parliaments only as far as they are willing to go. As I have shown in displaying the catalogue of the tools that activist courts are using to constrain the political branches through aggressive expansion of the constitutional-judicial domain, politics isn't always the winner. But neither are courts.

The most important question about judicial independence, I would submit, is not about whether judges are free to resolve individual cases according to the law; it is about being bound rigidly by a certain form of law in the first place. If judges have to take a positivist attitude toward law and simply follow the rules laid down by the political branches, then they are not really independent of politics but (as the soviet example clearly shows) completely subservient to it. In a constitutional order, or in any field where judges have judge-made law to soften the edges of the political demands, other legal resources can be brought to bear in establishing some judicial spaces less susceptible to direct political pressure.

At its highest reaches, then, the independence of judges requires some legal and institutional mechanisms through which the political branches can actually be challenged in their ability to dictate to judges the entirety of the law they are to apply. Without the independence to make at least some of the law themselves, judges are almost as much at the mercy of political commands (even political commands framed as statutes) as they would be through the direct political intervention in every case. Compared with the ability to engage in at least some lawmaking, the judicial ability to decide cases according to the rules laid down pales in comparison, and may itself be reduced to insignificance if the law can accomplish just what telephone justice would otherwise do—transmit current political preferences directly to the judges.

If there is no struggle between the political branches and the judicial branch over the meaning of the law and the way that it is to be applied in concrete cases, then there is not only no meaningful separation of powers but also no meaningful distinction between law and politics. Only when judges are empowered to resist direct commands through invoking the power to make law themselves can they be truly independent within a broader legal order.

∞ **Notes**

---

1. For this distinction, I am indebted to Peter Russell's useful introduction, "Toward a General Theory of Judicial Independence" (Russell, 2001). Russell notes that institutional features that enable the judiciary to be independent of other branches of government may not automatically lead to the independence of individual judges from those institutional constraints imposed by the organization of the judiciary itself. Similarly, a judge may feel independent—and even act independently—in the absence of institutional guarantees that buffer the judge from pressures.

2. Perhaps *especially* in America in the age of Chevron. See *Chevron USA, Inc. v. Natural Resources Defense Council*, 1984.

3. But see Inge Markovits, 1996. Markovits shows how the practice of telephone justice in the former East Germany was almost surely exaggerated as well as being widely resented and even evaded by self-respecting judges.

4. There's a complicated role for legislative history here. Often a statute or a regulation is enacted because of some public flap over a specific instance in which it becomes clear that the law has to be changed. If the law is in fact changed, then it is clear that it should apply to cases just like the one that caused the change of law in the first place. But what if the Parliament puts into the legislative history a whole series of hypothetical cases about how, in the view of the legislators, the courts should understand the new law in cases like these? If the Court takes direction from a legislative history, does this infringe the independence of a court? There are sharply different answers to this question. In England, for example, references to the Hansard (parliamentary record) were until recently forbidden; in Justice Antonin Scalia's world, legislative histories fare no better. But some judges (and

some topics) generate much more attention to legislative histories. In American evidence law, for example, it is relatively common for judges to rely on the notes of the Advisory Committee for understanding the Federal Rules of Evidence, even though the Advisory Committee's democratic pedigree is nonexistent. When House or Senate Judiciary Committee reports contradict the Advisory Committee, however, courts are supposed to defer to those over Advisory Committee notes in their understanding of the legislative history. But they don't *have to* pay attention to any of the legislative history at all.

5. I've elaborated this heretical view in the context of a review of Inge Markovits's book; see Scheppele, 1996.

6. I use "lawmaker" here in the sense in which it is usually used in continental legal systems to represent a complex process of parliamentary and executive action as if it were the will of a lone individual.

7. There is also, speaking specifically about soviet-style systems, a further complication in noting that the party and the government were always in some tension. The party possessed the real power; it duplicated and superceded the institutions and tasks of the government. Who "the lawmaker" was, then, was always a bit of a shell game. Parliaments were the nominal locations of lawmaking; the real power to draft laws, however, stayed with the party. My discussion about the lawmaker in World A and World B elides this distinction, and in many ways it is crucial to the point about legitimate lawmaking. For now, however, I assume things are much simpler.

8. In soviet-style systems, ordinary cases and politically sensitive cases were often handled by separate institutions, precisely so that ordinary judges would not come under direct political pressure as a routine matter. As Inge Markovits notes in her analysis of the East German legal system, there may have been more of a commitment to the rule of law than most outside observers (on the other side of the Cold War) could; see Markovits, 1996.

9. In fact, even in quite elaborated legal systems, the pardon power is the surviving element of a time when executive and judicial functions were merged. If a president (or queen) has the power of pardon, it means that he or she can override the judicial branch, at least when it comes to criminal sentencing. If this power were used extensively, it would pose a different sort of threat to judicial independence. Lest one think, however, that the separation of executive and judicial functions has long since been assured, recall that Montesquieu in his famous discussion of separation of powers referred to the three powers that should be separated as (1) the legislative, (2) the executive in matters of domestic policy, and (3) the executive in matters of international policy. The "executive in matters of domestic policy" became the judiciary by the end of his discussion. But that just shows how flexible the categories have been; see Montesquieu, 1873.

10. I am using "division of powers" here rather than the more usual "separation of powers" precisely because the sort of powers that I am talking about here—converting political judgment into decisions in concrete cases—cannot be separated in theory or in fact. They can be divided across numerous actors and, in fact, it is the nature and extent of this division that concerns us here. Also, because most readers will have some strong ideas about "separation of powers," the advantage in "division of powers" is that it strikes most ears as strange and therefore open in meaning. The purpose of this chapter is in large measure to fill in the range of what that meaning has to be in order for judges to be considered independent.

11. For the moment I am leaving aside what it takes to make a case "clear." Facts themselves can be interpreted just as much as legal rules can be, and one other avenue for judges to escape specific statutes is to interpret around the facts of the case. I have taken this subject on at some length in Scheppele, 1990.

12. The 1950s social norms that the Burns and Allen show presupposed in aiming its humor can no longer be presumed in turn-of-the-century postfeminist American public culture. Now, from the present historical perch, Gracie looks like a victim of male domination. In the 1950s, I suspect, the question was more tantalizingly open, especially in light of everything else she did in that show that was far from docile and obedient. And so the understanding of what Gracie's "good night" might signify has changed.

13. For an analysis that is quite relevant in this connection, see Hutcheon (1994), in which she shows how the identical statement spoken against a different background context can come to have a meaning opposite that superficially stated. Such a reversal, however, depends on a solid sense of shared understandings between speaker and audience about what that speaker means in the context. Irony is not a formal property of a statement, but instead a deeply contextualized one.

14. For a related argument about moral judgment, see Waldron, 1981. Waldron argues that contained within the meaning of what it is to have a right is the implicit assumption that one must also have the protected possibility of doing wrong. If the thing one has to do is settled (e.g. "you must always do the right thing"), then an element of coercion appears in the choice over what one should do with the right, negating the voluntariness underlying the idea of a right in the first place. In short, if one doesn't have also the "right" to make wrong choices, it makes no sense to speak of having a right in the first place.

15. The idea of the hard case and its interpretive possibilities has been raised most explicitly by Dworkin, 1978, pp. 80-130.

16. I found some evidence of these directives also when I worked at the Hungarian Constitutional Court and learned that lower-court judges in the soviet time expected as a matter of practice to be given more specific directives about how to decide specific cases. Some of those directives persisted into the post-soviet time because they were so much a matter of course that all of the judges had gotten used to them. Of course, all of these systems were civil law systems without formal and binding published judgments. I wondered how different much of this was from the more familiar American practice of binding lower-court judges to the concrete decisions of those courts above them in the legal hierarchy.

17. A word of explanation is needed here. Positivism was a view strongly rejected by most soviet legal writers. It was associated for them with the ideology of bourgeois law, in which law was proclaimed to be neutral but in fact benefited only those possessed of capital and property. Positivism, then, was seen as an ideological force directing the attention of judges away from law's concrete effects. By contrast, soviet legal writers stressed that socialist law was substantive and antipositivist because it was aimed at different results— the empowerment of workers and peasants. But there was a strange disconnection in the writings of soviet jurisprudes between positivist theories of lawmaking (in which "neutral" law was actually bourgeois law in disguise, according to the soviet writers, and ought to be rejected forcefully) and positivist theories of judging (in which judges were supposed to ask only validity questions about the law before they applied that law and that was mandatory). In respect of judging, soviet writers were perhaps even more positivist than were those from liberal legal systems.

18. L. S. Jawitsch (1996), for example, noted that "the law-making power of judicial bodies is often used by ruling classes to break and circumvent laws adopted by sovereign bodies, but in these cases it is a matter of the extreme process of the counterposing of judicial activity to statute law" (translated and quoted in Butler, 1996, p. 373). This "extreme process" was required, according to Jawitsch, when statutes got out of step with the interests of the dominant class: "The more legislation lags behind the dynamics of social relations and society's needs, the broader judicial lawmaking is" (Jawitsch, p. 375). For Jawitsch, this was clearly a problem to be remedied. Judges were tempted to go beyond the law when

the law failed to keep up with social change, and that required the lawmaker to get busy, in order to direct the courts.

19. Of course the mechanisms of oversight and the consequences for failure to do one's job correctly were different in the Soviet Union and in liberal legal systems. I don't mean to understate those differences. But in attempting to ensure that judges followed the rules and didn't deviate from them in individual cases, both soviet and liberal legal systems share the sense that a judge who failed to follow the rules would not be a proper judge.

20. This may be understood as a restatement of H. L. A. Hart's (1961) famous conceptualization of positivism. The rule of recognition specifies the pedigree that a norm must possess to be a law and the judge is therefore authorized to apply only those norms that meet the test.

21. There was, on occasion, some way to avoid the literal interpretations of the laws. For example, in Hungary, a criminal defendant could be found guilty, not guilty, or "guilty but not dangerous." This latter category enabled judges to find the defendant had literally violated a specific criminal statute but that the conduct did not amount to a challenge to society. In those cases, the defendant would not be punished even though he had violated the law.

22. Oushakine, under review.

23. There seems to have been a large amount of discretion wielded by prosecutors in determining which cases to pursue and which to drop and that was no doubt a process in which personal connections and other such factors made a huge difference.

24. Having read a lot about soviet law, I was surprised to learn about this system for monitoring judges for it wasn't written about in any of the books I had read. I learned about it instead from talking to Russian lawyers. They have asked me whether the United States keeps track of judicial "mistakes" as Russia does. Not fully understanding the question, I said that there was a clear sense in the relevant professional community about which judges were better than others, but that such judgments got to be more and more politically based the higher one went in the legal order. One Russian lawyer to whom I said this found it highly surprising that Americans would not keep such statistics because how else, after all, should one measure the performance of judges to know if they are doing their jobs well or not? Doesn't every accountable legal system need to do that? When I insisted that no such statistics were kept, he clearly couldn't imagine how a legal system could be effectively run without such measures. And he was a professor of constitutional law at one of the most prestigious legal academies in Russia.

25. Here again, however, there is at least one feature of this that is not too different from the way American law works. Judicial appointments are more politically contested and politically significant the higher up one goes in the judicial order. In the American federal system, judges (or prospective judges) on the Supreme Court are closely watched for their political leanings, and those political leanings take on significance precisely because a majority of such leanings in this Court bind all of the judges below. Lower court judges' politics are likely to be less sharply reviewed and therefore considered less significant in general precisely because the appeals process is supposed to reign in deviant judges.

26. Vyshinskii (1996), Stalin's Minister of Justice, wrote in the *Law of the Soviet State*, "Soviet law is the law of the socialist state of workers and peasants, born in the fire of the October Revolution which cast down the authority of the bourgeoisie and confirmed the authority of the workers and peasants" (p. 357). The primary difference, then, between bourgeois law and socialist law was in the content of the norms and which class was most benefited by those norms.

27. Perhaps the strongest contemporary advocate of the "higher law" model of constitutionalism is Ackerman (1991) who argued that constitutions should be thought of

not just as some other source of law on a special topic (i.e., government) but instead as a law of a different order, one that should be seen as creating and making enforceable limits on what government can do in the first place. The argument has its roots in the earlier work of Corwin (1928/1929), in which he argued that the Constitution did not just create a government and set limits for its operation, but instead that the Constitution created a moral community that set certain principles above the push and shove of daily democratic politics.

28. As I will show, not all governments that adopt this view put down all constitutional understandings in a single written document labeled a Constitution. Even countries that have such a text will find that there are invisible amendments to that text as courts elaborate what a constitutional understanding should be.

29. In a practical way, Dworkin was responding as an American constitutionalist to H. L. A. Hart's British positivism. In British constitutional law, with parliamentary supremacy allowing no higher law, judges apparently had no other alternative than to follow the rules laid down. The constitutional attitude suggested by Dworkin has only now become officially possible for British judges. Since October 2000, judges have had the possibility of applying the European Convention on Human Rights directly in British courts, which gives a sort of higher law constraint on the application of statutory rules. It falls short of full judicial review but it may just give British judges an ability to gain a critical distance on statutes. One might guess that British judges, with their ability to draw from and elaborate the common law, in practice always had this wiggle room, however.

30. I do not mean to suggest here that constitutions are the only device through which judges can gain such a critical distance from statutes. The common law performed the same function, especially through such judicial maxims as "a statute in derogation of a common law rule shall be narrowly construed." If judges have the power to make law through their own decisions, then obviously giving more weight to those decisions than to the statutes that attempt to change their direction allows judges to get some traction in the struggle with politicians. For present purposes, the common law provides a major source of perspective for judges in doing something other than following the rules laid down—by politicians.

31. For more detail, see Scheppele, 2001, pp. 1370-1395 for an account of the way that Germany, Hungary, Poland, and Slovenia have read these sorts of principles into their constitutional "rule of law" clauses.

32. Constitutional courts, unlike supreme courts, are typically courts of limited jurisdiction that hear only constitutional matters. Most constitutional courts can consider abstract challenges to laws, if brought by the appropriate parties. In abstract challenges, the court rules on whether a statute or other positive legal enactment is facially consistent with the constitution without needing a concrete case or controversy or even an actual or imminently anticipated harm to reach the question. Some constitutional courts can reach questions of the constitutional application of laws as well. In general, however, constitutional courts are separated from the ordinary judiciary and behave more like political bodies than like routine courts. See Alec Stone Sweet (2000, pp. 32-38) for a fuller general explanation.

33. There may be occasions when courts gain critical distance on statutes without going beyond the statutes themselves by activating the preamble to the *statute*, or by giving special force to aspects of the statute's legislative history. Alternatively, common law courts might also interpret the common law as a sort of preamble to every statute, so that statutes that sweep too broadly into the territory of the common law are interpreted narrowly in light of prior legal developments. Although I talk specifically about constitutional preambles in this section, I also want to argue that this is a more general technique of using language and the invocation of broader principles in the vicinity of a positive legal enactment to justify a particular shift in the statute's meaning.

34. See Lindseth, 1996/1997, for an account of the historical background to the Decision of 16 July 1971, which declared an amendment of the 1901 Law on Associations to be unconstitutional. The original law of 1901, regarded as a triumph of the Third Republic's commitment to liberalism, allowed organizations to register and be recognized as having legal personality with purely formal registration procedures. It was widely seen to embody a crucial liberal commitment to freedom of association. But following the uprisings of 1968, the conservative Parliament sought to amend the law to allow the public prosecutor to initiate judicial proceedings during the registration process that would inquire into whether a particular organization was formed for an illicit purpose before it would be allowed to register legally. The previously established free registration of organizations would then allow political inquiry to determine the acceptability of the organization before its official registration. It was this political situation that pushed the Constitutional Council beyond its toleration point into being an active player in French politics. See also Bell, 1997.

35. The Council's decision is even more stunning when one considers that the documents from the Constituent Assembly in 1958 clearly show that the preamble was never meant to be part of the legally enforceable text. Moreover, the materials from the 1946 Constituent Assembly that put a whole series of new rights into the preamble of that Constitution clearly reveal that the 1946 lists of rights was never meant to be a legally enforceable part of the 1946 Constitution either. Thus, in the associations case, the Constitutional Council announced for the first time on its own initiative that rights were to be a crucial part of the French constitutional order even though two successive constituent assemblies had overtly reached the opposite conclusion. For the constitutional history, see Sweet, 1992.

36. The figure comes from Sweet, 2000, p. 63.

37. For example, the preamble guarantees "justice, liberty and equality" and "secur[es] the dignity of the individual and the unity of the nation." When the battle between the government and the Court became one of the causes of the state of emergency from 1975 to 1977, the government passed a constitutional amendment that added the word "socialist" to the preamble and removed the right of private property from the constitutional text. The Supreme Court after the emergency then switched abruptly from being a Court that had used the right of private property to stop the government's socialist proposals to being a Court that recognized and enforced social rights and pushed the government toward recognizing more and more social entitlements. See, for example, Austin (1999) for an account of the battles between the government and the Court and the effect of the state of emergency on later court jurisprudence.

38. See the discussion of this case in Hofnung, 1996.

39. For a discussion of this case, see Kommers, 1997, p. 48.

40. The reason why the case is confusing is detailed in Austin (1999, Chapter 11): "Redeeming the Web: The Kesavananda Bharati Case" on which I have relied for much of this account.

41. The law that the Supreme Court invalidated in *Kesavananda* involved putting certain other laws under "Schedule 9" of the Constitution. Schedule 9 was itself added to the Constitution by amendment and allowed any law placed under that category to evade judicial scrutiny for its limitation on fundamental rights. Through *Kesavananda*, the Supreme Court established its power to examine those things which the Parliament wanted it to be barred from recognizing.

42. For information on the Nepalese developments, I am indebted to Richard Stith, 1996.

43. *Proceeding Concerning the Constitutional Complaint of Publishing Company "Die Welt" and Mr. K.-H. V.* [BverfGE] [Federal Constitutional Court] 34, 269 (F.R.G. Feb. 14, 1973) [also known as the *Soraya Case*], in Schlesinger et al., 1988.

44. For a discussion of the line of cases, see Sweet, 2000, pp. 119-121.

45. The Canadian approach to this question is detailed in Beatty, 1998.

46. The South African Constitution, Section 8(2) says: "A provision of the Bill of Rights binds natural and juristic persons if, and to the extent that, it is applicable, taking into account the nature of the right and of any duty imposed by the right." The section does not say that it only binds in constitutional cases.

47. For an account of this, see Klug, 2000, pp. 164-166.

48. See, for example, László Sólyom's introduction to Halmai, Paczolay, Bálogh, Bitszky, & Scheppele (Eds.), 1996. As the first casebook in Hungarian constitutional law, this book made a statement about what the most important principles of Hungarian constitutional law were and Sólyom's introduction had an important symbolic role because he was president of the Court at the time.

49. For a description of the Court's practice, see Scheppele, 1996/July.

50. For a fuller discussion of this issue, see Mayer, 1994.

51. Although India has a federal system, it has a unitary judiciary, and all cases are brought in a single legal system that culminates in the Indian Supreme Court. In small deference to principles of federalism, every Indian state has a High Court that itself possesses the power of judicial review over state laws, though an appeal lies from every one of those cases to the Indian Supreme Court.

52. For a succinct description of the case law and results, see Jain, 2000, pp. 76-86.

53. Gelpe cites H.C. 910/86, *Ressler v. Minister of Defense,* 42(2) P.D. 441, translated in 10 *Selected Judgments of the Supreme Court of Israel* 1 (1988-93).

54. Decision 4/1997: On the Review of International Treaties, translated and excerpted in Sólyom and Brunner, 2000, pp. 356-363.

55. During 1989, the states of East-Central Europe broke away from soviet control, or at least took steps down that road by developing ways that the communist party in each place could be challenged by those in the opposition.

56. The Soviet Union itself fell apart in 1991, following a putsch against Mikhail Gorbachev by hard-liners within his own party, followed by an opportunistic seizing of power by Boris Yeltsin. The states that emerged from this unplanned and rapid change found it harder than did the states in East-Central Europe to make the democratic transition well.

57. For more detail on this, see Schwartz, 2000, pp. 3 ff.

58. See Dimitrov, 1999, for details of this struggle.

59. In Hungary, for example, "anyone" can challenge the constitutionality of a law; in Russia, anyone who feels that his or her rights have been violated by an organ of state (including a court) can go to the Constitutional Court for redress.

60. Well, at least so it seems. However, a disturbing thing occurred when I worked at the Hungarian Constitutional Court in the mid-1990s. The Court had issued a set of forceful decisions in early summer 1995, striking down various aspects of the government's austerity program. The government had not really wanted to undertake substantial reform of the social welfare system quite so thoroughly at that time but had been strongly urged (some would say threatened) to do so by the various international financial institutions that managed Hungary's ability to borrow to pay for its debt. After the law was struck down as unconstitutional, judges at the Court received phone calls from World Bank representatives asking if these representatives could come and give presentations at the Court on the economics of Hungary's welfare system. Most judges refused to talk to them, but the effort to influence the Court was quite explicit. As the only American working in the building, I was asked whether my government always operated this way and whether Americans really believed in the rule of law.

61. The Hungarian Constitutional Court is unusual in having only the power of abstract review and not the power to hear concrete constitutional complaints. The Court is also unusual in that any person can challenge an existing law in Hungary and the Court has no discretion to refuse to hear such challenges. These two features of Hungarian constitutional jurisprudence meant that the Court had a broadly democratic mandate to engage in far-reaching judicial review. Ordinary citizens could, and did, write letters to the Court, expecting that the Court would take seriously their claims that new or old laws violated the new Constitution. And this the Court did with a vengeance.

62. I use the past tense here because this practice has largely changed since 1998 under a new set of judges picked by the Parliament precisely so that they would not exercise this degree of activism. For an account of the changes on the Court, see Scheppele, 1999.

63. For a more elaborated version of this sequence of cases, see Halmai & Scheppele, 1996, pp. 155-184.

64. The Polish Constitutional Tribunal did something similar when they declared that the system of welfare payments to families had to be constitutionally protected and then, confronted with a huge state budget deficit, had to back down and say that the state should pay welfare benefits when it could. The Court did reserve for itself the right to look over the state budget to check the state's claims that it really couldn't pay these benefits, however. See Brzezinski & Garlicki, 1995.

65. The information reported here was based on data I collected while on a trip to the Russian Constitutional Court in December 2000.

ᘒ References

Ackerman, B. (1991). *We the people: Foundations*. Boston: Harvard University Press.

Adam, R. (2000). Government failure and public indifference: A portrait of water pollution in Israel. *Colorado Journal of International Environmental Law & Policy, 11*, 257-376.

Austin, G. (1999). *Working a democratic constitution: The Indian experience*. Oxford: Oxford University Press.

Barak, A. (1996). Constitutional human rights and private law. *Review of Constitutional Studies,3*, 218-281.

Barak, A. (2000). Law, justiciability and judicial activism, *Iyunei Mishpat, 17*, 475-502.

Beatty, D. (1998). Canadian constitutional law in a nutshell. *Alberta Law Review, 36*, 605-629.

Bell, J. (1997). *French constitutional law*. Oxford: Oxford University Press, Clarendon Books.

Brzezinski, B., & Garlicki, L. (1995). Judicial review in post-communist Poland: The emergence of a Rechtsstaat? *Stanford Journal of International Law, 31*, 13-59.

Chevron USA, Inc. v. Natural Resources Defense Council, 467 U.S. 837 (1984).

Corwin, E. S. (1928-1929). The "higher law" background of American Constitutional law (Pts. I & III). *Harvard Law Review, 42*, 149-185, 365-409.

Declaration of Independence of the State of Israel. (1948). [On-line]. Available: www.yale.edu/lawweb/avalon/mideast/israel.htm

Dimitrov, H. D. (1999). The Bulgarian Constitutional Court and its interpretive jurisdiction. *Columbia Journal of Transnational Law, 37*, 459-505.

Du Plessis v. De Klerk, (5) BCLR 658, 1996 SACLR LEXIS 1 (1996) (South Africa).

Dworkin, R. (1978). *Taking rights seriously*. Boston: Harvard University Press.

Fitch, D. (1997). Du Plessis v. De Klerk: South Africa's Bill of Rights and the issue of horizontal application. *North Carolina Journal of International Law and Commercial Regulation, 22,* 1009-1037.

Frank, J. (1973). *Courts on trial: Myth and reality in American justice.* Princeton, NJ: Princeton University Press.

Fuller, L. (1964). *The morality of law.* New Haven, CT: Yale University Press.

Gelpe, M. (1999). Constraints on Supreme Court authority in Israel and the United States: Phenomenal cosmic powers; Itty bitty living space. *Emory International Law Review, 13,* 493-559.

Golak Nath, S.C.R. 1643 (1967) (Israel).

Gomez, I. (2000). Declaring unconstitutional a constitutional amendment: The Argentine judiciary forges ahead. *University of Miami Inter-American Law Review, 31,* 93-119.

Gorlé, F. (1987). Criminal law. In F. J. M. Felbrugge (Ed.), *The distinctiveness of soviet law* (pp. 227-268). Dordrecht: Martinus Nijhoff.

Halmai, G., Paczolay, P., Bálogh, Z., Bitszky, B., & Scheppele, K. L. (Eds.). (1996). *Alkotmányos elvek és esetek (Constitutional principles and cases).* Budapest, Hungary: Constitutional and Legislative Policy Institute.

Halmai, G., & Scheppele, K. L. (1996). Living well is the best revenge: The Hungarian approach to judging the past. In A. J. McAdams (Ed.), *Transitional justice in new democracies* (pp. 155-184). Notre Dame, IN: Notre Dame University Press.

Hankiss, E. (1990). The loss of responsibility. In I. Maclean, A. Montefiore, & P. Winch (Eds.), *The political responsibility of intellectuals* (pp. 29-52). New York: Cambridge University Press.

Hart, H. L. A. (1961). *The concept of law.* Oxford: Clarendon.

Hausmaninger, H. (1995). Towards a "new" Russian Constitutional Court. *Cornell International Law Journal, 28,* 349-386.

Hofnung, M. (1996). The unintended consequences of unplanned constitutional reform: Constitutional politics in Israel. *American Journal of Comparative Law, 44,* 505-564.

Hungarian Constitutional Court. (2000). Decision 4/1997: On the review of international treaties (2000). In L. Sólyom, & G. Brunner (Eds. & Trans.), *The constitutional judiciary in a new democracy,* (pp. 356-363). Ann Arbor: University of Michigan Press.

Hutcheon, L. (1994). *Irony's edge: The theory and politics of irony.* New York: Routledge.

Jain, M. P. (2000). The Supreme Court and fundamental rights. In S. K. Verma Kusum (Ed.), *Fifty years of the Supreme Court of India* (pp. 1-100). Oxford: Oxford University Press.

Jawitsch, L. S. (1996). In W. E. Butler (Ed. & Trans.) *Russian legal theory* (pp. 369-410). New York: University Press Reference Collection.

Kashyap, S. C. (1994). *Our Constitution: An introduction to India's Constitution and constitutional law.* India: National Book Trust.

Kesavandanda Bharati v. State of Kerala, AIR (SC) 1461 (1973) (India).

Klug, H. (2000). *Constituting democracy: Law, globalism and South Africa's political reconstruction.* Cambridge, UK: Cambridge University Press.

Kommers, D. (1997). *The constitutional jurisprudence of the Federal Republic of Germany* (2nd ed.). Durham, NC: Duke University Press.

Lindseth, P. (1996/7). Law, history and memory: "Republican moments" and the legitimacy of constitutional review in France. *Columbia Journal of European Law, 3,* 49-93.

Maneka Gandhi v. Union of India, AIR 1978 SC 597, (1978) (India).

Markovits, I. (1996). *Imperfect justice.* Oxford: Oxford University Press.

Mayer, A. E. (1994). Universal versus Islamic human rights: A clash of cultures or a clash with a construct? *Michigan Journl of International Law, 15,* 307-404.

Montesquieu, C. (1873). *The spirit of the laws* (T. Nugent, Trans.). Cincinatti: Robert Clarke.

Oushakine, S. A. (under review). *The hypocrisy of a chameleon: Detecting crime in late soviet society.*

People's Union for Democratic Rights v. Union of India, AIR 1982 SC 1473 (1982) (India).

Radkov, V. P. (1977). Socialist legality in soviet criminal procedure. In J. N. Hazard, W. E. Butler, & P. B. Maggs (Eds. and Trans.), *The soviet legal system: Fundamental principles and historical commentary* (3rd ed., pp. 67-68). Dobbs Ferry, NY: Oceana Publications. (Originally published 1959)

Russell, P. (2001). Toward a general theory of judicial independence. In P. H. Russell & D. O'Brien (Eds.), *Judicial independence in the age of democracy: Critical perspectives from around the world* (pp. 1-24).Charlottesville: University Press of Virginia.

S. v. Makwanyane, (3) SA 391; 1995 (6) BCLR 665 (1995).

Scheppele, K. L. (1990). Facing facts in legal interpretation. *Representations, 30,* 42-77.

Scheppele, K. L. (1996). The history of normalcy: Rethinking legal autonomy and the relative dependence of law at the end of the soviet empire. *Law and Society Review, 30,* 627-650.

Scheppele, K. L. (1996, July). *Imagined Europe.* Plenary address given at the international meetings of the Law and Society Association, Glasgow, Scotland.

Scheppele, K. L. (1999). The new Hungarian Constitutional Court. *East European Constitutional Review, 8*(4), 51-87.

Scheppele, K. L. (2001). When the law doesn't count: The 2000 election and the failure of the rule of law. *University of Pennsylvania Law Review, 149,* 1361-1437.

Schlesinger, R., et al. (1988). *Comparative Law* (5th ed.). Mineola, NY: Foundation Press.

Schwartz, H. (2000). *The struggle for constitutional justice in post-Communist Europe.* Chicago: University of Chicago Press.

S.P. Gupta v. Union of India, AIR 1982 SC 149, (1982).

Stith, R. (1996). Unconstitutional constitutional amendments: The extraordinary power of Nepal's Supreme Court. *American University Journal of International Law & Policy, 11,* 47-77.

Stone, A. (1992). *The birth of judicial politics in France: The constitutional council in comparative perspective.* Oxford: Oxford University Press.

Sweet, A. S. (2000). *Governing with judges: Constitutional politics in Europe.* Oxford: Oxford University Press.

Vyshinskii, A. Y., (1996). Law of the soviet state. In W. E. Butler (Ed. & Trans.) *Russian legal theory* (pp. 321-367). New York: University Press Reference Collection.

Waldron, J. (1981). A right to do wrong. *Ethics, 92,* 21-39.

Appendix

Conference Participants

On March 31-April 1, 2001, the American Judicature Society and the Brennan Center for Justice at NYU School of Law cosponsored a conference entitled *Judicial Independence at the Crossroads: Developing an Interdisciplinary Research Agenda.* The chapters in this volume emerged from the conference. Participants are listed below, with their affiliations at the time of the conference.

Professor Lawrence Baum
Department of Political Science
Ohio State University

Professor Jenna Bednar
Center for Political Studies
University of Michigan

Professor Robert G. Boatright
Department of Political Science
Swarthmore College

Professor Stephen B. Burbank
University of Pennsylvania School of Law

Professor Gregory Caldeira
Department of Political Science
Ohio State University

Professor Charles M. Cameron
Department of Political Science
Columbia University

Professor Oscar Chase
New York University School of Law

Professor Lee Epstein
Department of Political Science
Washington University

Dr. Kevin M. Esterling
University of California, Berkeley
School of Public Health

Professor William E. Forbath
University of Texas School of Law

Professor Charles H. Franklin
Department of Political Science
University of Wisconsin-Madison

Professor Barry Friedman
New York University School of Law

Professor Tracey E. George
University of Missouri School of Law

Professor Charles Gardner Geyh
Indiana University School of Law

Deborah Goldberg
Brennan Center for Justice
at New York University School of Law

Professor Mark A. Graber
Department of Government and Politics
University of Maryland-College Park

Edward Hartnett
Visiting Professor of Law
University of Pennsylvania School of Law

Professor Geoffrey Hazard
University of Pennsylvania School of Law

Professor Deborah R. Hensler
Stanford University School of Law

Professor Gary King
Department of Government
Center for Basic Research in the Social Sciences
Harvard University

Joel F. Knutson
American Judicature Society

Professor Lewis Kornhauser
New York University School of Law

Mark Kozlowski
Brennan Center for Justice
at New York University School of Law

Professor Terri Peretti
Department of Political Science
Santa Clara University

Hon. Louis H. Pollak
United States District Court
Eastern District of Pennsylvania

Malia Reddick
American Judicature Society

Professor Gerald N. Rosenberg
Northwestern University School of Law

Professor William G. Ross
Cumberland School of Law

Professor Edward Rubin
University of Pennsylvania School of Law

Professor Philippe Sands
University of London (School of Oriental and African Studies) and
New York University School of Law

Professor Kim Lane Scheppele
University of Pennsylvania School of Law

Professor Jeffrey Segal
Department of Political Science
SUNY at Stony Brook

Professor Louis Michael Seidman
Georgetown University Law Center

Allan D. Sobel
American Judicature Society

Professor Pablo T. Spiller
Haas School of Business
University of California, Berkeley

Professor Emerson Tiller, II
Department of Management Science and Information Systems
University of Texas

Index

About the Editors

Stephen B. Burbank is the David Berger Professor for the Administration of Justice at the University of Pennsylvania. A graduate of Harvard College and Harvard Law School, he served as law clerk to Justice Robert Braucher of the Supreme Judicial Court of Massachusetts and to Chief Justice Warren Burger. He was General Counsel of the University of Pennsylvania from 1975 to 1980. Professor Burbank is the author of numerous articles on federal court rulemaking, complex litigation, international civil litigation, and judicial independence and accountability. He was the principal author of *Rule 11 in Transition: The Report of the Third Circuit Task Force on Federal Rule of Civil Procedure 11* (1989) and a principal author of the *Report of the National Commission on Judicial Discipline and Removal* (1993). Professor Burbank is a member of the Executive Committee of the American Judicature Society, for which he also serves on the editorial committee, as chair of the amicus committee, and as cochair of the Center for Judicial Independence Task Force. He has served as a Visiting Professor at the law schools of Goethe University (Frankfurt, Germany), Harvard University, the University of Michigan, and the University of Pavia (Italy).

Barry Friedman (A.B. 1978, University of Chicago; J.D. 1982, Georgetown University) is Professor of Law at New York University School of Law, where he writes and teaches in the areas of constitutional law, federal jurisdiction, and criminal procedure. His areas of specialty are judicial review and federalism. His most recent project has been an extended political history of judicial review. From there he is turning to a project discussing the difficulty with modeling judicial review; this project delves deeply into the empirical and game theoretic literature on the subject. Professor Friedman also practices law, both privately and pro bono, and has litigated in all levels of the state and federal courts, including on issues of judicial independence and federalism. He has testified before Congress on the same subjects. He speaks regularly at judicial conferences, at academic gatherings, and before other groups. Friedman is completing a term of more than eight years as an officer and executive committee member of the American Judicature Society. He remains the cochair of AJS Task Force on Judicial Independence.

About the Contributors

Charles M. Cameron is Associate Professor of Political Science at Columbia University. He has been a National Fellow at the Hoover Institution and a Research Fellow at the Brookings Institution. He is the author of *Veto Bargaining: Presidents and the Politics of Negative Power* (2000) as well as many articles in journals of political science, economics, and law.

Lee Epstein (http://artsci.wustl.edu/~polisci/epstein/) is the Edward Mallinckrodt Distinguished University Professor of Political Science and Professor of Law at Washington University. Recent and current research projects include *The Norm of Consensus on the Supreme Court* (coauthored with Jeff Segal and Harold Spaeth, forthcoming), which considers whether justices serving on Supreme Courts of the 19th (and into the 20th) century disagreed over the outcomes of cases but masked their disagreement from the public by producing consensual opinions; *Strategic Defiance of the U.S. Supreme Court* (with Segal and Charles Cameron), which seeks to address the question of why lower courts defy (or comply with) precedent established by the Court; and *What Role do Constitutional Courts Play in the Establishment and Maintenance of Democratic Systems of Government?* (with Jack Knight and Olga Shvetsova, forthcoming), which answers the primary question via a model that assumes strategic behavior on the part of the relevant actors (including judges, executives, and legislatures) and assesses the predictions generated by the model against data drawn from Russia. She also is working on a paper (with Gary King) that adapts the rules of inference used in the natural, physical, and social sciences to the special needs, theories, and data in legal scholarship, and explicates them with extensive illustrations from research in the law reviews.

Charles H. Franklin is Professor of Political Science and a faculty affiliate of the Institute for Legal Studies at the University of Wisconsin, Madison. His research on courts has focused on how the U.S. Supreme Court affects public opinion and how public awareness of Court decisions is shaped. He is also current president of the Society for Political Methodology and the American Political Science Association's Political Methodology Organized Section.

Charles Gardner Geyh (pronounced "Jay") (J.D. 1983, University of Wisconsin) is Professor of Law at the Indiana University School of Law in Bloomington. He is the Reporter for the American Bar Association Commission on the Public Financing of Judicial Elections and a consultant to the Parliamentary Development Project on Judicial Independence and Administration for the Supreme Rada of Ukraine. He formerly served as Director of the American Judicature Society Center for Judicial Independence; Reporter to the ABA Commission on Separation of Powers and Judicial Independence; task force reporter to the Constitution Project's Citizens for Independent Courts initiative; assistant special counsel to the Pennsylvania House of Representatives on the impeachment and removal of Pennsylvania Supreme Court Justice Rolf Larsen; consultant to the National Commission on Judicial Discipline & Removal; legislative liaison to the Federal Courts Study Committee; and as counsel to the U.S. House of Representatives Committee on the Judiciary. His work on judicial independence and accountability has appeared in books, reports, and articles published by the New York University Law Review, the University of Pennsylvania Law Review, the Georgetown Law Journal, and other law reviews.

Deborah Goldberg (Ph.D. 1980, The Johns Hopkins University; J.D. 1986, Harvard Law School) is the Deputy Director of the Democracy Program at the Brennan Center for Justice at NYU School of Law. She oversees the Center's Judicial Independence Project, which employs scholarship, legal action, and public education in efforts to protect judges and the judiciary from politically motivated attacks, to ensure that federal and state judicial selection processes do not interfere with independent judicial decision making, and to defeat improper attempts to constrict judicial power. Ms. Goldberg is the editor and principal author of *Writing Reform: A Guide to Drafting State & Local Campaign Finance Laws.* She provides legal counseling and legislative drafting assistance to advocates seeking to improve state judicial campaign financing and has testified before the ABA Commission on the Public Financing of Judicial Elections. She taught ethics and political philosophy for three years at Columbia University before entering law school.

Jack Knight is the Sidney W. Souers Professor of Government and Chair of the Department of Political Science at Washington University in St. Louis. He has a B.A. and a J.D. from the University of North Carolina at Chapel Hill, and a M.A. and Ph.D. from the University of Chicago. His primary areas of interest are modern social and political theory, law and legal theory, political economy, philosophy of social science. His publications include *Institutions and Social Conflict* (1992), *Explaining Social Institutions* (with Itai Sened, 1995), and *The Choices Justices Make* (with Lee Epstein, 1998), as well as articles and chapters in various journals and edited volumes.

Lewis A. Kornhauser (J.D., Ph.D. University of California, Berkeley) is an economist and Alfred and Gail Engelberg Professor of Law at New York University. His work includes extensive economic modeling of judicial behavior, including: *Adjudication by a Resource Constrained Team: Hierarchy and Precedent in a Judicial System*, 68 S. Cal. L. Rev. 1605 (1995); *An Economic Perspective on* Stare Decisis, 65 Chi.-Kent L. Rev. 63 (1989); *Modeling Collegial Courts I: Path Dependence*, 12 Int'l Rev. L. & Econ. 169 (1992); *Modeling Collegial Courts II: Legal Doctrine*, 8 J.L. Econ. & Org. 441 (1992).

Terri Jennings Peretti received her undergraduate degree in political science from the University of Kansas and her M.A. and Ph.D. in political science from the University of California, Berkeley. She has taught American politics, constitutional law, and judicial process at Santa Clara University for 12 years. Her publications, most recently *In Defense of a Political Court*, focus on judicial review and judicial selection.

Edward L. Rubin is Professor of Law at the University of Pennsylvania Law School. Rubin received his undergraduate degree from the Princeton University and then worked for the New York City Board of Education as a curriculum planner. He attended Yale Law School, where he was Note and Comment Editor of the Yale Law Journal, and graduated in 1979. After clerking for Judge Jon O. Newman, United States Court of Appeals for the Second Circuit, he practiced entertainment law in New York City for two years as an associate at Paul, Weiss, Rifkind, Wharton & Garrison. He joined the faculty of the University of California, Berkeley School of Law (Boalt Hall) in 1982 and served there until 1998, when he moved to Penn. Between 1990 and 1992 he was the Associate Dean at Boalt. Rubin teaches administrative law, constitutional law, and commercial law. He is the author of *Judicial Policy Making and the Modern State: How the Courts Reformed America's Prisons* (with M. Feeley, 1998) and *The Payment System: Cases, Materials and Issues* (with R. Cooter, 1994), the editor of *Minimizing Harm: A New Crime Policy for Modern America* (1998), and the author of numerous law review articles. He administered the Japanese-American Legal Studies program at Boalt Hall, and has served as a consultant to the governments of the Russian Federation and the People's Republic of China.

Kim Lane Scheppele is Professor of Law and Sociology at the University of Pennsylvania. She came to Penn in 1996 after 12 years at the University of Michigan, where she held appointments in the political science department, the School of Public Policy and the Law School. At Penn, she teaches comparative constitutional law, post-communist law and society, constitutionalism and evidence. Her current research focuses on the new constitutionalism in the post-soviet world. She spent four years doing research at the Hungarian Constitutional Court and is about to go to Russia for similar work at the Russian Constitutional Court. She is interested in the development of popular constitutional consciousness and its impact on developing constitutional jurisprudence of the new constitutional courts in the post-soviet world. The author of numerous articles in law reviews and social science journals, Professor Scheppele is also the author of *Legal Secrets: Equality and Efficiency in the Common Law* (1988), coeditor of *Alkotmanyos Elvek es Esetek* (the first casebook on Hungarian constitutional law) and a contributor to recent volumes on the Rule of Law and Transitional Justice. She is the treasurer and 2001 program cochair for the Law and Society Association, a former chair of the Sociology of Law Section of the American Sociological Association, and cofounder of the Conference Group on Jurisprudence and Public Law of the American Political Science Association.

Olga Shvetsova is Assistant Professor of Political Science at Washington University in St. Louis. She received her Ph.D. in 1995 from Cal Tech. Her areas of interest include comparative politics, political institutions, political economy, and formal political theory. The most general description of her research is the study of institutional determinants of multipartism. More specifically, she is currently working on several projects, one of which is the study of complex mechanisms motivating political competition and political entrepreneurship in democratic federations. Together with several coauthors, she offers a new typology of federal systems based on the representational properties imbedded in their electoral and constitutional systems. On this foundation they are able to derive the differences in the dynamics of federal political competition which can lead to cementing or, on the contrary, destabilizing the federal arrangements.